Japan

FROM PREHISTORY TO
MODERN TIMES

MICHIGAN CLASSICS IN JAPANESE STUDIES
NUMBER 7
CENTER FOR JAPANESE STUDIES
THE UNIVERSITY OF MICHIGAN

Japan

FROM PREHISTORY TO MODERN TIMES

by John Whitney Hall

CENTER FOR JAPANESE STUDIES
THE UNIVERSITY OF MICHIGAN
ANN ARBOR, MICHIGAN

Originally published in Germany under the title
DAS JAPANISCHE KAISERREICH
Copyright © 1968 by Fischer Bücherei GmbH,
Frankfurt am Main, Germany

Reprinted by arrangement with S. Fischer Verlag, Frankfurt am Main, Germany
Reprinted in 1991 by the Center for Japanese Studies, 108 Lane Hall, The University
of Michigan, Ann Arbor, MI 48109

Library of Congress Cataloging-in-Publication Data
Hall, John Whitney, 1916 –
    Japan, from prehistory to modern times / by John Whitney Hall.
        p.   cm.   — (Michigan classics in Japanese studies ; no. 7)
    Reprint. Originally published: New York : Delacorte Press, 1970.
    Includes bibliographical references and index.
    ISBN 0–939512–54–8 (paperback)
    1. Japan — History.   I. Title.   II. Series.
[DS835.H23   1991]
952 — dc20   91 – 4231
                                                                    CIP

The paper used in this publication meets the requirements of the ANSI Standard
Z39.48-1984 (Permanence of Paper).

Printed in the United States of America

Contents

CONTENTS

List of Illustrations

[*between pages 242 and 243*]

ILLUSTRATIONS

Maps

Maps by Harald and Ruth Bukor

Foreword

My decision to write the volume on Japanese history for the Delacorte World History series was elicited by my good friend Etienne Balazs, who had just been commissioned to prepare the volume on China. His death soon after his visit to America came as a great shock, and I find myself completing this work as though in his memory. There is little to explain about the work itself. Its general structure, with its heavy emphasis upon the premodern period of Japanese history, has been set by the nature of the series in which it finds itself. No attempt has been made to provide the usual kind of textbook completeness. My own fascination with Japanese history lies primarily with the manner in which Japan's political and social institutions have changed and diversified over time and how this fundamentally "Eastern" culture gave rise to a modern world power. The evidence I cite in this volume is largely subordinated to my attempt to explain this remarkable phenomenon in analytical terms.

My acknowledgments go first to my students at Yale University, particularly Robert Bockman, Harold Bolitho, Susan Hanley, William Hauser, and Jeffrey Mass, who read the manuscript while it was in progress and offered valuable suggestions, and to Bernard Susser who helped to prepare the bibliography. Second, I wish to thank Shōgakkan Publishers of Tōkyō for supplying the majority of the photographs that appear in this volume. To Mr. Kanai Madoka who arranged for permission to use the photographs goes a special word of thanks.

Morse College, Yale University   JOHN WHITNEY HALL
June, 1967

Japan
FROM PREHISTORY TO
MODERN TIMES

1

Introduction:
Japan's Historical Position

When in the middle of the nineteenth century European and American travelers pressed their attention upon the isolated islands of Japan, they little imagined that within a century the mysterious "Land of the Mikado" would have transformed itself into one of the leading nations of the modern world. In the 1850's, Japan was, in the eyes of the West, a little-known and backward country that had insisted on secluding itself from foreign view for over two centuries—the farthest removed of the lands of the Far East. Yet today Japan stands third among the industrial nations of the world and bears the memory of a violent attempt at military expansion that made its cities the first targets of atomic warfare.

Japan is today a modern nation in the full sense of the term. Yet its history is less familiar to us than the histories of those Western powers that it has now outstripped, or of the other countries of Asia that have gained recognition as the birthplaces of ancient civilizations or world religions. Japanese history does not force itself upon the world's attention as does the mainstream of European history or the exotic chronicles of China or India. Its significance has become apparent only in proportion to the recognition Japan has gained as a modern state and as scholars have begun to place Japanese history within a world context.

Admittedly, Japan has not been a major creative force in

1

world history, at least until recent times. The slender arc of islands gave rise to no classic civilization of its own that could impose its style upon surrounding peoples. The Japanese achievement has been more confined. It has been the particular destiny of the Japanese that they have lived within two contrasting great traditions (Chinese and Western), and it has been through their genius that, while accommodating to both, they have achieved some stature and distinction in each. From the sixth century until the middle of the nineteenth century, Japan was immersed in the Chinese zone of civilization; after 1854, hurried modernization assimilated Japan within the expanding frontiers of Western influence. In each of these contexts, Japan played an important, though not commanding, role. In East Asia, from at least the eighth century, Japan ranked high among the countries surrounding China in its political and cultural achievements. The Japanese absorbed many elements of Chinese civilization—the written language, techniques of government, styles of architecture and art, and systems of philosophy and religion. Yet in almost every field, they placed their own imprint upon what they had learned, and thus retained a cultural style of their own. A thousand years later Japan led the way among East Asian countries in adjusting to Western civilization. But again, as any visitor to Japan must agree, the resulting cultural fusion is something that bears the distinct stamp of Japan's own historical heritage.

Yet while Japan's role in history cannot be considered dominant, Japanese action has in a number of circumstances determined the course of events in its corner of the world. Japan's successful defense against the Mongols in the thirteenth century was a significant turning point in Mongol history. Hideyoshi's invasion of Korea at the end of the sixteenth century contributed both to the weakening of the Ming dynasty in China and to the subsequent decline of Korea. Portuguese and Spanish ambitions in East Asia were to some extent thwarted by Japanese hostility in the early seventeenth century. Japan's expansion as a modern power after 1868 thrust its armies into Korea, Manchuria, and China, upsetting both the national ambitions of these peoples and the balance of power among Western interests in East Asia. Japan played a major role in World War II both as a stubborn opponent of the United States and as a major disruptive force in China and Southeast Asia. The work of its armies contributed to both the Communist conquest of mainland China and to the fall of the colonial empires in Southeast Asia.

By the latter half of the twentieth century, Japan had regained a ranking position among the industrial nations. But because of its lack of military buildup following its defeat in World War II, and because of the shadow of the great Chinese colossus that looms behind it, Japan has been content with a rather ambiguous international position. A nation of subdued political influence in the world of the atom, it is the nature of its modern transformation that makes it a very special member of the advanced nations of the world.

But Japan's history has intrinsic qualities that can inform the mind and excite the imagination irrespective of where Japan stands within the hierarchy of world powers. For if history is a glass through which man learns to know himself and his society, then Japan offers the historian lessons of profound value. Its comparatively long and isolated history provides the elements of a remarkably rich and accessible case study of national growth and development. In the first place, the isolation of the Japanese islands has made for an unusually unified and self-contained history. Protected from the play of competing civilizations or the periodic disruption of foreign invasion, the Japanese people in historic times have lived a relatively undisturbed existence. Yet their culture has undergone a succession of fundamental changes that transformed it from a primitive tribal society prior to the sixth century into a nation of aristocratic bureaucrats from the seventh through twelfth centuries; later, into a land of contending feudal powers; and finally, into its present condition as a nation state. The process of change in Japan has not been cyclical, but rather one of linear development and cumulative growth. And perhaps because of the factor of isolation and the relatively homogeneous social and cultural conditions that have prevailed in Japan, the historian is better able to follow the

3

process, identifying with relative ease the effect of foreign influences or the interrelated pattern of decay and regeneration among indigenous institutions.

Secondly, a position on the extreme fringes of the Chinese zone of civilization has made it possible for the Japanese, though absorbing Chinese culture in great quantity, to yet retain a firm hold on their own essential institutions and values. Japanese institutional history contrasts fundamentally with that of China, despite the heavy overlay of Chinese influence. Far from giving rise to simply a minor version of Chinese civilization, the Japanese developed certain social attitudes and patterns of government that surprisingly seem more comparable to those of Europe. Japan's feudal institutions, its maritime orientation, and its strong sense of nationality are historic qualities that contrast sharply with Chinese tradition and may help to explain why the Japanese, of all the East Asian peoples, were best prepared to meet the Western impact.

Thirdly, there is the slow organic quality that has distinguished Japan's political and social evolution, again partly as a result of long periods of isolation. The Japanese people have escaped the experience of a major revolution or of devastating foreign invasion. Throughout their premodern history, structural changes have come slowly and have been brought about more by internal forces than external pressures. And this has resulted in the tendency for superseded institutions to be discarded and pushed to the side, but seldom swept away completely. Art and architectural treasures have been kept in repair for centuries, just as certain family lines or certain symbolic offices have been kept alive though shorn of power and influence. The Japanese imperial house can without question claim the longest continuous reign of any ruling house in the world today. Factors of continuity thus constantly run through the fabric of Japan's cultural history and reveal the warp upon which the woof of change can be traced.

But of course, it is the fact of Japan's emergence as a modern nation that most excites our interest in Japan's past. For as Japan has become a recognized member of the modern world, its history has become relevant to us and to all other modern societies. Japan's social and institutional history, once simply an exotic curiosity, is now added to the total body of evidence on how nations have entered the modern condition. The relevance of Japanese history is assured despite the fact that it comes into the stream of world history from so distant a source. It is this view of Japanese history, important in its own right and relevant to the modern world, that has motivated the writing of this book. The drama of Japanese history may not compare with China's in terms of sheer breadth or violence of action; yet, in the more muted tones that so typify the Japanese landscape, it is not without its heroes and noble monuments. The temples of the ancient capital of Nara still stand today, as do the great castles around which the epic battles of the sixteenth-century wars of unification were fought. The *Tale of Genji* in modern translation can draw our imaginations back to the court society of the eleventh century. The study of Japanese history can be a humanistic experience of real delight. The process of Japanese cultural development has been continuous yet changing; and the Japanese, for all their isolation from the rest of the world, mastered the techniques of life through the ages in ways that must earn our respect and our curiosity.

2

Japan's Historical Setting

The size and location of the Japanese islands have provided a distinctive home for the Japanese people. The four major islands, Hokkaidō, Honshū, Shikoku, and Kyūshū, and over a thousand smaller ones that comprise the Japanese archipelago, extend in an arc between the tip of Sakhalin to a point south of the Korean peninsula. In latitude they stretch from the 45th parallel at the northern tip of Hokkaidō to the 31st parallel, which touches southern Kyūshū. The total area is small, approximately 142,700 square miles, and the highly mountainous nature of the islands leaves only about 16 per cent of the land arable. On the other hand, the islands lie, for the most part, within the monsoon zone of East Asia, and the overall climate is significantly moderated by the strong ocean currents that circulate along their entire length.

These basic facts about the Japanese islands have remained unchanged throughout Japan's historical period. Yet their significance has varied in relation to the changing conditions of life in Japan and in the surrounding world. Today Japan may be described geographically as a country of medium size, larger than Britain, but smaller than France. Its location off the northeast coast of Asia has placed it in a strategic position either to engage in continental affairs, or to maintain a position of detachment. But above all, Japan has been able to exploit its opportunities to become a maritime power, making up through trade and shipping the severe lack of natural resources upon which modern industry must thrive.

Until a hundred years ago, Japan would have to have been described quite differently. In terms of size, it was fairly large and prosperous by Asian standards, but it was also the most remotely and poorly situated with respect to the center of continental civilization. What is now considered a scarcity of natural resources was not then a handicap, since in terms of the prevalent technology Japan was rich in land, water, sun, and manpower. The early Japanese themselves were pleased with their homeland, calling their islands the land of "luxuriant rice ears." Historically, therefore, isolation and a relatively productive agricultural base were the two outstanding determinants in Japan's geographical setting. These factors combined to permit the Japanese to develop a high level of cultural life in touch with, but not overwhelmed by, continental influence.

The shift in geographical determinants that has occurred in the last century has been accompanied by a change in cultural milieu of even more dramatic proportions. A century ago, Japan could be regarded as simply a member of the East Asian community. And for the greater portion of Japanese history, it was the East Asian cultural environment that most powerfully conditioned the Japanese way of life. Fifty, or even thirty, years ago the remnants of this style of life were so much in evidence in Japan that an understanding of so-called "Asiatic" patterns of economy and society was considered the essential foundation for any inquiry into Japanese life, however contemporary. Today one is less apt to think in terms of absolute dichotomies between Eastern and Western modes of behavior, but for the historian it is well to keep in mind the broad features of the dominant cultural environment that enveloped Japan for so many centuries.

The development of an intensive style of agriculture based largely on the cultivation of rice by irrigation was common to the regions affected by the monsoon winds and rains. Even today the Japanese farm family makes a living off of, on an average, just over two-and-one-half acres of cultivated land, feeding more than ten times as many individuals per acre as even the most efficient farm in the United States. This is

7

made possible by the perfection of an intensive technology dependent on irrigation and the heavy input of manpower, as contrasted with the extensive techniques of Europe, which have relied on natural rainfall and the labor-multiplying effect of machines and draft animals.

While less mechanized than European agriculture, the Asian style of cultivation was certainly not in any way primitive, for it operated upon a highly sophisticated base of social organization and water control. Irrigation networks, which were developed over the course of centuries, served elaborate field systems, nourishing the young rice plants and replenishing the soil so as to provide a rich base upon which a dense sedentary population of farmers could subsist. The cultivators, grouped into tightly packed villages, formed cooperative units through which they could channel the maximum labor to the requirements of cultivation.

Common to most of historic monsoon Asia, then, was a peasant base characterized by a high ratio of cultivators to units of land, and a high ratio of agricultural production to that of the total economy, which was made possible through a highly sophisticated system of water control and village and family organization. This peasant "folk" base, as anthropologists have termed it, remained relatively immobile, rooted to the soil, and preoccupied with the problems of land and water.

Common also to the peoples of East Asia, as it was, of course, to most premodern societies, was the sharp distinction between the peasant base and the ruling stratum of families who served as bearers of the higher culture. Primary reliance on a land economy placed a heavy burden on the peasant population, which supported the upper 10 per cent or so of land owners, fighters, priests, and officials. It would seem that the slow development of commerce and industry or other alternative sources of wealth permitted a more authoritarian relationship between the dominant ruling class and the subservient agricultural producers. Government was characteristically despotic, unchecked by competitive interests of church or law.

Confucianism, which in East Asia served as the chief philosophical receptacle for the attitudes toward government and

8

society that emerged from such an agrarian culture, justified government in benevolent but authoritarian terms and conceived of society as consisting of a naturally ordained hierarchy of classes: the ruling elite, the farmers, the artisans, and the merchants. Traditional society in East Asia was vastly different from the pluralistic, individualistic society that was to emerge in the countries of the West. In its underlying philosophy, its legal institutions, and its deepest attitudes toward family and individual, it established norms that differed fundamentally from those upon which modern European society is based.

Historically Japan grew up within a cultural environment in East Asia in which China was the center. Yet the haste with which Japan exchanged elements of its traditional cultural style for those newly acquired from the West must to some degree be a measure of Japan's historic independence from the influence of China. In origin the Japanese people were not of Chinese stock. The style of primitive life that characterized the Japanese before their contact with China differentiated them from the Chinese in a number of basic ways. Language was the most obvious difference, but basic religious beliefs, social patterns, and concepts of government were also essentially different. But not only did these differences exist in primitive times, many of them were stubbornly preserved by the Japanese throughout their historic development.

Historians have often commented upon the "special characteristics" that have distinguished the Japanese from other East Asian peoples. Sir George Sansom wrote about the "hard, non-absorbent core of individual character" that resisted and worked upon foreign influences. Some writers have emphasized the continuing "primitiveness" of Japanese social customs and religious beliefs. Others have observed that the Japanese retained warlike qualities from their early tribal heritage. The Japanese themselves would rather wish to be thought of as peculiarly attuned to nature and beauty or as having a genius for assimilating foreign cultural influences into a synthesis uniquely their own. In modern times, writers have resorted to the idea of "national character" to explain Japanese behavior patterns. The historian, of course, is wary of using such impressionistic instruments of analysis. But he need not deny the existence of a number of historical continuities within Japanese culture that stem from sources quite different from the dominant continental norm and that provide the basis for Japan's individuality among the peoples of East Asia.

A syndrome of related attitudes and practices associated with the primitive religious beliefs and social organization of the Japanese people has remained most persistent in this respect. The practices of Shintō, which ranged from simple communal worship of local spirits to the politically oriented beliefs surrounding the Sun Goddess and the imperial line, have remained central to the Japanese orientation toward government and community despite the influence of Confucianism and Buddhism. The continuity of the imperial house is clearly a fundamental fact of Japanese history. It symbolizes the homogeneity of the Japanese people and the unbroken unity of the Japanese polity. However, it does more. The continuity of dynasty in Japan helps to explain a number of significant features of Japanese political organization. Until recent times, the holders of political power in Japan have consisted of a single hierarchy of families presided over by the imperial house. The structure of this aristocratic hierarchy showed certain distinct characteristics from the time of its first appearance as a primitive tribal hegemony. Ruling families organized themselves into extended clanlike lineages over which chieftains held both political authority and religious sanction. Religious influence and social prestige derived from the powers of the ancestral deities that the chieftain worshipped. Thus the kinship-based authority structure through which the imperial house first established its hegemony over the Japanese islands was backed by the sacerdotal powers of the ancestral Sun Goddess. This, the earliest form that sovereignty took in Japan, was to persist until modern times.

The early Japanese elite were warriors as well as rulers. And while the influence of Chinese civil administration was to suppress the warrior tradition in Japan for some four centuries or more after the seventh century, the warrior-aristocrat was to reappear in the twelfth century in the person of the samurai, to remain the most distinctly Japanese type of leader down to modern times. It was under samurai leadership that those particular features of Japanese society that so contrasted with the Chinese model were to emerge, notably the strong emphasis on political as against personal or family loyalty, the militant sensitivity to national honor, the rough but direct and effective system of local administration that the military aristocracy provided. The Japan that met the impact of the West in the nineteenth century was conscious of its difference from China and had in fact begun to cultivate a certain disdain for China's "foreignness" and "backwardness."

It is significant that the main islands of Japan in historic times were unified either under a single political authority or under a homogeneous ruling society. The three islands of Kyūshū, Shikoku, and Honshū upon which the first Japanese state emerged were never to develop into separate and competitive regions, nor were they to produce separate sovereignties as did the British Isles. On the other hand, the mountainous and variegated topography made for the division of the Japanese homeland into numerous small localities that could maintain their identities as provinces or feudal domains. The story of Japanese political history has been played out upon this variegated topographical base. First to be settled and to be politically organized were the regions of northern Kyūshū and the shores of the Inland Sea. This became the "core region" of old Japan, centered on the Kinai Plain and oriented toward the distant continent. It was here that the seat of political authority was first established and flourished. Only after the twelfth century did the great eastern plain of Kantō begin to compete with the central core, and only in the nineteenth century did the Kantō, centered upon the great city of Tōkyō, dominate political and economic affairs of Japan. In fact, today the traditional elements of Japan's geographical and cultural orientation have been almost totally negated, for the country now looks out upon the Pacific for its link to the out-

side world, while within, the sinews of modern communications and the expanding machinery of local administration
have increasingly obliterated the historic geographic divisions
that played such an important role when culture was still a
matter of land, water, and aristocratic families.

3

Origins of the Japanese People and Their Culture

One would wish to be able to begin the story of Japanese history with an exact statement of origins. The historian's quest for absolute starting points and the temptation to look for explanations of the very recent in terms of the very remote may be, as Marc Bloch has remarked, an "idol of origins." Yet the search for certainty about the genesis of the Japanese people is not an idle one, particularly since the geographical isolation of the Japanese has helped preserve various early elements in their culture far into their later history. An exact knowledge of the original racial composition of the Japanese and the sources from which the early culture was compounded would help immensely to get us started with the telling of their history; but such knowledge is as yet denied us.

The Japanese islands, like the British Isles, obviously became the home of a mixture of peoples who arrived at various times and from various places on the continent, and, perhaps, even from islands to the south. By historic times this mixture had produced a relatively homogeneous people who stood out distinctly from their continental neighbors, such as the Chinese, the Koreans, or the Mongols, in terms of language, physical type, religion, and political and social structure. These early distinguishing traits were to continue to identify the Japanese. But their origins are not precisely known, nor is it clear how long the process of amalgamation required, nor

13

precisely when the early inhabitants may be said to have become Japanese.

The geological soils of Japan have yielded the skeletons and
tusks of Ice Age animals that tell us that during the Pleistocene
age the Japanese islands were joined to the continent by land
bridges similar to the one that joined Asia to the New World.
These connections probably remained until the first primitive
man entered the area of the Japanese islands. Japanese
scholars have discovered what they believe to be the petrified
bones of premodern hominids who may have roamed the area
as far back as 200,000 years ago, but the identification is still
tenuous. Meanwhile, archaeologists, beginning with the ex-
cavation at Iwajuku in Gumma Prefecture in 1949, have found
and identified a rapidly growing number of stone tools that
remain from a preceramic culture dating back to between
100,000 and 200,000 years ago. The stone implements are
roughly flaked, and among them certain large stone tools appear similar to the *chopper-chopping* implements found
throughout China, Southeast Asia, and India. Yet another
preceramic culture of a considerably later time has also been
identified. But this culture, distinguished by smaller flake tools
and sharp-edged projectile points (microliths), has also failed
to leave positive skeletal evidence. It may be supposed, however, by reference to similar continental evidence, that its
bearers were of modern physical type.

It is with the bearers of various neolithic cultures that the
more probable ancestors of the Japanese of today came into
the archipelago. By this time, of course, the land bridges had
submerged under water and the most feasible approaches required crossing the narrow stretch of sea separating Japan
from the Korean peninsula, or migrating along the island
chains that arced up to Japan from the south or down from
the north. Our knowledge of the movements of the early neolithic peoples of East Asia is still extremely vague, but if we
broaden our view to take in the extended sweep of all the
eastern half of Asia, we may obtain some sense of the possibilities of how Japan was peopled.

From about 20,000 years ago, it appears that successive

14

waves of people, differing in physical characteristics, moved out of south-central Asia in an easterly direction. The earliest were of proto-Negroid and proto-Caucasoid stock, and it is presumed that survivals of the former are found in the remoter parts of Malaya, New Guinea, and the Philippines and that remnants of the latter are found in the Ainu of northern Japan and the Bushmen of Australia. A later influx into East Asia brought the ancestors of the Mongoloids, who swept in several waves across the continent pushing the former inhabitants before them or assimilating them in greater or lesser degree. Today the Mongoloids thoroughly dominate East Asia. Their ancestors, as they themselves are today, were divided into a number of subgroups, distinguished by physical type, to be sure, but, more importantly, by language and culture traits. Three prime linguistic divisions of the Mongoloids have roughly geographical identities. In the northern steppe and forest lands were various groups that spoke languages in the Altaic family, a group of associated languages that today includes Turkish, Mongolian, Korean, and Japanese. Most of central and southern continental East Asia were occupied by the speakers of the Sinitic group of languages. Of this group, Chinese, which in itself is a family of languages, is most widespread, but important sub-families are found in Tibet, Burma, and Indo-China. The third major group of Mongoloid languages is variously termed Austronesian or Malayo-Polynesian. Its speakers have come to occupy the southern half of the Malay Peninsula and the islands of Southeast Asia as far east as Polynesia.

Related in counterpoint fashion to the contours of the linguistic map is the evidence of early cultural differentiation among the neolithic inhabitants of East Asia. The northern forest lands became the home of groups of hunters whose social organization was tribal and matrilineal. The steppes were occupied by nomadic groups whose tribal organization was more commonly based on patrilineal succession. The vast Yellow River Plain gave rise to a more sophisticated culture based upon the growing of wheat and millet and the organization of society into villages. The early inhabitants of what is

15

today south-central China and the southern coastal area developed a maritime culture that also knew about the growing of irrigated rice. And finally, in the islands to the south and southeast were found predominantly fishing communities, highly skilled in the design of boats, and with a social system characterized by the ritual segregation of the sexes.

We have little precise evidence on the movement of ethnic groups on the Asian continent until fairly recent times. We know, however, that by at least the second millennium B.C., with the emergence of a bronze culture supporting an extensive development of government in the Yellow River area, Chinese civilization began to exert a constant pressure upon its frontiers both northward and southward. Such pressure, and the periodic warfare between the Chinese and the tribal groups of the northern steppe and forest lands, was to create a constant impetus for movement among the people who resided on the periphery of the main body of Chinese civilization.

We may presume, then, that the peopling of the Japanese islands took place first as a result of the dimly observable ethnic movements on the continent, and then as the result of smaller, more localized migrations, perhaps in response to the pressure created by the expansion of the Chinese people. Ultimately the flow into Japan tapered off into occasional sporadic wanderings or flights of refugees. But essential information on the timing, origin, and composition of these formative population movements is still lacking, leaving us with a number of puzzling problems.

The question of when the Japanese people actually formed into a coherent national mix cannot be given an exact answer. Was it as early as the sixth or seventh millennium B.C. with the appearance of the first bearers of neolithic culture, or was the composition not set until the third century A.D., after successive waves of migrants had each contributed essential ethnic and cultural elements? Another major mystery is the identity of the Ainu, an aboriginal group now consisting of about fifteen thousand individuals at the extreme north of the Japanese islands. The once commonly accepted assumption that the Ainu—considered to be survivals of a remote proto-Caucasoid

16

wave of migrants—were also the descendants of the first neo-lithic pople who had inhabited the entire island chain, has been largely abandoned. But the role that the Ainu played in Japanese history is still uncertain. Finally, a major contro-versy persists over whether, among the possible sources of Mongoloid stock, the Japanese were formed exclusively from peoples entering from the north, that is, from the Altaic-speak-ing tribal communities, or whether a significant influence is traceable to the Malay-speaking maritime communities to the south. For while in language, social customs, and religious beliefs the early historic Japanese appeared to affiliate most strongly with the peoples of northeast Asia, their style of living and language contained tantalizing evidence of southern influence.

The archaeological record, once we enter the phase of cul-ture marked by the manufacture of pottery, is extremely rich. Pottery was introduced in Japan perhaps as far back as 4,500 B.C. (possibly even earlier) and is associated with a hunting and gathering culture whose remains have been found from the southern Ryūkyūs to northern Japan. Technically at the Mesolithic stage of development, since they did not practice agriculture, these people lived on game and nuts in the up-lands, or on fish and shellfish along the seacoast. The most common evidence of their existence is found in refuse heaps—chiefly shell mounds—which they left scattered about their settlements. Fortunately the remains of settlements have occa-sionally been identified and excavated, giving evidence of com-munities of small, sunken hut-dwellings. Their inhabitants used tools of stone and bone, including fishhooks and harpoon points; they had developed a laminated bow similar to the typical Japanese bow of historic times; they apparently had domesticated the dog; and they made a variety of handshaped pottery of remarkably sophisticated design. It is from this pottery that the people were given the name Jōmon, or "cord pattern," since much of their work is marked with an overall ropelike design. Archaeologists set the disappearance of Jōmon pottery in western Japan at about 250 B.C., but the pottery and its attendant culture lingered much longer in the north before it was finally superseded by the wave of a more advanced culture. The considerable chronological and regional variation in the Jōmon culture style has led archaeologists to postulate several stages of historical development, as well as the possible existence of several differing streams of immigration. As for origin, it has generally been supposed that the Jōmon people were most closely related to those of the forest cultures of northeast Asia and even America. Jōmon sites have produced numerous small, grotesque female figurines, and it is believed that these may be evidence of a matrilineally based society. Recently scholars have begun to claim the discovery of related cultures in New Guinea and even Peru. What is certain, however, is that the Jōmon people lived and developed in Japan for several millennia and became the creators of one of the most remarkable styles of pottery known to the Stone Age. In richness of design and ingenuity of pattern it remains unsurpassed.

In the third century B.C., Jōmon culture was disrupted by an influx of a people of startlingly different cultural type. These new people, known as Yayoi, from the name given their style of pottery, had mastered the use of agriculture and brought with them the technique of irrigated rice cultivation. Their coming marked both an ethnic and technological revolution. Yayoi pottery, though less elaborately ornamented, was of superior manufacture, being made on the wheel and turned out in a more varied assortment of sizes and shapes. The Yayoi people were clearly of Mongoloid stock. They were also quite clearly in touch with the higher Chinese civilization of the continent from which their agricultural techniques may have come and which was the origin of their early, largely ritualistic use of bronze objects.

Excavations of Yayoi settlements, such as the amazingly complete one at Toro in Shizuoka Prefecture, reveal that these people lived in villages with closely grouped earthen-floor huts. The huts were of thatch placed over structures of wooden posts and beams. Such villages were clustered along streams or on coastal plains where it was possible to build paddy fields inclosed by stockade-style dikes and fed by irrigation ditches.

The Yayoi people brought with them the horse and the cow, though not in abundance. Their implements were chiefly farm tools: wooden hoes, rakes, and spades, stone celts and harvesting knives. But they also produced stone arrow points and fishing implements. It appears that from the beginning the Yayoi people were able to smelt iron and forge simple tools, and an occasional hoe was tipped with iron. The Yayoi dead were buried more ostentatiously than Jōmon dead, who were interred at their campsites. Stone and earthenware jars were used as coffins in burial sites, which were removed from the village. Low mounds placed over the graves seem to presage the practice of dolmen building, which flourished between the third and sixth centuries A.D.

The spread of Yayoi culture into Japan was rapid. From its beginnings in northern Kyūshū it probably reached the Kantō Plain by the end of the first century B.C. Beyond the Kantō, a distinct frontier came into existence; however, it had Jōmon remnants, perhaps intermixed with Ainu groups, to which the Japanese gave the name Emishi, or Ezo—a frontier that was not entirely eradicated until the ninth century. While the two cultures were different and appear to have been carried by people of different ethnic composition, there is no need to postulate a violent confrontation between them except in this northern region. Rather, throughout western and central Japan, Yayoi people and their culture overlaid and fused readily with the existing Jōmon inhabitants.

To say that we have no clear evidence of the original provenance of the Yayoi people is not to deny the evidence that they probably moved into Japan from southern Korea or that the general occasion of such movement is surmisable, for the third and second centuries B.C. were turbulent ones in East Asia. The extensive wars that united the Chinese kingdoms into the Ch'in Empire in 221 B.C. had raged for nearly two centuries and had been accompanied by constant military activity against the nomadic tribes to the north. Unity had thrust Chinese armies even farther afield toward northern Korea, and, as a result, Chinese immigrants had begun to flow in that direction. The succeeding Han dynasty actually invaded the

19

Korean peninsula, conquering the state of Chosŏn in 108 B.C., and establishing the commandery of Lo-lang with its capital at modern P'yŏngyang. Thus the period of unification and expansion of the Chinese under the Ch'in and Han emperors set up new movements of peoples along the expanding frontiers and sent out new waves of cultural influence that affected both Korea and Japan.

These events on the continent were reflected not only in the original migration of the Yayoi people but their subsequent cultural development as well. In later Yayoi sites, numerous Chinese objects are found, such as bronze coins and mirrors from the former Han dynasty (202 B.C. to A.D. 9), and the influx of such objects continued for many centuries. But before two centuries had elapsed, the Yayoi people themselves began to cast bronze artifacts of types and uses only remotely related to possible continental models. Particularly distinctive were large bronze "bells" and broad, thin ceremonial "weapons" such as spears, swords, and halberds. The casting of weapons predominated in northern Kyūshū and the Inland Sea region; bells have been found more prevalent in the eastern end of the Inland Sea and farther to the east. While bronze weapons have been found in Korea and bronze bells were common in China, these were functional implements, whereas in Japan, both types of bronze castings were completely nonfunctional and appear to have been used for symbolic purposes only. Whether the two regions marked out by differences in bronze artifacts reveal variations in the origin or ethnic composition of their inhabitants is not ascertainable, but there is evidence that the Yayoi people were of many subgroups, perhaps organized into tribes that were sometimes at odds with each other from the time they moved into the Japanese islands.

The archaeological record in Japan continues to offer evidence of successive cultural changes in the third and fourth centuries A.D. About the middle of the third century, members of the ruling elite in the Yamato Plain area, the highly developed region at the eastern end of the Inland Sea, began to erect huge earthen mounds as burial tombs. Within another half century this practice had spread westward into north

Kyūshū, moving against the easterly direction that had commonly marked the flow of technological innovation up to this point. The great tumuli, called *kofun* by Japanese scholars, were often imposing structures larger in mass than the pyramids of Egypt. The greatest of them, the tomb of Nintoku, stands today nearly fifteen hundred feet long and over one hundred feet high. Tombs were built in several forms, round or square, but the most distinctive shape was the "keyhole," which appears to have had no counterpart in other mound-building cultures. The appearance of these tombs has been taken to mark the beginning of a third distinct period of prehistoric development in Japan, to which archaeologists have given the name Tomb (or *Kofun*) culture. The building of such tombs continued into the seventh century when, under Buddhist influence, the practice was abandoned.

The tumuli of the third to sixth centuries are literally treasure stores of information on the life and customs of the Japanese elite of the time. Into the great mounds passage-graves or spacious megalithic chambers were cut where the bodies of the dead were laid. With the bodies were placed objects of great variety, from symbols of wealth and authority such as mirrors, crowns, or strings of precious stones, to objects of everyday use such as swords, armor, horse trappings, pottery vessels, agricultural tools. Outside the tomb, set up in rows around the slope of the mounds, were placed pottery cylinders capped with pottery figurines called *haniwa*. These figures provide the most vivid insight into the way of life of the tomb builders. Here are men in the tailored, quilted clothing typical of the northern, nomadic, horse-riding peoples. They protected themselves with slat armor and helmets, carried long iron swords and long recurved bows. Their horses were elaborately harnessed and provided with stirrups. They decorated themselves with *magatama*, or curved jewels, and sometimes by tattooing. Their houses, now raised off the ground, were roofed in heavy thatch in a way reminiscent of present-day Japanese farm houses. Their increased use of iron in agricultural implements indicates a considerable advance in farming techniques, while their pottery, similar in shape to the

21

Yayoi ware, was a much harder and more highly fired, bluish ware known as *sue* and was worked into more technically perfect and complex shapes. The tomb finds clearly reveal a class of warrior aristocrats who possessed the power to rule over a thickly settled countryside and to draw upon the agricultural produce of the regions they controlled.

The tombs and their contents present us with a further puzzle. Was the Tomb age brought to Japan by yet another wave of continental invaders, Tungusic men of the northern steppe, perhaps set adrift by the breakup of the Han Empire? Did such invaders ride down the Korean peninsula with their iron swords and superior armor and then subdue the Yayoi inhabitants of Japan, imposing upon them a new form of autocratic government? There are many signs of close contact between the Tomb culture and Korea. Tombs similar to those erected in Japan are also found in Korea—with the exception of the keyhole shape. *Magatama* are found in the golden crowns of the Korean kingdom of Silla. But such similarities, while indicating cultural affinity, do not offer conclusive proof of a distinct ethnic conquest. Tomb culture can, in fact, be accounted for as an evolutionary phase of Yayoi culture itself, enriched by continental contact, to be sure, but not dependent on any new wave of invaders from the continent. If Tungusic elements must be accounted for, Japanese historians are inclined to argue that they were already present in the original Yayoi culture.

There are a number of pieces of evidence that appear to support the theory of indigenous evolution. First, let us recall that the earliest tumuli were found in central Japan, not in Kyūshū where an invading group would have started its conquest. The first tombs are also found to contain mostly Yayoi-style objects. It is not until the fourth century that *kofun* begin to contain the new objects of continental origin. As we shall note later, the fourth century witnessed the final dissolution of the Chinese colony at Lo-lang. The Korean peninsula had been divided for some centuries between the kingdoms of Koguryŏ, Paekche, and Silla. Historic records attest to the involvement of Japanese forces in the wars between these kingdoms. The Japanese themselves claim to have established during the middle of the fourth century a military foothold in Kaya (or Mimana) along the southern Korean coast. It is possible to suppose that the change in character of the Tomb culture was the result of some sort of Japanese advance into Korea and the consequent absorption of continental influence by the Japanese leaders whose aggrandizements both at home and abroad were revealed in the increasing size of the great tumuli.

We have begun to talk by now of the Japanese people as though by this time their identity as a people had been established, and surely it had by the time of the tomb builders. But we must return to the question of racial composition with which we began this section. When did the Japanese people emerge as a fully identifiable group? Were the Jōmon people directly ancestral to the Japanese today? Some Japanese scholars have claimed that the evidence shows a Jōmon physical type sufficiently like the Japanese to justify such a claim. But whatever the ethnic relationship, it is clear that the Jōmon culture disappeared without contributing a significant element to the later Japanese way of life, with the possible exception of certain language survivals and, of course, genetic legacies, for instance lower stature and more abundant body hair. With the Yayoi people, it is a different matter; they are much more clearly ancestral in terms of general physical type, culture, and language. Techniques of glottochronology suggest that the Japanese speech community separated from Okinawan some eighteen or nineteen hundred years ago. Such a date would seem to fit the sequence of development as the joint Yayoi ancestors of the Japanese and Okinawans moved into their homelands and subsequently lost contact with each other. Thus by the age of the great tomb builders, the Yayoi people, by virtue of how much fusion with the earlier-Jōmon inhabitants and by how much subsequent absorption of immigrants through Korea we do not know, had become the historic Japanese.

4

Formation of the Early Japanese State

Against the archaeological background we have just surveyed, we must now attempt to pick out the outline of the history of the formation of the first unified political order in the Japanese islands. The written record is scanty, and at crucial points it is unreliable. The art of writing was transmitted rather late to Japan, the oldest remaining inscriptions being on swords and mirrors of the fifth and sixth centuries, and the oldest extant works of historical narrative were set down only in the eighth century. However, Japan's two earliest histories, the *Kojiki* (*Record of Ancient Matters*) compiled in 712 and the *Nihon shoki* (*Chronicles of Japan*) compiled in 720, while obviously containing a great deal of myth and legend and even of purposeful fabrication, were also based on historical memories and genealogical traditions of some reliability, and accounts of events after the fifth century were based on written records where possible. There are also historical records and inscriptions preserved by the Chinese and Koreans against which the Japanese histories can be checked.

When in 1940 the Japanese government with great publicity celebrated the 2,600th anniversary of the "founding" of the Japanese state, it was following with literal credence the chronology of the *Nihon shoki,* which placed the ascension of the first Japanese "emperor" in the year 660 B.C. The date was an obvious fabrication, arrived at by projecting backward with the use of a system of historical cycles imported from China. Historians today agree that the achievement of political unity in Japan more likely occurred at the end of the third century or the beginning of the fourth century A.D., at a point marked by the appearance of the *kofun* tumuli. Not only do the Chinese records seem to support such a supposition, but events on the continent appear to bear them out. The end of the Chinese commandery of Lo-lang in A.D. 313 had resulted as much from the competitive pressures of the newly forming Korean states as from the ebbing of Chinese support. Thereafter the three native Korean kingdoms fought among themselves while strengthening control over their own territories. Political unification was in the air, and, as we have seen, the Japanese, having achieved some measure of unity at home, were soon to become involved in Korean affairs. A stone monument erected in 414 to the king of Koguryŏ on the banks of the Yalu states that in A.D. 391 the Japanese crossed over into Korea and defeated the armies of Paekche and Silla.

Mention of Japan is found in Chinese histories as early as the first century B.C., at which time the *Han shu* describes the land of "Wa" as consisting of a hundred or more "countries," some of which sent tribute to the Chinese court. The name Wa, perhaps signifying "dwarf," was to remain the Chinese and Korean designation for the Japanese well into historic times. Other Chinese accounts report the existence of general warfare during the last half of the second century A.D. The most complete of the early descriptions is found in the *Wei chih,* a Chinese chronicle compiled before A.D. 297. It contains information, presumably from officials or traders who had visited Japan, and describes the route to Japan and to several of the centers of government, mentioning the country of Yamatai governed by an unmarried queen named Himiko.

The *Wei* record describes a well-ordered society with strict distinctions of rank in which social respect was shown by squatting down by the side of the road. The people were given to strong drink, but were rigorous in the maintenance of laws. They used divination and various practices of ritual purity. Within the "countries" were officials, and taxes were collected.

25

Some "countries" had kings, and others queens, a fact that may indicate that the elite society was in a state of transition from matriarchy to patriarchy at that time.

Unfortunately, the geographical information in the *Wei chih* is inaccurate or garbled, so that the location of Yamatai and the identity of Himiko cannot be determined accurately. Japanese historians have been intrigued by the possibility that Yamatai refers to Yamato, the old capital district in central Japan, and that Himiko may be a rendition of Himeko or "sun princess," a title later used by members of the ruling Japanese family. The Himiko story contains further tantalizing details, for the *Wei chih* states that in order to put an end to the warfare among the countries of Japan, the kings formed a union under the leadership of Himiko. The queen lived as a priestess and governed by spiritual power, and when she died, a huge mound was heaped over her. The fact that the Japanese ruling house traced its descent from a shamanistically conceived Sun Goddess and that the age of the great tomb builders was about to begin can only excite the imagination at this point. The link between the Chinese reports and the legendary Japanese accounts are too tenuous to permit more than speculation. Yet an underlying fact remains, that from whatever direction we view the period of transition from Yayoi culture to that of the tomb builders, and from the period of warring groups to that of general unity, our attention is directed inward to the domestic history of the Japanese.

Among the mythologies of the world, the legends that begin the narrative of Japanese history seem primitive and lacking in variety and imaginative detail. There are no culture heroes, nor are there deities who remain on high to direct the destinies of man. The problem of creation is simply and naïvely disposed of, and the legendary stories appear most concerned with the ancestral identities and genealogies of the ruling families of early historic times. The accounts, as set down in the *Kojiki* and *Nihon shoki,* are obviously attempts to make a coherent narrative out of a number of legend cycles, and the folklorist is able to distinguish in them several stages of human development and several localities, perhaps reflecting the movement of the early ancestors of the Japanese.

The legends begin with the opening of heaven and earth. Out of a vagueness emerge two deities, brother and sister, named Izanami and Izanagi, who create the Japanese islands by catching up pieces of land as though fishing. Next are born the deities of the "Plain of High Heaven" (*Takamagahara*), a land beyond the ocean and above the habitat of man. Among these are Amaterasu Ōmikami, the Sun Goddess, and her brother, Susa-no-ō-no-Mikoto, a god of storms and violence. Together these deities produce the next series of deities, who seem to be ancestral to the main lineage groups that later appear as participants in the struggle for power in Japan. In the long and intricate genealogical details and the regional local color these accounts contain, we find exemplified the main characteristics of the Japanese legends.

The later chapters of the legendary story contain several cycles but focus upon three main localities: northern Kyūshū, Izumo, on the Japan Sea, and Yamato. The first and the last of these locations are associated with Amaterasu, while Izumo is the home of Susa-no-ō's descendants. The sister and brother appear in perpetual conflict. She acts in many ways like a typical shamanistic chieftain, dressing as a warrior, using magical powers, and possessing symbols of authority such as a mirror of bronze and a necklace of curved jewels. And it is she who becomes the progenitor of the main line of rulers on earth, a group of families known as the *tenson,* or "sun line." Susa-no-ō likewise becomes progenitor of the Izumo line of rulers. Ultimately, the struggle between the deities is transferred to earth. Amaterasu sends her grandson Ninigi-no-Mikoto down from Takamagahara, having bestowed on him "three treasures" as symbols of his authority. He is accompanied by numerous groups of warriors and servants who make up his retinue, and whose presumed descendants make up the later Yamato aristocracy. He settles down in northern Kyūshū. Two generations later, Ninigi's grandson Kamu Yamato Iware Hiko leaves Kyūshū and fights his way up the Inland Sea to occupy Yamato. There he establishes his seat of government and is recognized as Japan's first "emperor," Jimmu ("Divine Warrior"). Jimmu's successors eventually conquered Izumo and other unpacified parts of Japan to bring the process of nation building to an end. The Izumo leaders, though stripped of political power, were allowed to continue the worship of the shrine of Susa-no-ō.

Here, then, between the archaeological record, the Chinese chronicles, and Japanese legendary history, we see the establishment of the first Japanese state revealed. How much of the legendary story is to be taken seriously is a matter of controversy, but its outlines have a way of being authenticated as more evidence is assembled from other sources. The name Jimmu and the concept of a ruling emperor are, of course, later creations by Japanese historians who sought to emulate the Chinese dynastic tradition. And historians have cast doubt upon the historicity of Jimmu himself and on his eastward expedition. However, there is no disputing the appearance of a powerful group of families in Yamato led by the chieftain of the Sun Line. Here indeed was the origin of the first political hegemony in Japan holding sway over what we may describe as the Yamato state.

Up to this point, we have sought to visualize the formation of the Yamato state from records that were basically external to the process of political and institutional integration itself. But it is also possible to reconstruct the story from the inside, building upon our knowledge of the structure of primitive Japanese society and the process of consolidation that it underwent. As we have noted, the Chinese sources referred to the strong separation between the ruling families and the common people. Careful analysis of the Japanese records by Japanese historians and sociologists has taken us much farther toward an understanding of the organization of early Japanese society. From the structural point of view, we know, first of all, that three types of social groups, *uji, be,* and *yatsuko,* comprised the community.

The first of these, *uji,* is generally translated as "clan," though "lineage-group" is probably more appropriate. *Uji*

28

were certainly not clans in the sociological sense of being exogamous divisions of a tribe. They were instead large groups of families related by real or fictional blood ties to a main-descent lineage and held together by the patriarchal power of the lineage head. They formed the characteristic units into which the upper class was organized. Being of the upper class, the members of the *uji* possessed surnames and bore titles of respect. Within the *uji*, members worshipped a common tutelary deity, the *uji-gami,* often the supposed progenitor of the group. They obeyed the head of the main house of the prime lineage, who held the status of *uji-no-kami,* or "chief." The *uji* chief, as presumed direct descendant of the *uji* deity, served both as patriarchal head and as the chief priest in the conduct of services of veneration to the deity. As such, his authority was both hereditary and sacerdotal and was vested in certain symbols, for instance, a mirror, arrow, or precious stone.

As a ruling class, the *uji* depended upon a sub-stratum of common workers. These were the *be* or communities of workers who were grouped by locale or occupation. To an extent, *be* members were not free since they were bound to the service of superior *uji.* Like the *uji,* they acquired a common religious focus: a local spirit (*ubusuna-gami*) or the *uji-gami* of the particular family they served. Most *be* were organized as agricultural communities producing rice for themselves and their superiors; but others specialized in certain services such as weaving (Hatoribe), pottery-making (Suebe), fishing (Ukaibe), the making of bows (Yugebe), or household functions such as military or domestic service.

The third social category of this time, *yatsuko,* consisted of slaves attached mainly to *uji* households. All told, they may have accounted for 5 percent of the population. They were used chiefly as domestics, and there is little evidence that the Japanese relied upon a system in which large groups of slaves performed essential economic functions.

During the years in which the Yamoto hegemony was taking shape, then, the basic social complex that possessed political and military power was the *uji* together with its attendant *be* and attached domestics. In time some *uji* became quite power-

29

ful, and as they did, they also gained control over neighboring *uji*, enlisting lesser families under their authority into larger, more complex, regional hegemonies. It was such a process that gave rise to the local political communities in early Japan. Foɪ as groups of *uji*, organized under the command of powerful leaders, began to fill out the contours of the many small regions into which Japan's mountainous topography naturally fell, we can see the beginnings of the small political units that the Chinese called countries. Such local clusters of *uji*, then, were the "hundred or more countries" identified by the Han historians. Presumably at first they were independent of one another, but soon larger geographical coalitions were formed, and these in turn awaited only the assertion of a superior force or leadership to be brought under a single authority.

The rise of the chiefs of the Sun Line to power in Yamato followed some such process. First as heads of a small local hegemony, then as predominant powers in central Japan, the chiefs extended their influence by reducing to submission or by securing the allegiance of surrounding *uji* and enlisting them into a household organization of increasing size and strength. By military conquest, assimilation through marriage, and the assertion of superior spiritual powers deriving from the prestige of the Sun Goddess, the members of the Sun Line achieved a position from which they could claim to be sovereigns of all of Japan. It is interesting to note that the rise of the Sun Line "dynasty" came about in a way quite unlike the establishment of the imperial dynasties of China. It resulted not from the massive conquest of the country by a single superior military force with the consequent imposition of a powerful centralized authority, but rather it took shape slowly as, step by step, one group of *uji* struggled to the top of a hierarchy of ruling families in Japan. The Sun Line chieftains did resort to military force in the struggle, but they also used conciliation and diplomacy where possible, attempting to win the allegiance of hostile *uji* by assertion of superior sacerdotal prestige. Most often, therefore, competitors were not eliminated but were incorporated instead into a balance of power over which the chieftain played the role of *suzerain* and peacemaker. The resulting

30

political structure was something especially congenial to the Japanese and it originated a pattern that was to be repeated many times in Japanese history.

Once formed, the Yamato hegemony took on certain structural characteristics. At the top of the hierarchy of power was the chief of the main house of the Sun lineage. Around him a loose cluster of intimately related houses comprised the Sun Line *uji* itself. Supporting the ruling *uji* was a large number of service or what we might call "vassal" *uji*, generically known as *miyatsuko*. (Since some of these service *uji* bore surnames that ended in the word *be*, we can imagine that they either supervised groups of *be* attached to the sovereign house, or may themselves originally have been the heads of *be* communities.) Of the direct vassals of the Yamato chief, some were relied upon for contributions of a functional nature such as military, priestly, or craft service and were known as "attendant families" (*tomo-no-miyatsuko*). Others were relied upon as regional supporters of the Yamato hegemon and were referred to as "territorial families" (*kuni-no-miyatsuko*).

The Sun Line group and its vassals and retainers (to use the terminology of feudalism in suggestive fashion only) were poised at the top of a balance of political and military power. The balance was made up on the one hand of a group of closely related branch *uji*, and on the other of a much larger body of formerly subjugated but now allied *uji*. We may suppose that, in its formative stage, the driving force in the expanding Yamato coalition was the combination of members of the Sun Line *uji*, its offshoots, and its vassals, but this group at no time constituted an overwhelming military force in the country. Hence the element of coalition and compromise entered the structure, and the unrelated, subjugated houses became as much an essential part of the balance as those with direct blood relationships to the Sun Line. The subtle play of competing interests between the various *uji* groups over which the Yamato chieftain served as peacemaker thus created a dynamic tension that gave stability to the edifice, and, in fact, prevented the Sun Line from ever being dislodged from its supreme peacemaking position.

There were, of course, other stabilizing elements in the Yamato political structure. The whole hierarchy of power was linked together, when possible, by family or simulated family connections. By skillful techniques of intermarriage or by taking "tribute" males and females from vassal *uji* into service, the Sun Line cemented close ties with its subjugated and allied families and acquired means of intimate control over them. Where possible, authority was asserted along family lines and justified on a familial basis.

Religion also played an important role in providing a sanction to the evolving hegemony and offered a rationale that united the community with the authority structure. The primitive religion of the Japanese people has retained a remarkable vitality in Japan, even to this day, under the name of what is now called Shintō. While today a great variety of religious beliefs and practices are subsumed under this name, the early religious practices of the Japanese were much more simply conceived and were directly associated with the efforts of the early Japanese to integrate themselves to their homeland and their social and political community. Lacking creed, scripture, or a developed metaphysic, Shintō's two prime features were a rather naïve belief in the protective or baneful effect of supernatural powers and a close association with the social community, whether in terms of locale or of family. The early Japanese confronted the unknown spirits directly and joyfully and reinforced through worship their deepest feelings of communal togetherness.

The essential elements of Shintō belief are contained in a relatively few basic concepts and sacred objects. Worship was directed toward *kami*. Often translated as "god," "deity," or "spirit," *kami* can best be described as localized spiritual forces of either natural or human origin. *Kami* were believed to possess generalized powers usually confined to specific localities or categories of human activity. The *uji-gami* venerated by members of certain *uji* were human or totemistic progenitors of lineages and were presumed to possess protective powers over the *uji* and its territory. A localized spirit could protect a village or a larger region depending on its particular potency. In addition, certain generalized spirits such as Inari (the rice spirit) could be worshipped throughout the land.

Kami, it was believed, became manifest in certain concrete objects known as *shintai* (literally "kami body"). Such objects could be found in nature, i.e., a rock, tree, mountain, or waterfall. They could be symbolic objects such as a mirror, a precious stone, or a crude statue. Most *shintai* that were objects of communal or family veneration were placed in shrines (*miya*) where they became the objects of worship (*matsuri*), which consisted of ritual prayer and ceremonies of purification. The sign of the existence of a *miya* was usually the *torii* or simple gateway.

The religious beliefs and practices of the early Japanese were closely integrated with the structure of the political community. Among the common inhabitants of the agricultural and craft villages, local *kami* were worshipped for protection and a sense of group identity. The local chieftain's worship of his *uji* duty through the agency of the *shintai* that was peculiar to his lineage served both to symbolize his authority over the members of his *uji* and to justify the territorial influence he and his family came to possess. Thus, as the Yamato chieftain asserted authority over the entire Japanese islands, his rituals before the shrine of Amaterasu became an integral part of the conceptions of sovereignty that backed his claim to political supremacy in Japan.

It is in these rituals that we see most clearly the manner in which spiritual power drawn from the *kami* was brought to the support of political authority. As we know, the chief of the Sun Line held three sacred objects as symbols of his spiritual and secular position. Of these, the mirror can be conceived of as the literal "body" of Amaterasu. The sword of Susa-no-ō was evidence of the Yamato conquest of Izumo. But it was the necklace that most directly served as the symbol of succession passed from Amaterasu to each succeeding head of the Sun Line *uji.* Thus the necklace became the most important emblem of enthronement for the emperors of Japan. The *tama,* or jewels, in the necklace were thought to represent the soul-spirit, which could enter the body of its possessor and make

33

him a "living god" in full communion with the great spirit of Amaterasu. Therefore, while it became the practice of the Sun Line to enshrine the mirror at Amaterasu's shrine at Ise and the sword at Atsuta Shrine, the necklace was retained in the sovereign's direct possession.

In terms of Shintō belief, then, the early Yamato state assumed the following form. The chief of the Sun Line, through the efficacy of Amaterasu, offered protection to the entire country, while the lesser *uji* chiefs, through the power of their lesser and more localized *uji-gami,* assured local protection and assumed the right to local rule. Governance and worship of the *kami* went hand in hand, and, in fact, the same word, *matsuri goto,* served for both functions. Political authority, whether acquired by force or through long-established social prestige, was thus sanctioned by religious belief. The importance of the early legends with their elaborate genealogical data was that they wrote into the spiritual world a hierarchy of *kami* that matched the socio-political order that had come into being under the Yamato hegemon.

It is apparent that the social structure, the political organization, and the religious beliefs of the Japanese people of the second through fifth centuries were singularly different from comparable practices that were current on the continent at the same time. It is for this reason that the details of life in the early Yamato age assume such importance, for it was during the early centuries of relative isolation from China that the Japanese people evolved their first political system and defined their distinctive cultural identity. In the succeeding centuries, despite the powerful influence of Chinese civilization, the essential features of the style of political and social organization institutionalized by the Yamato state were to remain relatively undisturbed. The *uji* system of elite family organization and particularly the form of the Yamato sovereignty, in which a peacemaker, priest-chief ruled over a coalition of elite families, was to remain characteristic of the Japanese political style until modern times.

5

The Yamato State and the Spread of Chinese Influence

Twice in their history the Japanese people have given the appearance of having been totally engulfed by foreign influence: once in the seventh century when the country wholehcartedly embraced Chinese civilization, and then in the nineteenth century when Japan absorbed the impact of Western expansion into East Asia. How is one to interpret the eager and seemingly uncritical welcome the Japanese gave these influences from abroad? Is it, as some have unkindly suggested, that the Japanese are essentially imitators without a sufficiently creative vigor to sustain an independent culture of their own; or is the picture of imitativeness an illusion created by the fact of Japan's geographical isolation, a condition that has served to accentuate the contrasts between periods of rapid borrowing and those of apparent domestic quiescence? Sir George Sansom has written of the seventh and eighth centuries as a time when Japan awoke dramatically to the superiority of Chinese culture. Arnold Toynbee has conceived of Japan as entering for the first time upon the stage of high civilization under Chinese tutelage. To both historians, Japan was overwhelmed by the example of China and thus driven to imitation and emulation.

But to view the seventh and eighth centuries exclusively in terms of Sinification neglects the all-important domestic factors in Japan's history. These same centuries were marked by major political and social changes that cannot be explained simply as byproducts of a radical turn toward Chinese culture. The Taika *coup d'état* of 645 that traditionally signals the beginning of Japan's conscious emulation of China, was also the start of a major effort to centralize power and to institutionalize the privileges of a newly emergent aristocratic class. Japan's efforts at Sinification cannot be understood without reference to the deep currents of indigenous change that were affecting the Yamato state and its social base in the sixth century.

From the time of the establishment of the Yamato state in the third century, the Sun Line chieftains and their supporters worked persistently to extend their influence and consolidate their hegemony. The annals of the early "emperors" as recorded in the *Kojiki* and *Nihon shoki* are of uncertain authenticity, but they tell the story of a constantly expanding authority in which military expeditions worked outward from Yamato to gain, or in some instances regain, control of outlying districts. The fifth century probably brought the power of the early Yamato state to its peak. It begins with the ruler Nintoku, whose spacious tomb is said to have taken twenty years to complete. It ends with Yūryaku, the eccentric despot, who worked incessantly to increase the flow of tribute. His boast, repeated in the Chinese records, was that he held sway over fifty-five provinces to the east, sixty-six provinces to the west, and fifteen across the sea in Korea. Chinese sources mention five "kings" of Japan during this century who sent tribute embassies to China.

By the sixth century, the outlines of a more advanced structure of government had become discernible. The head of the Yamato confederation, styling himself a true sovereign (*sumera-mikoto*), had begun to claim more abstract and absolute prerogatives of authority over the assemblage of *uji* chiefs, claiming that they were in fact his officials and accountable to his pleasure. A more precise set of titles of rank (*kabane*) had also been evolved. Of these, *Atae, Sukune, Mabito,* and *Ason* ranked highest and were given to families close to the main line of the Yamato *uji. Omi* became the common

36

designation of important chiefs more distantly related to the sovereign line; and *Muraji* became the highest title held by great chiefs among the unrelated and vassal *uji*.

Ultimately a council of state was organized under the sovereign, in which the great chiefs were represented. Later still, spokesmen chiefs, *Ō-omi* and *Ō-muraji,* were named to serve as chief ministers of state. Simultaneously the effort was made to bring local administration under more direct central authority. The entire country was divided into units known as *kuni* (roughly equivalent to the spheres of influence of the major territorial *uji*), and within these units the ruling chiefs were reduced to the status of *kuni-no-miyatsuko.* In other words, they were treated, where possible, as though they were appointive officials, though in origin they may well have been reluctant subordinates to Yamato authority. Meanwhile, the ruling house constantly expanded its wealth by acquiring new agricultural and craft *be* both in Yamato and other more distant *kuni.*

The trend toward economic aggrandizement was not restricted to the ruling family. As can be seen in the wide distribution of huge burial mounds dating from this period, the great *uji* chiefs, beginning in Yamato but also in a number of outlying *kuni,* were rapidly increasing their control over the manpower and productive resources of their locales. As local leaders in their own right, they joined their forces to the Yamato expeditions to Korea or, on occasion, disputed the authority of the Yamato chief. Thus the Yamato rulers were frequently obliged to rely on their special guard units or to call on the forces of their two chief military *uji,* the Otomo and Mononobe, to maintain the balance of power.

In the sixth century Japan was not an insignificant member of the East Asian community of states. Since the previous century, the Japanese had been active in Korea and had acquired a base of operations in the territory of Mimana. This Japanese foothold on the peninsula apparently played an important role in the triangular struggle between Koguryŏ, Paekche, and Silla. Historically the Japanese most frequently allied themselves with Paekche, perhaps because its location

37

was so strategically placed along Japan's sea route to China, but also because it seems to have maintained a higher level of cultural achievement. But in 532 the forces of Silla and Paekche attacked Mimana, and Japan lost half of its Korean sphere of influence. Thirty years later, in 562, the Japanese were driven from Mimana entirely. But strong interest in the continent continued. A new center of foreign relations was established at Dazaifu, in North Kyūshū. Sporadic efforts to regain the Mimana foothold continued for yet another century, but Japan's final disengagement from the peninsula became unavoidable after 668 when Silla, with Chinese aid, united all of Korea.

The military exploits of the sixth-century Japanese reveal the considerable resources they had at their disposal. We hear of fleets of several hundred ships and armies of several tens of thousands of men. Furthermore, behind the military operations, there emerges a picture of growing Japanese maturity as a state and a rising level of cultural accomplishment. Mimana was of as much interest to the Japanese as a base for the acquisition of new knowledge and skilled workmen from Korea as for its military value. Naniwa, the port of Yamato at the eastern terminus of the Inland Sea, was the scene of a constant going and coming of tribute missions between Japan and China or the courts of the Korean kings. Refugees or captives from the continent were willingly absorbed into the Yamato system, and those of rank or accomplishment were given honorable titles under a special category of "foreign" *uji*. Their surnames such as Hata (using the character for Ch'in) and Aya (using the character for Han) revealed to later generations their origin from the Chinese dynasties. Others were enlisted as craft and service *be* and placed under the supervision of Yamato service *uji*.

During the fifth and sixth centuries, then, a steady stream of continental immigrants entered Japan, and with them came the spread of new technologies and ideas. Knowledge of Confucian books was, according to the *Nihon shoki*, introduced to the Yamato aristocracy by the scholar Wani at the beginning of the fifth century. This is a convenient time from which to date the spread of the use of Chinese writing in Japan; but the ability to write was probably limited for some time to Korean or Chinese immigrants who served the ruling elite as scribes. The name "scribe" (*fuhito*) became one of the noble titles assigned by the Yamato rulers. These early centuries also saw the introduction of new irrigation techniques, improved systems of paddy field organization, a more exact calendar, and a variety of other innovations. The transmission of the Buddhist doctrine to Yamato, probably in 538, brought to a high point this early absorption of Chinese civilization through Korea.

However, changes in Yamato culture and outlook could go only so far without bringing powerful stresses to bear upon the structure of government and society and to the prevalent system of religious beliefs. While the Yamato rulers sought to convert the lineage-based federation of *uji* into a more centralized and tightly administered state structure, the great *uji* by private aggrandizement were beginning to reduce the head of the Sun Line to a powerless figurehead. As new families rose to influence in Yamato or to independent power in more distant territories, the system of authority based on the fabric of kinship ties and Shintō beliefs began to break down. The sixth century was a particularly unsettled time in Japan as enmities split the Yamato coalition and revolts broke out in outlying areas or among the Japanese military forces in Korea. In fact, it was the rebellion of a Kyūshū chieftain by the name of Iwai that accounted for the failure of the Japanese to retain their hold in Mimana in 562. The Yamato political order was clearly in danger, and the question of whether it was to dissolve into a chaos of contending groups or was to evolve into a new and more firmly centralized state organization was in serious doubt for several decades. Yet ultimately the thrust toward centralization won out, and this outcome was greatly assisted by new influences that reached Japan from China.

By the end of the sixth century, China, which had been disunited since the fall of the Han dynasty in the third century, was again in a phase of resurgence under the Sui (581–

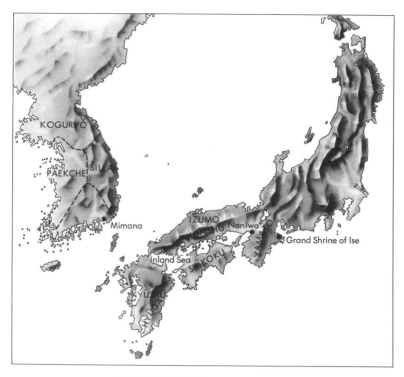

JAPAN DURING THE YAMATO PERIOD, CA. 500

618) and T'ang (618–907) dynasties. The grandeur that was imperial China was again made visible in monuments of cultural achievement: in cities, palaces, and works of art, in vast new public works and in massive armies sent forth across the borders of the empire. The Japanese were dazzled by such grandeur, to be sure, but two features of the new "Far Eastern" culture, as Toynbee has called it, were to prove most significant to the Japanese. These were the institutions of government, particularly as perfected under the T'ang dynasty, and the doctrines of Buddhism, as institutionalized under the power of the Chinese emperors and the Sinified sectarian orders.

It was the genius of the T'ang rulers that they were able to organize to a high degree of symmetry and effectiveness the government machinery of imperial China: perfecting the organs of the central bureaucracy which supported the emperor and his authority, elaborating the machinery of local admin-

40

istration and taxation, and embodying both theory and practice of government in a systematic set of legal codes. This theory, which had been evolving through the course of Chinese political history, rested on three central principles that contrasted fundamentally with those upon which the early Yamato state rested. These were the concept of an absolute sovereign legitimized in ethical terms as receiving the Mandate of Heaven; the conception of a government of imperial servants —that is, trained officials serving at the pleasure of the emperor—and the principle that the empire should be impartially regulated under the uniform laws of the emperor. These were ideal principles from which the Chinese often deviated, and T'ang society was in fact much more aristocratic in its structure than the ideal would seem to permit. Yet, however faulty the practice, the model represented a system vastly more effectively centralized and bureaucratized and much more efficient as a means of organizing the resources of the state than anything the Japanese of the Yamato period could imagine.

Powerful religious forces were also bent to the support of the Chinese state. Buddhism, having been introduced into China by at least the first century B.C., had undergone a long period of doctrinal and organizational development, as well as adjustment to the interests of the state. A religion of universal appeal, Buddhism had produced in China elaborate sectarian divisions, networks of temples and monasteries, a numerous priesthood, a rich body of scriptures, and a complex and beautiful iconography. Buddhism had become a major force in China and Korea by the sixth century. Especially noteworthy, however, was the manner in which T'ang rulers succeeded in harnessing Buddhism as an instrument of state, adding its ritual and its universal spiritual appeals to the support of the absolute ruler and extending its doctrines to buttress the moral foundations of a united empire.

The introduction of Buddhism into Japan in 538 had immediate political as well as religious repercussions. To the elite families of Yamato who based their claims to prestige on descent from their ancestral *kami,* Buddhism presented a real threat. For if the Buddha had powers superior to all local

41

deities, as was claimed, then what was to happen to their *kami*-based authority? In the middle of the sixth century when the Yamato sovereign put to his advisors the question of whether to worship the Buddhist images received from Korea, he precipitated a major conflict among the great families of Japan. The division of opinion thrust the Soga family, a relatively recent and ambitious offshoot of the Yamato line who served as *Ō-omi*, against a conservative coalition of families of long service to the Yamato line, chief among whom were the *Ō-muraji* Mononobe (hereditary generals) and the Nakatomi (Shintō ritualists). The quarrel between these factions divided Yamato for several decades; but in 587, the Soga, who steadfastly championed the cause of the new religion, defeated the Mononobe in battle and assured the acceptance of Buddhism.

The victory of 587 also made the Soga all-powerful in Yamato, and for the next seventy years successive Soga leaders were able to dominate Yamato affairs, even to the point of near usurpation of sovereign authority. In 592, Soga-no-Umako (?–626), to whom belonged the credit for the annihilation of the Mononobe, was able to maneuver the assassination of the Yamato chief (his nephew) and replace him with a female ruler, Suiko (his niece). Suiko's nephew, Umayado-no-toyotomimi-no-mikoto (574–622, posthumously known as Shōtoku Taishi), was concurrently named regent. Fortunately for the Yamato *uji*, Shōtoku Taishi, though married to a Soga lady, jealously guarded the interests of the ruling family. At least during his lifetime, Soga aggrandizement was placed under restraint.

Whether all the acts attributed to Shōtoku Taishi were indeed his own is not of prime importance. For certainly during his lifetime the leaders of the Yamato *uji* came to appreciate the role that Buddhism could play as a buttress to government and an ordered society. They must have glimpsed as well the possibility of creating an "imperial state" based on the Chinese model in which a sovereign emperor would be served by loyal subjects. If we are to believe the traditional and undoubtedly idealized story, Shōtoku Taishi dedicated his life to increasing the prestige of the *mikoto* of Yamato both at home and abroad. In his youth he fought, alongside the Soga, to gain the acceptance of Buddhism as a religion of state, and in his later years he richly endowed Buddhist institutions in order to make his family the prime patron of the new religion. For some years he worked to recapture Japan's lost power on the continent, sending expeditions to retake Mimana in 595 and 602. Then, abandoning his military efforts, he opened direct communication with the reunited Chinese empire in 607.

Shōtoku Taishi was less successful in securing the political reforms that he hoped would bolster the authority of his family in Yamato. He attempted, however, to gain recognition for the Yamato sovereign as a ruler in the imperial sense, endowed with the moral attributes of sovereignty and supported by a court and administrative officials. He announced in 603 a new system of twelve court ranks, presumably so that the sovereign might determine a new order of official precedence. In 604 he issued a code of seventeen articles of government with which he hoped to establish a new tone of political ethics. Borrowing Confucian theories of state, he likened the relationship between sovereign and subject to that between Heaven and Earth. In official correspondence he worked for the acceptance of a new terminology of sovereignty, employing the concepts of imperial China and asserting for the Yamato chief the dignity of "emperor" and "son of heaven."

The death of Shōtoku Taishi in 622 and the passing of Soga-no-Umako from the political scene soon after, plunged Yamato into a state of bitter political rivalry. From this point on, the process of institutional and cultural change under Chinese influence became more closely interwoven with the political factionalism which divided the great chiefs. Cautiously there began to emerge a coalition of families, led by Naka-no-Ōe, an imperial prince, and Nakatomi-no-Kamatari, which was determined to crush the main Soga faction and carry forward the political and administrative reforms Shōtoku Taishi had envisioned. The close contact that this group had with advisors who had returned from firsthand study in T'ang China led them to the conclusion that fundamental institutional reforms must accompany any direct action on their part. In 645, at a state ceremonial, Naka-no-Ōe himself took a hand in the assassination of Umako's grandson, Soga-no-Iruka, and thus prepared the way for the elimination of Soga influence. This act so stunned the great chiefs that the victorious faction was able to proceed rapidly with its plans for political reform. On New Year's Day of 646, the group issued the famous edict that announced a new year-name, Taika (literally, "great change"), and promulgated an ambitious reorganization of the political order. Following Chinese precedent, it called for the abolition of all private holdings of rice land, as well as the *be* communities that supported the *uji*. It asserted the rights of the sovereign over the land resources of the country. It called for the establishment of a permanent imperial capital and the administration of the country through a system of provinces, districts, and villages. It ordered the drawing up of a population census and the systematic allotment of land to cultivators after it had been fully surveyed and graded by quality. Taxes were to be systematically imposed, and the upper class was to be assigned official posts and receive stipends according to rank and status.

The *coup d'état* of 645 and the edict of 646 dramatically united the drive for possession of power by what we may now call the Japanese imperial family and the desire to emulate China. It goes without saying, however, that the country was not transformed overnight. (In fact, modern historians cast some doubt on the authenticity of the reform edict and hence on the existence of a preconceived reform plan.) Reforms were effected slowly and pragmatically. The effort to bring rice land under public regulation was initiated by Prince Naka when he voluntarily gave up his own private lands to the state. Lands held in the name of the sovereign were also easily brought under official title and management, but others were acquired with greater difficulty. An imperial capital laid out in Chinese style with palaces, and public buildings had been erected at Naniwa in 645. In 649, eight departments of central administration were created and officials named to staff them. In 652, the first large-scale land distribution was completed in the capital area. By 668 Prince Naka was able to ascend the throne as Emperor Tenchi (r. 668–671), with the satisfaction that a number of important steps toward centralization of political authority in the hands of the emperor had been taken.

But upon Tenchi's death, a serious succession dispute broke out that engulfed central Japan in several months of bloody warfare and apparently jeopardized the reform policies. Yet it was this civil war, known as the Jinshin disturbance, that brought to the throne an emperor who possessed all the attributes of absolute authority. The emperor Temmu (r. 673–686) swept to power as much on the basis of military strength as any Japanese ruler since early historic times. For the first time in several centuries, the head of the imperial family had sufficient power in hand to exert real leadership. Temmu, therefore, was able to complete the program begun by Prince Naka-no-Ōe and to push through measures that had long been opposed by vested interests among the *uji* elite. Within a few decades after his death in 686, the imperial city of Heijō (more commonly known as Nara) had been established with a fully developed officialdom, and a systematic set of codes had been promulgated for the regulation of administrative procedures, local government, taxation, and military affairs. These final steps in the great reform were carried out by Temmu's successors with zeal and a remarkable degree of initial success.

There is, however, a question that remains to be asked. If the reforms of the latter half of the seventh century did not occur simply as the result of irresistible Chinese influence or as the product of pressures exerted by an all-powerful central authority in Japan, why was there not more opposition to them, especially from the *uji* chiefs? The answer undoubtedly lies in the broader social implications of the reforms, for these measures, despite what must have been their initial unpopularity for the more independent of the great *uji*, ultimately worked to the benefit of the entire ruling class, helping to convert it into a securely established civil aristocracy.

The breakdown of the traditional Yamato authority structure during the seventh century must have given as much concern to the *uji* chiefs as to the sovereign family itself. Thus we can imagine that the *uji* chiefs were not reluctant to see the appearance of a more powerful central authority and the adoption of new and more effective techniques of local administration and land control. Moreover, the Taika reforms did not strip the great families of all hereditary influence or wealth. In most instances the former chiefs were confirmed in their privileged positions and given access to the imperial government. In essence the new polity merely interposed the public institutions of a centralized state between the *uji* chiefs and the sources of their wealth and political power. Where formerly the prestige and authority of these families had come from their historical claims to local preeminence and to their own private military forces, they were now backed by the full weight of an imperial system, its laws and its machinery of government, and, above all, its capacity to collect taxes systematically.

In the long run, these conditions proved advantageous to the former *uji* elite, particularly to those families within reach of the imperial court. These soon moved into the capital city to form a new aristocracy strategically placed to benefit most from the imperial benefice and from the tax income that flowed to Nara from the rest of the country. The great public works, the palaces, government offices, temples, roads, and irrigation works that marked the heyday of the Nara period were the visible signs of a new concentration of power that was for and of the aristocracy. Japan not only had transformed its political system and its cultural style, but it had created a new structure of society that was to endure for another five centuries.

In the long sweep of Japanese history, the seventh century may best be looked upon as the time of transition to an aristocratic style of culture. During this century the former *uji* elite converted themselves into a civil nobility (called *kuge* by the Japanese) that centered on a new imperial court, divesting themselves of their former localized and warlike qualities. The *uji* elite took with them into the aristocratic age their lineages (some eleven hundred are listed in the ninth-century

Shinsen shōjiroku, or *Register of Genealogies*). While they left behind their sources of independent military and economic strength, they gained new prestige and security by their association with the new central government and by their access to a highly sophisticated way of life. And so long as they were able to maintain a reasonably effective machinery of government, they were able to give peace and stability to the nation. Historically, their political powers proved inadequate only after the twelfth century, and their social status was not abolished until 1945.

6

The Aristocratic Age

Nara and the Institutions of Taihō

Of the achievements of the seventh and eighth centuries, which marked the beginning of the aristocratic age in Japan, those in public architecture and Buddhist art continue to attract the greatest attention, not only because of their aesthetic excellence, but because many of them are still visible as historic monuments in present-day Nara and its environs. Yet achievements in the field of government undoubtedly had more widespread and lasting effect upon the historical development of the Japanese people. Despite the fact that the specific governmental forms of the eighth century—the administrative codes and tax procedures—fell into disuse in time, they nonetheless laid the base for Japan's legal institutions until the fifteenth century and set for a much longer time the Japanese conceptions of authority, administrative organization, taxation, and judicial process. The institutions of the Taihō era (put into effect in 702), like Roman Law in Europe, clearly served as the continuing basis of administrative practice throughout a subsequent feudal era. And when in 1868 the Japanese aspired to a reassertion of national prestige under imperial authority, they briefly reverted to the nomenclature of the Nara system of bureaucracy.

The two great political monuments of the early aristocratic age were the capital city of Nara, completed between 708 and 712, and the Taihō Codes. The capital, a rectangular city roughly two and two-thirds miles by three miles, laid out with palaces, government buildings, roads and temples, was the physical embodiment of the new power and wealth of the state and the symmetry of the administrative and social conceptions that were contained in the Taihō Codes. Its lack of an outer defensive wall is a reminder of Japan's safe isolation from foreign invaders and even from domestic enemies of any consequence.

The institutions of Taihō reveal the new government that occupied Nara in its ideal and most developed form. In them the subtle play of Chinese influence upon Japanese political realities is clearly visible, for however much the Japanese strove to emulate China, they were equally careful to protect the inner recesses of their political and social traditions. The Taihō Codes consisted of two parts: the *ritsu,* or penal laws, and the *ryō,* or administrative institutions. To these were added later supplementary precedents and regulations known as *kyaku* and *shiki.* For many modern Japanese historians the early aristocratic age is sufficiently colored by the Taihō institutions to be called the *ritsu-ryō* age.

In Nara, what had formerly been the priest-chief of the Sun Line had become, in reality, an emperor reigning through a centralized bureaucracy with absolute authority over the destinies of his country. The Japanese sovereign now adopted the style of "son of heaven" (Tenshi) or "heavenly sovereign" (Tennō) and was supported in his legitimacy by borrowed concepts of heavenly mandate and rule by virtue and benevolence. But the Japanese sovereign did not lose his original role as hereditary high priest, as his continuing sacerdotal functions and his reliance on the concept of descent from the Sun Goddess attest. Here was the first of many adjustments the Japanese made in Chinese state theory. While relying upon certain features of the Chinese system, they managed to preserve the hereditary inviolability of the imperial house by the claim that the mandate was in fact given in perpetuity to the imperial line by Amaterasu and that the reigning emperor was *by definition* virtuous.

Along with these additions to the concept of sovereignty came changes in social, or class, theory and in the concepts

49

that governed the relationship of the people to sources of wealth and power. The Taihō institutions cut through the practices of localized independence (the primitive feudalism) that had characterized *uji* society and created instead a body of subjects of the throne classified on the basis of their differing relationships to the sovereign. The laws recognized three basic categories: the emperor and his immediate family; free subjects (*ryōmin*), divided into officials and state tenants; and unfree subjects (*semmin*).

The imperial house and the officials who served it comprised an aristocracy. Distinguished by their special social status and their privileged relationship to the government, the structure of this group is best revealed in the hierarchical system of court ranks that took shape at this time. Four ranks of princes, reserved for members of the imperial family, were placed above eight ranks of subjects, which in turn were subdivided so as to make thirty grades in all. The aristocracy as a whole, however, fell into three general divisions. The first three ranks were especially privileged and were available to only a few of the families closest to the imperial house at the time of the Taika and Jinshin incidents. The fourth and fifth ranks, which were filled by the general run of the pre-Taika *omi* and *muraji,* formed the bulk of the court aristocracy. Below this level, privilege fell off rapidly for the lower court aristocracy and for the descendants of the old *kuni-no-miyatsuko* who gave rise to what might be described as a local gentry.

Aristocratic rank and government office brought perquisites and emoluments that varied according to rank. High rank was accompanied by certain quotas of personal retainers, the profit from assigned lands, certain exemptions from taxation, a share in the state's foreign trade, and the privilege of having sons inherit rank. Lower aristocracy and gentry received office land but few other privileges.

The structure of government as prescribed by the institutions of Taihō was specified at both the central and local levels. The central government, while similar to the T'ang model in terms of symmetry and functional rationale, had few points of exact identity and, in fact, retained many strictly Japanese features. For instance, in contrast to the Chinese imperial system, the central government under the emperor was separated into two major divisions, the Office of Deities (*Jingikan*) and the Grand Council of State (*Daijōkan*). The first of these was put in charge of the emperor's Shintō rituals, the second encompassed the civil administration of the state. The civil bureaucracy, rather than being capped by a group of policy and administrative boards as in China, was headed by three ministers. These were the Grand Minister (*Daijōdaijin*), the Minister of the Left (*Sadaijin*), and Minister of the Right (*Udaijin*). Since the Grand Minister was generally an honorific appointment, real administrative power resided with the Minister of the Left, or of the Right in his stead, an arrangement similar to that of *Ō-omi* and *Ō-muraji* under the Yamato system.

The ministers, working through Executive Officers (*Benkan*), superintended eight Ministries (*Shō*). These were divided left and right as follows: Central Secretariat, Ceremonies and Personnel, Aristocratic Affairs, Popular Affairs (chiefly land, census, and taxes), War, Justice, Treasury, and Imperial Household. A Censorate was established on paper but had little significance in practice. Capital Guards were recruited from the provinces.

The central government was staffed in the main from out of the court aristocracy. Since ranks tended to remain hereditary, officials at each administrative level were recruited from among the families that held the necessary court rank to qualify for appointment. Thus while the political system was not strictly hereditary, since there was considerable choice among candidates for any given post, there was little possibility of individual mobility within the official hierarchy. The Chinese practice of recruitment on the basis of ability and by examination was never adopted. Although a college was established in the capital, it served mainly to educate sons of the court aristocracy, whose positions were already assured.

Local government began at the center with the administration of the capital, divided into left and right districts, and proceeded outward to the provinces (*kuni*). Although retaining the old name, the new provinces were each made up of several of the older *kuni*. In the ninth century they numbered sixty-six. They were administered by Governors (*Kokushi*) who were sent out from the capital to occupy seats of provincial authority (*kokufu*), newly built as miniature replicas of the national capital.

Provinces were divided internally into districts (*kōri* or *gun*) and these in turn into administrative villages (*ri,* later *gō*). Since district boundaries tended to coincide with those of the old *kuni,* it was common for members of the pre-Taika *kuni-no-miyatsuko* families to serve as District Heads (*Gunji*). The new system, by imposing a centrally appointed governor holding high court rank over district heads who received only gentry status, was designed to bring a heavy weight of central authority to bear at the provincial level. To facilitate supervision of the provinces from the capital, a road system was created and the provinces organized into administrative groups. The Capital Provinces (*Kinai*) surrounding Nara were treated as a separate and special category. Beyond them the outlying provinces were grouped into five Circuits served by five main highways.

From the government's point of view the ultimate purpose of the newly systematized local government was to improve the efficiency of land management and to increase the state revenue. Following the Taika incident, the government had enunciated the basic principle that the resources of the state (paddy land in particular) were the property of the emperor. In keeping with this principle the government sought to put into effect a land-tax system resting on three new procedures: full control of manpower (based on the census), equitable distribution of the productive base (by land allotment), and uniform taxation and equitable distribution of revenue. That these procedures were enforced with any degree of success is one of the remarkable aspects of the early aristocratic age in Japan. Population censuses were carried out beginning in 670 and periodically, though with decreasing frequency, into the ninth century. On the basis of these, the rural populace was

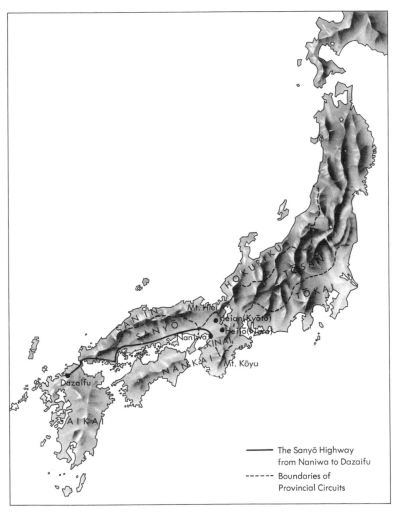

Mt. Hiei

Heian(Kyōto)

Heijō(Nara)

Naniwa

KINAI

SAN IN

SANYŌ

NANKAI

Mt. Kōya

Dazaifu

SAIKAI

HOKURIKU

TŌSAN

TŌKAI

——— The Sanyō Highway
from Naniwa to Dazaifu

------ Boundaries of
Provincial Circuits

JAPAN UNDER THE TAIHŌ INSTITUTIONS

registered by households (*ko*) and organized into villages. Households served as basic units of land allotment and tax collection.

To facilitate the equitable distribution of land, rice land, now considered public domain, was systematically divided into fields of equal size under what was known as the *jōri* system. Accordingly, rice lands were divided into squares roughly half a mile to a side. These squares were divided internally into thirty-six equal and numbered squares (called *tsubo* and equal in area to one *chō*), and each of these was cut up into ten strips of one *tan* each (at that time approximately .3 acres). These strips became the basis of periodic allotments to the cultivators. The land so apportioned was known as *kubunden*. Today in Japan from parts of southern Kyūshū to north of the Kantō Plain the outlines of the *jōri* system are still in evidence. And since there is little indication that the country was greatly agitated by any sudden attempt to enforce an unwanted system of field division during the seventh and eighth centuries, we must suppose that systematic rationalization of rice fields was a practice which had begun to be adopted before the Taika Reform and which probably recommended itself to the Japanese on its own technological merits.

Under the allotment system cultivators were assigned equal portions of paddy land according to certain categories: a male six years old and over received 2 *tan,* a female received ⅔ of the male allotment, etc. Those who received *kubunden* were obliged to keep the fields cultivated and to pay taxes in the form of a grain tax (*so*), a textile produce tax (*yō* and *chō*) and corvée (*zōyō*) or military service (*heishi-yaku*). While taxes in kind were collected, the transportation system did not permit the easy circulation of bulk commodities. Thus the main emphasis of the tax system was on labor, either directly in the form of corvée and military service or indirectly in terms of household production, especially textiles. Silk cloth served the purpose of currency to large extent and was used quite generally as a means of commuting labor service.

The Nara experiment with a conscript army was undoubtedly the least successful aspect of the Taika reforms. Military service was considered a duty of male subjects and was exacted in lieu of produce and corvée taxes. In theory one third of the mature males of a province were placed on the list of conscripts (*heishi*) and were liable to be called up in rotation for service in the provincial military unit. During the years of liability (from age 20 to 59) each conscript was expected to serve one year at the capital and three years on the frontier. While on active service, conscripts were required to provide their own equipment and provisions, a burden which fell upon the census group (*ko*) from which the conscripts were drawn. There were, of course, many adjustments for age and circumstance, and always the possibility of commutation to produce or payment for a substitute. The armies which resulted lacked discipline and fighting spirit and eventually degenerated into little more than labor gangs.

The city of Nara (officially known as Heijō) which served as capital of Japan from 710 to 781 both exemplified and epitomized the new advances that Japan was able to make under Chinese influence and aristocratic leadership. Its noble palaces and public buildings gave evidence of a new imperial dignity and a newly gained national power. During the city's heyday Japan became a major participant in the affairs of East Asia, sending nine official embassies to T'ang China (two more followed in the early ninth century) through its port of Naniwa, and opening up official relations with the state of Po-hai in what is now Manchuria. Out of Nara, also, newly formed conscript armies moved against Japan's frontiers with the Ezo to the north of the Kantō and the Hayato in southern Kyūshū, expanding the scope of the imperial sway.

Remaining from ancient Heijō today are evidences of outstanding cultural and intellectual achievements: the exquisitely designed wooden temples of Yakushiji, Shinyakushiji, and Tōshōdaiji; the artistic marvels of Buddhist sculpture and iconography found at Tōdaiji or the more intimate artifacts contained in the imperial treasurehouse of Shōsōin. The latter, with its more than nine thousand objects, many of which had been in the possession of the Emperor Shōmu (r. 724–756), reveal the skill of the native craftsmen as well as the breadth

55

of Japan's overseas contacts. For in the storehouse, objects from China, India and even Persia stand beside works of domestic manufacture in the continental manner. In it are to be found the products of foreign trade and of state artisans: brocaded silks, vessels of gold and bronze, objects of lacquer, mother of pearl, and glass.

Important too are the works of history and literature produced by the Nara artistocracy. The writing of official histories in the Chinese style began with the *Nihonshoki* (720), which sought to establish the historical position of the Japanese state and of the imperial house. Eventually six such histories were compiled, covering the events of the imperial court to the end of the ninth century. Provincial gazetteers, known as *Fudoki* (commissioned in 713), recorded as well the history, topography, and special products of the newly formed provinces. Meanwhile the aristocracy bent the Chinese written language to its own use to set down a wealth of poetic expression in the *Man'yōshū* (c. 760). An anthology of over four thousand poems in the Japanese manner (as contrasted to the Chinese), this work reveals most intimately the vigor and breadth of sentiment displayed by the Nara aristocracy as it went about the tasks of government, foreign affairs, and travel to distant official posts or to far off military frontiers.

The high period of Chinese influence in Japan was also marked by the acceptance of Buddhism both as a dominant religion and as a powerful establishment. The adoption of a new universal religion must be considered a major turning point in the evolution of any people's cultural history, and the arrival of Buddhism to Japan, like the spread of Christianity to the British Isles, was such a turning point. Some historians, in fact, have written of the early history of Japan as being divided into two distinct parts: Japan before and after the introduction of Buddhism. The impact of Buddhism on Japan was certainly more profound and lasting than it was on China itself, and Japan still stands as one of the major strongholds of the Buddhist religion in the world today.

After the initial success that Buddhism enjoyed under the

patronage of Shōtoku Taishi and the Soga house, the new religion was assured of the favor of the central Yamato nobility. Splendid temples were erected at government expense and richly endowed with lands; impressive Buddhist ceremonies were woven into the court ritual; and noble families, turning from the building of *kofun,* began to direct their resources to the patronage of family temples. Buddhism as a religion and as a cultural force became an integral part of aristocratic life. By the eighth century the Buddhist establishment, entrenched in the capital area and with strong roots in the provinces, enjoyed an official position in many ways stronger than that afforded the native Shintō shrines.

Yet Buddhism did not disestablish Shintō. Both in terms of belief and practice it came into Japanese life at a different level from that served by Shintō, meeting different spiritual needs without subtracting from the validity of the older tradition. The Buddhist overlay proved in most instances quite congenial to the Japanese, as for example the custom of establishing "family temples" (*uji-dera*), which fitted naturally into the practice of maintaining family or ancestral shrines. In the course of time we shall see that various efforts were made to achieve a complete fusion of the two religions, but Shintō remained the essential link of the Japanese people to their social system and to their homeland.

Buddhism in Japan came to play three major roles. First as a religion it brought to Japan a new system of beliefs and pious attitudes. Secondly as a religious establishment which spread to Japan from the continent it was a major carrier of Chinese civilization to Japan. Thirdly, having established itself as a religious organization with social influence and economic power on Japanese soil, it became a major force in the nation's political affairs.

As a religion, Buddhism in the seventh century was of course far different from what it is today. In these early years metaphysics was little understood, except by some portions of the priesthood, and the idea of personal salvation had yet to be widely developed. Buddhism was viewed with awe primarily for its presumed magical powers and its capacity to ward off calamity or to reward the faithful and the good. Thus the earliest aspects of Buddhism to be worshipped were such manifestations of Buddha's immediate availability as Yakushi (Buddha of Medicine), Shitennō (the Four Heavenly Rulers), and Kannon (Buddha of Mercy). Temples were endowed and staffed with priests for the purpose of reading sutras which were believed to have protective powers. The Six Sects of Nara, essentially groups of priests devoted to the study of certain sutras, were conceived of as an essential apparatus for the protection of the state. An entire network of "state protective" (*gokoku*) temples was eventually to be erected. Buddhism in these first centuries of its existence in Japan had little "life influence," in other words, for the layman.

Buddhism's role as a carrier of Chinese civilization was more readily apparent. The assimilation of Buddhism into Chinese culture meant that its architecture, iconography, and priestly orders were all highly colored by the Chinese style, and the scriptures of Buddhism arrived in Japan in Chinese translation. Among the educated Chinese who came to Japan during the Nara age most were Buddhist priests, driven to attempt the dangerous sea crossing by the zeal of their faith. By contrast, not a single outstanding Confucian scholar is known to have immigrated to Japan. Thus much of what the Japanese learned of T'ang China was filtered through the eyes and minds of the Buddhist priesthood. In Japan Chinese priests disseminated knowledge about Chinese literature, art, mathematics and medicine and helped draw plans for bridges or irrigation works. In all of this, of course, the Japanese proved ready pupils, so that today some of the best examples of T'ang architecture and art are to be found in the environs of Nara.

The emergence of a Buddhist establishment endowed with economic and political powers came about slowly as a result of public and private patronage for purposes of spiritual protection and the enhancement of secular prestige and well-being. The intermingling of political and religious interests was present from the start. It could be seen most clearly in the city of Nara, where forty-eight temples were eventually built, in large part under state patronage. Among these the great Tōdaiji, chief of state temples, served as the family temple of the imperial family. The significance of Tōdaiji as the center of the state religious observance on behalf of the emperor and for the protection of the country requires further elaboration.

The official policy of calling upon Buddhist orders to read protective sutras had an early beginning in Japan, but it was probably with the introduction of the Kegon sect in 736 that the practice was systematically adopted as a matter of state policy. It was the Kegon sect (Hua-yen in Chinese) which had also best served the needs of the state in China. In 741 the Nara government provided endowments for the establishment of temples of this sect, one to a province throughout Japan, in close conjunction with the provincial capitals. These were to consist of a Provincial Monastery (Kokubunji) and Nunnery (Kokubun-niji) and were to be on call to read protective sutras at appointed times throughout the year and in times of national emergency.

Tōdaiji was the Kokubunji of the capital province of Yamato and also head of all Kokubunji. It was in 747 that the Emperor Shōmu gave the order to begin work on a gigantic statue of Rushana (Vairocana) Buddha, the central figure in the Kegon pantheon, to be placed in the Great Buddha Hall of Tōdaiji. The huge figure, fifty-three feet high, is said to have required over three million pounds of copper, tin, and lead and some fifteen thousand pounds of gold. It taxed the resources and energies of the new nation to the limit. But at the grand ceremony of "opening the eyes" in 752, Japan literally became the center of the Buddhist world in East Asia, for official representatives and monks arrived in Japan from as far away as Champa and India. But the chief significance of the Great Buddha was that it represented Rushana, the universal Buddha and symbol of the spiritual unity of the universe. The Emperor Shōmu, by calling himself the "slave" of Rushana, could nonetheless claim to be his earthly counterpart. For as Rushana presided over the universe

59

in all its manifestations, so did the emperor assure the harmony of his state. Here was the ultimate use of religious symbolism for support of the state.

In Buddhism, the imperial government thus acquired, above and beyond Shintō, a powerful set of religious sanctions. And it is important to note that the relationship between the temporal authority and the Buddhist establishment remained similar to that which existed between the state and Shintō. The Buddhist priesthood did not acquire a spiritual authority, as did the papacy in Europe, which presumed to be superior to the powers of the secular ruler. To this extent the Japanese emperor served as his own high priest. But there was always the danger of priestly interference in governmental affairs through favoritism or infiltration into high office. And to this the Nara government was especially vulnerable.

Patronage of Buddhism by the imperial family and the Nara officialdom ultimately led to difficulties. Not only did the needs of the Buddhist establishment drain off the resources of the state, but the priesthood became increasingly involved in governmental affairs, for which the casting of the Great Buddha had opened new opportunities. While the Taihō Codes had contained explicit regulations for control of the priesthood, and while ordinations into the priesthood were strictly controlled by the state, there was little real effort to keep the civil and religious establishments separate. This was particularly true at the top where the priesthood was constantly being replenished by members of the Nara nobility. The Buddhist priesthood either directly or vicariously provided an attractive way of life for the nobility, and emperors and empresses retired to the priestly life or sent surplus members of their families to become priests or nuns. For the ambitious members of the lesser nobility, also, the priesthood provided the one way of advancement not restricted by family status.

The dangers of priestly interference in government were suddenly and dramatically revealed in the notorious relationship between the Empress Kōken and the priest Dōkyō. Under her favor, Dōkyō in 764 was appointed Grand Minister, and in 766 he was given the title of Hōō, traditionally reserved for priestly emperors. In 770 Dōkyō made a dramatic play for the throne itself, but the resistance of court leaders together with the timely death of the empress brought his downfall and banishment. This event set in motion a strong reaction within the imperial family and its court supporters against the political influence of the Buddhist priesthood. Whereas in China the imperial government eliminated the Buddhist threat by a series of drastic persecutions and confiscations of property, in Japan the solution to this political problem was handled in characteristically roundabout fashion. The emperor and his court were shortly to abandon Nara in favor of a new capital city from which the Nara temples were physically excluded.

Heian and the Fujiwara Ascendancy

Following the Dōkyō incident the imperial family made a strenuous effort to escape the influence of the Buddhist monasteries. Fortunately, the Emperor Kammu, who came to the throne in 781, was a strong leader willing to take firm direction of state affairs. Kammu's reign (781–806), and to lesser extent those of his three successors, brought on a period of government strengthening and institutional innovation which briefly revitalized the power of the imperial government. Kammu's first act was his most dramatic. Nara was abandoned as a capital in 784. An effort to reestablish the court at Nagaoka ended in failure when the supervising officials quarreled. Another site was found, and the new capital of Heian (the present Kyōto) was entered in 794. The new city was larger than its predecessor, being some three by three and one-third miles in size. It was situated safely out of reach of the great Buddhist monasteries of Nara, which were precluded from transferring their headquarters to the new capital.

From Heian, Kammu gave his attention to several critical problems of statecraft. To tighten the central administration, he established new organs of government which, while bypassing much of the machinery of the Taihō bureaucracy, put more direct and effective power in the hands of the sovereign and his close advisors. What had been an irregular body of Court Councillors (*Sangi*) now became a primary advisory board; a new executive chancellery, called the Bureau of Archivists (*Kurōdo-dokoro*), centralized the executive function of government; and a new enforcement agency, the Office of Imperial Police *Kebiishi-chō*), was developed as the most effective agency available to the central government for law enforcement and prosecution of crimes. In an effort to improve provincial administration and tax collection, Circuit Inspectors (*Kageyushi*) were appointed to audit the accounts of retiring provincial governors and in time became the primary link between the central government and the provinces. Frontier wars with the Ezo were pushed with new vigor under the leadership of Sakanoe-no-Tamuramarō (758–811). As a consequence of initial failures, the cumbersome and ill-trained conscript armies were abandoned in 792 in favor of a system of local militia (called *kondei*) recruited from the provincial gentry. The system proved effective, and as we shall soon see, was to have far-reaching influence upon the political development of the provinces.

Finally Kammu and his advisors were instrumental in the patronage of two new Buddhist sects which, both in terms of doctrine and willingness to remain aloof from political affairs, better suited the needs of the court. Of these, the Tendai sect was founded in 805 by Saichō (or Dengyō Daishi, 767–822) who, having just returned from a year of study in China, was permitted to establish the monastery of Enryakuji on the slopes of Mount Hiei just north of the capital. The monk Kūkai (better known as Kōbō Daishi, 744–835) returned from China in 806 to found the Shingon sect. His headquarters monastery was built on Mount Kōya in the interior of Kii province to the south of the capital. Both new sects broke with the tradition of city-based temples which had brought the Nara sects in such close proximity to the center of political activity. When in 827 the Tendai monastery on

Mt. Hiei was permitted to establish an independent ordination platform, the monopoly of the Nara sects was effectively broken.

The new capital and its reinvigorated court presided over nearly half a century of stable government still dedicated to the principles set forth in the Taihō Codes. But thereafter, while the prestige of the Heian court remained unchallenged for yet another three centuries, the nature of Japanese government and the style of aristocratic life underwent profound changes. Evidence of an underlying reordering of Japanese life appeared slowly at first, but the direction of change was soon unmistakable. At the top of the structure of state, the gradual abandonment of the Taihō concept of a strong emperor ruling through his personal bureaucracy brought on a realignment of power in which the person of the emperor lost most of its political influence to the competitive interests of the great court families and the Buddhist monasteries. Ultimately the Fujiwara family gained a position of supremacy at court, and as a consequence, the emperor, though still the undisputed sovereign, was again reduced to a role similar to that which he had held in the late Yamato period: that of sacred peacemaker, and symbol of ultimate legitimacy.

Meanwhile a general drift toward decentralization and patrimonialism in government affairs became apparent as the aristocratic families entrenched themselves within the capital and in the provinces. Ultimately the Taihō system of land control was abandoned in favor of a form of private proprietorship known as *shōen*. And then, as centralized control over the country began to weaken, a military aristocracy began to take over in the provinces. But these changes, while they put an end to the Taihō institutions as such, did not immediately detract from the power or the wealth of the court aristocracy. In Kyōto, the *kuge* continued to live an affluent and refined life which, being now all but cut off from China, inclined more and more to native tastes, especially in the arts and letters. The tenth and eleventh centuries brought the culture of the Heian court to its epitome. The life of the

63

kuge, as depicted in the great eleventh century novel *The Tale of Genji,* continues to live in Japanese memory as the true ideal of the Japanese aristocratic style.

The rise of the Fujiwara family to preeminence within the Heian court came about in a fashion quite typical of the slow tempo which characterized so much of the political process in Japan. Nor was the imperial family at first disturbed by the possibility that the Fujiwara might prove dangerous competitors, since for many centuries the Fujiwara served the emperors loyally and frequently supported them in their effort to control the balance of power at court.

The origins of the Fujiwara go back to the Taika *coup d'état.* Among the leaders who plotted against the Soga was Naka-tomi-no-Kamatari, who subsequently received high posts and honors and acquired the surname Fujiwara. Three of Kama-tari's granddaughters married into the imperial family. Throughout the Nara period, members of the growing Fujiwara lineage frequently appeared as leaders in the affairs of state and continued on occasion to provide consorts for the reigning emperor. But during the seventh and eighth centuries the imperial house succeeded in retaining an effective supremacy over the other noble families, including the Fujiwara, either through the capabilities of its own members who served as ministers of state or through the backing of the Buddhist priesthood.

Both of these sources of support proved unreliable, however, as the end of the Nara period approached. The threat of encroachment by the Buddhist priesthood was eventually met by relocation of the capital. Maintenance of strong imperial leadership was constantly threatened by factionalism and rivalry among claimants to the throne. It was to reduce this threat that the Emperor Shōmu began the practice of degrading excess members of the family and giving them surnames as "subjects" of the emperor. This was the origin of such lineages as Tachibana, Taira, and Minamoto—families whose new position as members of the court nobility denied them access to the throne but whose direct descent from the imperial line was expected to make them loyal supporters of the imperial prerogatives. But the imperial house was never a sufficient power bloc within the court to stand by itself. And throughout the Nara period, the Fujiwara continued to maintain a leading place among the aristocracy. It was a Fujiwara, in fact, who had led the opposition to Dōkyō and still another who was the prime mover in the decision to move the capital from Nara. As a consequence, imperial reliance upon Fujiwara support tended to increase toward the end of the eighth century.

Shortly after the move to the new capital, the internal rivalry which had divided the Fujiwara into a number of competitive factions was resolved, and what was known as the Northern, or Hokke, branch gained undisputed control of the lineage. The Fujiwara now presented a unified front at court. Yoshifusa (804–872), serving as a favored imperial advisor, marked the initial ascendancy of his family when he received the unusual distinction of being named Grand Minister in 857. The next year he succeeded in having the infant Emperor Seiwa, his own grandson, placed on the throne, while he himself took the title of Regent (Sesshō). Not only was the enthronement of a minor considered irregular, but this was the first time a person other than an imperial prince had held the post of regent. Even more irregular was the continuation of the regency after the emperor had come of age. When in 884, Yoshifusa's successor as head of the Fujiwara, Mototsune (836–891), became regent for Emperor Kōkō (r. 884–887), he took the title of Kampaku, which hereafter became the usual designation for the regent of an adult emperor. From this point on, the Fujiwara monopoly of these combined titles (Sesshō-Kampaku) and the privileges of supplying consorts to the imperial line became the basis of a powerful hold over the imperial throne and the court at Heian, a hold that was to last for the next two centuries.

This is not to say that the Fujiwara were now without rivals. From time to time, the imperial family was able to play off other houses against the Fujiwara or avoid the appointment of a Kampaku. And eventually, the imperial house itself created a base detached from the person of the emperor from which it could engage effectively in the rivalry for power at court. This was the Office of the Retired Emperor (*In*), established in 1086, from which successive ex-emperors were able to conduct family and administrative affairs in competition with the Fujiwara.

But for roughly a hundred years after 986, when the Fujiwara won a decisive victory over their remaining court rivals, their hold was nearly despotic and few appointments could be made to high office without their approval. The climax of this era of Fujiwara ascendancy came under Michinaga (966–1027), who virtually ruled the Kyōtō court for thirty years. Four emperors were his sons-in-law and three others were his grandsons. A poem attributed to Michinaga expresses the feelings of one who had achieved the ultimate: "When I reflect, this world is indeed my world, nor is there any flaw in the full moon."

The rise of the Fujiwara to positions of public power was accompanied by a number of fundamental changes in the style of Japanese government. Decentralization of political authority led to the appearance of a type of patrimonial "house government" quite reminiscent of the old *uji* system. It may in fact have been simply a reappearance of a manner of administrative procedure which had persisted within the aristocratic families from very early times. As, in the words of E. O. Reischauer, the noble families and monasteries became "multiple successors of the old centralized state," they were obliged within their own establishments to make provisions for a wide array of administrative and managerial functions. Thus, we may suppose that the "private" managerial organs by which the great *uji* had conducted their affairs were again thrown into public view when, as in the case of the Fujiwara house, these began to serve openly as branches of government. Orders from the Fujiwara Administrative Office, the *Mandokoro*, thus carried the weight of official sanction. And just as the Fujiwara were no usurpers of imperial prerogatives, so the exercise of "private" authority was included within the legitimate realm of responsibility which the possession of high rank and office and of vast territories conveyed.

By the middle of the tenth century the Japanese state and its government had come a long way from adhering to the bureaucratic idea which had been given shape in the Taihō institutions. First of the Chinese concepts of government to lapse was perhaps the most fundamental, namely the principle that the state had an existence of its own over and beyond the body of nobles who comprised its officialdom. During the ninth century, the abandonment of such practices as the redistribution of land, the minting of coins, the preparation of official histories, and the sending of embassies to China gave evidence not only of an estrangement between the Kyōto court and T'ang China but also of deep-seated changes in the relationship between political power, social status, and landed revenue within the Japanese ruling stratum. Court society had begun to restructure itself in such a way that the social and political hierarchies had again, as in the days before the Taika Reform, become very nearly identical. As a result, the formal machinery of government embodied in the Taihō Codes became increasingly superfluous. Yet in typical Japanese fashion, this machinery was never really abolished. It was merely relegated to a ceremonial status where it served for some centuries as a mechanism for the legitimization of the newly emerging "private" centers of power and as a framework within which the real struggle for power went on.

The Fujiwara family offers only the most conspicuous example of the way in which court families literally became public institutions with their own built-in administrative organs. From the Fujiwara we learn that the aristocratic houses in Japan continued to be organized on the *uji* pattern whereby branch families were clustered around a central figure who served as head of the *uji*. In the Hokke Fujiwara *uji*, the chief authority continued to rest with the head of the main Hokke line. The *uji* chief (now called *uji-no-chōja*) no longer functioned as a priest, but the family maintained its ancestral shrine, Kasuga Jinja, and its family temple, Kōfukuji, both located in Nara, and the *uji* head was naturally expected to maintain the family rituals and engage in conspicuous patronage of these and other religious institutions.

The head of the Fujiwara lineage served as the arbiter and Administrator (*Bettō*) of the family interests. He presided over the family Council (*Hyōjōshū*) and coordinated the activities of various managerial offices, such as the Administrative Office (*Mandokoro*), the Office of Military Affairs (*Samurai-dokoro*), and the Court of Appeal (*Monchūjo*). Similar offices were in evidence when the imperial house established its Office of the Retired Emperor, so we may presume that other court families, and also monasteries, used this pattern of simple but direct administration to oversee their internal affairs and to supervise their expanding land holdings. Land management was, in fact, to become a prime matter of concern for all the aristocracy as the fiscal basis of government became decentralized under the *shōen* system of proprietorship.

The growth of the proprietary domain was the result of no single failure in the Taihō institutions nor any particular form of exploitation by the aristocracy. Rather, the spread of private rights upon which the proprietorships were based, occurred at many levels, and resulted from a number of parallel developments. At the top, among the aristocracy, there was a natural tendency for the sustenance, rank, and office lands assigned for official support to slip back into conditions of possession in perpetuity. At the other end of the scale of land rights, there was the slow but persistent growth of permanent tenures among the cultivators. This resulted both from the gradual abandonment of the practice of land redistribution (the last recorded instance in the home provinces was in 844) and from the ability of cultivators to acquire private rice lands outside the public domain, generally by reclamation.

The opening up of new fields, in fact, provided the most direct and least ambiguous means of acquiring private possession of rice lands. The constant demand for more allotment land obliged the government to encourage reclamation and frequently to offer inducements in the form of special rights over new fields. Thus, land reclaimers were at first permitted to retain possession of their fields for one, two, or even three generations. Then when in 743 the Emperor Shōmu exempted newly reclaimed land from being absorbed into the allotment (*kubunden*) system and permitted its retention by the reclaimer in perpetuity, the fundamental conception of public domain was violated.

But the most basic divergence with the Taihō system came as various tax immunities were secured in addition to private tenure. First, as tax exemptions were permitted, then as immunities from civil or criminal jurisdiction of local officials were granted, step by step the vital elements of independent state authority over the land were dissipated. The process of acquiring exemptions from land taxes began with the privilege of exemption from the grain tax and then extended to other categories. Temples and shrines normally carried immunities of some sort for their lands. The court nobility were also permitted exemptions on certain holdings. All such immunities could be extended by official action or influence at court. The ultimate immunity, and the one which converted immune lands into true private proprietorships, was protection from official entry and inspection by the cadastral (land-tax) inspectors and police officers of the provincial government. Ultimately it was the acquisition of these combined immunities which served to withdraw the ever expanding private holdings from the purview of imperial local government. This was the origin of what the Japanese called *shōen*, territories under private proprietorship in which the proprietor assumed most of the duties of governance as well as all of the fiscal rights which had once belonged to the central government.

Proprietorships of this type appeared sporadically in the eighth century in Japan but grew steadily thereafter. As the privileges and immunities which were available to *shōen* proprietors were made secure by official recognition, several other related processes combined to add to the size of the *shōen* and also to their territorial homogeneity. There was some accretion through purchase, and of course some illegal absorption of public lands, but it was largely through commendation that immune lands gathered up neighboring holdings into ever larger parcels. By the thirteenth century, when this process had run its full course, it is estimated that the entire country was divided into approximately five thousand separate *shōen* jurisdictions. The number of major proprietors being but a few hundred, the pattern was clearly one of widely scattered multiple holdings. For instance Fujiwara Yorinaga in 1150 held twenty *shōen* in nineteen provinces. Around 950, Tōdaiji of Nara held *shōen* in twenty-three provinces with a total area of over 14,000 acres, while the Iwashimizu Hachiman shrine controlled thirty-four *shōen* in six provinces.

While the impression is often given that the *shōen* were illegally acquired by selfish court and religious interests, in actual fact most *shōen* came into being legitimately as recognized creations within the legal framework of the Taihō institutions. As a consequence, they came to incorporate into their own internal organization many of the administrative and taxation procedures which had existed under the imperial system of local government. The "*shōen* system," in other words, became a structure of government in itself, evolving directly out of the old imperial institutions of local administration and land management.

Commonly, the *shōen* system placed several levels of "proprietors" and several classes of managers over the workers who made up the bulk of the *shōen* inhabitants. At the top was the main proprietor (*ryōshu* or *ryōke*) in whose name special immunities had been granted. Often, however, such a proprietor made a further commendation of his holdings to a "protector" (*honke*) whose high status at court would provide an ultimate guarantee of legality. Since most proprietors were absentee residents of the capital area, they depended on a class of officials (*shōkan*) to administer their lands and to collect dues and recruit corvée labor. Through the *shōkan*, the proprietors provided the elements of fiscal management, police protection and general surveillance which normally comprise the elements of local government. The actual workers of the land (*shōmin*) were peasant owners (*myōshu*) in possession of certain rights of tenure, or their dependent cultivators.

According to *shōen* procedure, each status in the hierarchy of relationships to the land, whether *ryōke, shōkan,* or *myōshu,* was endowed with certain rights or obligations which in turn permitted certain claims upon the fruits of the land. The nature of these relationships and the extent of these claims was expressed in a concept which became a pivotal part of *shōen* practice, namely the idea of "function" or *shiki.* Within the *shōen* the idea of *shiki* served to define legally the relationship between land rights and income. For example the *ryōshu* possessed what was known as the *ryōshu shiki,* which specified the nature of the proprietorship (*ryōchi*) as well as the types and amounts of proprietary dues such as the land rent (*nengū*), the produce payment (*kajishi*), and the service payment (*kuji*). Thus Japanese proprietors received a portion of the production of the entire proprietorship, not the income from specific lands or desmenes, as was common in Europe. *Shiki* also defined the rights and incomes of the lesser "functions" within the *shōen,* such as those of managers or cultivators. Each type of *shiki* received the income proper to its designated share. *Shiki* thus became equivalent to landed property itself. They were heritable, divisible, and even alienable within the limitations which applied to each level of function within the overall system.

In the final analysis, of course, the *shōen* gave rise to a style of land-law and local administration which proved quite alien to the spirit of the Taihō institutions. On the one hand, authority relationships within the *shōen,* though capable of legal definition under imperial law, were the products of private agreements and were both personal and heritable. On the other hand, status within the system was recompensed not by the receipt of office salaries derived from taxation but rather in the form of dues. In the *shōen* the cultivator no longer resided under an impersonal officialdom which imposed a uniform set of taxes. He conceived of himself, rather, as owing certain agreed-upon dues to certain superiors in return for personal benefices. The *shōen* system thus lay at the bottom of a wide-scale return to patrimonialism in government and in social relationships.

The changes in government structure and land-tax proce-

dures which had occurred by the middle of the Heian period
need not be looked upon simply as a falling off from the
bureaucratic ideal which had marked the eighth century. While
it is true that the court families and the great monasteries were
now engaged in a direct and seemingly cynical competition for
the country's resources, yet these same aristocratic interests
must be credited with providing some three centuries of stable
rule for the country as a whole. Their provincial operations,
moreover, were to help raise the level of the cultural and
economic life of the countryside even in the remoter provinces.
For the avid competition for lands was to send a constant
stream of courtiers into the provinces intent on pushing back
the frontiers of cultivation. Roads and waterways were improved in order to transport the produce of distant *shōen* to
court proprietors. *Shōen* were encouraged to become centers
of craft production and commercial activity. Little noticed, at
least by comparison with the more dazzling happenings at the
capital, was a gradual, but quantitatively significant, flow of
the elements of higher civilization to the provinces.

But it was the court families, of course, which were the first
beneficiaries of the shift to patrimonialism in government and
economy. The period of Fujiwara dominance, when the great
court families subsisted on the ample flow of goods and services
from their country proprietorships, brought to a climax an era
of high aristocratic culture which has come to epitomize for
the Japanese people their ideal of courtly life and aristocratic
values. The combination of affluence and cultural independence from China led to the flowering of a style of life which
differed remarkably in content and mood from that of Nara.

We know, of course, much more about the court life of
the eleventh century than of the eighth. There are detailed
paintings and marvelously intimate descriptions of the Heian
scene in the prose writings of the time. Yet we must be on guard
lest we assume that all Heian enjoyed, as did Hikaru Genji, hero
of *The Tale of Genji*, a life dedicated to the pursuit of female
companionship and aesthetic beauty. Behind the court "mimes,
pageants, and processions," behind the lacquered temples and
palatial residences, there was a workaday world of *shōen*
administrators and gangs of laborers brought up from the

provinces. There was lumber to be dragged and tiles to be hauled for the newly building temples and residences. There was guard duty to perform before the palace gates, and much going and coming between Kyōto and the provinces.

The most evident feature of Heian court life which distinguishes it from that of the Nara period is that much of its obvious reliance on Chinese models had worn off. Chinese civilization had by now been assimilated beyond the point of conscious imitation. Heian court culture was both relaxed and inventive. Its style of palace architecture (known as *shinden-zukuri*), using unpainted woods and thatch roofs, achieved a natural integration of building to surrounding landscape through a studied asymmetry in the distribution of rooms and causeways about a garden or pond. A new so-called "Yamato style" of domestic painting which excelled in illustrated narrative scrolls (*emakimono*) turned frequently to local domestic scenes or historical incidents for subject matter.

But it was in literature that the most remarkable and enduring products of court culture are to be found. This flowering of aristocratic literature was prepared for by the development of a native syllabary (*kana*) which permitted the Japanese to write their language much more simply than through the cumbersome use of unmodified Chinese characters that had been used in the *Man'yōshū*. Outstanding as examples of Heian literature are the imperial anthology of poetry, *Kokinshū* (compiled in 905) and the works of the female prose writers: *The Tale of Genji* (*Genji Monogatari*, ca. 1002–ca. 1019), by Murasaki Shikibu and the *Pillow Book* (*Makura no sōshi*, ca. 1002) by Sei Shōnagon. Toward the end of the eleventh century male authors were more in evidence and their interests turned more to narratives of historical and political events. The *Tale of Glory* (*Eiga Monogatari* ca. 1092) tells of the colorful rise of Fujiwara-no-Michinaga and of his ostentatious life.

Heian court life gives evidence of a noticeable assimilation of Buddhist beliefs. The complex mysteries of Tendai and Shingon doctrine, of course, still remained quite external to the inner thought-life of most Japanese. The Buddhist priesthood continued to be looked to for magical powers to ward off evil or to cure illness, while temple rituals and esoteric iconography were admired chiefly for their aesthetic qualities. But in the tenth century new and more accessible teachings began to gain currency among the aristocracy. Among these was the worship of Amida, the Buddha of the Pure Land (Jōdō) or Western Paradise, and the idea of salvation by faith in the vow which Buddha had made to save all creatures. These ideas were spread by such priests as Kūya (d. 972), who took his message into the streets of Kyōto, and Genshin (942–1017), whose work the *Essentials of Salvation* (*Ōjō yōshū*) became a popular tract. Genshin's highly accessible portrayal of the horrors of hell and the ecstasies of paradise, his explanation of the efficacy of calling on the name of the Buddha (*nembutsu*), and his emphasis on the idea of degeneration (the idea of *mappō*, i.e. that the world was approaching the decline of the "law") had great influence upon the mood of the times. The popularity of the idea of salvation is illustrated in the many paintings of "Amida's welcome" (*raigōzu*) which were placed beside dying persons to bring them hope in their last hours.

In yet another way as well, Buddhism penetrated the common religious beliefs of the Japanese by further assimilation with Shintō shrine worship. By Heian times the Buddhist priesthood had taken over administration of a sizeable number of local shrines. The idea that Japanese *kami* were actually local manifestations of Buddhist deities—that in fact Amaterasu was Dainichi (Great Sun), the alternative name for Rushana, the universal Buddha—helped to justify the fusion of the two religions. By the twelfth century, a syncratic theory called Ryōbu Shintō had been systematized by Shintō priests. Buddhism, in other words, had found yet another way to adapt itself to Japanese culture.

7

The Feudal Age

The Bushi and the Kamakura Shogunate

Two major facts dominate the history of the twelfth century in Japan. One was the breakup of the monopoly of power held since the eighth century by the court-based aristocracy and the central monasteries. The second was the appearance of the new institutions of political authority and land control to which historians have given the name feudalism. The first of these developments is a particularly good example of the historical process of indigenous political and social evolution in Japan. For while the *kuge* were to suffer loss of their dominant position in the country, they were never fully eradicated. The social process was typically slow and roundabout, so that the court nobility were first bypassed, then relegated to a respected but impecunious place of ceremonial isolation. The manner in which this came about was also characteristically slow and undramatic. There was no conspicuous turning point, no invasion to contend with. And even the outbreaks of civil lawlessness and warfare which marred the twelfth century seemed at the time of rather uncertain significance.

Yet by the end of the twelfth century Japanese society and its manner of government had changed significantly. And the agents of this change were clearly visible: the increasing role of a provincial military aristocracy (the *bushi* or samurai) in national affairs, the establishment of a military headquarters with broad civil powers (the Shogunate), and the increased reliance on the "lord–vassal" relationship in the exercise of

75

power. Together these signified basic transformations in the composition of society, the structure of power, and the legal foundations upon which political authority was exercised.

To say that these developments represented the intrusion of feudal practice into the Japanese political order implies first of all a comparison between the institutions of Taihō and certain newly emerging administrative practices, the essence of which was a new nexus of authority between military superior (lord)and follower (vassal). This was only incidentally a result of the spread of the *shōen* system. For the *shōen* grew up within the Taihō legal framework and might have continued to support an imperial government had the court families given sufficient attention to the maintenance of a central bureaucracy and its local branches. But the organs of imperial government, robbed of attention and fiscal independence, gradually lost their ability to maintain law and order, particularly in the rural areas. It was this turn of events which led to the privatization of the enforcement apparatus and ultimately to the militarization of administration at the local and then the national level.

But the appropriateness of the use of the term feudalism requires further explanation and calls for further comparison between Japanese institutions and those of medieval Europe. The transference of the European concept of feudalism originated with the mid-nineteenth century Western visitors to Japan who were first impressed by the similarities they saw between the Japan of that day and the idealized feudalism they remembered from their historical reading. In time the term was adopted by both Japanese and Western historians and passed into common parlance, but not without accompanying abuse. The term feudalism as an explanatory concept in Japanese history has too often been used uncritically, and this in turn has given rise in recent years to disagreement among historians as to its appropriateness in the Japanese case. But the political institutions developed by the military aristocracy of the thirteenth century in Japan are undoubtedly sufficiently similar to those of feudal Europe so that the problem is largely semantic and definitional. In other words, a carefully conceived model of feudalism may be applied to both Japan and Europe.

And for the historian with theoretical and comparative interests, it is at this point that Japanese history becomes particularly relevant in world terms. On the one hand, the similarities, as Professor Asakawa sought to discover, can lead to a solidly based conception of feudalism as a general historical phenomenon. And on the other, dissimilarities which one inevitably finds help to illuminate basic differences between Japanese and European cultures and to bring out the special features of Japanese history.

Perhaps the most useful way to conceive of feudalism is the simplest, namely that it is a condition of society in which there is at all levels a fusion of the civil, military, and judicial elements of government into a single authority. This fusion of public and private functions being achieved in the person of the locally powerful military figure, it is also natural that military practices and values become predominant in the total society. It is probably true, as Asakawa has suggested, that the appearance of feudal conditions requires certain preconditions: a land-based economy, the "ghost" of a previously centralized state which can provide a legal base or framework, and the existence of a sharp gap in military technology between the fully equipped fighter and the rest of society. The condition of "barbarization" or the "tribal element" emphasized by European scholars appears less significant in the Japanese case.

If in Europe the spread of feudalism resulted from both the dissolution of Roman society and the intrusion of new peoples, in Japan the civil nobility appears simply to have given way to a military aristocracy which emerged out of the lower strata of the old nobility. As a newly emerging ruling class the military aristocracy were distinguished by their rural origins and by the fact that they tended to organize themselves into groups held together by personal bonds of agreements in arms. Authority within the group was exercised as between lord and vassal—not as between civil bureaucratic officials. In the typical lord-vassal relationship the lord (*tono* in Japan) required loyal service (*hōkō*) of his vassal (*kenin,* literally "houseman") and rewarded him with support, most often in the form of a fief (*chigyōchi*). The fief holder, by exercising localized military rule, thus laid the basis for a system in which social distinction and the capacity to exercise public powers coincided with the holding of private tenures of land. Most of the above conditions were, of course, implicit in the spread of the *shōen* system, except for the military element. The early benefices held by vassals of their lords were simply *shiki* rights within certain *shōen*. But the *shōen* performed a transitional economic function. For as *shiki* rights were granted as part of the fabric of military allegiances, they eventually became the basis for the appearance of the true landed fief.

The spread of the particular practices which identify the feudal syndrome did not occur suddenly or uniformly throughout Japan, nor was there any sudden "break" with the imperial system. The encroachment of feudal practices, as identified with the ascension of the *bushi* (or samurai) into political and economic leadership, came slowly over the course of many centuries. Historians have customarily divided this process into three: the Kamakura period (1185–1333) when the military leadership and feudal practice existed in equilibrium with those of the Kyōto court; the Ashikaga (or Muromachi) period (1338–1573) during which the *bushi* took over the remnants of the imperial system of government and eliminated most of the court proprietorships, the Tokugawa period (1603–1867) when the *bushi* class stood unchallenged as the country's rulers but relied increasingly on non-feudal means of government. In all of this the Japanese military aristocrat, the *bushi,* was the key figure, and it is to the origin of the *bushi* that we must now turn.

To the court nobility, the *bushi* appeared as an unexpected problem in the eleventh century. But it is probably true that the provincial aristocracy was never far from the surface of military affairs in Japan. Although the establishment of a conscription system had technically disarmed the provincial aristocracy, local scions of the *uji* elite continued to play a prominent role in the armed forces. In fact military service was probably the most attractive career open for ambitious members of the provincial aristocracy in Nara times. Thus in 792, after the breakdown of the conscript system, families of provincial district heads were again called upon to serve as the prime source of military manpower. The idea of the elite fighter was thereby revived. And with it the "technological gap" in military training and equipment which characterized a military aristocracy came into being. It was the spread of this new local military upper class and its encroachment upon what had been the purely civil functions of government that marks the so-called "rise of the *bushi*" and the general return to private arms-bearing in Japanese society.

It was during the ninth century that we first hear of provincial governors requesting permission to arm themselves and their staffs so as better to carry out their assignments. This practice, which began in the eastern provinces, was an early indication of the weaknesses of civil military and police units in the provinces. As local conditions worsened, the central government deputized provincial governors or members of their staffs with military and police powers in the form of special titles such as sheriff (*ōryōshi*) or military police (*tsuibushi*). Such appointments were at first temporary, giving civil officials the needed authority to recruit and use armed bands for defense or police action. But as the provincial official class held its posts increasingly on a hereditary basis and as local disturbances extended over long periods of time, military titles became permanent and began to overshadow civil appointments.

In the *shōen,* too, members of the managerial class found it necessary to arm themselves and their subordinates when officials of the provincial administration proved less and less able to assure local protection. As a consequence, then, both within the provincial governments and in the *shōen*, superiors began to draft fighters from among their subordinates, forming armed guards on a regular basis and punitive forces as the occasions arose. Military duty became a regular form of service within the *shōen* system and the remaining organs of the imperial government. And provincial families of means and status were encouraged to train their members in the technically demanding skills of archery, swordsmanship, and horsemanship, and to acquire the costly equipment of horse and armor which were to make of them a military elite.

All of this bore directly on the relationship between civil authority and the power of enforcement at other levels of government. For as increasingly the capacity to exercise authority came to rest upon the force of arms, officials appointed to civil posts began to acquire their own concurrent military or police powers. And hence at every level of central and local government, offices recruited bands of fighters for private use. At the capital, toward the end of the ninth century, the Bureau of Archivists assembled its own military guard; the capital Imperial Police likewise drew their own recruits from the provinces; the Fujiwara attached their own private troops to their military headquarters and organized family guards (their "claws and teeth") for use by the regent or other leading members of the family; the six palace guard groups became the private bodyguards of members of the imperial family; and even the temples and monasteries assembled large bodies of armed men from their *shōen* for purposes of protection.

The transformation of the provincial upper class into a military elite did not immediately disrupt the existing order, for it simply carried the trend towards privatization exemplified by the *shōen* into other features of the government. The *bushi* were simply officials who engaged professionally in military service as well as local administration. Their military service was performed within one or another of the existing command systems centering in the court. But ultimately the *bushi* were to prove a problem as they began to develop new interests and new ties of association which cut across the old power structure and particularly as they created bands or cliques with local interests which conflicted with those of the court.

During the tenth century bands of *bushi* known as *tō* began to form in the provinces. They were drawn together by many differing bonds of mutual interest or family association. Most of them had at their center a core of kinship or ritual-kinship relationships of the kind which had characterized the Japanese familial structure from earliest times. The head of the familial group formed a unit with members of his immediate family (*ichimon* or *ichizoku*). Branch families were treated as patrimonial followers (*ienoko*) and non-kin followers were called housemen or retainers (*kenin*). Thus kinship terms were used to define associations which were not necessarily based on consanguinity, and the head of the group continued to serve as a leader in religious rituals before family patron shrines or before local protective deities. It is for this reason that the *bushi* bands of this time are so often referred to as clans.

To this family-based organization was added the element of the military association. Military action drew together men from widely scattered localities around a single outstanding leader. The agreements in arms formed on such occasions tended to be personal and enduring. It was the private military bond—equated with the European practice of vassalage—which became the key feature of a new authority system. Large regional bands of military families generally resulted from periods of extended domestic disturbance and tended to form around members of the court aristocracy who had moved into the provinces to take command of special military or police forces. Such families possessed the combination of military titles and social prestige which gave them an advantage few purely local leaders could match. Members of the Fujiwara, Taira, or Minamoto families, served increasingly as members of the *shōen* managerial staffs, or as deputy governors or resident officials of the governor's staff. As such they were quickly able to gain a following among gentry families of long residence in the provinces and to emerge as regional leaders.

Several disturbances during the tenth and eleventh centuries provided the occasions for the rise of a number of potent military leaders who stood at the centers of regional cliques of extended size. The first of these was the affair of Taira-no-Masakado in the eastern provinces. Masakado, a strongheaded leader with great personal ambitions, was a fifth generation descendant of the emperor Kammu. In 935 he attacked and killed his relative Taira-no-Kunika, deputy governor of the province of Hitachi, and in 939 he captured the provincial capitals of Shimotsuke and Kōzuke, claiming mastery of the eight Kantō provinces. He even styled himself a "new emperor." He was eventually killed and his rebellion put down by Fujiwara-no-Hidesato (newly appointed "Constable of Shimotsuke") and Taira-no-Sadamori, son of Kunika. Sadamori was rewarded for his action by the prestigious post of General of the Pacification Headquarters (*Chinjufu-shōgun*). Meanwhile in western Japan along the Inland Sea the increase of piracy had presented a problem because of its interference with tax shipments. Fujiwara-no-Sumitomo, sent out from the capital to pacify the pirates, himself turned brigand and began to terrify the area. He and his followers were killed or scattered only after a new delegation of military authority had been made in 939 to members of the local aristocracy. One of these was Minamoto-no-Tsunetomo.

In the aftermath of these incidents we find members of the Taira and Minamoto families assuming increasing importance in the provinces. Tsunemoto's son, Mitsunaka, allied himself with the Fujiwara house and soon had served in a variety of provincial posts and acquired a large number of *shōen* from which he recruited fighting forces for the Fujiwara guards. Before long, men of his branch of the Minamoto (the Seiwa Genji) were serving as court-appointed officials both in Kyōto and in the provinces. The Taira descendants of Sadamori (of the Kammu-Heike line) became prominent in the eastern provinces, but other lines having the Taira surname gravitated to the Inland Sea region. A series of disturbances which kept military action going in the eastern provinces from 1051 to 1088 provided further opportunity for the Minamoto leaders to advance their prestige in the Kantō. By the end of the century two major cliques were beginning to develop separate identities, the Minamoto under Yoshiie establishing strong bases in the Kantō, while the Taira under the patronage of the retired emperors had entrenched themselves in the home provinces.

By the middle of the eleventh century it was obvious that the new provincial aristocracy were serving not only as keepers of peace in the provinces but as participants in the power struggles which were occurring with increased frequency at court.

Thus the time was approaching when a member of this new class could assemble enough of the elements of power for himself to take a leading hand in court affairs. Yet another century was to pass before the court families had so weakened themselves by factionalism and inattention to administrative affairs, that this possibility became a reality.

By the middle of the twelfth century, however, Kyōto was in a state of turmoil as conflicting centers of influence—the Office of Ex-emperors, the Fujiwara, and the great temples—quarrelled among themselves. Court interests, relying more and more upon their provincial subordinates to handle local affairs and to staff their private military guards, had begun to lose effective control over the course of events in the capital. Meanwhile, the great monasteries of Enryakuji and Kōfukuji added to the trouble by pressing demands upon the court and using masses of rowdy troops for intimidation. The time was at hand when someone in command of the armed guards would take fortune into his own hands and defy the court. The man to first exploit this situation was Taira-no-Kiyomori (1118–1181), leader of the dominant Taira faction.

Kiyomori succeeded to the head of the Kammu-Heike lineage in 1153. He had served prominently in several provincial posts, and as governor of Aki had attained fourth court rank, an unusual privilege for one of provincial origin. In 1156 a conflict of interest between the retired emperor Sutoku and the reigning emperor Go-Shirakawa precipitated the first occasion in which a court faction resorted to open military action. In the resulting Hōgen conflict Kiyomori, who supported emperor Go-Shirakawa, won a decisive victory. On the losing side was the Minamoto leader Tameyoshi. His subsequent execution greatly weakened the position of the Minamoto at court. In 1159 Minamoto-no-Yoshitomo, the sole remaining Minamoto leader of note, joined a conspiracy to eliminate Kiyomori. But Kiyomori again triumphed, and with the death of his chief rival, he found himself without military opposition at court. Kiyomori's subsequent promotion to Counsellor (*Sangi*) and to the third court rank, for the first time put a man of the provincial aristocracy into the upper level of the court nobility and within the policy organs of the court. It was a position from which Kiyomori proceeded to dominate Kyōto.

The Taira hegemony rested on a power base which drew from extensive *shōen* holdings and the support of strategically placed provincial officials. Kiyomori's strength came from his superior military forces. But his legitimacy was acquired in the manner of the Fujiwara, by infiltration of the court itself. Like the Fujiwara leaders, Kiyomori relied chiefly on the acquisition of high posts in the central government and exploiting the possibility of intermarriage with the imperial family. He himself became Grand Minister, his son became Inner Minister (*Naidaijin*), sixteen of his near relatives were made high courtiers, thirty became middle-rank courtiers, and many others became provincial governors or heads of the capital guards. By 1180 he was able to place his infant grandson on the imperial throne as Emperor Antoku, thereby attaining de-facto supremacy at court. Kiyomori's palace headquarters at Rokuhara thus superseded both the Fujiwara *Mandokoro* and the ex-emperor's office as the prime locus of political power in the capital. The period from 1160 to 1185 is therefore sometimes called the Rokuhara era by Japanese historians.

The Taira hold over the court did not last long. Kiyomori's rude dictatorship immediately aroused the bitter opposition of the court and priesthood. Go-Shirakawa, his onetime patron, became a major source of opposition. Yet it was not until 1180 that a conspiracy against the Taira involving some Minamoto remnants, the priests of Onjōji and Kōfukuji, and Go-Shirakawa's son Prince Mochihito came into being. The plot was put down with great brutality, but a call to arms, sent out in the name of Mochihito, reached other members of the Seiwa-Genji in the eastern provinces. Presently Yoritomo (1147–1199), heir to the headship of the Seiwa Minamoto line, raised his standard in Izu. Ironically he had been spared death in 1160 because of his youth. Yoshinaka (1154–1184), a more distant kinsman, raised a following in Shinano. By 1181, when Kiyomori died, the Taira found themselves on the defensive against the Minamoto.

The war between the Minamoto and Taira (the Gempei War) lasted from 1180 to 1185. Beginning in the Kantō, it ultimately shifted its focus to central and western Japan where the main Taira strength was concentrated. By 1183 Yoritomo controlled the Kantō, Yoshinaka had occupied Kyōto, and the Taira had fallen back upon their bases in the Inland Sea. At this point Yoritomo became suspicious of Yoshinaka's actions in Kyōto and dispatched against him an army of Kantō fighters under command of his younger brothers Yoshitsune and Noriyori. Yoshinaka was eliminated in 1184, and Yoshitsune went on to lead the Kantō forces in a series of brilliant victories against the Taira as they retreated down the Inland Sea. At Dan-no-ura the Taira forces, now almost entirely confined to ships, met the Minamoto for the last time and were annihilated. In the naval battle that ended the Taira hegemony the Emperor Antoku was drowned and with him was lost the sword which formed one of the three sacred regalia of the Japanese throne.

The Gempei War comprises a particularly romantic chapter in Japanese history. A major war between large forces drawn from many corners of Japan, it engaged the military elite in the most general and sustained military activity that the country had yet seen. Moreover, because of the style of combat, in which heavily armored fighters challenged their opponents in single combat, it gave rise to a host of heroic episodes. The poignancy of the war was heightened as well because, by the time they faced the Minamoto, most of the Taira leaders were thoroughly converted to the ways of the Kyōto court. The picture of the rough fighters of the Kantō confronting the refined Taira converts to courtly ways has lent a pathos to the telling of the exploits of the Gempei struggle. The war thus made a strong impression on the Japanese imagination and gave rise to a romantic literature (particularly the *Heike Monogatari*) out of which was to emerge both an idealized version of *bushi* behavior and numerous stories which were to form the basis of later dramatization in the *nō* and *kabuki*.

From a historical point of view the fighting between these two great *bushi* factions had significant implications as well.

The Gempei War served in large degree to establish the new position of the *bushi* in the country's leadership, leading to the establishment of the first national military hegemony under Yoritomo. For Yoritomo was to assert his mastery over the country in a manner quite different from Kiyomori. By setting up a separate military headquarters at Kamakura, far from the city of Kyōto, he began the process by which the court was bypassed and its powers drained off by the newly emerging military aristocracy.

Minamoto-no-Yoritomo had begun in 1180 to raise forces against the Taira in the province of Izu. His original intent, in response to the mandate from Prince Mochihito, had been simply to revive the fortunes of his house and to clear the eastern provinces of the Taira. He ended by forming a military protectorate over the entire country. By contrast to the Taira, who had concentrated their attention on infiltrating the civil organs of government, Yoritomo exploited to the limit the military and police powers which he wrested from the court during the unsettled years of military struggle. Yoritomo's establishment of the shogunate was, strictly speaking, not a usurpation of authority, for it received the sanction of the imperial system. Yet the process by which Yoritomo gained power was almost exactly the reverse of that employed by the Taira: remaining outside the court, he first built up the military might and personal organization with which he later acquired court honors, titles, and finally legitimacy.

Of the Minamoto leaders, Yoritomo seems to have had the clearest insight into the "political necessities" of the time. Thus after his early successes he rejected the temptation to proceed to Kyōto to gain the titles by which a more rapid rise might have been achieved. He also left to others the glamor of battle while he turned to the more exacting task of consolidating his base in the Kantō area. Throughout the Gempei War Yoritomo therefore stayed in the east, confirming landholdings, rewarding followers and building up a loyal band of "housemen" (*gokenin*). His military headquarters at Kamakura took on more and more of the characteristics of an administrative center for the area.

As the recognized head of the Minamoto lineage, the final victory over the Taira in 1185 redounded to Yoritomo's credit and resulted in his receiving a broad delegation of powers from the court. And while these powers were largely confined to the military and police functions of the state, they included certain responsibilities for the facilitation of *shōen* tax payments as well. By taking the title of *Sō-tsuibushi* (Chief of the Military Police) in 1185, he received the authority to make military appointments in the western provinces and the right of interference in the *shōen* holdings of the court and monastic proprietors. These powers were further extended when in 1190 he received the titles of *Sō-shugo* (Chief of the Military Governors) and *Sō-jitō* (Chief of Military Land Stewards). They were given final legitimization by the grant of the title of Shogun in 1192.

Meanwhile Yoritomo's status was enhanced by receipt of high court rank and his wealth by the acquisition of numerous *shōen*. By the time he became Shogun, he was in fact a major power within both the civil and military sectors of government. Chief of the Seiwa Minamoto lineage and holding senior second court rank, he possessed directly a large number of *shōen* (perhaps 120 pieces in 39 provinces) confiscated from the Taira and confirmed to him by Office of the Ex-emperor, in addition to many other *shōen* which had been commended to him by his followers. As Shogun he became "proprietor" (*kokushu*) of the eight provinces in the Kantō and Bungo in the west, and proprietor in all but name of seven others. In these provinces he had the authority to appoint governors, civil officials, and even certain *shōen* officials. Elsewhere his powers were more limited and were closely related to his right to set up two new classes of officials: Military Governors (*shugo*) and Military Land Stewards (*jitō*). These appointments were the hallmark of Yoritomo's extended system.

Justified originally in 1185 to aid Yoritomo in cleaning up the remnants of military resistance, the *shugo* were set over most provinces, where they could superintend provincial military and police affairs. At the same time *jitō* were placed over the land in order to aid *shōen* officials in collecting land dues and to exact an emergency military tax which Yoritomo claimed was necessary for his mopping up operations following Dan-no-ura. The new military appointments which Yoritomo made from out of his band of *gokenin* did not displace the existing provincial civil administration or the *shōen* managers but were set alongside them. To the Shogun they formed a network of provincial connections which gradually extended over the entire country. And it was this network of appointments which ultimately converted the Kamakura headquarters into more than a mere regional power and gave it the dimensions of a national administrative agency.

In his rise to power, Yoritomo had claimed to serve the imperial regime as protector, not destroyer, and he was careful to seek legal sanction for his actions. Thus the Kamakura shogunate rested legally on a delegation of authority from the court. Yet the Shogun found himself in possession of an organization capable of assuming nearly all the functions of local government, and furthermore one which was vastly more effective than the weakening machinery of government over which the court nobility presided. Thus Yoritomo had brought into being a system of administration based on a feudal command system which was eventually to displace (or absorb) the organs of civil government which had their center in Kyōto. The establishment of Kamakura as the center of these new institutions and as the city of the *bushi* class marked a major turning point in Japanese history.

Kamakura Under the Hōjō

The outstanding feature of the century and a half which followed the end of the Gempei War was the balance in both political and cultural influence which existed between the two centers: Kyōto and Kamakura. The balance at first was more or less equal. Kyōto retained its prestige as the city of the court nobility and the center of high culture. The wealth of the nobility and their ability to maintain a life of elegance had not been drastically reduced by the ascendance of the provincial *bushi*.

Their farflung *shōen,* now managed more firmly because of the efforts of the military stewards who had been placed at the side of the old managerial staff, continued to support their aristocratic way of life. Yet civil authority was unquestionably at a disadvantage against the growing power of the military aristocracy, and the balance of political influence during these years was to shift constantly away from Kyōto towards Kamakura. A major turning point occurred in 1221, when Ex-emperor Go-Toba raised an armed force from nearby imperial *shōen* and certain Buddhist monasteries in an effort to destroy the shogunate. The Kamakura leaders, in return, dispatched a large army which easily put down what they claimed was the emperor's "rebellion." In the resulting settlement, the shogunate confiscated still more *shōen* from the *kuge,* established the office of the Deputy Shogun (*Tandai*) in Kyōto (located at Rokuhara, the old Taira headquarters), and further extended the stewardship system throughout Japan. The balance of power was tipped distinctly in favor of Kamakura which began to interfere increasingly in such court matters as succession to the throne or to the Fujiwara regency.

Kamakura, as a new political center, embodied two primary institutions. It was the headquarters of the Minamoto band, a group of perhaps two thousand military houses in Yoritomo's day, who had pledged their allegiance to Yoritomo or in other ways had been enlisted as housemen (*gokenin*). It was also the administrative headquarters of the shogunate. Kamakura itself grew from a simple fishing village into a town of some size where important Minamoto vassals built their residences and new Buddhist sects erected their headquarter temples. The shogunate, or *bakufu,* as an administrative organization was less complex than the imperial government. Staffed almost entirely by *gokenin* appointees, the shogunal organs of administration, in line with the "house governments" of the Fujiwara and the In, tended to be simple and functional.

First of the *bakufu* agencies to come into existence historically was the Office of Samurai (*Samurai-dokoro*), which Yoritomo had created at the start of his campaign against the Taira. Gradually it developed into a military and police headquarters charged with strategy, the recruitment and assignment of military personnel, and the general superintendence of *gokenin* affairs. Its chief officer was first selected from the Wada family, one of Yoritomo's chief vassals. The Office of Administration (*Kumonjo*, later named *Mandokoro*) served as a general administrative and policy-making board. Over it Yoritomo had placed an expert on legal matters recruited from the Kyōto court, Ōe-no-Hiromoto. The Office of Inquiry (*Monchūjo*) served as a court of appeals, enforced penal regulations, and kept various judicial and cadastral records. Its first head was also an administrative specialist from Kyōto, Miyoshi-no-Yasunobu. These three offices made up the higher administrative apparatus of the shogunate in Yoritomo's time, and the three office heads, acting under the chief (*Shikken*) of the Office of Administration, served as an advisory board which debated policy in the Shogun's presence. These simple organs of central administration served the needs of the shogunate throughout most of its existence.

Outside of Kamakura, the Shogun's men occupied a variety of local positions, often within the preexisting framework of imperial provincial administration and *shōen* management. As provincial governors, as sheriffs deputized by the Kyōto government, or as managers of *shōen*, they performed services as though they were civil officials. It was in addition to these existing functions that the new appointments of Military Governor and Military Land Steward were made. *Jitō* served as local officials with functions similar to those of *shōen* managers or provincial tax officers. Their prime distinction was that they were assigned by the shogun and remained accountable to Kamakura, not Kyōto. *Jitō* at first served to reinforce the existing local administration and had the responsibility of seeing to it that the land dues were faithfully collected and apportioned. But this service did not come free of charge. *Jitō* were consequently recompensed, generally through the splitting off to suitable *shiki*. Those newly appointed after 1221, for instance, commonly received one-eleventh of the land dues and "one-half of the produce of mountain and stream." A military surtax (*kachōmai*) of about one-fiftieth of the land dues was also collected to support the military establishment centered on Kamakura. Thus the absorption of *shōen* income by the military officials was not inconsiderable.

Above the *jitō*, and often selected from among the more powerful among them, were the Military Governors. These were appointed to one or more provinces each, and placed alongside the now powerless civil governors as superior enforcement officers. One of their prime duties was to supervise the local members of the Shogun's band and to make assignments to the various military guard groups.

Yoritomo, for all his astuteness as a leader, failed to assure the perpetuation of his own succession. Having killed off all rivals within his immediate family, he left at the time of his death in 1199 two unworthy sons, utterly lacking in ability to control the Minamoto band. A struggle for power consequently ensued among Yoritomo's former vassals. In time Yoritomo's widow, Hōjō Masako (1157–1225), and the male members of her family were able to grasp power. Masako's father in 1203 became head (*Shikken*) of the Office of Administration, and by so doing established what amounted to a regency over the Shogun. Through this post successive members of the Hōjō family were able to dominate the Kamakura shogunate until its demise in 1333. In 1219, a figurehead Shogun, in the person of an infant Fujiwara courtier descended from Yoritomo's daughter, was brought to Kamakura, and after 1252 imperial princes serving as Shogun provided a facade behind which the Hōjō ran the *bakufu*.

The Hōjō regency lasted for well over a hundred years and gave Japan a period of vigorous government and reasonable stability. Ironically the Hōjō were of Taira lineage, a family firmly entrenched in the province of Izu before its alliance with the Minamoto through Yoritomo. As the power behind the shogunate the Hōjō produced a succession of able heads who successfully built up the political status of the Kamakura *bakufu*. Increasingly, however, the Hōjō absorbed other posts in the shogunate, taking over control of the Office of Samurai, the Deputy Shogun in Kyōto, and a majority of the country's provincial Military Governorships. The creation of a Council of

State (*Hyōjōshū*) in 1225 was largely an effort to provide broader participation in the policies and operations of the shogunate by non-Hōjō families. But ultimately this body was also dominated by the Hōjō.

One of the most impressive features of the Kamakura administration was the relatively impartial and effective attention it gave to the maintenance of peace and the keeping of order within the provinces. The members of the Shogun's vassal band, serving as provincial officers or as military governors and land stewards, developed a rough and empirical system of administration particularly when it came to enforcing the rights of proprietorship and tenure. By this time the technical provisions of the old Taihō Codes had little application to conditions in the provinces. And for this reason the Hōjō drew up in 1232 a simple code of administrative principles and regulations for the guidance of *gokenin* serving under the shogunate. This was the *Jōei Code* (*Jōei-shikimoku* or more properly *Kantō goseibai shikimoku*) which became the first codification of customary "feudal law" in Japan. It established as basic principles that the interests of religious institutions and court proprietors should be protected; it enjoined the warrior aristocracy to abide by the provisions of *shōen* law and to respect higher authority; and it clarified the duties of *jitō* and *shugo* and the functions of the Kamakura courts.

The most dramatic test of the effectiveness of Hōjō leadership came toward the end of the thirteenth century when the Japanese fighters met the massive amphibious efforts of the Mongol leader Kubilai Khan to subdue Japan. Kubilai, having overrun most of China and all of Korea, sent envoys in 1266 to demand that the Japanese enlist themselves among the tributary vassals of the Mongol state. If left to the imperial advisors in Kyōto, the Japanese undoubtedly would have acquiesced, but the Hōjō Regent Tokimune brusquely turned the envoys away. Kubilai consequently prepared for an invasion of Japan, requisitioning ships and seamen from the recently conquered Chinese and Koreans. In 1274 a mixed force of perhaps 30,000 Mongols and Koreans sailed from Korean ports against Japan. They effected a brief landing on the shores of north Kyūshū near Hakata where they were met by Japanese forces assembled by Kamakura from its vassal supporters. A timely storm, however, drove the invasion fleet back to Korea with heavy losses.

Kubilai was now even more determined to bring Japan to its knees. While pressing his conquest of south China, he continued to send envoys to Japan and to make preparations for a second expedition. Tokimune was also active. The envoys sent from Kubilai were promptly beheaded. A long defensive wall was built along the coast of Hakata Bay, a military headquarters was established in Kyūshū, and new concentrations of troops were placed in readiness and even trained in the new group-combat techniques which had been demonstrated by the Mongols. In 1281 Kubilai dispatched from Korea and China a massive force said to number 140,000 men. Although able to make limited landings, the wall and the fighting qualities of the Japanese prevented the Mongols from penetrating inland. When after about two months of fighting another storm broke up the great invasion fleet, those who could fled back to Korea, leaving the remnants to be slaughtered by the Japanese or captured and enslaved. The Japanese had successfully defended themselves against what was surely the largest overseas expedition in history up to modern times.

Thus the Japanese accounted for one of the few defeats suffered by the Mongols under Kubilai's leadership. The Mongols continued to smart under their failure, and in 1283 Kubilai set up a headquarters to prepare for yet a third expedition. But it was disbanded after his death in 1294. In Japan, however, the military alert imposed by the Hōjō continued until 1312. The clash with the Mongols had had a deep and enduring effect. Mingled with the satisfaction of having saved their country was also a continued sense of apprehension particularly in the minds of the military leaders. Kamakura furthermore was left with two unexpected problems. On the one hand the temples and shrines, which during the invasion had kept up a din of sutra reading and incantations, took credit for the defeat of the Mongols, claiming that it was the result of spiritual forces, particularly the "divine wind" (kamikaze), which Japan's protective kami had generated against its enemies. On

93

the other hand, the families of the men who had actually done the fighting and dying, concentrated largely in Kyūshū, required compensation; and since the invading force left no land as spoils of war, Kamakura had little with which to keep its Kyūshū vassals content. Thus despite the success of the Hōjō defense against the Mongols, an important region of Japan had been disrupted and the Hōjō had been left with problems which were to be their undoing.

The fighting men of Japan who in this episode appeared upon the stage of world history were a very special product of Japanese culture. The *bushi*, or samurai, stood out from among the types of leaders produced by East Asian societies as something quite distinct. Certainly the *bushi* had little in common with the scholar-officials of China and interestingly enough compared more closely in style of life and basic values to the European knights of roughly the same period. Products of a feudal environment, they contrasted also with the older court aristocracy which remained in control of the city of Kyōto. By the end of the twelfth century, the *bushi* had become a major element in Japan's higher culture, not just in political and military affairs. And while the way of life represented by the *bushi* had not by any means become predominant in Japan by this time, the national cultural scene was increasingly affected by the tastes and values of this new class of leaders.

The *bushi*, although of the ruling class, lived a life which contrasted greatly with that of the court nobility. He was essentially a provincial aristocrat dedicated to the bearing of arms, and, by contrast to the *kuge*, was preoccupied with the problems of the sword and the land. Most *bushi* were directly involved in affairs of land management, living on or close to the land. The court nobility lived off the land in their own isolated world of the capital. The *bushi* therefore emphasized, in contrast to the genteel accomplishments of the *kuge*, such skills as horsemanship, archery, swordsmanship, and the leading of men. They exalted such personal qualities as loyalty, honor, fearlessness, and frugality. The two prime symbols of this class were the sword (the soul of the samurai) and the cherry blossom (whose petals drop at the first breath of wind, just as the samurai gives his life to his lord without regret). Between the requirements of serving his lord and reflecting honor on his family name, the *bushi* was constantly entwined in a network of strenuous obligations. The *bushi* was also obliged to live a life of physical hardship in the field (or else imposed upon himself by contrived conditions of discipline), enduring such rigors in the belief that he was thereby "building character." Frugality was a major precept, not only because the *bushi* lived from the limited produce of the soil, but because luxury presumably led to weakness. He thus tended to scorn the easy life of the courtier as soft and lacking vigor. He even scorned an easy way of taking his own life. For the *bushi* brought back into vogue the resort to suicide as "the honorable way out" and as a means of showing "earnestness" or opposition to a superior. But the accepted method of taking one's life, by slashing the bowels (*seppuku*), imposed the most gruesome and lingering of deaths. Here to some extent was evidence of brutalization. The *bushi* lived a rigidly disciplined life under absolute demands of authority, with the constant threat of death about him. Roughness, directness, and above all *action* was demanded of him.

In time, as the *bushi* class absorbed more and more of the powers of government, they came to develop a mystique about themselves as the only competent leaders of Japanese society. Scorning the effete courtiers and the money-tainted merchants, they held to a pride in a profession which, in theory at least, was dedicated to the general welfare. Such sentiments were not fully developed by the thirteenth century, but they were in the making. It was not until the seventeenth century that the idealized cult of the *bushi* (*bushidō*) was expounded, by which time principles derived from Confucianism were introduced to provide more generalized ethical supports.

Like medieval Europe, the early feudal age in Japan was also a time of deep religious fervor. The religious awakening of the Kamakura period was not simply the result of the rise of a new class, but it was certainly intimately associated with the changing patterns of life and culture and the sense of instability which the wars between the Taira and Minamoto and the shifting power balance between Kyōto and Kamakura had brought about. For many, the times were out of joint and could only elicit pessimistic thoughts. Apprehension over the "end of the Law" continued, and those who looked at the world from the declining city of Kyōto could well imagine that Japan had come upon unfortunate days.

But the spread of new sects and the deep penetration of Buddhist beliefs into Japanese society had more positive causes. The new awakening met the needs of new classes and new sections within the country. The warrior aristocracy, for all their rough ways, were deeply attracted to Buddhism, and many among them retired into the priesthood in their later years. Within *bushi* society the monastic orders played an important role: the priesthood provided a pool of educated men who could serve as scribes or advisors to unlettered military administrators; the monasteries served as a refuge for arts and letters and afforded a quiet life for those who eschewed the warrior's existence. The new awakening was indicative also of a rising standard of life and cultural attainment in the provinces, for much of the new religious activity and the leadership which gave it energy came from the peasantry and lower samurai. By the middle of the thirteenth century the Buddhist establishment had become an integral part of Japanese life at all levels, from the lowest village community to that of the Kamakura and Kyōto aristocracy, and religious centers of importance had sprung up almost uniformly throughout the provinces.

The Kamakura awakening was also in part a reaction against the established Buddhist order, against the esoteric concepts of Tendai and Shingon and the hierarchic view of life held by the six Nara sects. For the new sects which emerged in the thirteenth century brought Buddhist teachings within the comprehension of the most humble layman and opened the path to salvation to all. The new sects carried forward a popularization of Buddhist tenets and a liberalization of doctrine in favor of more direct emotional expressions of faith. The new leaders, often of humble origin, encouraged the translation of sutras into simple Japanese, ministered to lay congregations, and even declared that priests should marry and have families in order to better understand the problems of the common people.

The religious ideas about which the new sects were organized were, of course, not original to the times. The Kamakura awakening had long been prepared for it in the monasteries of the Heian period, where the cult of Amida and techniques of Zen meditation were both well known. What happened during the Kamakura period was that these ideas which had been kept within the established monastic orders as minor doctrines were now, in the hands of new leaders, made the basis of independent sects. The first such leader to break with the establishment was Hōnen Shōnin (1133–1212), the founder in 1175 of the Pure Land (Jōdō) sect. Inspired by the earlier teachings of Genshin, Hōnen taught of man's inability to attain salvation through his own efforts, for it was only by relying on forces outside himself that man could be saved. In man's search for relief from suffering and mortality, he claimed, man must realize that salvation can come only through faith in Buddha's original vow. Such faith is expressed by repeating with utmost sincerity the name of Amida (nembutsu). To Hōnen, then, the nembutsu was all sufficient. Nothing else was needed, neither temples, monasteries, rituals, or priesthood. Moreover all were equal in the eyes of Buddha, high or low, male or female. These extreme views were naturally opposed by the older sects, and in 1207 Hōnen was exiled from Kyōto. But the result of his subsequent travels into the provinces was to further spread and popularize his teachings.

Meanwhile one of Hōnen's pupils, Shinran (1173–1262), further simplified these teachings by declaring that a single sincere call upon the name of Amida was sufficient for salvation. He strenuously argued against the establishment of monasteries; he led the way in breaking the traditional discipline by marrying, eating meat, and living a normal secular life. He believed that if a good man could be saved "how much more so a wicked one." Shinran founded a separate sect from that of Hōnen which he called the True Pure Land sect (Shin Jōdō

Shū) or more simply the True sect (Shinshū). The sect was more popularly known as the Single Minded sect (Ikkōshū) in later centuries. Both the Pure Land and the True sects became immensely popular, and while denying the necessity of a priestly organization, nonetheless gave rise to large communities of believers served by temples and priests. The Shin sect has the largest number of adherents in Japan today, and the Jōdō sect ranks second.

Also relying on the act of faith but directed toward a different object was the Lotus (Hokke) sect founded in 1253 by Nichiren (1222–1282). A Kantō man of bellicose nature, Nichiren taught his followers to chant "Hail to the Lotus Sutra" (*Namu myōhō-renge-kyo*). Convinced that his was the only true path to salvation, both for the individual and the nation, he bitterly attacked all other sects and denounced the country's leaders for their support of any but the Lotus sect. He even criticized the shogunate and predicted foreign invasion if the other doctrines were not suppressed. Nichiren's sect, generally known by his name, is known as the most militant and nationalistic of the Buddhist groups. His name, which translated literally means sun lotus, may be taken to signify "Japanese Buddhism." Extremely nationalistic in his thinking, he frequently expressed the conviction that Japan was the land of the *kami* and that Japanese Buddhism was the only true Buddhism.

It is interesting to note, as Professor Reischauer has done, that the popular Buddhism of Kamakura times had come to resemble Christianity in a number of ways through its emphasis on a single saving deity (Amida), the portrayal of heaven, hell, and the narrow path to salvation, the stress on faith, the display of religious zeal in public preaching and chanting, and in many other forms of popularization already mentioned. The three popular sects also led to the formation of religious congregations which became important organs of the intellectual and cultural life of the lower classes in the coming centuries. In time some, particularly the Ikkō groups, organized themselves politically and served as agencies of self-protection and self-government against higher authority. During the fifteenth century Ikkō communities under priestly leaders seized control of the two provinces of Kaga and Noto and administered them for nearly a century. And during the late sixteenth century the great temple-castle of Ōsaka stood off the attacks of the most powerful feudal armies for over a decade.

But while the new faith sects gained in popularity it should not be imagined that the older sects were completely moribund. In fact a considerable revival and counter-reform took place, particularly among the Tendai and Shingon orders, whose local branch temples also became centers of education and charitable works. During the first few decades of the Kamakura period a nation-wide effort was made to rebuild the Tōdaiji of Nara which had been destroyed during the Gempei War. Funds were solicited throughout the country, and Yoritomo proved most supportive of the venture. The resulting interest in temple architecture and Buddhist sculpture led to the development of a "neo-classical" revival of considerable vitality.

In a sense bridging the gap between the new popular sects and the earlier monastic orders was yet another sectarian movement in Kamakura times, namely Zen. The meditative school of Buddhism had been known in Japan since the seventh century, but it was not until the twelfth that renewed contact with China encouraged two Tendai priests to establish separate Zen sects outside the traditional orders. Eisai (1141–1215) twice travelled to China and after his return in 1191 began his advocacy of Zen practices, founding the Rinzai sect in opposition to Tendai authority. His pupil Dōgen (1200–1253) founded the Sōtō sect of Zen after his return from China in 1227. Eisai, like Hōnen, was expelled from Kyōto for his ideas, but unlike Hōnen he travelled to Kamakura and obtained the patronage of the new military government. He thereby inaugurated a close relationship between the shogunate and the Zen monastic order. Returning to Kyōto with the backing Kamakura, Eisai established Kenninji, the first temple dedicated exclusively to Zen practices, and began a movement which was to lead to the creation of the Five Official Temples (Gozan) in Kyōto and Kamakura, and the ultimate spread of sectarian Zen throughout Japan.

Zen too was a reform sect in terms of its rejection of the older sects, chiefly their ritualism and scholasticism. It was the aim of Zen meditation to return to the original experience of the Buddha by inducing the personal experience of enlightenment (*satori*). To acquire enlightenment, Zen adherents were expected to undergo a rigid spiritual and physical discipline which emphasized meditation (*zazen*) and the study of intellectually insoluble problems (*kōan*), the latter as a means of jarring the individual out of his reliance on the intellectual process. It was in Zen, perhaps, that the main contrast between Christian and Buddhist behavior is best illuminated. For while the attainment of enlightenment was to some extent like the "sudden conversion" of medieval Christianity, its consequences were less public and social. The enlightened individual was given no mission of social service, but rather the capacity to live life existentially without anxiety or "attachment." It was this quality which became so attractive particularly to the warrior aristocracy. For if Zen through mental discipline created men of self-understanding and self-reliance, it produced men of action and strong character as well.

While Zen was anti-intellectual in its religious premises it did not urge withdrawal from the real world of action or of the arts and letters. In fact it was the Zen priesthood and the Zen monastic establishment which played the most vital role in the encouragement of higher culture during the late Kamakura period and the succeeding centuries. Zen monasteries were established close to the cities of Kyōto and Kamakura and within the main provincial centers, but unlike the Nara sects they kept their distance from political affairs. The Zen temples remained available but on the outskirts of the affairs of the warrior aristocracy, adopting the names of hills to indicate their withdrawal to nature. Thus it was the Zen monasteries which served increasingly as the main refuge of scholarship and art in the world of the *bushi,* and it was the Zen priesthood to which the *bushi* most frequently retired. The tie between Zen and the Hōjō regents was especially close. Zen priests were used as scribes, educators, and advisors by the Hōjō, while the regents themselves became lay members of the sect, relying on its discipline for spiritual strength. Hōjō Tokimune, who so stoutly resisted the Mongols, is usually depicted in his Zen priestly robes.

The establishment of the network of officially supported Zen temples in Kyōto and Kamakura together with the spread of popular sects and the revival of the traditional orders added immensely to the volume of Buddhist activity in Japan and to the role of religion in the life of the Japanese people. The comparison with Europe is again brought to mind. Buddhism in feudal Japan had a place similar to that of the Christian Church in Europe, as the conscience of society and as a refuge from the world of warfare. But the relationship of the religious establishment to the state remained quite different within the two cultures. Buddhist temples might continue to grow wealthy, and individual priests might gain the ear of the militarily powerful, but the Buddhist establishment as a whole acquired no place outside the political order from which to influence the behavior of the state. It did not anoint the ruler in Japan, and no distant Pope attempted to interfere with political decisions either in Kyōto or Kamakura. The state continued to dominate religious institutions more fully in Japan than in Europe.

But religion was clearly the dominant influence in the higher cultural achievements of the period. In literature, art, and architecture, Buddhism provided the content. And most frequently the creator came from the priesthood as well. Typical of the product of the Kyōto court was the *Hōjōki* (*Record of a Ten-Foot-Square Hut*) by the retired Shintō priest Kamo-no-Nagaakira (1155–1216?), who looked back upon court society from his position as a religious recluse. In *Tsurezure gusa* (*Idle Jottings*) by Yoshida Kenkō (1282–1350), a celebrated poet and court official, who retired into the Buddhist priesthood, wrote his melancholy reflections on the passing of aristocratic life. Characteristic of the *bushi* society was a genre of battle tales in which didactic messages of Buddhist inspiration were interspersed in dramatic tales which related the military exploits of the warrior class. The *Heike monogatari* (*Tales*

101

of the Heike), created in the early thirteenth century, was the most famous of these works. It told of the struggle between the Taira and Minamoto, and particularly the final defeat of the Taira. The *Heike Monogatari* provided a storehouse of plots for later Japanese writers, but its main importance at the time of its writing was its substructure of Buddhist commentary on the behavior of the warrior class.

The Ashikaga Hegemony

For roughly a hundred years after the founding of the Kamakura shogunate, civil and military systems of authority reinforced each other in Japan to give the country a reasonable political stability. By the fourteenth century, however, there were disquieting signs of political breakdown and social unrest. In Kyōto the court was further split into factions whose quarrels seemed to grow in intensity as income from the civil proprietorships began to dwindle. In 1259 the practice of primogeniture in the imperial succession was violated and the imperial line broke into two competing branches: the "senior" or Jimyōin and "junior" or Daikakuji. Between these the Hōjō had managed to impose a precarious compromise of alternate succession in 1290. Meanwhile the Fujiwara house had split into five branches (*gosekke*) in 1252 from which the post of Imperial Regent was also filled in rotation.

Kamakura was no less rent by factionalism. Long-time vassals of the Shogun, having extended their powers in competition with the Hōjō, expressed open resentment over the way in which the Hōjō monopolized the affairs of the shogunate or apportioned among themselves the majority of provincial Military Governorships. The Ashikaga family, for example, strategically based on both sides of Kamakura as *shugo* of Mikawa and Kazusa, had built up powerful provincial followings which made them increasingly reluctant to accept the dictates of the Hōjō *shikken*. Families such as the Ashikaga gave evidence that a new kind of military leadership was emerging outside of Kamakura. The original *gokenin* band based on direct loyalty to the Shogun was beginning to fall apart regionally. And families, generally of *shugo* status, were emerging as intermediary powers between Kamakura and the provinces.

The weakening of the *gokenin* system was hastened as well by the dissipation of the independent strength of the smaller military houses that served as land stewards. The cause was in the main economic, for as the generations passed from the time of the first *jitō* appointments, and as the original houses broke into numerous branches, what were once ample patrimonies became fragmented into dangerously slender inheritances. Added to this was the strain of defense against the Mongols. Thus by the end of the thirteenth century many of the Shogun's housemen were finding it difficult to keep up their service toward Kamakura. Instead they became dependent upon the local *shugo* or *jitō* to whom, in exchange for economic support and protection, they began to transfer their feudal allegiances.

Underlying most of the political and social problems of fourteenth-century Japan, however, was the tension which was building up between civil and military proprietary interests in the *shōen*. The system of dual land management had been precarious from the start, and now in every quarter the *jitō* were demanding larger shares of the proprietary income, either to satisfy their economic appetites, or because they were in fact performing most of the managerial work in the *shōen*. By the fourteenth century many court families had been obliged to divide their *shōen* physically into halves (under a procedure known as *shitaji-chūbun*), one half paying dues to the court proprietor and the other to the *jitō*. And increasingly the Kyōto courtiers complained that the Military Stewards failed to deliver even the rents due on the halves which were rightfully theirs.

The event that destroyed the Kamakura shogunate and became the occasion for a thorough reshuffling of the political and economic order, is known in history as the Kemmu Restoration. Set off in 1331 by Emperor Go-Daigo (r. 1318–1339), of the junior or Daikakuji line, the restoration was as much an anachronism as it was a failure. Yet it was to have the most far-reaching consequences. For, in his ambition to prevent the senior line from returning to the throne, and in dreaming of the possibility of recovering the imperial powers of former days, Go-Daigo set in motion a chain of events which was to lead beyond the destruction of the Hōjō family to a fundamental reordering of the country's polity.

The fall of the Hōjō was sudden and unexpected. Go-Daigo had begun a rather clumsy revolt in 1331. Defeated and captured by Kamakura forces, he was exiled to the island of Oki. From there, however, he managed to publicize his cause, and when in 1332 he escaped from exile, he found himself at the head of a full-scale uprising. To his side flocked a number of powerful military leaders who had grievances against the Hōjō, among them Ashikaga Takauji, who captured Kyōto for Go-Daigo, and Nitta Yoshisada, who destroyed Kamakura and exterminated the Hōjō family.

From 1334 to 1336, Go-Daigo held Kyōto and sought to fulfill his plans for a restoration of imperial government. From the first, however, a deep cleavage of interest divided him and the military leaders upon whom he depended. Go-Daigo intended not only to reinstate the old organs of imperial government, but to reassert control over the military sector as well. Thus he granted the title of Shogun to his son, Prince Morinaga, and freely appointed courtiers as provincial Military Governors. Conversely the rewards he gave to his military supporters were far below their expectations. In 1335, the disaffected Ashikaga Takauji turned against Go-Daigo and proceeded to create a new shogunate of his own. Having captured Kyōto from Go-Daigo in 1336, he set up the emperor Kōmyō of the senior Jimyōin line to legitimize his position. Two years later, in 1338, he acquired the title of Shogun.

The failure of Go-Daigo's restoration and the establishment of the Ashikaga shogunate did not immediately bring peace to the country. For Go-Daigo and his court followers managed to fortify themselves in the hills of Yoshino from where they and their successors continued to claim that they were the rightful sovereigns. For the next six decades, two lines of emperors disputed the throne of Japan, and within the country at large, the existence of two imperial causes provided the excuse for the sporadic fighting referred to as the war of the "North and South Dynasties." The disturbance which began in 1331 was not fully resolved until 1392, during which time a new balance of political power, inclining ever more toward localism and feudal authority, had been brought into existence.

The most significant feature of the new political order which resulted from the passing of the Hōjō hegemony was symbolized by the fact that Kyōto, not Kamakura, had become the seat of the shogunate. Military power had now encroached completely upon the imperial capital. Vestiges of the imperial central government were preserved, to be sure. The emperor was still looked to as sovereign, the provinces retained a hazy identity as administrative subdivisions of the state, and *shōen* law served as the basis of land management. But though the court families might still hold high ranks and titles and claim proprietary rights over distant *shōen,* they now had lost all political power and nearly all capacity of interference in the administrative and fiscal affairs of their lands. They were by now completely dependent upon the Military Land Stewards for whatever income they might receive from the provinces. Conversely the Ashikaga Shoguns, though they coveted high court rank and posts, no longer depended upon such appointments to justify their exercise of authority. The Shogun was now admittedly the only real power in the nation and was able to issue orders in the imperial name.

It is interesting to reflect that while the ultimate encroachment of military over civil authority was probably inevitable, the process had been greatly, and unwittingly, accelerated by Go-Daigo himself. For in his effort to reestablish a unified system of government, he coalesced civil and military administration wherever possible. Civil governors were not appointed to the provinces, for instance, because *shugo* (often in the persons of court nobles) were assigned to take their place and serve both in civil and military capacities. Thus when the restoration failed, the military governors inherited a greatly enlarged sphere of authority.

In somewhat the same manner the imperial family lost its

status as an independent political and economic force in the capital. The Office of the Ex-emperors had been abolished in 1321, and many of the imperial proprietorships were turned over to the public treasury, all in an effort to revive the ideal form of centralized government. All such lands were lost to the imperial family when Go-Daigo was driven from Kyōto. Thus began the period of real economic embarrassment for the imperial family and the *kuge* population of Kyōto which was to force the court increasingly upon the charity of the military houses. Kept alive chiefly as symbols of a bygone court culture, the *kuge* were eventually relegated to the same style of ritual existence that the imperial family had long accepted.

Despite its acquisition of most of the superior rights of government, however, the Ashikaga shogunate had difficulty in exercising an effective hold over the country. The collapse of the imperial government had destroyed the legal and institutional structure within which "military government" had operated during the Kamakura period. The vassals of the Kamakura Shogun had been individually weak, but they were able to exert a national influence because of their strategic placement within the local organs of the old imperial system. After 1338, the old regime was destroyed and the only real authority in the land was that of the Shogun and his vassal *shugo*. The Ashikaga hegemony rested solely upon the Shogun's ability to control his vassals by force and through the system of feudal alliance. The Ashikaga family, while superior in wealth and military resources to any one of its vassals, was nonetheless not powerful enough to dominate the country single-handedly. For the military houses which served the Shogun as vassals were themselves regional hegemons of considerable power. The balance of strength between the Shogun and the vassal *shugo* houses was from the first a delicate one. The Ashikaga shogunate therefore took on the form of an uneasy alliance of powerful military houses over which the Shogun frequently held but a precarious pre-eminence.

From time to time, however, the Ashikaga Shoguns were able to put together a coalition which held the peace for a number of decades at a time. The most notable of such periods began in 1392 during the latter part of the life of Yoshimitsu (1358–1408), the third Shogun, and lasted another fifty years under his two successors. By 1392 the southern court had capitulated, Kyūshū had been pacified, and recalcitrant *shugo* such as the Yamana had made their peace with the Ashikaga. Yoshimitsu, more than any head of the Ashikaga house before or after was able to act as the absolute hegemon of the country. It is at this time that the political structure of the shogunate is seen in its most complete form.

Perhaps the most distinctive quality of the Ashikaga system of government arose from the role played in it by the *shugo* who served both as high officials of the central government and as local military governors. The central organs of the *bakufu*, since they were staffed by the Shogun's great vassals, thus inevitably became units in the Ashikaga balance of power as well. First among the central offices was that of Chief Administrator (*Kanrei*), assigned normally to one among the three most powerful of the Shogun's vassals: the Shiba, Hatakeyama, and Hosokawa. As a group these three families known as the *"sankan"* commanded a significant balance of power among the Ashikaga vassals. They thus formed an inner line of support for the Shogun, which, when they acted together, gave him the necessary backing to dominate the rest of his vassals.

Below the Chief Administrator the most important office was that of Head (*Shoshi*) of the Office of Samurai. The *Shoshi* was customarily selected from one of four families (Yamana, Isshiki, Akamatsu, and Kyōgoku) and had the responsibility of military planning, discipline, and police protection. He also superintended the *shugo* of the home province of Yamashiro and commanded the Shogun's Kyōto guard force. These four families served as a second line of support for the Ashikaga house and together were referred to as the "four shiki" (*shishiki*).

The Administrative Office (*Mandokoro*) was now primarily responsible for shogunal finances, while the Document Office (*Monchūjo*) served as a secretariat and repository of cadastral records. A Judicial Board (*Hikitsuke-shū*) settled disputes, usually over land problems, and determined punishments.

107

General administrative policy was debated in the Consultative Board (*Hyōjōshu*), a council of high officials. The Shogun also relied on a large number of executive officials (*bugyō*) who performed particular functions. These tended to be drawn from his own household retainers rather than from among the *shugo*.

Another special feature of the Ashikaga system was the number of regional deputies who represented the Shogun's authority outside of Kyōto. The post of Governor General of the Kantō (*Kantō kanrei*) was set up in Kamakura much as the Hōjō had established a deputy in Kyōto. The importance of this office is indicated by the fact that it was first assigned to Takauji's son. The Governor General maintained what amounted to a secondary *bakufu* with prime responsibility for the eight Kantō provinces. Other Deputy Officers were established in Kyūshū, west-central Japan and in the far north. These posts were generally assigned to vassal houses which concurrently served as *shugo* in these localities.

By the time of Yoshimitsu, most of the *shugo* had been carefully selected by the Shogun and were considered trustworthy. The majority were in fact relatives of the Ashikaga family. While they bore quite different surnames, they were all members of a group of cadet branches referred to as *ichimon*, "the first circle." The remaining *shugo*, being from unrelated families, were referred to as "outside lords" (*tozama*). Primary reliance was naturally placed on cadet members of Ashikaga lineage, and families such as the Hosokawa, Shiba, Hatakeyama, Isshiki, Yamana, and Imagawa, who had followed Takauji out of Mikawa and Kazusa, were relied on as the core of the Ashikaga power structure and the heads of the main organs of shogunal administration. *Tozama shugo* were of two different types and received treatment accordingly. Those far distant from Kyōto, such as the Shimazu and Ōtomo, had simply been confirmed in territories which they had long occupied. They thus retained a wide area of independence but were almost entirely excluded from shogunal affairs. Those who held provinces close to the capital, such as the Kyōgoku, Rokkaku, Akamatsu, Toki, and Ōuchi, had come to the support of

Ashikaga Takauji early in his career and were considered more dependable. They were consequently assigned to positions of responsibility within the *bakufu*.

By the end of the fourteenth century the *shugo* had developed into true regional rulers, for in effect they had gained possession of the combined powers of the earlier civil and military governors and the military land stewards. *Shugo* jurisdictions were referred to as *kankoku* or *bunkoku* ("assigned provinces," reflecting the concept of proprietary governorship of the late Heian period). The increased powers of the *shugo* were not arbitrary, and in most cases found justification in the Ashikaga legal institutions. Specifically provided for in the Ashikaga decrees were new rights of pursuit of criminals and settlement of land disputes, both of which gave the *shugo* entrance into the lands of civil and military proprietors. Supervisory powers over temples and shrines and the authority to carry out land surveys were absorbed from the provincial governors. Within the military sphere of authority, too, the *shugo* now confirmed the holdings of *jitō*, or more likely absorbed the functions of stewardship under their own command. Military service was now recruited in the name of the *shugo*, who thus became the heads of local military units. The Shogun's armies were consequently made up of separate contingents led by the *shugo*. When the *shugo* gained the ability to distribute lands captured in war or left vacant as a result of military action, their local independence was nearly complete.

The *shugo*'s advances in the acquisition of local fiscal and proprietary rights had been greatly facilitated by a practice known as *hanzei*, or half-rights. Legalized by Ashikaga Takauji early in his drive for power as a means of securing military support, it permitted *shugo* to hold back "for military purposes" one-half of the *shōen* proceeds destined for absentee proprietors. Permission was at first given on only a limited and temporary basis, but ultimately it became general practice. This was naturally a heavy blow to the court families, many of which had already lost half of their lands to the *jitō* under the *shitaji-chūbun* system of division. But of greater significance was the fact that *hanzei* rights were exercised by the *shugo*, not the *jitō*. This meant that the provincial Military Governors automatically acquired fiscal rights in all non-military *shōen* within the area over which they held jurisdiction. Increasingly, the *shugo* were becoming the real masters of the countryside, converting themselves into what Japanese historians have called *shugo-daimyō;* that is, regional hegemons with extensive territorial holdings.

Yet having noted the growing power of the Ashikaga Military Governors, it is equally necessary to understand the particular problems and weakness with which they were obliged to cope. The units of *shugo* jurisdiction were provinces, in other words territorial divisions of the state, over which they in theory exercised certain legal powers vested in them by the Shogun. In most cases, a sizeable gap existed between the *shugo*'s power in hand and his jurisdictional authority. The imperial system was now in effect dead, but the system of military allegiances and feudal controls had not fully matured. Within his province of assignment, moreover, the *shugo* held only a portion of the land as a direct proprietorship, and often his major holdings were located elsewhere within some other province. Nor were all the military families within his jurisdictional territory pledged in loyalty to him. Thus, like it or not, the *shugo* was forced to rely upon the Shogun's support in local affairs, and it was this necessity which obliged him to keep a hand in the politics of the Ashikaga shogunate. This conflict between central and local interest was ultimately to be the undoing of the great *shugo* houses. For as they turned their attention increasingly to the affairs of Kyōto, they faced the danger of losing touch with their provinces. But this was not to become a serious problem for roughly a century, until the time of the Ōnin war which began in 1467.

Running through the entire Ashikaga political history, therefore, was the continued conflict between feudal power and the remnants of the imperial system. The transitional nature of the early Ashikaga polity is illustrated as well in the lives of the military aristocracy who assembled in Kyōto. Beginning with the Shogun, the great *shugo* families came out of the provinces to take up residence in Kyōto. There they began to assume the cultural guise of the old nobility, building palaces, patronizing temples, dressing and behaving in courtly fashion. In their lives the *shugo* thus sought to exemplify the new status they had achieved.

Of the Ashikaga Shogun, Yoshimitsu best illustrated the fusion of high aristocratic style and elements of military power. Having succeeded his father as Shogun at the age of nine, he spent his early years under the regency of Hosokawa Yori-yuki, the *Kanrei*. His early years were also ones of constant military struggle. In 1379 he successfully faced a threatened revolt of the Shiba, Toki, and Kyōgoku families and thwarted the effort of the Kantō branch of the Ashikaga house to pull back to Kamakura the main center of *bakufu* power. In 1390 he destroyed the rebellious Toki Yasuyuki, *shugo* of Mino and Owari; the next year he successfully met the obstreperous Yamana Ujikiyo, *shugo* of eleven provinces in central Japan, and cut him back to the two provinces of Hōki and Tajima. In 1392 he managed to resolve the conflict between the contending imperial dynasties, and in 1399 he defeated Ōuchi Yoshi-hiro, *shugo* of six provinces in western Japan.

Meanwhile Yoshimitsu had embarked upon a number of imposing tours of inspection throughout Japan. In 1388 he toured the Fuji provinces in great pomp, taking the occasion to consolidate his grip on the Kantō. The next year he visited Kōyasan, the great Shingon monastery to the south of Kyōto, and the Itsukushima shrine in the central Inland Sea region. In 1390 he turned his attention to the provinces on the Japan Sea, visiting Echizen in that year and Tango in 1393. The same year took him to the imperial shrine of Ise. Each progress was calculated to identify the Ashikaga house with some important religious symbol and to impress the local military families of the Shogun's power and prestige.

Yoshimitsu worked constantly to improve his court status as well. Having received the titles of Inner Minister and Minister of the Left, in 1394 he turned the office of Shogun over to his son in order to accept the post of Grand Minister of State and the highest court rank. By this move he ascended the pinnacle of both political systems, military and civil, a condition which

111

he publicized by the adoption of two separate forms of his official signature. Having greatly expanded his residential estate on the outskirts of Kyōto at Kitayama, and having built there in 1397 the Golden Pavilion (Kinkakuji), Yoshimitsu lived and entertained in the grandest style. On occasion he rode about in Chinese costume, in the ceremonial clothing received from the Ming Emperor. At other times he entertained the emperor as though his equal. In 1407 Yoshimitsu succeeded in having his own wife named empress dowager to succeed the late Empress Tsūyōmon-in. The celebration of his son's coming of age in 1408 was carried out in the presence of the emperor in a manner appropriate to princes of the blood. Such intimate relations between subject and sovereign had no precedent, and in fact it was never to recur with such lavish and open display

Yoshimitsu died in 1408 and was succeeded in turn by his son and grandson. The latter died in 1428, by which time the stability of the shogunate was beginning to deteriorate as a result of worsening political and fiscal conditions and weakening Ashikaga leadership. The sixth Shogun Yoshinori (1428–1441) showed signs of vigor. Alarmed by an unsettling quarrel in the Kantō, Yoshinori in 1439 sided with the Uesugi against Ashikaga Mochiuji, the *Kantō Kanrei*, and helped to exterminate the Kantō branch of the house. Three years later in 1441, Yoshinori was assassinated by one of his chief retainers, Akamatsu Mitsusuke. *Shugo* of three provinces in central Japan, Mitsusuke had apparently felt the restraining hand of the Shogun too frequently. His action proved a major blow to the power of the Ashikaga house.

Yoshimasa, the eighth Shogun (r. 1443–1473) exemplified the courtly ineffectiveness to which the Shogun was eventually relegated. During his tenure of office, quarrels broke out regularly among his vassals, and the fiscal foundations of the shogunate were shaken by civil disorder. Between 1467 and 1477 the great *shugo* exhausted themselves fighting in the streets of Kyōto. In the process half of the city was destroyed. Yet Yoshimasa himself lived quietly as a lay priest in his estate in the Higashiyama suburb of Kyōto, emulating Yoshimitsu by building his Silver Pavilion (Ginkakuji). During the years between his retirement in 1473 and his death in 1490, he lavished his attention on the arts to become the foremost patron of one of the most creative periods of cultural flowering in medieval Japan.

Cultural Development and Economic Growth

One of the fascinating and seemingly paradoxical aspects of the history of the fourteenth and fifteenth centuries in Japan is that, despite the instability of the political order, the country at large gave evidence of remarkable cultural and economic growth. When viewed across the subsequent stretch of time, these centuries stand out as having produced the art forms and clarified the aesthetic values which to this day are most admired by the Japanese. The same centuries saw Japan emerge as a major maritime power in East Asia activated by a vigorous internal economic expansion.

Of course the paradox is partly the historian's own creation. For he has tended to exaggerate the destructive extent of the warfare which prevailed during these centuries and has too readily assumed that decentralization of political power was necessarily bad for the country. Yet decentralization was undoubtedly one of the contributing factors to the cultural and economic growth of these centuries. For it was under *shugo* patronage that Japan became a multi-centered economy and was able to support new cultural capitals in the distant provinces.

The Ashikaga cultural flowering which centered on the Shogun's residences in Kyōto, and to a more limited extent on the provincial headquarters of the *shugo,* was the result of three prime factors: it was a product of the fusion between the two main bodies of the aristocracy, civil and military; it was nourished by new influences from China, and it reflected the new and expanding cultural role played by the Zen monasteries. Its historical importance derived in the main from the fact that it was infused with certain universal qualities that

113

could weather the centuries and remain relevant to later generations of Japanese. For while the Heian period gave rise to a more absolute aristocratic ideal, the model it produced remained unattainable in later centuries, based as it was on sources of wealth, prestige, and leisure which only a nobility could command. The Ashikaga product was not so specifically restricted to the "noble" way of life and contained common human elements quite accessible to later generations and to all classes of Japanese society.

Symbolizing the fusion of the two levels of aristocratic society was, as we have noted, the transfer of the *bakufu* from Kamakura to Kyōto. Up to the fourteenth century the *kuge* had monopolized Japan's higher culture, and even in Kamakura only a few of the military houses had lived up to the level of the nobility. With the entrance of the *bushi* into the city of the emperor and the Fujiwara, they now became full participants in the polite society of the court. The Ashikaga military aristocracy thus took on the ways of the *kuge,* receiving instruction in etiquette, poetry, music, or literature, and adding court rituals to their own ceremonial occasions.

The new Chinese influence was not the result of any sudden revival of contact with China. Since the end of the Heian period the tempo of communication with the continent had been building up. During the thirteenth century numerous priests went back and forth between Japan and China. The Mongol invasion attempts greatly accelerated Japan's shipbuilding and seafaring capacities. Thus by Ashikaga times, and particularly after the establishment of the Ming dynasty in 1368, regular communications began to build up between Japan and China and between certain of the Zen temples of Kyōto and those of south China. The sending of the Tenryūji trading ship to China in 1342, the mission of the Emperor Hung-wu to Japan in 1373, and the final acceptance by Yoshimitsu of the status of tributary "king of Japan" under the Ming emperor in 1401, are milestones in the development of this regular communication. As a result Japanese again were able to gain direct knowledge of Chinese civilization. But whereas in the seventh century it was governmental institutions that attracted the attention of the Japanese, seven centuries later it was in the realm of religion, the arts, and technology that the Japanese found greatest interest. Chinese influence is visible in nearly every aspect of the Ashikaga cultural flowering. And to some extent this may account for the more eclectic and universal qualities which gave the Ashikaga achievements their historical staying power.

Indispensable to the cultural world of the Ashikaga Shoguns was the Zen priesthood and the great Zen monasteries which fringed the city of Kyōto. The Ashikaga Shoguns patronized the Zen establishment more compulsively and more lavishly than the Hōjō, converting the sect into something of an official organ of the shogunate. Musō Kokushi (1275–1351) became the chief spiritual advisor to Ashikaga Takauji, and it was he who suggested that Takauji establish the monastery of Tenryūji in memory of the dead Go-Daigo. Thereafter successive Shoguns took Rinzai sect priests as their advisors. In 1386, Yoshimitsu adopted a system of official organization for the Zen order. The "Five Temples" (Gozan) were given special status as official temples. Under the great Nanzenji which served as headquarters were ranged in hierarchical order the Kyōto five—Tenryūji, Shōkokuji, Kenninji, Tōfukuji, and Manjūji—and the five temples of Kamakura. Below the Gozan came the "Ten branches" (Jussatsu) consisting of over sixty provincial temples, and below these were some two hundred local temples. The provincial branches had been established in somewhat the same manner as the Kokubunji of Nara times, although the immediate model for the practice seems to have come from Sung China. Called "State Pacification Temples" (Ankokuji) they were in fact looked upon as protective and pacifying influences. The shogunate not only supported but supervised the Zen establishment, prescribing the system of ranks and salaries and placing the whole system under the control of a *bakufu* official.

The Ashikaga Shoguns used the Zen priesthood even more than did the Hōjō, as the literate branch of their government. In Kyōto, the temple of Shōkokuji served as a center of foreign relations where diplomatic documents were drafted and from

115

which priests serving as agents of the Ashikaga prepared to sail for China. But it was chiefly as spiritual advisors and as companions in aesthetic pastimes that the Ashikaga Shoguns turned to the Gozan priesthood. Such reliance on priestly advisors appears to have been motivated by serious religious concerns. Takauji, for example, having spent his entire life in battle and having shown himself an entirely unscrupulous leader by betraying both the Hōjō and Go-Daigo, lived in an atmosphere of considerable spiritual insecurity. In his later days he began to fear for his spiritual future and surrounded himself with Zen priests, among them Musō Kokushi. If the Hōjō regents used Zen to give them strength with which to deal with real problems, the Ashikaga Shoguns clung to Zen in a spirit of mysticism and escapism. After Yoshinori the heads of the Ashikaga house retired more and more to the seclusion of the semi-priestly life, shutting themselves off from the unpleasant realities that surrounded them.

The two high points of the Ashikaga cultural flowering occurred under the patronage of the third and eighth Shoguns, Yoshimitsu and Yoshimasa. Yoshimitsu's years of retirement to his villa have given the name Kitayama (Northern Hills) to the first of these culminating points, and the location of Yoshimasa's villa has given the name Higashiyama (Eastern Hills) to the second. These two men exemplified the contrasting qualities of the shogunal patronage of the arts just as their villas symbolized the full range of aesthetic qualities admired at the time. Yoshimitsu, the successful ruler, lived in luxury and ostentation. His monument was the Kinkakuji, a pavilion covered with gold and surrounded by a spacious pond and deer park. Here he collected art from around the world, and gave lavish entertainments enlivened with dances and dramatic presentations. His tastes were eclectic, and he was pleased by the colorful and exotic. Yet for all the display and search for novelty, Yoshimitsu and his followers were men of disciplined taste. The Kinkakuji despite its splendor was designed to take its place in a natural setting.

Yoshimasa, living in the declining years of shogunal power, himself a weak person physically and morally, drew about him, as if in compensation for the hopelessness of the times, a sophisticated coterie of priests and artists who among themselves developed a highly refined appreciation of the arts. His monument, the Ginkakuji, expresses the mystical quality which the connoisseurs of the time looked for in all the arts. The effort to find an "inner meaning" in nature and the artistic creations of man stemmed from the deeply introspective quality of Zen Buddhism.

Between the two expressions of Ashikaga culture we see the happy coincidence of aesthetic motivation and taste which combined the elegance of the nobility, the vigor of the *bushi,* and the depth of Zen monastic life. This syndrome of sensibilities was given expression in an aesthetic vocabulary which has endured to modern times as being particularly Japanese: *yūgen,* the mystery behind appearances; *wabi,* the mystery of loneliness; and *sabi,* the mystery of change. In all there was an eschewal of the realistic or the obvious in favor of the symbolic, the suggestive, and the profound.

Among the arts and pastimes of the Ashikaga period perhaps the tea ceremony (*cha-no-yu*) is central to an understanding of the other elements. The drinking of tea as a social pastime among members of the *bushi* aristocracy had a considerable vogue in the early Ashikaga period. It generally was accompanied by the conspicuous display of tea paraphernalia, pottery bowls, and lacquer containers. In Yoshimasa's time, however, under the influence of the priest Murata Shukō (1422–1502) it became a semi-religious aesthetic pastime in which a small group gathered in a quiet retreat to drink ritually prepared tea and to appreciate the objects of art which decorated the retreat or which were used in the serving of the tea. The tea ceremony thus became the vehicle for the dissemination of artistic tastes in a wide variety of fields such as architecture, painting, flower arrangement, ceramics, and lacquer ware.

The architecture of the Ashikaga period is characterized by the use of natural woods and the subordination of building to the surrounding natural setting. Two influences appear to have combined to produce a style of domestic construction which was to become directly ancestral to the modern domestic

117

style. South Chinese influence appears in the temples of the Gozan with their heavy roofs supported by darkened unpainted pillars and white plaster walls. The native palace style was seen in the villas and pavilions. The so-called "studio style" (*shoinzukuri*) popularized the use of *tatami* to cover the entire floor and the *tokonoma* as a special alcove for display of art objects. The two most famous buildings of the period are, of course, the Gold and Silver Pavilions. Both were essentially viewing towers from which to contemplate surrounding gardens of water, rocks, and pines. Both were planned and laid out at great expense to recapture the world of nature and to suggest to meditative minds the relationship between man and his environment. The art of landscape gardening progressed along with architecture and led to the creation of a great variety of contemplative gardens, many of which remain today. At Saihōji is a garden in which the floor is entirely covered with moss. The garden at Ryōanji uses simply sand and rocks to create the illusion of islands in a wide expanse of sea. But of whatever size or style, the gardens of the Ashikaga period held to the principle of condensing the larger world into the manageable confines of man-sized space.

The greatest art of the Ashikaga period was undoubtedly painting. Although largely derivative of Chinese landscape style, the new manner of ink painting suited the mood of the time perfectly and inspired Japanese artists, many of them Zen priests, to a remarkable mastery of technique and fresh creative imagination. The new monochrome style known as "water and ink" (*suiboku*) eschewed vivid colors and placed its emphasis upon skilled brushwork. In the hands of a Sesshū (1420–1506) it gave rise to impressionistic "ink-splash" sketches or extremely realistic renditions of the snow covered hills and valleys of his native land.

An art form with a completely different style of appeal and one which more nearly exemplified the grand manner of the social life of the *bushi* aristocracy was the dramatic form known as *nō-kyōgen*. *Nō*, or serious religion-based dramatic performances, and *kyōgen*, or comical interludes, formed the heart of the great displays with which the Shogun and *shugo*

MEDIEVAL JAPAN

119

entertained. Yet again, it was only as a number of dramatic ingredients were woven together by men who emerged from out of the religious institutions surrounding Kyōto that the new art form was perfected. By the Kamakura period the court tradition of masked dances and various Shinto and Buddhist ritualistic dances and didactic plays had developed into a number of dramatic styles, some serious and others popular and comic. Four guilds of dance-actors attached to the temple of Kōfukuji in Nara were especially advanced in these techniques. It was from one of these guilds that Kan'ami (1333–1384), a Shintō priest by profession, and his son Seami (1363–1443) were taken under the patronage of Yoshimitsu. They were instrumental in uniting elements of dance and music available to them into the *nō* as we know it. The resulting dramatic form was an extremely stylized music drama in which elements of music, dance, poetry, costume, and masks were harmoniously combined. As in the Greek drama, to which it has been likened, the masks play an important role; there is no scenery, and a chanting chorus frequently picks up the theme of the play.

Nō, while basically Shintō and Amidist in inspiration, was perfected in the Zen-dominated atmosphere of Yoshimitsu's court. Thus it exemplified the combination of "splendor used with restraint" which typified the Kitayama period. The actors in their costumes of gold brocade and vivid colors present a lavish elegance, yet against the bare stage, there is no sense of gaudiness. The scripts are lyrical and highly poetic; the dance is refined and beautiful. The messages of the plays are either strictly Shintō in their evocation of some particular *kami*, or deeply infused with the Amidist compassion and the search for salvation. Action is always symbolic and suggestive rather than realistic. It is this combination of rich, poetic elegance and sense of mystery that most typified the quality of *yūgen* which Seami strove to achieve in his performances. The *Kyōgen* mimes, many of which were takeoffs on contemporary high *bushi* society, exemplified the encroachment of elements of the lower classes into the world of higher culture. Interspersed between the serious numbers of a *nō* performance, they served to lighten the atmosphere, and often to cast humor upon the very members of society who were the prime patrons of the *nō*.

We should not suppose that Japan remained economically stagnant during the Kamakura period, and it is in the early years of the Ashikaga period that our attention is again attracted by evidence of dramatic economic growth in Japan. Evidence of expanded production leading to new commercial activity appears first in the field of agriculture. Under the encouragement of regional military leaders Japanese farmers began to adopt a number of improvements in farm technology. Better farm tools, new crops such as soy beans and tea, and the greater use of draft animals appreciably changed the style of agricultural technology. New irrigation works and better control of rivers helped to increase the area under cultivation, so that agricultural production in many areas was literally doubled. Commercial farming and handicraft production also became possible on an expanded basis, as goods formerly produced simply for local consumption or for the household use of *shōen* proprietors were introduced into an emerging commercial market. Raw silk, hemp, linen, paper, dyestuffs, lacquer, vegetable oils, and many other subsidiary products of village economy were now produced in surplus for general sale.

Specialization of function at the village or *shōen* level produced new groups of artisans as well. Carpenters, thatchers, potters, smiths, weavers, and brewers became detached from their positions within the *shōen* as part-time specialists in the agrarian community. Increasingly they formed organizations of their own which offered them protection in their chosen specialization. Guild organizations known as *za* probably started during the mid-thirteenth century, when the Hōjō set aside certain commercial quarters in Kamakura and assigned artisans and merchants to particular locations. During the fifteenth century the *za* proliferated enormously and developed a pattern of organization remarkably similar to that of certain medieval European guilds. *Za* consisted of a closed member-

121

ship community of merchants or artisans who claimed monopoly rights to the sale or manufacture of particular commodities. These rights plus an element of protection were guaranteed by a patron—a great temple, a shrine, or a noble family. In an age when legal protection was of little real significance, such a system of strength in numbers and attachment to a patron became the main reliance of commercial and artisan groups. *Za* tended to cluster around the prestigious establishments of Kyōto, Nara, and Kamakura. With the rise of the great *shugo*, provincially based *za* with local patrons also made their appearance. Trading *za,* specializing in particular commodities or local products thus provided the first extended network of commercial distribution on a market economy basis. Shipping lines and packhorse services became generally available rather than being limited to certain *shōen* for tax delivery purposes.

An important indication of the growing trade economy was the increased use of coins for currency and exchange. Since the Japanese government had long since given up the minting of coins, the new circulatory medium was made up chiefly of imported Chinese cash, though unminted gold and silver were used by weight. Money became a necessity as the limits of a barter economy were stretched and goods were purchased from great distances. Increasingly even taxes may have been collected in coin from farmers. During the sixteenth century feudal lords began the practice of measuring their fiefs in terms of strings of cash (*kan*) rather than measures of grain, though this did not mean that land dues were necessarily collected in coin.

Use of money, either by farmers or feudal proprietors, required the conversion of produce to cash and this gave rise to groups of money changers and pawnbrokers serving the merchant and peasant classes. The two most common types were the local moneylenders, usually village warehouse merchants or *sake* brewers, and the large town merchants who often specialized in financial transactions with the feudal authorities. Temples also served an important function in these days, since they had the ability to accumulate reserves and the prestige and moral authority to demand repayment on loans. The large headquarter temples with their bases in Kyōto and Kamakura and their many provincial branches were even able to develop systems of letters of credit and means of facilitating the movement of large sums of capital.

The increase in trade, of which the spread of money was a symptom, brought with it a number of major consequences. Wealth, for instance, was no longer tied solely to the land but could be accumulated in other ways and stored in the form of precious metals or goods. A merchant class, congregating in a few important administrative and trade centers, was able to establish itself as a class of wealth outside of the confines of aristocratic society. But the aristocratic houses and temples also derived profit from association with trade and usury. The *za* were a source of profit to their patrons, while territorial authorities were able to impose transit fees or taxes on commercial activity within their spheres of control. The Shogun and *shugo* were not slow in tapping sources of income from foreign trade or domestic monopoly. The close association between feudal authority and commercial activity which distinguished the development of commercial economy in Japan, thus had its origins at this time.

In Japan as in Europe the growth of the commercial and service classes was marked by the rise of new towns and cities which contrasted sharply in their prime functions with the older administrative centers. Whereas up through the Kamakura period, only the three major urban concentrations of Kyōto, Nara, and Kamakura existed, by Ashikaga times numerous provincial towns had come into being, and in addition sizeable communities had grown up around some of the temples and shrines and at major ports and marketplaces. The latter, being removed from the direct presence of either feudal or religious power, were able to gain a degree of self-government and political autonomy. The merchants of Sakai, Hakata, Ōtsu, Ujiyamada, and Muro, for instance, formed independent commercial communities. Sakai even acquired its own military protection and ran its own affairs under a council of thirty-six senior citizens. But the parallel with Europe cannot be pushed further. Merchant independence did not grow within the sphere of feudal authority to provide the basis of a commercial estate with special privileges and political representation in the councils of the Shogun or *shugo*. The commercial sector remained undeveloped and dependent upon feudal support to such a degree that in the sixteenth century it was easily brought under the firm control of military authority.

One of the problems which the rising merchant class faced in its effort to create its own economic base was the difficulty of entering trade with the continent from its isolated position on the fringe of East Asia. To be sure the expansion of trade with the continent was one of the more remarkable developments of the fourteenth and fifteenth centuries, but by comparison with the opportunities open to the Italian merchants of the day or the Portuguese or English of later times, the Japanese traders were at great disadvantage. For many centuries, in fact, the sea gap between Japan and the continent had been bridged chiefly by Korean and Chinese sailors and by Chinese and Korean ships. It took the Mongol emergency to cause the Japanese to develop their own merchant marine. And it was only in the decades following the Mongol invasions that any significant numbers of Japanese from coastal communities, mostly in the Inland Sea region and Kyūshū, began to venture into the China Seas. The early fourteenth century saw the Japanese engaged in a form of freebooting trade mixed with coastal plunder and piracy which gained for the Japanese ships the name of Wakō (Japanese pirates). This in turn was a reflection of the generally undeveloped trade practices in East Asia where, especially in Korea and China, the authorities frequently looked upon trade as undesirable and hence to be avoided or drastically restricted. By the time of the establishment of the Ashikaga shogunate, the various political and religious groups in Japan had learned to appreciate the profit which could be obtained through trade, and they therefore saw a value in bringing this freebooting activity under some sort of control. The Shogun and other Kyōto groups soon entered into a sponsored trade with China and simultaneously made the effort to control all foreign trade under an official license system. The "alliance" between feudal and merchant interests that developed at this time was as much desired on the part of the merchants who lacked capital and needed protection as it was coerced by the feudal authorities.

How successfully the Ashikaga authorities and the *shugo* managed to control the Wakō is a moot question, but the development of official trade with China is well documented. In 1342 Ashikaga Takauji was persuaded to send a trading ship to China and apply the profit from the venture to the building of Tenryūji. Further "Tenryūji ships" followed and other monasteries in the Kyōto area joined with merchants of Sakai to enter the China trade. Meanwhile the first Ming Emperor Hung-wu sent two monks as envoys to Japan in 1373 to request cessation of the Wakō activities. The Shogun Yoshimitsu was in no position to do anything at the time. But after 1392 when the Yung-lo emperor renewed pressure on the Japanese, Yoshimitsu succumbed to considerations of profit and entered into a tributary arrangement with China. In 1401 he sent a mission to China pledging his effort to control the Wakō. The mission returned in 1402 with Yoshimitsu's investiture as "King of Japan" and subject of the Ming. In 1404 an agreement was reached which set up an official "tally trade" with China. Yoshimitsu has been severely criticized by Japanese historians for his submission to China and his consequent disregard of Japan's national honor. But the trade profits were enormous, and the priests who mediated between the Ashikaga court and the Ming capital softened the problems of honor for the Japanese Shogun.

Although the agreement of 1404 called for only one official trading mission in ten years, six voyages are recorded between 1404 and 1410. In the latter year the Shogun Yoshimochi broke off the agreement with China on grounds of honor. Subsequently, however, with the ascension of a new Ming emperor in 1425 and Yoshimochi's death in 1428, negotiations were reopened, and a more liberal trade agreement was finally reached. Trade resumed in 1432 under an arrangement whereby official embassies composed of several ships might be sent every ten years. The mission of 1454, for instance, contained ten ships: three "Tenryūji ships" patronized by the Ashikaga, two "Ise ships" for the imperial family, one by the Governor General of Kyūshū, one each by the Shimazu, Ōtomo, and Ōuchi families, and one by the Tonomine temple of Yamato. Behind this list of patrons, however, was the activity of the merchants of Sakai and Hakata who fitted out the ships and shared in the profits.

That such trade was immensely profitable to its patrons goes without saying. We know also that increasingly, as the land revenues of the shogunate and the imperial court were depleted or cut off at their source, commercial income became the main support of both the civil and military aristocracy in Kyōto. The trade also reveals a great deal about the state of the Japanese economy. Exports to China were now mass commodities and artifacts such as refined copper, sulfur, folding fans, screens, painted scrolls, and above all swords. Single missions carried tens of thousands of Japanese steel swords to China. In return the Japanese ships returned with strings of cash (50,000 strings in 1454), raw silk, porcelains, paintings, medicines, and books. All of this gave evidence that Japan was no longer an under-developed member of the Chinese world order. In fact the limited trade permitted by a reluctant China was eventually to prove too restrictive for the Japanese. After 1551 the tally trade broke down, and Japanese traders in unrestrained numbers began to ply the China Seas, only to be faced with competition from a most unexpected source. Already European traders had penetrated the Straits of Malacca and had made their presence known in the ports of Southern Kyūshū.

The Rise of the *Sengoku-Daimyō*

A shogunal succession dispute followed by a quarrel between the Hosokawa and Yamana houses led to open military action in the city of Kyōto in 1467. The Shogun Yoshimasa, unable to control his two great vassals, called upon the remaining *shugo* to suppress the quarrel. As a result the entire Ashikaga following split into two rival factions and engaged in a bitterly-drawn-out war which lasted for eleven years. On

126

the Hosokawa side were ranged the *shugo* of twenty-four provinces with an estimated manpower capacity of 160,000 men. On the Yamana side were the *shugo* of twenty provinces with the capacity of mustering 110,000 men, though perhaps only half of these numbers were committed. The war raged sporadically in and out of the city of Kyōto, leaving half of the city devastated and most of its great monuments burned. The warfare came to an end in 1477, but it had resulted in utterly destroying the power of the shogunate. Yoshimasa retired to his suburban villa, and though his son served as Shogun, his authority extended no further than the limits of the home province of Yamashiro. The provinces had fallen into the independent hands of the *shugo* or their successors, and a state of complete decentralization was in the making. The Ashikaga house and the remaining court nobility were now completely cut off from their provincial sources of income and were obliged to live their powerless though still symbolically significant lives at the sufferance of the regional military powers which were beginning to emerge.

The hundred years from the beginning of the Ōnin war to Nobunaga's entrance into Kyōto in 1568, which marked the beginning of the reunification of Japan, define a period in Japanese history known as Sengoku, "the Warring States." The name is appropriate, for warfare was endemic. But the prevalence of warfare was not the most important feature of this age. The Ōnin war, first of all, proved to be a major breakpoint in Japanese political history. It unquestionably marked the end of an effective Ashikaga hegemony and the beginning of the fully decentralized phase of Japanese feudalism. But it stands for more. It marked the end of a major cycle in Japanese institutional history, as the remaining elements of the imperial system were finally eradicated to be entirely replaced by feudal authority. After 1467 the Military Governors, who up to that time still had relied on certain features of the imperial local administration, were superseded by a new type of local authority, the true *daimyō*. Within the daimyo domain the *shōen* disappeared, to be replaced everywhere by the fief. And throughout Japan basic changes in the structure and the composition of social classes gave evidence of the fact that Japan was becoming "completely feudal."

But again the process of change was not violently revolutionary. Both emperor and Shogun remained in Kyōto as symbols of residual sovereignty, though their political power was now completely shorn away. After the death of the Shogun Yoshimasa in 1490, the shogunate possessed neither the prestige nor the strength to impose upon a province a *shugo* who was not already established as a local hegemon. The last remnants of centralizing authority had been dissipated, and the country literally dissolved into autonomous territories. And yet the remnants of the old authority structure lingered on to keep alive a shadowy conception of legitimacy. However far the idea of a unified state was stretched, it was somehow not destroyed. The "state" was not divided, and the traditional locus of sovereignty was not challenged.

What happened at the top of the state was reflected at lower levels as well. The destructive Ōnin war had all but exhausted the *shugo* and had drastically weakened their powers of control over their provincial jurisdiction. The ensuing years saw a rapid break-up of the *shugo* houses and the provinces over which they had been placed. In almost every part of Japan the territories to which the *shugo* had been assigned split up into smaller domains either among contending branches of the old *shugo* lines or among contending vassal houses. Thus the Hosokawa lost their territories to the Miyoshi and Chōsokabe while the Yamana were superseded by the Mōri and Amago.

The new political units which resulted from the breakup of the *shugo* holdings were smaller but they were more easily held than the military governorships. Their appearance coincided with the rise of a whole new group of locally powerful military families which historians have called *sengoku-daimyō*. The traditional writers of Japanese history have lamented the passing of the Ashikaga *shugo* houses and the aristocratic culture they stood for, and they have described the process by which they were eliminated as one of *ge-koku-jō* (the revolt of vassals against their lords). The passing of the Ashikaga military

128

houses was indeed at the hands of their inferiors, but the success of the daimyo cannot be explained simply as the result of treachery. They rose to power both because of certain fundamental weaknesses in the power structures over which the previous generation of *shugo* presided and through their own ability to exploit new and more effective means of organizing military power and of controlling territory .

The prevalence of warfare, or rather the constant need to defend land rights by force of arms, led to fundamental changes in the local basis of political life throughout Japan of the sixteenth century. While even as late as the beginning of the fifteenth century the country had retained most of the external administrative features which had existed in the thirteenth century, by the beginning of the sixteenth century the political topography of the nation had taken on a dramatically new appearance. The contours of real power no longer coincided either with the boundaries of the *shōen* or the old administrative jurisdictions. In the countryside the basic units out of which combinations of effective power were being built consisted of armed men, their castles, and their lands held in fief. Such units were more intimately related to the geographical or defense topography of the land than to the traditional contours of imperial administration or of *shōen* proprietorship. In actual practice therefore the domains of the Sengoku lords took shape from the inside out, not as legally defined grants or subdivisions of the state. Their shape conformed, in other words, to the territorial limits of the combined holdings of the vassals over which they exercised control. The true daimyo domain was simply a composite of separate fiefs over which the daimyo held the right of overlordship.

Within the *sengoku-daimyō* domain the elimination of the *shōen* in favor of the practice of enfeoffment was now complete. At the local level a process of consolidation of the *shiki* rights and the elimination of absentee privileges had long been at work. By this time the many separate levels of proprietorship, and the various managerial functions had been absorbed by the single authority of the daimyo who now could claim full

129

overlordship as defined by the feudal concept of the proprietary domain (*ryō*). Such a domain could be subdivided into fiefs (*chigyō-chi*) as he saw fit.

Also within the domain, a similar process of consolidation and simplification of rights and responsibilities was affecting the condition of the cultivator class. Concentration of authority in the hands of the daimyo had lifted the level of direct participation by the *bushi* class in rural affairs, drawing them toward the castled center of the overlord's domain and thus releasing the peasantry to work out their own self-management. At the same time the unsettled conditions in the countryside and the decay of the *shōen* system, together with the expansion of the farming class both in numbers and productivity, encouraged the formation of self-sufficient village communities. By Sengoku times daimyo came to depend more and more on the ability of peasant communities to manage their own affairs and to pay taxes on a village quota basis. The local populace, in such instances, was held accountable for purposes of administration, taxation, labor and military service according to village-size units. Such village units, called *mura*, were encouraged to develop their own organs of self-government and even of self-defense during the years of intense civil war which were to follow. And where this was not done, villagers often took matters into their own hands and asserted the rights of self-governance by violent means. Increasingly, then, the daimyo conceived of his territory as made up of a given number of *mura* producing a given amount of dues. He enfeoffed his vassals in terms of these village units and calculated their worth in terms of the tax quotas of such *mura*.

The daimyo domain, as it took shape during the sixteenth century, became in essence a petty principality. The European travellers who observed Japan at the end of the century called the daimyo "kings" and "princes." Over their territory the daimyo now stood as absolute masters. Their domains were theirs to govern and protect, with only the haziest reference to delegated authority and sanction from the Shogun and emperor. Such local rulers administered their domains through their bands of retainers (*kashin*) and by delegation through subinfeudation. Their techniques of administration were even more simple and straightforward than the house governments of the Fujiwara and the Minamoto, emphasizing military organization first and civil administration second. Yet the larger of the daimyo governed their territories in a manner both more comprehensive and more direct than had been possible under any previous system of government.

The degree to which the daimyo gave thought to the governance of their domains is revealed in the new "house laws" (*bunkoku-hō*) which began to make their appearance toward the end of the fifteenth century. Those of the Date, Imagawa, Takeda and Ōuchi, for instance, show the beginnings of a new administrative-legal system which recognized the ascendance of the feudal order and the need to establish a new legal base. A perusal of these house codes reveals the new powers to which the daimyo laid claim. In them the daimyo asserted what was tantamount to sovereign authority over the men and lands of the domain. He exploited to the full the rights of the lord to regulate the affairs of his vassals and to administer his territories. He provided for the systematic collection of taxes and the standardization of tax procedures, the regulation of markets, transport facilities, weights and measures. He laid down procedures by which his vassals could profit from their fiefs. He controlled marriage and inheritance among his vassals. He established penal laws and imposed strict discipline, relying on the use of joint or group responsibility. He claimed the right to regulate and protect religious institutions within his territory.

The nature of the daimyo's control over his domain is also clearly revealed in the changing nature of warfare in which he was engaged. The method of hand-to-hand combat in which the single armored samurai predominated had gone out with the Ōnin war. Now daimyo recruited large bodies of men from their territories and faced their enemies with lines of pike-wielding footsoldiers. The *bushi* had become in large part an officer class serving as captains over a new class of footsoldiers known as *ashigaru* ("light foot") who stood midway between the peasantry and the *bushi*. We hear now of armies of ten to twenty thousand being raised from the confines of a single province. It was the requirements of provisioning and garrisoning such bodies of troops that gave rise to the large castle towns which appeared in the centers of the daimyo domains.

The century of warfare known as Sengoku was the furnace in which the new domains were forged. And the constant struggle of contesting military leaders to defend or enlarge their domains, to ward off powerful neighbors or to gain mastery of the smaller military houses in their territories, provided the fuel. Most of the successful daimyo who remained after the middle of the sixteenth century had spent their entire lives in the field, and their territories had been crossed and recrossed by their armies as they tightened their grip upon the land. Warfare thus served as the ultimate destroyer of the old order as well as the creator of the new institutions of local rule which the daimyo used to control their territories.

It should not be supposed, of course, that the country fell apart into domains of equal size or even that all Japan by the 1560's had fallen under control of daimyo of large size. Many areas remained fragmented into extremely small holdings over which the control of a daimyo-sized overlord had not been extended. There were, as well, non-feudal interests which held out against the efforts of daimyo to absorb them. In Japan of the 1560's there were in all, perhaps, two hundred daimyo worthy of the name, and their territories may have extended over two thirds of the country, but this is simply a guess. The major daimyo who had managed to grasp large pieces of the old *shugo* territories are more readily identifiable, and these numbered less than thirty. In the far north the Date, with headquarters near present Yonezawa, distinguished themselves by issuing one of the first complete house laws, the *Jinkai-shū* in 1536. In the Kantō, the Hōjō (not descended from the Kamakura regents) with headquarters at Odawara, and the Satomi had become prominent. Branches of the Uesugi, who had once served as *Kanrei* under the Kamakura branch of the Ashikaga house, had now been pushed into the northeastern provinces where they adjoined the domains of the Takeda, the Suwa, Jimbō, and Asakura. On the eastern seaboard were the

Imagawa and the Oda; in the home provinces the Asai, the Hosokawa (reduced now to a minor holding), the Tsutsui, and Hatakeyama. The western provinces had given rise to a number of powerful daimyo: on the Japan Sea side, the Yamana still persisted but had lost most of their territory to the Amago; the Ukita, Kobayakawa, Ōuchi, and Mōri had emerged on the Inland Sea side. Shikoku saw the rise of the Miyoshi and Chōsokabe; Kyūshū was the base of the Ōtomo, Shimazu, Kikuchi, and Ryūzōji. A number of these families, as their names reveal, had been powerful during the Ashikaga period or were relatives or close vassals of the *shugo* of the fifteenth century. But the political map of the time showed few major remnants of the great families which had held power under the early Ashikaga Shoguns. And the round of further fighting which was to break out after 1568 eliminated nearly all of these.

The story of the sixteenth century is not told simply by reference to the rise of the daimyo. The warfare of the Sengoku period and the condition of political unrest led to other evidences of social and political change which appeared to move counter to the consolidating attempts of the daimyo. Uprisings among the common people or the acquisition of local political power by religious communities resulted in the establishment from time to time of regional groups which resisted daimyo authority. Famous in this respect was the great "provincial uprising" (*kuni-ikki*) which in 1485 put the province of Yamashiro under a locally organized government of peasants and petty *bushi*. The uprising successfully drove out the armies of the *shugo,* and for eight years the leaders refused to pay provincial dues. Similar revolts against military authority were frequent in the years immediately after the Ōnin war, when the *shugo* had so squeezed their territories for taxes and men. Of the religious-led uprisings, that of the Ikkō sect in Kaga was most noteworthy. In 1488 members of the sect under priestly leadership expelled the *shugo* from Kaga, and thereafter for nearly a century the province was governed through the priestly organization of the Honganji monastery in conjunction with the lesser samurai and village heads of the province. Such monk-led communities came into existence in other portions of the country or often held out as pockets within the expanding territories of the daimyo.

Japanese historians seriously debate the question of whether these indications of the rise of "popular power" in Japan constituted an anti-feudal force which might have had significant national consequences had not the daimyo suppressed them. Yet it is hard to see that an alternative form of government to the one being perfected by the daimyo was in the making. The Yamashiro uprising created a form of commune which regulated its affairs under a coalition of landowners and petty samurai. It eventually dissolved when the leaders of the commune extended their powers and saw the value of again accepting the superior authority of the rising *Sengoku-daimyō*. The Kaga religious administration also rested on the same class of petty military gentry, whereas the priestly leadership, centered in the Honganji temple itself, behaved in much the same manner as would a local daimyo. Religious establishments had become, in other words, the ruling headquarters of feudal territories similar in most respects to the daimyo domains.

8

The First European Encounter

The period of Japanese history from the 1540's to the 1640's has been called the Christian century. The designation is something of a Western conceit. To be sure, Christianity was introduced into Japan at this time and may by the second decade of the seventeenth century have touched close to two percent of the country's population. But the capacity of Westerners to interfere in the national affairs of Japan was slight, and their cultural impact was even less pronounced. The century of contact with Europeans was a significant chapter in Japanese history, but chiefly in terms of the internal dynamics of Japan's own gigantic struggles which led to the reunification of the country and to the reshaping of its basic social and economic institutions.

Yet in terms of world history, the sixteenth and seventeenth centuries in East Asia hold a special interest, for they witnessed the first extensive contact between Europeans and the Chinese and Japanese, and resulted in an initial rebuff of the Westerners by the two prime powers of East Asia. It is well to remember that the first phase of East-West contact involved a very different "West" from that of the nineteenth century. The Portuguese and Spanish who ventured to the Orient in the sixteenth century were stretching their capacities to the limit when they established their colonies in Malaya and the Philippines. Their manpower was limited and their staying power rested as much on the weakness of the peoples they conquered as on their special military superiority. The Dutch and the English who entered

Asian waters in the seventeenth century were not yet prepared to exert a major effort to penetrate the China and Japan trade. And so, after a century and a half both China and Japan were able to "control" the Westerners. The Portuguese were expelled from Japan and restricted to the small colony of Macao in China. The Dutch accepted a small, controlled trade with Japan at the one port of Nagasaki. Both China and Japan were able to return to their traditional policies of isolation.

What was it that differentiated this first encounter between Europe and East Asia from the one which came in the nineteenth century? From the Western side, it is generally explained in terms of the rise and decline of European trading activities and the rivalries between the Old World colonial powers and the Dutch and the English who followed. But conditions within China and Japan had a significant influence as well. It is well to remember that in the sixteenth century the Eastern countries were not so inferior to those of Europe in terms of their technologies of government and military defense. The early infiltration of the Portuguese into the China Seas had been facilitated in large measure by the internal weakness of both China and Japan. China was in the last stages of dynastic decline, while Japan was politically disunited and preoccupied by internal rivalries. Once both countries returned to full strength, China under the Ch'ing dynasty and Japan under the Tokugawa house, they regained the ability to control their own frontiers.

The Portuguese reached India in 1498. By 1510 Albuquerque had established a military outpost and trading center at Goa, which was to become the hub of Portuguese operations in the East. One year later the Portuguese captured Malacca from the Arabs and gained access to the spice trade and the China Seas. They are said to have reached China by 1514, and though they failed to obtain the commercial concessions they sought from the court at Peking, they were able to establish in 1557 a post at Macao from which they had access to trade with Canton. Shortly before this, in 1543, Portuguese traders landed on the small island of Tanegashima south of Kyūshū and made their first contact with the Japanese. The Spanish arrived in 1587, the Dutch in 1609.

THE FIRST EUROPEAN ENCOUNTER

These were years of confusion and high adventure in the China Seas. The official Japanese trade with China had broken down and the seas swarmed with Japanese and Chinese freebooters. The Japanese before long established bases in Annam, Siam, and Luzon and had entered the spice trade. The islands off the coast of China became the haunts of pirates, while Japanese ships so frequently carried out raids on the China coast that the weakening Ming government in desperation forcibly rolled back the coastal population of central China several miles inland. China remained an important element in the Japan trade, since the chief profit for Japanese traders came from importing Chinese silk and gold to Japan in exchange for Japanese silver and copper. It was into this regional trade that the Portuguese intruded themselves.

Portuguese trade with Japan began in 1545, and soon the daimyo of Kyūshū were vying with each other to lure the Europeans to their ports. Within a decade the Portuguese had practically run the Chinese traders out of Japanese ports by their more aggressive tactics and because of the greater maneuverability and greater size of their ships. The novelty of the European commodities which the Portuguese brought to Japan was also a major attraction. European firearms, fabrics such as velvet and wool cloth, glassware, clocks, tobacco, and spectacles appealed to the Japanese and their eclectic tastes. Ports of entry shifted frequently and often depended on the whims of local daimyo. Kagoshima seems to have been popular in the 1550's with Hirado and Fukuoka gaining favor in the 1560's. With the opening of Nagasaki as a major port in 1571, it became the main Portuguese center in Japan.

The effect of this trade upon Japan was considerable. For one thing, it accentuated the commercial factor in the national economy, making it possible for great wealth to be accumulated by trade rather than exclusively by control of land. The growth of trade was not a sudden phenomenon, of course, and it was not just the arrival of the Portuguese that brought into being the flourishing activity in the ports of Kyūshū. But the Europeans enlivened the trade and helped to augment its disruptive aspects. The manner in which certain of the lesser daimyo of

Kyūshū were able to increase their military power out of all proportion to their territorial size eventually became a major concern for the land-based daimyo of central and eastern Japan who led in the process of military unification after the middle of the sixteenth century.

There were other measurable influences, of which two need particular attention: one was the introduction of new firearms and military technology, the other was the introduction of Christianity. The Japanese were not ignorant of gunpowder, which they had faced in the Mongol invasions. The freebooting Japanese Wakō were also frequently subjected to explosive missiles from Chinese and Korean coastal defenses. But the Portuguese arquebuse was the first accurately firing weapon the Japanese had witnessed. Its introduction into Japan had an immediate impact on the nature of Japanese warfare. Within ten years after the Japanese first caught sight of the arquebuse at Tanegashima, the daimyo of western Japan were avidly importing Western arms, and Japanese artisans were turning out replicas in large numbers. The "Tanegashima" became the new weapon of the rising daimyo. The Ōtomo of north Kyūshū apparently were the first, in 1558, to put cannon into the field. By the 1570's musket corps were entering the battle lines of troops along with pikemen and archers, and in 1575 Oda Nobunaga won a major battle against the Takeda forces by employing three thousand musketmen in recurring waves. This was something of a turning point in the warfare which preceded Japan's military unification. Thereafter superior firepower was to determine the contest of strength, and the small mountain castles which had held out against the bow and the cavalry-fighter were brought within reach of musket and cannon. Daimyo were obliged to build massive castles with far-flung battlements and moats to protect their forces. Only the daimyo with the greatest of resources were able to survive. The importation of the musket probably hastened by several decades the ultimate unification of the country.

The impact of Christianity upon the Japanese of the sixteenth century was largely a product of the Jesuit missionary

THE FIRST EUROPEAN ENCOUNTER

effort. The tremendous vitality of the European missionary activity is seen when we realize that only nine years after the founding of the Society of Jesus in 1540, Francis Xavier, one of its founders, was preaching in Japan. Xavier (1506–1552) arrived in Goa in 1542. Disappointed in the Indian response to his message, he eventually made his way to Japan guided by a Japanese castaway named Yajirō. He arrived at Kagoshima in 1549. Here he was welcomed by the daimyo who hoped trade would follow when he granted Xavier permission to preach. Within a year Xavier had been expelled from Satsuma and was obliged to move to Hirado. From there he travelled through Hakata and Yamaguchi to Kyōto where he attempted to obtain a license to preach from the Ashikaga Shogun. Failing this he returned to Kyūshū through Sakai, established the first church in Yamaguchi and obtained the support of the Ōuchi and Ōtomo houses. He left Japan in 1551 with the hope of carrying his message to China, but died near Canton in 1552.

The brief two years during which Xavier travelled in Japan laid the basis of the greatest missionary success the Jesuits had in all of Asia. Yet he and his successors faced insuperable odds in conveying the Christian messages to the Japanese. Handicapped by the difficulty of making Christian principles comprehensible to the Japanese, it is probable that for many years they could achieve no meaningful appeal other than through personal conduct and example. The Japanese called the Portuguese and Italians "Southern Barbarians" (Namban), noting their arrival from the south seas, and at first considered Christianity just another version of Buddhism. Yet for some reason the Japanese were attracted to the men from afar. Their frankness and resoluteness, their absolute faith and strength of character were attractive features in an age of warfare when the Buddhist priesthood showed signs of materialism and corruption.

The missionaries were also men of learning who brought with them knowledge of a new civilization. Xavier, who had begun his mission with the attempt to reach the common man by streetcorner preaching, learned quickly to make his appeal to the ruling class and to coat his religious message with the attractions of European material civilization. Missionaries therefore brought trade in their wake and entered their audiences with the daimyo bearing curious gifts. Several daimyo of Kyūshū, in large measure influenced by thoughts of trade, adopted the new religion and some even ordered all their subjects to follow suit. The arrival of Father Gaspar Vilela (1525–1572) in Kyōto in 1560 established the capital as a second major center of Christian activity, and for a time the Jesuit missionaries had the active support of Oda Nobunaga, one of the prime military leaders of Japan.

Three daimyo of Kyūshū provided the most conspicuous support of Christianity. It was Ōmura Sumitada who in 1570 created the port of Nagasaki, permitted the Jesuits to establish a church there, and in 1579 turned over the administration of the town to the missionaries. Having become Christian in 1562 he later ordered his entire domain to do likewise. Arima Harunobu and Ōtomo Yoshishige (better known by his Buddhist name of Sōrin) made up the rest of the so-called "Three Christian Daimyo." These men in 1582 sent a group of four Japanese Christian envoys to the Papal court in Rome by Spanish galleon. Itō Mancio, Chijiwa Miguel, Nakaura Julian, and Hara Martino returned to Japan in 1590 after having crossed the Pacific to Acapulco and then on across the Atlantic to Spain and Italy. In 1613 Date Masamune sent a similar mission around the Cape of Good Hope to Lisbon and thence to Rome. By 1582 when the Jesuit Visitor Valignano (1537–1606) reported on his findings in Japan he estimated that there was a total of two hundred churches and 150,000 converts, all the work of seventy-five priests.

But already the willingness of the Japanese leaders to tolerate the foreign religion had begun to change. For as the tide of unification and consolidation swept over the country, the open conditions which had greeted the Western traders and missionaries began to disappear. Christianity was not to be interdicted until 1587, and the first persecutions were not to come until 1597. But after 1612 the Tokugawa authorities set to work to exterminate the religion with ruthless determination and great loss of life. Foreign trade was still encouraged for several decades more, but it too was placed under heavy restriction as the newly established central authority jealously prohibited the Kyūshū daimyo from enriching themselves through foreign contact. By 1640 Japan had adopted a rigid policy of national seclusion and suppression of Christianity.

9

Nobunaga, Hideyoshi and the Pacification of the Daimyo

By 1560 Japan stood on the threshold of an epic turning point in its political history. During the next forty years powerful military forces driving out of east-central Japan under the leadership of three successive military geniuses were to beat the daimyo into submission and impose a rough unity upon the country. The "three unifiers" who accomplished this feat—Oda Nobunaga (1534–1582), Toyotomi Hideyoshi (1536–1598) and Tokugawa Ieyasu (1542–1616)—were daimyo, and the unity they achieved took the form of a military hegemony over the remaining daimyo. By the time of Ieyasu the hegemony was firmly established and legitimized in a new shogunal authority which managed to keep the peace for over two centuries and a half.

When precisely the daimyo first saw the possibility of achieving a national hegemony is hard to say. Nobunaga was not the first, and he and his successors fought out their lives with numerous powerful competitors. Once under way, however, the process of consolidation proceeded along certain clearly discernible lines. A base had been laid during the early sixteenth century with the appearance of the *sengoku-daimyō*. As these regional lords of new and militant type filled out their territories and added to their resources, they began to fall upon each other in an effort to extend their frontiers or to gain control of their neighbors. Within each region the most power-ful daimyo, reducing surrounding daimyo to submission, formed leagues of military houses over which they served as overlords. As of 1560 the trend towards the clustering of daimyo had just begun, but a number of powerful regional leaders had already emerged. Houses such as the Hōjō, Uesugi, Imagawa, Ōuchi, and Shimazu each had acquired control over the daimyo of several provinces and were able to put coalition armies of formidable proportions into the field. They possessed, in other words, the requisites for national conquest. It was among these regional daimyo clusters that the final contest for control of Japan was fought.

As had so often happened in Japanese history, military conquest proceeded hand in hand with the acquisition of legiti-macy. As the regional leaders sensed the possibility of further aggrandizement, their eyes turned toward Kyōto and the neg-lected symbols of authority which resided there. Uesugi Kenshin (1530–1578) who in 1558 made a trip to Kyōto and returned to his home territory of Echigo with the long empty title of Governor General of the Kantō (*Kantō Kanrei*), im-mediately laid claim to the Kantō provinces and began to attack the Hōjō and Takeda territories. But it was for those closer to the home provinces to attempt the capture of Kyōto itself. The move came in 1560 when Imagawa Yoshimoto (1519–1560) at the head of some 25,000 men sought to cut his way to Kyōto over the territory of Oda Nobunaga. Yoshi-moto never reached the capital. Oda Nobunaga with but 2,000 men suprised the great Imagawa army and routed it.

With this one battle Nobunaga was projected into the ranks of the major contenders for power. Moreover, his lands were well placed strategically, since Owari, his home province, was within easy reach of the capital yet sufficiently removed to permit him to stay aloof from the constant strife which kept the central provinces in turmoil. By 1568 Nobunaga was ready to proceed against Kyōto. Entering the capital at the head of 30,000 men, he posed as protector of the emperor and cham-pion of Ashikaga Yoshiaki, a rival claimant to the Ashikaga

143

shogunate. Once in command of the capital, he installed Yoshiaki as Shogun, exacting from him a sworn statement that he would refer all political decisions to Nobunaga alone. A base had been laid for the eventual conquest of all Japan.

But Nobunaga's task was just begun, and numerous obstacles lay in the way to national hegemony. In the capital area he was opposed by the monks of Enryakuji on Hieizan who stubbornly resisted his occupancy of the capital. Across Lake Biwa stood the rival daimyo Asakura Yoshikage and Asai Nagamasa who frequently joined with the Hieizan forces against Nobunaga. Southwest of Kyōto the merchants of Sakai remained hostile. The fortress of Ishiyama, defended by the fanatical community of Ikkō adherents, was strategically placed to obstruct Nobunaga's expansion toward the Inland Sea. Ishiyama and Sakai were both supported in their resistance to Nobunaga by the daimyo of the Inland Sea region and the priests of Negoro who controlled much of Kii to the south. Behind the first ring of enemies were the menacing shadows of more distant powers such as the Takeda, Uesugi, and Hōjō to the east and the Mōri and Shimazu to the west. But Nobunaga was fortunate in one thing. Having obtained as ally Tokugawa Ieyasu, daimyo of Mikawa, he was reasonably assured that his rear would be protected from his Kantō rivals.

Concluding that his first problem was the elimination of Buddhist power in the capital area, Nobunaga fearlessly struck at the centers of monastic strength. In 1571 he performed the most terrifying act of his career. Closing his mind to all religious scruples, he put the torch to the monasteries of Hieizan, destroying three thousand buildings and slaughtering thousands of monks. In the same year he dealt a heavy blow to the priestly communities of Negoro. The next year the Ikkō communities of Eichizen and Kaga were brought to their knees. In 1573 Nobunaga crushed the Asai and Asakura, adding their territories to his domains. Meanwhile, his armies, sometimes numbering 60,000 men, had encircled Ishiyama castle in an investment which, though not completed until 1580, was to end for all time the temporal power of the Ikkō (Honganji) sect. In 1573, having driven the Shogun Yoshiaki out of Kyōto,

Nobunaga brought to an end the Ashikaga shogunate and stood de facto hegemon of the country.

For the next few years Nobunaga put his main effort into developing the resources of his new territory. Between 1576 and 1579 he built his great castle of Azuchi on the shores of Lake Biwa, thereby opening a new chapter in Japanese military history. Azuchi castle was built to sustain the force of firearms. A massive citadel with a seven-story central keep surrounded by stone walls and defensive strong-points, it rose out of the Ōmi plain to become the symbol of a new age. Around his new castle Nobunaga arranged his conquered territories, reserving the choicest lands for himself and enfeoffing his vassal daimyo as castellans in the fortresses of his conquered rivals. Daimyo who submitted to him without resistance were accepted as allies and their loyalty tested by successively being placed in the vanguard of his armies in the field.

By 1577 Nobunaga was ready to move against his more distant rivals, and since his rear was still fairly secure he proceeded westward from the capital with the ultimate objective of eliminating the Mōri, master of some twelve provinces at the end of the island of Honshū. Against the Mōri Nobunaga now sent his chief general Hideyoshi. Nobunaga's armies swept with comparative ease through Tamba, Tango, Tajima, Inaba, and Harima and in 1578 secured the capitulation of the Ukita of Bizen and Mimasaka, beyond which were the lands of the Mōri. The encounter with the Mōri proved long and costly, and in 1582 Hideyoshi, finding himself still locked with the enemy at Takamatsu, called for reinforcements. Nobunaga responded with a force of his own from Azuchi. But while passing through Kyōto he and his eldest son were slain by a treacherous general, Akechi Mitsuhide. Hideyoshi, on hearing the news, broke off contact with the Mōri and returned by forced marches to the capital where he met and quickly destroyed Akechi. Thus Nobunaga, first of the unifiers, was killed at the age of forty-nine, well on his way to securing his goal of national conquest. Cut down in full career, his work had been chiefly military and destructive, but it had laid the basis of the unification which was to follow. At the time of his death he had secured control of approximately one third of the provinces of Japan, and moreover he had set the institutional pattern for the unified regimes of his successors.

Although Nobunaga had had little time to devote to administrative matters, he nonetheless began some institutional innovations of great consequence. The new style of mass warfare which he used so skillfully and the castle construction exemplified in Azuchi began the trend toward concentrating large standing armies at castle headquarters with the consequent withdrawal of the military aristocracy from the land. Within his territories Nobunaga also began a new and more systematic method of village organization and tax collection. In 1571 he required the submission of cadastral registers from his newly acquired territories, and he started his own re-survey (*kenchi*) of the home province of Yamashiro, using a new system of measurement and assessment. In 1576 he began to disarm the peasantry in some of his territories, thus anticipating the more complete separation between peasantry and warrior accomplished some twenty years later.

In the field of commerce and trade Nobunaga also attempted to lay the foundations for a national policy. Within his territories he ordered a unification of weights and measures and abolished the guilds and barriers which had obstructed the free circulation of goods. On the other hand he began the direct patronage of the merchant community by offering them special privileges and free markets within his castle towns. Thus he accelerated the process which was to bring the entire merchant class under the control of the daimyo as a service corps for the military establishment. But it is probably for his ruthless attack on the Buddhist establishment that Nobunaga is most remembered. For by the time of his death he had ended for all time the independent power of the great sects. By confiscating large portions of temple territory and by placing his own agents over the religious establishments, he began the process which was to draw both Buddhism and Shintō securely into the service of military government.

After Nobunaga's death his chief vassals met to decide the succession. A youthful grandson was named heir and a board of four regents created to serve as guardians. Hideyoshi, as one of the four, was given the responsibility of protecting the capital. Within three years, however, Hideyoshi had made himself undisputed successor to Nobunaga. By 1584 he had eliminated the other three guardians, had taken a permanent grip on Kyōto and had established as his headquarters a new and formidable castle built at Ōsaka, site of the fallen Ishiyama fortress. By 1585 he had concluded alliances with Tokugawa Ieyasu and Uesugi Kagekatsu and had secured the allegiance of all of Nobunaga's former vassals including even members of the Oda family. Simultaneously he was able to dignify his position with court rank and the title of Imperial Regent (*Kampaku*).

By 1585 Hideyoshi was ready to take up the task of unification where Nobunaga had left off. Around him stood nine major daimyo coalitions headed by the Hōjō, Takeda, Uesugi, Tokugawa, Mōri, Chōsokabe, Ōtomo, Ryūzōji, and Shimazu. Since three of these, the Uesugi, Tokugawa, and Mōri, were pledged as allies, the task which faced Hideyoshi was the reduction of the remainder. He began with the Chōsokabe. In 1585 he threw 200,000 men into Shikoku. The Chōsokabe capitulated. Two years later he headed a force of 280,000 men into Kyūshū. The Ōtomo and Ryūzōji of northern Kyūshū were destroyed, leaving the Shimazu to submit to Hideyoshi's overwhelmingly superior force. By 1590 Hideyoshi was prepared to face his most formidable enemy, the Hōjō of Odawara. With 200,000 men he marched into the Kantō, overran the Hōjō domains and settled down to the investment of Odawara castle. Two months later the Hōjō capitulated, and the few remaining hostile daimyo quickly pledged their allegiances. The military unification of Japan was complete, and all territory now either belonged to Hideyoshi or was held in the form of his grant in fief to daimyo who were his sworn vassals.

Historians have asked why Hideyoshi made no attempt to extend the process of unification so as to eliminate the daimyo and make himself a monarch in the absolute sense. The answer must come from a reflection upon the process of unification itself. From the outset the forces which had contended for mastery of Japan had consisted of coalitions of daimyo held together in loose feudal alliances. Each successive round of expansion for such coalitions had confirmed the pattern of dividing territory into the lord's domain and those of enfeoffed vassals. The constant pressure of civil war and the dangerous rivalries which surrounded each aspirant to national hegemony induced each to continue to work through alliance and conciliation and avoid as much as possible the necessity of fighting to the finish. Moreover, even for Hideyoshi, when extermination of rival daimyo was found necessary, as in the case of the Hōjō, the task was done through the force of a winning alliance, not by his own personal army. Such an alliance was held together in large part by the lure of reward in territory which awaited the successful campaign. Nobunaga, Hideyoshi, and later Ieyasu each rose to hegemony step by step, growing from small daimyo into large, and from large into heads of daimyo clusters. For Hideyoshi to have turned, even at the height of his power, to the elimination of his daimyo allies would have been impossible without some basis of power outside the alliance system itself. This neither he nor his successor possessed in sufficient quantity.

Under Hideyoshi, then, a new national structure of government had been created. The country had been conquered by one daimyo league whose overlord was now the foremost power in the land. The country was thus both completely decentralized and yet fully unified. At the basis of this new power structure was the disposition of territories between Hideyoshi and his vassal daimyo. Hideyoshi's systemization of land practices, which we shall describe shortly, had provided a new method of land measurement for the entire country. By now all cultivated land was assessed in terms of *koku* of rice. (The *koku* was approximately five bushels.) By definition a daimyo was a territorial lord who possessed lands assessed at 10,000 *koku* or more, the total national assessment in 1598 being about 18.5 million *koku*. Hideyoshi's own holdings consisted of lands assessed at 2 million *koku*. Though widely scattered they were strategically concentrated in the capital area and in Ōmi and Owari, thus giving him possession of the extremely rich lands around Lake Biwa as well as the key cities of Kyōto and Sakai. In Kyūshū Hideyoshi had also gained control of the ports of Hakata and Nagasaki.

Hideyoshi's vassal daimyo in 1590 numbered somewhat fewer than two hunderd. If we make allowance for the meager holdings of the imperial court and the drastically reduced lands of the temples and shrines, we can see that the territorial lords together held something under 16 million *koku*. The daimyo, of course, differed greatly in size and also in their relationship to Hideyoshi as overlord. The greatest and also the most independent of the daimyo were those like Tokugawa or Mōri who themselves had been leaders of powerful daimyo leagues. Against these were ranged the large number of Hideyoshi's "house" daimyo who, though of small size, were closely dependent upon him. The balance of power and loyalties and of strategic disposition between these differing groups of daimyo gave a certain element of stability to Hideyoshi's position.

Hideyoshi's position was in fact none too secure. His house daimyo, located mostly in the central block of provinces from Kai to Harima and northern Shikoku were all of small size, and only a few were assessed at over 100,000 *koku*. Foremost among these were Katō (250,000) and Konishi (200,000), Hideyoshi's two trusted generals whom he placed in Kyūshū, Asano (218,000 at Kōfu in Kai), Mashida (200,000 at Kōriyama in Yamato), and Ishida (194,000 at Sawayama in Ōmi). Daimyo who had come over to Hideyoshi from Nobunaga, constituting a second group of trusted vassals, were by now reduced in numbers. Only Maeda (810,000 in Kaga) had remained as a major power. The majority of large daimyo, who together retained the bulk of the territory of the country, were "outside" vassals to Hideyoshi. They were all houses which had been in existence at the time Nobunaga began his rise to power, and they had all at one time in the past faced Hideyoshi as enemies. Such were the Tokugawa (2,557,000 at Edo in Musashi), Mōri (1,205,000 at Hiroshima in Aki), Uesugi (1,200,000 at Aizu in Mutsu), Date (580,000 at

Ozaki in Mutsu), Ukita (574,000 at Okayama in Bizen), Shimazu (559,000 at Kagoshima in Satsuma), and Satake (529,000 at Mito in Hitachi). The territories of these daimyo in fact consisted of rear-daimyo clusters which had been absorbed whole by Hideyoshi in the process of his hasty conquest.

Hideyoshi had used what power and skill he had in working his band of vassals to his own advantage. Where possible he rearranged the disposition of daimyo either for strategic reasons or to cut them away from their locales of major strength. The most dramatic move of this sort was the transfer of Tokugawa Ieyasu from his home provinces of Mikawa and Tōtōmi into the former Hōjō territories in the Kantō. Thus the Tokugawa were removed from central Japan and placed in an environment where they could be watched by surrounding house daimyo. Hideyoshi's most trusted generals were enfeoffed, as we have noted, in central Japan, while his heir, Hidetsugu, was placed in Owari, Nobunaga's home province. Among the original band of commanders who had become daimyo in Hideyoshi's service, Kinoshita was placed in Harima to guard the approaches from the west, and Katō and Konishi were set in Kyūshū as a balance to the Shimazu and Nabeshima.

Hideyoshi's hegemony rested essentially on conquest and the feudal bonds which united him and his vassals. All daimyo had been required to swear oaths of fealty to him and seal their pledges by giving hostages. Ōsaka castle first served as a residence for hostages, and here the daimyo sent their wives, heirs, or principal vassals as tokens of loyalty. Later, daimyo were obliged to build residences around Hideyoshi's palace at Fushimi where they were within reach of his call and where wives and children were kept on a semi-hostage basis. The marriage alliance was also a favorite device for reinforcing the feudal bond, as was the ceremonial granting of Hideyoshi's surname or a character out of his given name.

Beyond such strictly feudal techniques, however, Hideyoshi sought to create a structure of legitimacy which would support his hegemony. Neither he nor Nobunaga laid claim to the status of Shogun—Nobunaga perhaps because he deposed a shogun to gain his de facto power, Hideyoshi presumably because he failed to gain entrance into the Minamoto lineage. Despite his humble origins, however, Hideyoshi had no difficulty in being adopted into the Fujiwara family and hence in qualifying for high court titles. He had taken the title of Imperial Regent in 1585 before he started his final campaigns and the next year received the title of Grand Minister of State. When in 1591 he retired in favor of his adopted son Hidetsugu, he was commonly known as the *Taikō*, or retired *Kampaku*. Thus it was chiefly as Imperial Regent that he laid claim to ultimate civil and military powers by delegation from the emperor. Hideyoshi made pointed and effective use of the imperial symbol. In 1588 on the occasion of a magnificent entertainment at his mansion at Fushimi attended by the emperor, he obliged all of his vassals to repeat their oath to him in the emperor's presence and to swear as well to protect the imperial institution. Thus he wove into the fabric of the lord-vassal relationship the traditional sanction and prestige of the throne.

Although Hideyoshi kept his daimyo under firm control, and although he acted the part of the absolute ruler of Japan, minting coins, making foreign policy, and issuing decrees which applied to the entire country, he left the administration of the country in the hands of his locally autonomous daimyo. Depending quite openly upon the daimyo to hold down their territories, he conceived of only the bare minimum of administration on a national scale. Through the administration of his own territories, of course, he was able to stabilize central Japan and the major cities. For this Hideyoshi relied on a simple house administration of the kind common to all daimyo of the time, which depended on vassals and retainers to perform military and civil functions. Thus Asano Nagamasa, one of the foremost "house daimyo," had been designated commissioner (*bugyō*) of Hideyoshi's lands and housemen. Maeda Gen'i, assigned to Kyōto as Deputy Military Governor (*Shoshidai*), administered the city and controlled the courtiers and priests. Natsuka Masaie served as *bugyō* in charge of finance and the domestic affairs of Hideyoshi's domain. Other designated

JAPAN DURING THE LAST YEARS OF THE ASHIKAGA SHOGUNATE

*Regional hegemon
**Lesser daimyō

retainers (often of less than daimyo status) handled such affairs as housing vassals, for construction, communications, military organization, supplies and other necessary functions. It was not until 1598, when Hideyoshi approached the end of his life and had settled his succession upon an infant son born to a favorite concubine, Yodogimi, that he attempted to formalize the balance of power among his vassals. He first named a board of Five Regents (*Go-tairō*) consisting of Tokugawa Ieyasu, Maeda Toshiie, Uesugi Kagekatsu, Mōri Terumoto, and Ukita Hideie. This group, comprised of the five largest outside daimyo, was obliged to swear a special oath to keep the peace and support the Toyotomi cause which would shortly be vested so precariously in a child heir. Next Hideyoshi placed in the hands of a board of Five House Administrators (*Go-bugyō*) the routine policy and administrative affairs of the realm. Then, between these two groups he inserted a board of three Mediators (*Chūrō*) in hopes that they could keep peace between the two other boards and mediate policy differences. The system, as can be imagined, did not function effectively beyond Hideyoshi's death in 1598.

However clumsy Hideyoshi's efforts at political organization may have proved, his domestic policies were of profound consequence to the development of the Japanese nation. Hideyoshi in fact presided over a major turning point in the history of Japan's institutions of cadastral management and social organization. His decrees brought to completion on the national level the basic administrative changes, begun by the great daimyo and further accelerated by Nobunaga, which finally swept Japan clean of the residue of *shōen* procedures and the remnants of the old imperial system of local administration.

In 1585 Hideyoshi began in earnest to carry out a new systematic resurvey (*kenchi*) of the land throughout Japan. By adopting a new unit of area measurement which differed from the one in use from Nara days, he literally forced the entire nation to reassess its land base. Superior, or proprietary, rights to the land were now completely redefined and vested solidly in the person of the daimyo and the national overlord.

153

The survey achieved yet another important institutional change by serving as the basis of a new village organization. Under the new system, fields were recorded in the name of the free cultivators (*hyakushō*) who tilled the land. *Hyakushō* families, furthermore, were grouped into villages (*mura*) which now became the standard fiscal and administrative units in the countryside. Village lands after measurement were evaluated by quality and productive capacity, and each parcel was assessed according to its yield as calculated in *koku* of rice. The combined yield then became the assessment figure (*koku-daka*) of the village and the basis for taxation. Villages were made responsible for their own self-government and the annual payment of their tax quotas. The village assessment figures were used as units for the allotment of daimyo domains and other smaller fiefs. Thus the entire system of land rights and local administration was restructured by the enforcement of what has been called the *Taikō-kenchi* (the Taiko's survey).

The resurvey had other profound social consequences, for it became the legal basis upon which a new separation of status between the peasant and the warrior-aristocracy came to rest. We have noted that the tendency of the samurai to move off the land, where they had served as land managers and tax collectors, and congregate in the daimyo's castles had begun in Nobunaga's days. But the *kenchi* served to hasten this process by forcing a complete and sometimes arbitrary division between cultivators and the professional military class. For once the *kenchi* had passed over an area, simply by definition, a line was drawn within Japanese society between the farming and non-farming populace. Those listed in the cadastral registers along with the assessed pieces of land, their families and other attached personnel, were the *hyakushō*. Those who were listed on the rolls of the daimyo as fief holders or stipendiaries were *bushi*.

This process of class separation was made final and irreversible by still another policy adopted locally by individual daimyo and eventually on a national basis by Hideyoshi, namely the effort to restrict the bearing of arms by any but the *bushi* class. "Sword hunts" (*katana-gari*), meant to disarm

154

the rural and urban populace, occurred sporadically during the 1580's. Hideyoshi ordered a nationwide sword hunt in 1588. Two years later, when defeat of the Hōjō gave him authority over all Japan, he issued the famous three-clause edict which froze the social structure and prohibited further class mobility or change of status. *Bushi* were prevented from returning to the villages, peasants were tied to their occupation and restricted from entering the trades or commerce, *bushi* were prohibited from leaving one master for another. Thus the basis was laid for the eventual perfection of a four-class social system wherein samurai, peasants, artisans, and merchants were given separate legal identities.

The imposing scope of Hideyoshi's domestic reforms was matched by the vigor of his foreign adventures. Hideyoshi was a product of the sixteenth century and its intense interest in foreign trade and overseas contacts. By mid-century, as we have noted, Japanese freebooters were busily engaged in their illicit trade with China and were probing the seas beyond Indochina. With the coming of the Europeans the competition for profit through trade was further intensified. Daimyo vied for the patronage of European traders and themselves commissioned ships for foreign trade. Hideyoshi with his castle at Ōsaka sat in one of the most active centers of foreign and domestic trade and hence was strongly motivated to turn Japanese overseas activities to his own profit. His own castle town of Ōsaka soon outdid Sakai as the major port of central Japan and became the new entrepot for the silk trade with China. In 1577 he gained direct control of Nagasaki and asserted his authority over its trading associations. From here he attempted to impose a national system of control over all overseas activity. Entering into diplomatic negotiations with China and other countries of East Asia, he attempted to obtain favorable, and legitimate, trading concessions from them. At the same time, he tried to suppress piracy and oblige all Japanese to obtain charters bearing his vermilion seal (*shuin*). Neither policy was fully successful, and China in particular steadfastly refused to negotiate with Hideyoshi.

Hideyoshi's eventual determination to conquer China

155

stemmed from a variety of motivations of which profit from trade may have been one. He had undoubtedly inherited from Nobunaga a dream of unlimited conquest. Having unified Japan he found the restless spirit among his daimyo unquieted and their thirst for reward unquenched. His megalomania was matched by his haughty lack of respect for the armies of the continent. In 1591, having been rebuffed in his demand for free passage through Korea, Hideyoshi boldly planned to cut his way through Korea, destroy the Ming dynasty and divide China into fiefs for his vassals. Setting up an invasion headquarters on northern Kyūshū, he ordered his daimyo to prepare ships and provide the troops and material for continental conquest. The first invasion force of some 200,000 men quickly overran the Korean peninsula in 1592 and struck to the Yalu River. But the Japanese generals were eventually met by large Ming forces and obliged to agree to a negotiated "victory" over the Chinese at P'yŏngyang. Hideyoshi demanded a Chinese princess as consort for the Japanese emperor, the equal division of Korea between Chinese and Japanese sectors, the establishment of a Japanese governor general in Korea, and free trade between Japan and China. The belated Chinese refusal of these demands occasioned the second invasion of 1597–1598 when 140,000 Japanese crossed over into Korea. But Hideyoshi's death brought an immediate close to what had proved to be a poorly conceived and reckless venture.

The forty years of Japanese history during which Nobunaga and Hideyoshi forged a new military unity probably constituted the most open and adventurous period that the Japanese people had yet experienced. It was a time when Japanese traders ranged the seas to Siam and India, when in excess of energy the daimyo had launched two massive overseas attacks, when European traders and missionaries freely roamed the streets of Ōsaka, Kyōto, and Nagasaki. Japan had become in fact an aggressive force in world history. The style of life of these years, particularly of the great unifiers, is legendary. No past rulers of Japan had commanded the personal might, autocratic power, and expendable wealth that men like

Nobunaga and Hideyoshi possessed. Self-made in the extreme, these men were their own masters; more forceful and less inhibited than earlier great leaders like Ashikaga Yoshimitsu or Fujiwara-no-Michinaga, they built on a grand scale and lived in imposing splendor.

While Kyōto remained during these years the great metropolis, the city of culture and the home of specialized artisans, the new centers of activity were the castle towns of the great daimyo. And since the outstanding establishments of this type were Nobunaga's castle at Azuchi and Hideyoshi's palace at Momoyama (Fushimi), historians have given the name Azuchi-Momoyama to this entire period. But the new daimyo-sponsored urbanization was not limited to central Japan or to the efforts of the national leaders. The great regional lords, from the Date in the north to the Shimazu in the south, built up new towns about their castles and created for themselves and their retainers regional replicas of life in the capital. In the history of Japan's urbanization no period is as active as the thirty years from 1580 to 1610 when the largest of the daimyo adjusted themselves into the national hierarchy and settled down to consolidate their military resources and their extended domains. First-ranking castles and castle towns such as Himeji, Ōsaka, Kanazawa, Wakayama, Kōchi, Hiroshima, Edo, Okayama, Kōfu, Fushimi (Momoyama), Sendai, Kumamoto, Hikone, Yonezawa, Shizuoka, and Nagoya, all came into being in this span of years and were to continue to flourish well into Japan's modern period. It is hard to think of a parallel period of urban construction in world history.

The castle town naturally derived its structure from the requirements of the new class of local rulers. As the daimyo had expanded their territories we found them, for instance, moving out of the narrow confines of mountain defenses to the larger moat-and-tower fortresses placed centrally so as to dominate the wider plains which served as the economic bases of their power. Here the daimyo could garrison their bands of vassals and their troops while creating communities of merchants and artisans to provide services for military and general needs.

157

Castle towns were planned cities, built from the center outward primarily to serve the needs of the lord. The town began with the great central keep, placed usually on a rocky promontory on the bend of the main river which watered the daimyo's plain. Around the keep were flung in concentric circles walled ramparts and moats to a distance sufficient to defend the keep from enemy cannon. Behind the walls were the residences of the daimyo and his chief vassals. Outside the walls was the town proper consisting of merchant quarters, further garrison quarters for samurai, and temples and shrines. Unlike either the Chinese or European walled city, no outer wall protected the townspeople or the religious establishments. Thus the castle towns came to reflect quite accurately the political absolutism and the social policies of the new military regime. The domain was the lord's, and the town grew up under the shadow of the lord's castle to serve his needs and those of the samurai aristocracy who surrounded him. Even the temples and shrines were obliged to erect their buildings at the lord's pleasure within the town where they would be available to the townspeople in times of peace but serve as defense outposts in time of war.

While the Ashikaga military elite emulated the way of the court nobility, the daimyo of the last half of the sixteenth century created their own style of grandeur and ostentation with little regard to traditional refinements. While priests were everywhere visible in the society of the time, and in the company of daimyo, they were no longer the respected advisors and the arbiters of taste they had been two centuries before. The style of Azuchi and Momoyama was designed to please the rude and self-made men who had fought their way to mastery of the country, and to demonstrate their power and wealth. The palaces which adjoined the great keeps were ornately decorated in gold and lacquer while the architectural elements of roofs and pillars adopted elaborately baroque features such as eccentrically curved rooflines, overall carved pillars, and the use of vivid primary colors.

The two most typical products of the taste of this age were the painted gold screens (byōbu) and panels which adorned

158

the daimyo's residences and the relief carvings which embellished the pillars and panels of the palaces and temples. The Momoyama style of screen painting developed by members of the Kanō school such as Eitoku (1543–1590) and Sanraku (1559–1635), are works in a grand style. Bold and colorful and lavish in use of gold leaf, they are nonetheless saved from pure ornateness by the breadth of their conception and their strength in detail. Examples which remain in Nishi Honganji or Daitokuji at Kyōto show a remarkable vigor of decorative design. The carvings were chiefly works of decoration or embellishment. Their special quality stems from the fact that while taken in the mass they give the impression of gaudiness and over-ornateness, as individual carvings they reflect the Japanese love of simplicity and stylization. Flowers, birds, and animals carved in sure deft lines reveal the skill of the Japanese craftsman.

The Momoyama screens and carvings reveal yet another feature of the period, namely the secular content of the life of the new aristocracy. The art which Nobunaga and Hideyoshi appreciated had little of the subtlety and none of the hidden mystical overtones of the products of the Higashiyama culture. Religion, to be sure, was not neglected, and Hideyoshi actually erected a great Buddha in Kyōto, larger than the one in Nara's Tōdaiji. But the venture was largely conceived as a means of enhancing his personal prestige. The statue, after twice being damaged by earthquakes, was melted down in 1662. The temple itself lost its standing with the rise of the Tokugawa house.

10

The Tokugawa Period

Establishment of the *Baku-han* System

The third of the great unifiers had the good fortune to out-live his rivals and the stubborn presence of mind to wait for the opportune moment to grasp control of the country. Tokugawa Ieyasu's career parallelled that of both Nobunaga and Hideyoshi, with whom he had been allied, but it extended eighteen years beyond Hideyoshi's death. He thus inherited the unity which his predecessors had created and went far beyond it to fashion a stable hegemony, one which was to last over two hundred and fifty years past the end of his own life.

Yet historians have dealt harshly with the Tokugawa regime, claiming that its conservative social policies brought about a "return to feudalism," or that its strenuous measures of political control imposed a tyrannous and despised garrison state upon the Japanese people. The final suppression of Christianity and the policy of seclusion adopted by the Tokugawa are pointed to as deliberate attempts to take Japan out of the mainstream of world history, so that for two centuries Japan literally stagnated in isolation.

There is no denying the conservative and restrictive nature of the Tokugawa regime. And there is no telling how differently Japanese history might have run had not the Portuguese and Spanish been expelled from Japan and had the daimyo of western Japan remained free to send their ships across the seas. Yet we must keep three points of qualification in mind. First, the disappearance of Western traders from Japanese

160

waters reflected to a large extent Japan's geographical isolation from the main trade routes of the world and the diminution of Western interest in the remote eastern fringe of Asia after 1600. Second, the Tokugawa desire to prevent the daimyo of western Japan from engaging in private trade reflected the degree to which central authority was still struggling against daimyo local autonomy. And third, we must realize that the consequences of the seclusion policy were not so comprehensive that the entire age was determined by them. They did not, in fact, force Japan into a totally rigid mold in the mid-seventeenth century thereafter to stagnate in isolation for two centuries.

The Tokugawa age proved to be a period of noticeable cultural and institutional development despite its seclusion from the rest of the world. To be sure, Japan was not strongly touched by those key scientific and political conceptions which in Europe laid the basis for modern society. But in a wide variety of other ways Japan strengthened its national and cultural foundations during these years. The "great peace" (Taihei), as it came to be called, permitted the Japanese to heal the wounds of civil conflict and to turn their attention to the peaceful needs of the country. While government remained in the hands of the military aristocracy, the samurai themselves underwent a radical change in their style of life and thought. They became in effect a bureaucratic elite under whose guidance the administration of the country was markedly systematized and rationalized. New laws and regulations clarified the status and responsibilities of the several estates and defined a philosophy of government, which though authoritarian, emphasized as well the responsibility of the rulers towards the welfare of the people.

Under the Tokugawa regime, the trend toward urbanization continued, and the economy was for the first time fully knit into a national entity. In the realm of thought, the spread of Confucianism affected the spiritual orientation of the entire Japanese people, laying the foundation of a more secular approach to life. The growth of educational facilities converted the samurai into a literate class and provided schooling for elements of the lower classes as well. In the cities the increasingly affluent merchants began to develop their own leisure pastimes, so that for the first time a "bourgeois element" was added to Japanese culture.

The Tokugawa family which succeeded to national hegemony in 1600 derived its name from a small village in Kōzuke province in the Kantō. At some undetermined time the family had moved into the province of Mikawa. Ieyasu's father was a *sengoku-daimyō* of moderate size, who from his castle headquarters at Okazaki had by 1500 gained control of about one half of Mikawa. He had submitted to the overlordship of the house of Imagawa whose territories adjoined his. But when Imagawa Yoshimoto was defeated by Oda Nobunaga in 1560, Ieyasu, who by then had become head of his house, threw in his lot with the victor. By 1568 the family's holdings had taken in the entire province of Mikawa. During the years of Nobunaga's conquest of central Japan, Ieyasu directed his attention to fighting off the attacks of the Takeda and Hōjō and absorbing as much of the former Imagawa territories as possible. By the time of Nobunaga's death, he had added Tōtōmi and Suruga to his holdings and was on the verge of acquiring Kai and Shinano. He had moved his headquarters to Sumpu, the old Imagawa capital.

In 1583, Ieyasu briefly attempted to dispute Hideyoshi's seizure of Nobunaga's mantle, but after some inconclusive engagements he came to favorable terms with Hideyoshi. For the next few years he cautiously continued to extend his territories, managing to avoid participation in Hideyoshi's Shikoku and Kyūshū campaigns. But against the Hōjō at Odawara he was obliged to make a major contribution, and when the campaign was over he was assigned 2,557,000 *koku* of vacated Hōjō lands.

Whatever Hideyoshi's motives had been in transferring Ieyasu to the Kantō, the move undoubtedly redounded to Tokugawa benefit. For besides placing Ieyasu in a position from which he could more easily decline participation in the Korean campaigns, it gave him a fresh base upon which to erect a more tightly organized administration. Reserving roughly 1,000,000 *koku* to his own direct control, he distributed the remaining lands, assigning lesser fief holders close to his new castle of Edo, and setting out his larger vassals as castellans on the more distant circumference of his territory. Several of his chief vassals were of considerable size by now: Ii received 120,000 *koku* at Takasaki, Sakakibara 100,000 at Tatebayashi, and Honda 100,000 at Otaki. All told thirty-eight of Ieyasu's vassals were castellans of daimyo size, that is they held fiefs which were assessed at more than 10,000 *koku*.

Hideyoshi's death immediately threw the hastily contrived Toyotomi power structure into peril. Almost immediately conflicts began to show up within the councils Hideyoshi had created before his death. Among the great lords of the Regency, the private ambition to succeed Hideyoshi led to mistrust and friction especially between Tokugawa, Maeda, Mōri, and Uesugi. Among the "house vassals" Ishida Mitsunari, distrustful of Tokugawa Ieyasu, worked tirelessly to organize a coalition against him. When in 1599 Maeda Toshiie died, a main element in the power balance upon which Hideyoshi had counted was destroyed. Ieyasu was now the obvious great power in Japan. Already he had begun to receive pledges of allegiance from other daimyo, and soon the Maeda faction sent hostages and made overtures of support. In the fall of 1599 Ieyasu entered Ōsaka castle and became in the comtemporary parlance "Lord of the Land" (Tenka Dono). By the end of the year nearly half of the daimyo of the Toyotomi league had submitted written pledges of allegiance to Ieyasu; many in fact had given hostages.

In the early months of 1600, Tokugawa Ieyasu was obliged to shift his main forces along with contingents from his allies into the Kantō to meet a threatened attack from the Uesugi. To Ishida this was the supreme opportunity. Gathering around him at Ōsaka an alliance of daimyo consisting of the Mōri, Ukita, Shimazu, Nabeshima, Chōsokabe, Ikoma and others of western Japan, he prepared to fall upon Ieyasu. Potentially the "western alliance" which Ishida headed had the chance of success, but it was badly led and split by factions, and some

JAPAN

of its key members were secretly in touch with Ieyasu. On the fifteenth day of the ninth month (October 21, 1600) the final meeting between these forces took place at the now historic battlefield of Sekigahara. The outcome was at first in doubt, but large segments of the western alliance never committed themselves, and at the critical moment Kobayakawa, one of Mōri's kinsmen, made good his prearranged defection. The western cause collapsed with great slaughter. Ten days later Tokugawa Ieyasu entered Ōsaka, the military master of the country.

Sekigahara brought about a drastic reordering of the political map. Around Ieyasu a new de facto hegemony was quickly created. In all, 87 daimyo houses had been extinguished and four (including the Toyotomi house) were reduced in their holdings. A total of over 7,572,000 *koku* had been confiscated, making it possible for Ieyasu to extend his private lands and to reward his loyal followers generously. Yet the Toyotomi line was not extinguished. Hideyoshi's memory was still fresh, and the young heir, Hideyori, had many supporters. As a consequence, Hideyori was able to retain Ōsaka castle and a 650,000 *koku* domain in the surrounding provinces.

Thus despite the victory at Sekigahara, the Tokugawa hegemony was not completely secure; nor was it legitimized. West of Ōsaka, Ieyasu's influence fell off sharply. The Tokugawa had not been able to place their house daimyo into the lands of western Japan where the network of oaths to the Toyotomi house was still strong. And so Ieyasu was obliged publicly to act out his continued loyalty to Hideyoshi. Yet while outwardly honoring Hideyori, he step by step acquired the power and legitimacy with which he could rightfully emerge as the sole hegemon of Japan. In 1603, he assumed the title of Shogun. As such he accepted the submission of all daimyo and began to assemble hostages at Edo castle. When he garrisoned Fushimi castle and placed his Military Governor in Kyōto in the newly built Nijō castle, his military position in the capital area was greatly enhanced.

In 1605 Ieyasu handed the post of Shogun over to his son Hidetada and established himself as the Ōgosho (Retired Shogun) at his family castle of Sumpu. From here he worked toward the final eradication of the Toyotomi house. His chance came in 1614, when on a flimsy pretext, Ieyasu was able to order the combined forces of his vassal daimyo to the attack of Ōsaka castle. The resulting engagement was bloodier than Sekigahara. Ōsaka managed to pit 90,000 desperate men against the 180,000 troops of the Tokugawa alliance, and a campaign fought in the winter of 1614 cost the Tokugawa allies 35,000 lives. Ieyasu, reduced to extremes, resorted to trickery, and in the "summer campaign" of 1615 managed to reduce Ōsaka and exterminate its defenders. The heir to the Toyotomi house had finally been eliminated, and Ieyasu stood supreme in the land. He died the next year secure in the knowledge that he had established an enduring regime.

Historians have given the name *baku-han* to the Tokugawa political system, indicating that it was based upon the parallel existence of a shogunate (*bakufu*) and some two hundred and fifty daimyo domains (*han*). The term *han*, meaning daimyo domain, was not to come into official use until the nineteenth century (the contemporaneous one being *ryō*), but it has been applied by Japanese historians retroactively in this case.

The particular form of government which evolved from the *baku-han* system was certainly unique to Japan, representing as it did the final maturation of two Japanese political institutions: the shogunate as national authority and the daimyo as regional administrators. The force of authority which united the system was at the top feudal, particularly as it applied to the relationship between Shogun and daimyo. Yet within the administrative subparts, within the direct jurisdictions of the Shogun or daimyo, authority was increasingly exerted through bureaucratic means. Certainly Ieyasu and his successors achieved a degree of power and nationwide authority far beyond that of previous military hegemonies. Yet the regime kept alive a dynamic tension between feudal and bureaucratic techniques and between decentralized and centralized authority.

The balance of power achieved by the Tokugawa house is most easily seen in the pattern of its territorial holdings. Since the initial redistribution made after Sekigahara the balance of territory had constantly shifted in favor of the Shogun. The destruction of the Ōsaka party in 1615 had vacated an additional 650,000 *koku*. But it was chiefly through means other than military action that over 10,000,000 *koku* were reassigned between 1600 and 1651, 4,570,000 *koku* coming from daimyo who died without heirs and 6,480,000 *koku* from confiscations for disciplinary reasons. All told twenty-four "outside" daimyo houses were eliminated in these years while the number of the Shogun's house daimyo increased proportionately. Meanwhile the Shogun's own domains (the *tenryō*) had risen from 2 to 6.8 million *koku*. These lands supported about 23,000 direct retainers. These included about 17,000 "housemen" (*gokenin*), who were without audience privilege and were usually stipended, and about 5,000 "bannermen" (*hatamoto*), who were privileged to come into the Shogun's presence and were mostly enfeoffed. Not only did the Shogun possess a formidable superiority in land and men over his nearest daimyo competitors (the largest daimyo was Maeda at 1,023,000 *koku*), but his territories included most of the important cities such as Ōsaka, Kyōto, Nagasaki, and Ōtsu and the mines of Sado, Izu, and Ashio. Thus the Shogun administered the main economic centers of the country and exploited the sources of precious metal whereby control of the country's currency could also be achieved.

The balance between Shogun and daimyo had numerous political and strategic nuances. Ieyasu had perfected an elaborate hierarchy of loyalties based upon the relationship which daimyo houses held to the Shogun. Closest to the head of the Tokugawa house was a group of twenty-three collateral houses (*shimpan* or "related *han*") headed by the so-called Three Houses (*Sanke*) who were directly descended from Ieyasu and bore the Tokugawa surname. These three houses, with domains at Owari, Kii, and Mito, were privileged to provide successors to the shogunate should the main Tokugawa line die out. The collateral daimyo held domains which totalled 2.6 million *koku*.

Next in the scale of importance to the Tokugawa house were

the "house daimyo" (*fudai*). These were houses which had received daimyo status from Tokugawa Ieyasu or his successors. Most of them had served as Ieyasu's retainers prior to Sekigahara. Numbering 145 in the eighteenth century, they were mostly small in size (the Ii house at Hikone was the largest with 250,000 *koku*), but their loyalty was considered absolute. Among them they held about 6.7 million *koku*. Finally there were the "outside lords" (*tozama*), houses which had achieved daimyo status either under Nobunaga or Hideyoshi, or in certain instances like the Shimazu, had an even earlier origin. Numbering 97 in the eighteenth century, these houses made up the bulk of the large daimyo, and in all they possessed 9.8 million *koku* of territory. As former enemies or as recent allies at Sekigahara, this group was treated much more generously and cautiously than the *fudai*.

The strategic disposition of *shimpan, fudai,* and *tozama,* so as to prevent the formation of hostile coalitions or to block the routes of military attack on Edo and Kyōto, was a matter of careful attention by the early Tokugawa leaders. Shogunal lands dominated the Kantō and central Japan, and strategic Tokugawa castles were maintained outside Edo at Ōsaka, Nijō (Kyōto) and Sumpu (Shizuoka). The Three Houses were placed east and west of Edo and south of Ōsaka. The *tozama* for the most part had grown up on the periphery of the Japanese islands. Here they remained, and where possible *fudai* were placed nearby to serve as checks. But as the Tokugawa discovered in the nineteenth century, western Japan continued to be loosely held. The shogunate had little direct military power west of Ōsaka. And it was in the far western portion of Japan, where *tozama* daimyo such as the Shimazu of Satsuma and the Mōri of Chōshū continued a tradition of hostility toward the shogunate, that the anti-Tokugawa leadership eventually re-emerged.

With these sources of real power, the Tokugawa shogunate created a machinery of controls which institutionalized the supremacy of the Shogun in all areas of government and national life. Evolved in the main by Ieyasu and his first two successors, the control system had reached maturity by the time of the death in 1651 of the third Shogun, Iemitsu. By that time the shogunate rested upon a secure base of regulations and precedents which assured the authority of the Shogun over the emperor and his court, over the daimyo, and over the religious orders.

The sixteenth-century unification movement had refocused attention on the emperor as the ultimate source of political sanction, and both Nobunaga and Hideyoshi had worked to enhance the public reverence paid the *Tennō*. Tokugawa policy continued the dual objectives of heightening the prestige of the sovereign while seeking to control him and isolate him from the daimyo. Thus the Tokugawa treated the emperor and his court with great outward respect, expecting the daimyo to do likewise. The court was assisted in rebuilding its palaces, and sustenance lands, which eventually totalled 187,000 *koku,* were granted to the imperial family and other *kuge* houses. Yet in reality the emperor and his court were closely controlled and cordoned off from free participation in the affairs of state. A shogunal Military Governor (*Kyōto shoshidai*) was established in Kyōto with a large garrison force at Nijō castle, adjacent to the palace enclosure. This officer worked through two court officials (*Kuge densō*) who acted as transmitters of the shogunal will to the court. Through them the *bakufu* was able to scrutinize all matters brought before the emperor and control the making of appointments or the granting of court honors. Contact between the court and the daimyo was also carefully regulated. Furthermore, in 1615 Ieyasu imposed upon the Kyōto nobility a seventeen-clause code (*Kinchū narabini kugeshū shohatto*) which rigidly prescribed the activities of the emperor to traditional literary pursuits and ceremonial functions, made mandatory prior *bakufu* consent for high official appointments, regulated the relationship between the imperial family and the great temples, and enforced a system of compulsory monasticism for certain of the imperial princes. Finally, utilizing the classical means of influence over the imperial family, the Tokugawa managed to have one of Ieyasu's granddaughters made imperial consort in 1619. But the practice of intermarriage was not actively pursued by later Shoguns.

Since all daimyo were the Shogun's vassals and in theory subject to his pleasure, control of the daimyo began with the Shogun's grant of investiture to them. While it was expected that daimyo held their territories as hereditary grants, in actuality their tenure was precarious. Confiscation or transfer was quite common at the beginning of the regime, and only a few of the most powerful *tozama* and *shimpan* daimyo remained permanently in their hereditary territories throughout the Tokugawa period. Towards the Shogun each daimyo swore a private oath in which he pledged to obey the Shogun's decrees, not to enter into collusions against the Shogun, and to serve the Shogun single-heartedly. In return the Shogun invested the daimyo as proprietor of his domain and specified his cadastral holdings. The daimyo's rights and responsibilities, though never specifically stated, were understood by custom to include: 1) the requirement of military (and for the *fudai*, administrative) service, 2) the duty to give special assistance when called upon, and 3) the expectation that the domain be peacefully and efficiently administered.

Aside from the private pledge, daimyo adhered to a public code of regulations known as the *buke shohatto*. This document first presented to the daimyo by Ieyasu in 1615, was modified to include, by 1635, twenty-one provisions. It was designed to regulate the private conduct, marriages and dress of the daimyo and prevent them from forming cliques or increasing their military establishments. It also contained specific regulations for attendance upon the Shogun at Edo and the giving of hostages, the prohibition against building ocean-going ships and the injunction against Christianity. It ended with the stipulation that the regulations of the Shogun be accepted as the supreme law of the land.

Of all control measures the requirement of alternate attendance (*sankin kōtai*) undoubtedly had the most far-reaching consequences. The practice of attendance upon one's lord and the giving of hostages to guarantee loyalty had been common

169

in the Sengoku period and had been utilized by Hideyoshi. After Sekigahara, the custom of sending hostages to Edo developed among the daimyo, at first voluntarily, and then after 1633 as a shogunal requirement. All daimyo were obliged to build residences (*yashiki*) in Edo where they kept their wives and children and an appropriate retinue which included a liaison officer to the Shogun's court. They themselves alternated residence between Edo and their domains. *Fudai* in the Kantō area alternated every six months. Daimyo more distant from Edo alternated every other year. This system proved extremely effective, not only as a means of keeping the daimyo under surveillance but as a means of knitting the country together despite the decentralizing effect of the daimyo system. The constant coming and going, and the constant attendance at the Shogun's court, meant that daimyo could not remain ignorant of the Shogun's decrees or fail to transmit them to even the most distant domains.

As a privilege of overlordship, the Shogun placed many demands upon the daimyo and subjected them to various forms of surveillance. Although the Shogun did not tax the daimyo directly, he exacted certain contributions from them, often on a fairly regular basis. Military and logistic assistance was of course assumed, and in time of emergency such as at Ōsaka in 1614–1615 the Shogun freely commanded his daimyo to fight on his behalf. Economic aid, particularly for the building of castles, roads, bridges, and palaces was also requisitioned by the Shogun from his vassal daimyo. Assessments of this kind, called "national service" (*kokuyaku*), were frequently used to weaken the more economically prosperous *tozama*. At the same time it made possible the building of gigantic fortifications, such as the shogunal castles of Edo, Sumpu, Ōsaka, Nagoya, and Nijō which overshadowed those of the rival daimyo.

Finally we find that the Tokugawa house tapped the well-springs of religious sentiment to enhance the reverence by which its members should be regarded. Tokugawa patronage of Buddhist and Shinto establishments was conspicuous, and calculated to reorient the great sects to the support of the

Tokugawa house. But it was the development of the cult of Ieyasu which centered on the great shrine of Nikkō that best exemplified this effort. Upon Ieyasu's death his spirit was deified as Tōshō-dai-gongen. The third Shogun, between 1637 and 1645, "established Ieyasu's spirit" on Mt. Nikkō in the mausoleum shrine-temple of Tōshōgū. Each Shogun thereafter made the effort to conduct a state pilgrimage to Nikkō, accompanied by the assemblage of daimyo and their retinues. In time, also, daimyo built replicas of the Tōshōgū in their domains and held annual ceremonies of reverence for Ieyasu.

But while it used religious beliefs and rituals to enhance the regime, the shogunate maintained strict control over the lands and affairs of the religious establishment itself. The military power of religious institutions had already been broken by Nobunaga, and Hideyoshi had undercut their separate economic existence. For as the land survey had swept across the country, the independent holdings of temples and shrines had been brought under the purview of the military hegemon and subject to the sanctions of his vermilion seal. In the process these holdings were drastically reduced. The Tokugawa continued the practice. In all, it is estimated that the lands of religious institutions during the Tokugawa period totalled hardly more than 600,000 *koku,* a very small figure when we consider the number of institutions supported by these lands. Only a few temples received grants equivalent to those of even the smallest daimyo. These were Kōfukuji (15,030 *koku*), Enryakuji (12,000 *koku*), and Kōyasan (11,600) *koku*). Tōdaiji of Nara, the greatest of the temples in former times, received only 2,137 *koku.*

The Shogun also placed the religious institutions under severe administrative control. Regulations issued in 1615 provided the basis for direct interference with the Buddhist orders. These restricted the relationship of the imperial family to the priesthood, enforced a complete centralization between home temple and provincial branches, and imposed rigid restrictions upon priestly activities. In 1635, all matters relating to the religious establishment were brought under the control of the shogunal Superintendent of Temples and Shrines (*Jisha bugyō*).

171

As a form of government for the country as a whole, the *baku-han* system provided Japan with a remarkably vigorous and comprehensive system of administration. By Tokugawa times government rested upon the simple fact that, above the level of the relatively autonomous village and town communities, the military estate had appropriated all superior rights, and administration was entirely in the hands of the samurai class. As commander-in-chief of the military class, the Shogun now possessed full powers of government. The Tokugawa regime represents, therefore, the rather unusual case of a civil government administered by a professional military caste. Being by profession a military aristocracy, all samurai were expected to stand ready to use their swords on call. But in peacetime they fulfilled additional tasks as civil or military officials. The convertibility of Tokugawa government from civil to military function was symbolized in the role of the Shogun as supreme commander of all Japan and the accountability of the daimyo to lead armies into the field on the Shogun's command. Thus Tokugawa government was literally the extension of military rule into times of peace.

Since the Tokugawa Shogun was in historical origin simply the greatest of the daimyo, and since the daimyo domain served as prototype for the organization of the Shogun's administration, it is best to start any study of Tokugawa administration by an inquiry into the nature of these local territories. While the *han* of the *baku-han* system were direct descendants of the militant domains of the sixteenth century, under the Tokugawa regime they lost their primary military function and were converted more and more into units of local administration. After 1615, in fact, each daimyo was permitted only one military establishment—a castle or a garrison headquarters—and was placed under exact restrictions as to the number of men-at-arms he could keep in readiness. The daimyo of course differed greatly in the size of their territories and in the specifics of their administrative procedures. Only one domain, Kaga, governed by the house of Maeda, was assessed at over 1 million *koku*. And only 22 were considered "great daimyo" with over 200,000 *koku*. Over half of the daimyo held territories of less than 50,000 *koku*. Thus if we assume a rough correlation between *koku* assessment and population, we can see that the people of Tokugawa Japan were governed under jurisdictional commands of great variety and often of minute size. It is in fact difficult to estimate the exact number of units of local administration which existed. The daimyo themselves varied in number from as many as 295 in the early seventeenth century, to 245 in the middle years, to 276 at the end of the regime. Added to these were the nearly five thousand minor fiefs of the *hatamoto,* and the many thousand jurisdictions of temples and shrines together with the even larger number of subjurisdictions within the Shogun's *tenryō* and the domains. Many domains, in other words, consisted of more than one non-contiguous piece. Thus the administrative map of Japan was extremely complex. But the pressures towards uniformity were such that these local units of administration acquired a great deal of commonality. In particular, uniformity and impartiality of administration grew up as daimyo and their retainer bands were moved from domain to domain. For as they did so the direct ties between the samurai class and the lower orders were gradually broken and the daimyo's band of retainers became increasingly a professional corps of administrators working under a fairly uniform set of legal presumptions.

Over his territory the daimyo exercised full rights of governance as prescribed in the shogunal grant. These rights were made implicit in the term *han-seki* (*han* signifying land registers and *seki* indicating census registers), which meant that the daimyo was charged with jurisdiction over "the land and people" of his domain. The daimyo administered his domain through his band of retainers (*kashindan*) who had been assembled at his castle headquarters. These were organized by rank, depending on size of fief or amount of stipend, and all were tied by oath to the daimyo and were enrolled upon the daimyo's register of men (*samurai chō*).

The highest level of retainers, generally called "elders" (*karō*), were usually enfeoffed vassals of independent stature. As a group they formed a council of advisors to the daimyo. As individuals they frequently acted as the daimyo's deputies or headed the domain's high court. In wartime the *karō* served as generals in the field. Next in the hierarchy of housemen was a more numerous group of high ranking retainers who served as heads of major divisions of the daimyo's government and military establishment. They commanded bodies of the standing army or the *han* guard, and superintended such functions of civil administration as finance, security, and shogunal liaison. Middle-rank retainers served in more specific administrative posts, undertaking a wide variety of civil functions such as the administration of the castle town, the rural areas, tax collection, the civil police, the daimyo's household affairs, military procurement, civil engineering, education and religious affairs. The lower ranks of the daimyo's men, such as foot-soldiers (*ashigaru*), pages (*koshō*), and servants, performed the more menial and routine tasks within the domain's administration.

The common "people " (*tami*) of the domain were conceived of as wards of the daimyo, who bore the responsibility of governing them with compassion. The daimyo's superintendent of temples and shrines oversaw the Buddhist and Shinto establishments. An office of rural administration superintended the villages (*mura*) through a network of intendents (*daikan*). A magistrate of the castle town exercised authority over the several wards (*machi*) of the town. Below the level of the daimyo's administration the farmers and urban populace lived in self-governing units (villages or wards) under the authority of their own headmen. Thus the *han* proved to be a remarkably tightly and comprehensively governed unit of local administration.

The organs of shogunal administration showed every sign of having evolved from the administrative practices devised by Tokugawa Ieyasu while he was still daimyo of Mikawa. The most important consequence of this was that as Shogun he relied for his administrative staff not on the entire 250 or more daimyo but simply on his "house daimyo" and his direct retainers, in other words, those houses which had been directly vassal to him when he was still daimyo. The *tozama,* therefore, remained outside the administration, and even the Tokugawa collateral houses were brought into it only as advisors.

Edo castle, which served as headquarters of the shogunate, was the largest and most impregnable fortress in the land. Within its farflung battlements and moats the assembled daimyo built their residences and the Shogun's higher retainers were assigned residential quarters. The city which formed around this vast assemblage of samurai quarters and official residences also became the largest in the land, so that at the end of the eighteenth century the commercial quarters alone accounted for a population of over 500,000.

Edo became not only the center of shogunal administration but the hub of a national network of roads and waterways which communicated with the distant daimyo castle towns. Five major highways radiating outward from Edo connected with the highways of central and western Japan which had served the early imperial state, creating the base for an official communication system over which the daimyo passed to and fro on their tours of alternate attendance.

Like the typical daimyo administration, the Edo *bakufu* was organized into its policy, civil administrative, and military functions. Policy and decision making was in the hands of a selected group of house daimyo who served as "elders." These were organized into two boards. The Senior Councilors (*Rōjū,* literally "elders"), who made up a supreme administrative council, were generally four to six in number and were selected from among *fudai* houses with domains of 25,000 *koku* or more. The *Rōjū* were given authority over matters of national scope, such as the affairs of the emperor and of the daimyo, foreign affairs, military affairs, taxation, currency, the distribution of lands and honors, and the regulation of religious institutions. Members of the group took monthly turns as duty officers, and in time it became customary to name one *Rōjū* as head of the board. Senior Councilors had the privilege of affixing the Shogun's seal to documents and hence were sometimes referred to as *kahan* (literally "seal affixer"). The post of Great Councilor (*Tairō*) was assigned from 1634–1684 and occasionally thereafter. During the last hundred years of the Tokugawa period the post, when assigned, was generally held by the head of the Ii house of Hikone. A second board of Junior Councilors (*Wakadoshiyori,* literally "junior elders") consisted of four to six *fudai* of lesser status and was given responsibility over the Shogun's housemen and bannermen. Under its purview also were the various guard groups, military units, the Shogun's private servants, pages, physicians, and the *metsuke* who served as inspectors and disciplinary officers.

Most of the functional administrative posts were placed under the board of Senior Councilors. A group of six or seven Chamberlains (*Sobashū*), headed sometimes by a Grand Chamberlain (*Sobayōnin*), served the administrative boards, arranging audiences and conveying messages. Nominally under the authority of the elders, they sometimes acted independently because of their ability to court the favoritism of the Shogun. Keepers of Edo Castle (*Rusui*) enforced military discipline in the castle, especially in the absence of the Shogun. Protocol Officers (*Kōke* and *Sōshaban*) handled the ceremonies and audiences between the Shogun and the Kyōto court and with the daimyo. Inspectors General (*Ōmetsuke*) maintained discipline over the daimyo. A large number of superintendents (*bugyō*) were placed over specific administrative functions. The Magistrates of Temples and Shrines (*Jisha bugyō,* usually four in number) ranked high in the *bakufu* hierarchy and in addition to supervising the religious affairs of the country served as judicial officers over the Kantō provinces. The Finance Magistrates (*Kanjō bugyō,* usually four) handled the Shogun's finances and oversaw the forty or fifty local Intendants (*Daikan*) who administered the Shogun's private domains. The City of Edo was administered by two City Magistrates (*Edo machi bugyō*) each placed over one half of the castle city. Magistrates of this type were assigned to all shogunal cities and towns including Kyōto, Ōsaka, Nagasaki, Nara, and Sumpu. The Nagasaki *bugyō* had the added duties of superintending foreign trade which was permitted under *bakufu* monopoly with the Dutch and Chinese. A host of other officials oversaw such matters as construction, buildings and grounds, military procurement, roads, and the like. The Magistrates of Temples and Shrines, of Finance, and of the City of Edo served as the core of a High Court of Justice (*Hyōjōsho*); in session they were joined by representatives of the Board of Senior Councilors and by Inspectors. Outside of Edo the main shogunal posts other than the city magistrates were the Governor General of Kyōto (*Kyōto shoshidai*) and the Keeper of Ōsaka Castle (*Ōsaka jōdai*). These two posts were placed immediately under the Shogun and ranked as nearly equivalent to that of Senior Councilor.

In a narrow sense, the *bakufu* with its headquarters at Edo was simply the Shogun's house government. Its powers of direct administration applied only to the Shogun's own domain (the *tenryō*). Yet this territory by reason of its size—roughly a quarter of the country—and its resources, which included the major cities in the land, placed the greater portion of the Japanese population within the scope of the Shogun's personal rule. Under the legal and de facto powers that accrued to the Tokugawa house, moreover, the Shogun assumed the role of chief of state in a variety of spheres, setting foreign policy, and taking prime responsibility for military affairs and national defense. Furthermore, while the daimyo realms were technically autonomous in their local affairs, they were subject to the limitations imposed upon them by the shogunal control system. The broad policy outlines laid down by the *bakufu* were generally accepted in the *han,* so that the laws and institutions of local government tended to follow Tokugawa precedents. The *baku-han* system acquired as a result a broad base of common legal assumptions and practices.

Legal and Religious Institutions

Under the Tokugawa regime, despite the political decentralization which resulted from the daimyo system, Japan acquired the rudiments of a unified national policy, enunciated through public laws and based on general principles. Since the Nara experiment in legal codification, Japanese government for

177

some seven centuries had moved increasingly in the direction of patriarchal and feudal privatization. It was not until the end of the sixteenth century that this current was finally reversed in the administrative procedures adopted by the great daimyo and then the Shogun. This is not to say that the Tokugawa rulers systematically set about creating a new legal framework for the Japanese state. Yet the vast quantity of laws, injunctions, and regulations which flowed from the *bakufu* and the *han* were the product of a conscious effort to bring order to society and to provide guiding principles for a well regulated administration.

The laws of Tokugawa Japan have been called minatory and repressive, even unnatural and reactionary. It is generally assumed that they were imposed upon a reluctant country largely to safeguard a rigid, unchanging political and social regime. Yet Tokugawa law was based upon certain broad principles which gave to it a universality not found in the localized rule of custom that had obtained during the previous centuries. Tokugawa legislation rested upon the philosophical premise of a natural order. Assuming that society by nature formed a hierarchy of classes, laws were directed toward fundamental social divisions and applied to individuals in terms of formally recognized status groups. Tokugawa government came to recognize four major estates and several minor groups as functionally and legally separate. The result has been called "rule by status," a legal practice considerably more impersonal in its application to the individual than the exercise of direct personal authority which had characterized the political system of the previous century.

Much of Tokugawa legislation was directed then to the clarification of the boundaries between the different classes and the effort to define behavior appropriate to each. At the center of the Tokugawa conception of class hierarchy was the so-called "four-class system," which placed samurai, farmer, artisan, and merchant in what was assumed to be a natural order of descending importance. It has been suggested that this conception of four classes or estates, which derived originally from China, was not entirely suited to the social realities in Japan. Unquestionably during the sixteenth century certain broad social divisions were beginning to take shape out of the heretofore undifferentiated localized communities. But the position of the merchant had been rather higher in the sixteenth century, and in fact continued to be higher in actual fact in the seventeenth and eighteenth centuries, than its position at bottom of the ideal scale would have it. Moreover in actual practice Japanese legislators frequently coalesced the artisans and merchants into a single urban class referred to as *chōnin*.

Tokugawa society, as reflected in legislation of the period, was conceived of, then, as falling into the following categories: the *kuge*, the samurai (including daimyo), priests, peasants, urban residents, and pariah (*hinin* and *eta*). For several of these groups the Tokugawa government laid down basic sets of regulations. Such were the code governing the emperor and courtiers (*kinchū narabini kugeshū shohatto*), the samurai code (*buke shohatto*), and the codes governing Buddhist sects and temples (*shoshū jiin hatto*) and Shintō shrines and priests (*shosha negi kannushi hatto*). Peasants were not placed under any single set of regulations, but the "Instructions of Keian" (*Keian no furegaki*) of 1649 made public most of the basic provisions of the village system in the Tokugawa territories and the style of life enjoined upon villagers in general.

By Tokugawa times the *kuge* had dwindled to a group of about three hundred families entirely confined to the palace enclosure in the city of Kyōto. Still awarded high respect because of their lineage and special court rank, they lived a life restricted by court tradition and removed from the centers of political power. The samurai, by contrast, were the active leaders of society. They formed a self-conscious upper class dedicated to military preparedness and civil administration. Privileged to bear a surname and to carry two swords, they possessed in theory the right, indeed the duty, to kill a disrespectful commoner on the spot. This was the so-called right of *kirisute-gomen*. Entrance into the samurai class was closed off once the wars of consolidation had ceased, and every effort was made to keep the class distinct from others. Only occasion-

179

ally did individuals from the highest levels of the peasantry or the merchant class obtain the privileges of "surname and sword" (*myōji-taitō*), and this usually only for the span of their own lives. Peasants (*hyakushō*), while ranked next to samurai in terms of their value to the society, were treated with obvious paternalism and great severity. They were expected to remain on the soil, to refrain from alienating cultivated land, to live frugally and work industriously. Through them every effort was made to keep the land base which formed the main source of samurai revenues at the highest level of productivity. Merchants and artisans were patronized for their services but confined to their special quarters within the towns. There they came under the provisions of numerous laws which restricted their style of life and the nature of their commercial activities.

The individual in Tokugawa Japan found himself governed in general terms by these broad class regulations, but he was most directly touched by the authority of the unit of administration or residence in which he found himself. Samurai were organized into bands of retainers (*kashindan*) and further into smaller personnel units (*kumi*) each with its unit head or disciplinary officer. Peasants were organized by village (*mura*) and further into mutually responsible groups (*goningumi*), usually consisting of ten families. Thus they came first under the authority of the group head and then the village headman (*shōya* or *nanushi*). The spirit of Tokugawa law was further revealed in the manner in which individuals were carefully registered by household within each of the above units and in the use of group responsibility and vicarious punishment in criminal or delinquency cases.

In actual fact, of course, the individual as such did not exist under Tokugawa law. The smallest unit of Tokugawa society was, rather, the family (*ie*), and the individual existed only as a member of the family—as family head, as son and heir, as second son, daughter, wife, and the like. Family status and the preservation of the family unit, to which all property and privileges adhered, became a matter of deep concern at all levels of society. Its importance for the samurai class was revealed in the prevalence of ritual suicide (*seppuku*) by which a samurai was able to expiate a crime while preserving the continuity of his family name.

The strict Tokugawa class system with its clearly defined sub-units made existence outside of the accepted estates and occupations extremely difficult. *Rōnin*, or samurai without position or status, for example, found life particularly hard. Such unattached samurai had been cast adrift in large numbers during the civil wars and the readjustment of domains which followed the establishment of the Tokugawa regime. They proved most troublesome during the Ōsaka campaign and again in 1651, when a *rōnin* plot against the Shogun was discovered in Edo. Thereafter every effort was made to absorb masterless samurai into the retainer bands of the Shogun or daimyo. But *rōnin* continued to emerge from out of the main body of the samurai class in small numbers. Few positions in society remained open for such individuals except the priesthood and certain professions such as medicine and teaching.

The concepts of natural law and social hierarchy which infused Tokugawa legislation reflected a number of significant developments in the ethical and religious foundations of Japanese society. Most conspicuous of these was the spread of Neo-Confucian doctrines and the accompanying turn toward more secular conceptions of man and society. The new interest in Confucian thought which began in the early seventeenth century resulted not from any particular renewal of contact with China as we might have expected, but from the internal needs of Japanese society itself. Confucian studies had long been kept alive by the Buddhist priesthood. But it took a special effort to draw Confucian doctrine out of its monastic habitat and make of it an independent school of thought with its own institutional supports and its independent body of professional expounders. The Confucian movement of the seventeenth century was both a product of spontaneous generation and of official encouragement. Its rapid growth was evidence that the Confucian tradition had something new to say to the Japanese of the Tokugawa period. For one thing, it is probably true that Japanese society in Tokugawa times had become more like that of China than ever before so that the relevance of Confucianism had become more immediately apparent. But also Chinese thought, once it gained acceptance by the Tokugawa rulers, and once it began to influence the laws of the land, fed on its own success, producing some of those very conditions which gave rise to the new sense of relevance. But however much the Tokugawa Japanese relied on Confucian doctrine, it was also inevitable that Confucianism in Japan took on features which would hardly have been recognized in contemporary China, as for example the Japanese insistence on retaining a martial spirit as part of the mark of the gentleman.

The man who emancipated Confucianism from Buddhist control was Fujiwara Seika (1561–1619), a Kyōto monk. Abandoning the Buddhist orders, he began to teach the doctrine of Confucianism openly as an independent philosophy which he claimed was particularly suited to the needs of the times. His student Hayashi Razan (1583–1657) was taken into Tokugawa Ieyasu's service in 1605 as an advisor on legal and historical precedents. He became the first of the line of scholars expounding the Shushi (or Chu Hsi) school of Confucianism who received hereditary appointment to the shogunate as Confucian advisors. In 1630 the Hayashi family was encouraged to establish a Confucian school, and this later became the official Tokugawa college, known as the Shōheikō. By 1691, official permission had been given to Confucian scholars to exist outside the Buddhist establishment. Meanwhile many daimyo had taken in Confucian advisors and had begun to give support to the founding of Confucian schools in their domains. It became possible as well for independent scholars to set themselves up in Kyōto, Ōsaka, and Edo as private teachers. By the middle of the seventeenth century Confucianism was fully accepted as the dominant lay philosophy, and its influence became a major impetus in the spheres of education and political philosophy.

The early Confucianists and their patrons were in many respects pioneers—creators of a new world for which a new world view had become imperative. The positivism of men like Hideyoshi and Ieyasu derived from the fact that they had indeed achieved a greater sense of power over their destinies than any rulers before them. The world to them and their contemporaries could be looked upon as something to be controlled and ordered. And to large extent it was this change in attitude which motivated the intellectual attack upon the Buddhist establishment and its mystical view of life. As Yamagata Bantō so succinctly put it "There is no hell, no heaven, no soul, only man and the material world." Confucianism satisfied the Tokugawa mind by providing a new philosophy of life and a new cosmology. Behind the universe, it claimed, there was reason (*ri*) which worked within matter (*ki*) to produce the world of man and things. Behind society as well there was reason and order if one could but comprehend it. Moreover, the order was a moral one. The importance of this Confucian message was that it provided for the time a new unity between thought and action, between philosophy and political system. Study of essential principles (*gakumon*) leading to learning (*bun*) could put man in touch with the essence of the moral order, and hence produce moral man. Government was essentially a task of facilitating the achievement of the moral order among men.

The spread of Confucianism thus went hand in hand with the formation of the new *baku-han* social and political order. For Confucianism, with its primary concern for political and social affairs, suited well the interests of the Tokugawa rulers and the samurai class. The early Tokugawa rulers faced very practical problems of bringing order out of military turmoil, and it was just such problems for which Confucianism prided itself on having the answers. The shift from a predominantly feudal and privatized society into one of classes and large groups required the enunciation of new and more general legal principles. The first steps away from the rule of man toward rule by law required the elaboration of new laws and administrative institutions. And since the Shogun and daimyo of this time found themselves to be much more "complete rulers" than their predecessors, they were obliged to be much more comprehensive in their legislation and more explicit in the rationale by which they justified their authority.

The significance of Confucianism for the Tokugawa political order was that it provided a new theory of government and a new vision of the harmonious society. The ideal social order which it envisioned took the form of a natural hierarchy of classes in which each individual occupied his allotted spot and strove to fulfill his mission in life. Thus, as we have already noted, Confucianism helped confirm the trend toward the separation of classes and the codification of conduct becoming each one. But it did more, for Confucianism was not simply a philosophy of social control; it postulated a moral order which stood above the ruler. It placed Shogun and daimyo under the responsibility to rule for the benefit of the people—to provide "benevolent administration" (*jinsei*) as it was called. Government might be absolute in principle, but it must justify itself by being responsible and humane in its application. The samurai could adhere to the tradition of the sword, but he must cultivate the way of the scholar-administrator as well. In Tokugawa Japan it became customary to use the Chinese character for gentleman when writing the word samurai.

Confucianism thus helped to give philosophical backing to the new legal and political order. And in an age when the basis of behavior was shifting from that of custom to principle, Confucian principles filled a void which Buddhism could not have done. Concepts of loyalty to the political order (*chū*) and to the family (*kō*) universalized the most basic social requisites of the age. Abstract concepts of status-conduct provided models for each class and profession. Each class was given its "way" (*dō*), such as *bushidō* (the way of the samurai) or *chōnindō* (the way of the merchant). *Bushidō* in particular, as the new code of a military class converted to peacetime administration, combined the necessary emphasis on military spirit with that on book learning, rationalizing thereby the contradiction in terms implied in the life of the samurai, the "warrior-administrator" of Tokugawa times.

While the spread of Confucianist thought was surely the most noteworthy intellectual development of the Tokugawa period, we must not suppose that the new philosophy accounted for the sum total of Tokugawa intellectual life. Buddhism and Shintō continued to serve the political community in important respects. Tokugawa society rested in fact on a balanced reliance on three spiritual systems in a complex yet eminently practical combination. In the eyes of the governmental authorities, Buddhism continued to serve as an important device for popular control. And the extreme compartmentalization of Tokugawa society into *han,* village, ward, and household gave force to the localized spiritual attachments which Shintō affirmed. Thus for the average Japanese of this time Buddhism and Shintō combined to fulfill his prime religious needs, while Shintō and Confucianism contributed to his ideas of the political order, and Confucianism and Buddhism instructed him in the values of social behavior. What has been described as the decline of Buddhism in Tokugawa times is thus a relative matter and reflects chiefly the degree to which it lost to Confucianism its primacy in the thought life of the educated classes.

Once the political and economic power of organized Buddhism had been broken in the sixteenth century, Japan's rulers began again to patronize the religion at the same time that they continued their policy of institutional control. In Edo, for instance, the Tokugawa house patronized a number of new temples, foremost of which was Kan'eiji of Ueno, established by the Tendai monk Tenkai as a protective temple for the city. The daimyo likewise encouraged the building of temples in their castle towns. By now, however, the prime motive for such patronage was to provide for the common rites of passage. Buddhist ceremonial dealt largely with marriages, burials, and memorial services, and the Buddhist priesthood was honored chiefly as the keepers of memorial tablets and graves.

Buddhism received its most extensive support from the Tokugawa regime as a result of the government's anti-Christian policy. By obliging all persons within the country to adopt a temple of registry (*dannadera*) as a means of demonstrating spiritual non-contamination, it automatically assured the support of tens of thousands of temples throughout Japan. In 1640 the shogunate required all Japanese to undergo temple registration and to submit thereafter to an annual scrutiny of religious beliefs (*shūmon aratame*). Thus by official command the Japanese populace became the spiritual wards of the Buddhist establishment (a few families were permitted registration at Shintō shrines). Moreover, since most temples of registry became the burial sites for their parishioners, the formal dependence of the Japanese people on Buddhist rites became almost complete.

The role of Shintō was somewhat different but no less pervasive. As a spiritual support to the political order and as an important tie between the individual and his community, Shintō continued to serve the Japanese people through a vast network of shrines. The emperor himself, of course, retained his position as Shintō high priest, performing ceremonies which invoked the spirit of the imperial ancestress enshrined at Ise. Most samurai families maintained ties with ancestral shrines as a token of dedication to the honor of the family's lineage, the most conspicuous of such practices being the Tokugawa ceremonial surrounding the shrine to Ieyasu at Nikkō. At the lower levels of society, guardian shrines served each village and each town ward, providing a cohesive element within the small compartments of Tokugawa society. Shintō retained its central position as a spiritual support to the Tokugawa political hierarchy and the community structure on which it rested. In the face of religious or philosophical systems which came to Japan from abroad, Shintō preserved a sense of national identity for the Japanese in a way which was to become increasingly significant as the Tokugawa period wore on. For in the isolated world created by the Tokugawa seclusion policy, the deepest feelings of "Japaneseness" fed by the Shintō tradition were to re-emerge at a critical juncture in Japan's history.

The final element in the Tokugawa intellectual environment was, then, the factor of isolation or closure. But the assumption that the Tokugawa rulers were predisposed to a policy of isolation because of a basic conservatism in their world view is not really tenable. Tokugawa Ieyasu showed himself anxious to develop foreign trade and for some time remained friendly to

186

the Christian missionaries. But his efforts to obtain full control of the destinies of the country and to assure complete loyalty to his regime led step by step in the direction of closure. The history of the adoption of the seclusion policy therefore shows an intermingling of three strands of concern: 1) the Tokugawa effort to secure internal political stability, 2) the Tokugawa desire to secure a monopoly of foreign trade, and 3) fear of Christianity.

Tokugawa Ieyasu was at first quite anxious to develop trade relations with foreign countries and he negotiated patiently with the Chinese, Spanish, English and Dutch. But he was unsuccessful in developing Edo as a port for foreign trade. European traders preferred the ports of Kyūshū, and China rebuffed Ieyasu's plea for an official trade conducted in licensed ships. Undoubtedly these failures turned Ieyasu and his successors toward the effort to secure monopoly control of the existing trade through regulated ports and licensed merchants. Thus in 1604, for instance, the league of silk merchants based at Sakai, Kyōto, and Nagasaki received special monopoly privileges over the import and distribution of Chinese silk thread (*ito wappu*).

Meanwhile the Christian problem had again arisen. Ieyasu, while friendly to the missionaries, had never rescinded Hideyoshi's edict of banishment of 1587. By 1612, however, the problems raised by certain Christian daimyo in Kyūshū and knowledge of the existence of Christian converts among the Shogun's *fudai* induced Hidetada, the second Shogun, to reissue the edicts and to order all Tokugawa retainers and persons living in Tokugawa territories to give up the alien religion. One minor daimyo, Takayama Ukon (1553?–1615), was deported to Manila in 1614 as the result of this more strenuous effort to clear the country of Christians.

From this point the desire for trade monopoly and fear of Christianity worked hand in hand toward the final adoption of a policy of strict seclusion. In 1616 foreign trade was restricted to Nagasaki and Hirado. In 1622 a major execution of Christians claimed the lives of 120 missionaries and converts. In 1624 the Spaniards were expelled from Japan. (The year before,

187

the English had voluntarily given up the effort to trade in Japan.) By now terrible tortures were inflicted upon Japanese suspected of being Christian, and many thousands were forced into abandoning their beliefs. A special way of testing for Christian belief was devised in 1629 by which individuals were obliged to tread upon bronze plaques (called *fumie* or "treading pictures") decorated with Christian figures such as Christ or Mary. Those who refused to tread on such plaques were presumed to be Christian and were subjected to torture and execution. The Catholic Church recognizes over 3,000 martyrdoms in Japan at this time.

The seclusion policy was crystalized between 1635 and 1641. In 1635 an edict prohibited any Japanese from traveling abroad and from returning to Japan once having gone. In 1636 the Portuguese were confined to Deshima, a small artificial island off the Nagasaki waterfront. Meanwhile, a revolt of disaffected peasants and a few masterless samurai in a heavily Christian area near Nagasaki shocked the *bakufu* into taking further action. The rebels, some 20,000 in number, seized an abandoned castle in the Shimabara Peninsula and, displaying Christian emblems, held out against an army of 100,000 men made up of neighboring daimyo contingents. In its extremity the *bakufu* even called upon the Dutch ships at Nagasaki to bombard the castle with their shipboard cannons. In the spring of 1638 the Shimabara rebellion was put down with great slaughter, and with it the Christian movement was extinguished. In 1639 the Portuguese were expelled from Japan, and when in the next year a Portuguese diplomatic mission reached Japan from Macao its leaders were executed. In 1640 the Tokugawa ordered the registry of all Japanese at temples of their choice (*tera uke*) and set up its Office of Religious Inspection (*Shūmon aratame yaku*). In 1641 the Dutch concession was restricted to Deshima and the Chinese to special trading quarters in Nagasaki. Japan's foreign associations were thereby limited to the Tokugawa monopoly at Nagasaki except for a restricted trade which the Sō, daimyo of Tsushima, conducted with Korea and the Shimazu of Satsuma conducted with the Ryūkyū's.

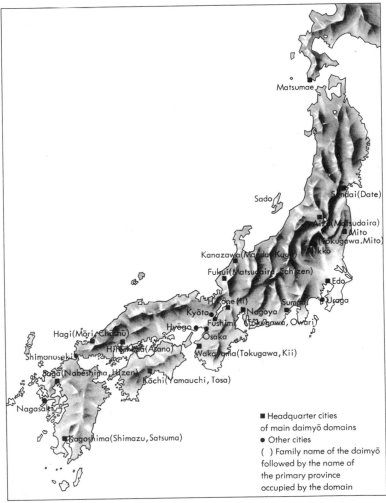

Matsumae

Sado

Sendai(Date)

Aizu(Matsudaira)
Mito
(Tokugawa,Mito)
Nikkō

Kanazawa(Maeda,Kuga)

Fukui(Matsudaira,Echizen)

Edo

Hikone(Ii)
Kyōto
Nagoya
Sumpu
Uraga
(Tokugawa, Owari)
Fushimi

Hagi(Mōri,Chōshū)
Hyōgo
Osaka

Shimonoseki
Himeji(Asano)

Saga(Nabeshima,Hizen)
Wakayama(Tokugawa,Kii)

Kōchi(Yamauchi, Tosa)

Nagasaki

■ Headquarter cities
of main daimyō domains
● Other cities
( ) Family name of the daimyō
followed by the name of
the primary province
occupied by the domain

Kagoshima(Shimazu, Satsuma)

JAPAN UNDER THE TOKUGAWA

189

There can be no denying that the adoption of the seclusion policy (*sakoku*) was a major turning point for Japan. The contrast between a Europe about to embark upon an era of important economic and scientific development and a Japan voluntarily closing its doors to the outside world, is quite dramatic. Moreover, fear of Christianity in Japan was such that within a few decades the authorities imposed a severe censorship on the importation of books and other written matter from the West. By restricting opportunity for trade, the Tokugawa authorities also arbitrarily limited Japan's potential for economic growth as well. Yet it is hard to predict what the consequences of a more open policy of foreign contact might have been, nor is there any assurance that Japan could have maintained free contact with the West and the Chinese without further debilitating domestic struggle. We do know, however, that closure insured peace and that in peace Tokugawa Japan had the opportunity to develop its political institutions and its economic and cultural resources.

Samurai Government and Its Problems

The more than two hundred years of domestic tranquility which the Tokugawa regime provided have confronted historians with a difficult problem of periodization, due in large part to the absence of obvious pivotal events. The standard treatments of Tokugawa political history have placed the Shogun at the center of their concern and have focused on the *bakufu*'s effort to perpetuate its dominance and ride above the currents of social and economic change. As a consequence the tale is told as one of gradual dynastic decline—as a sequence of minor routs and rallies leading to inevitable demise. The resulting periodization is suggestive but not fully appropriate to the dynamics of the political process, particularly if one's concern is with matters of institutional growth and structural change within the *baku-han* system. The assumption that fundamental changes in political institutions could take place only at the expense of the primacy of the Tokugawa house plays down the evidence of institutional growth and exaggerates the importance of the Tokugawa private interest. The story of the Tokugawa dynastic cycle should be told—but in context— as one aspect of the general development of government under samurai leadership.

The first three Shoguns, Ieyasu (1603–1605), Hidetada (1605–1623), and Iemitsu (1623–1651) have gone down in history as strong administrators. They devoted their energies to strengthening the *bakufu* and perfecting its control machinery. The next four Shoguns, Ietsuna (1651–1680), Tsunayoshi (1680–1709), Ienobu (1709–1712) and Ietsugu (1713–1716) were less forceful leaders. Having inherited a going concern, they found less need to involve themselves in affairs of state. They are criticized for having placed too much authority in the hands of special favorites selected from out of their personal retinues. After the assassination of Senior Councilor Hotta Masatoshi in the council chambers in 1684, for instance, Tsunayoshi withdrew entirely from the meetings of the Councilors and communicated chiefly through his grand Chamberlain, Yanagizawa Yoshiyasu (1658–1714), a minor retainer who had risen to high office in the *bakufu* through the Shogun's favoritism. Increasingly the Shogun's interests turned to cultural pursuits and Buddhist rituals.

Tsunayoshi's relaxed administration and unrestrained expenditures are blamed for plunging the *bakufu* into its first period of troubles. For it was in his time that the financial reserves of the *bakufu* became exhausted, and the shogunate resorted to currency debasement. Toward the end of his life Tsunayoshi began to issue Buddhist-inspired ordinances against the taking of life, which proved a great hardship to the Japanese people. Tsunayoshi himself was a vigorous person, and his personality kept the *bakufu* at the center of the political stage in Japan. But his capricious policies could not help but undermine popular confidence in the Tokugawa shogunate. The two men who succeeded Tsunayoshi were both short-lived in office and provided no noticeable leadership. Ienobu's advisor, Arai Hakuseki (1657–1725), a highly intelligent Confucian-trained official, pointed out the need for reform in

government, but without much effect. It was not until Yoshimune, the eighth Shogun, entered Edo castle that the first
major effort to reform the *bakufu* was attempted.

Yoshimune (1716–1745; d. 1751) came from the Kii
branch of the Tokugawa house and was already a mature
daimyo with set ideas when he became Shogun. He immediately took over personal command of the *bakufu* and set to
work on a series of drastic reforms to which the period
Kyōhō has given its name. His policies gave shape to the classic
style of reform by which the Tokugawa authorities were to
attempt from time to time to deal with their political and
economic difficulties. The fundamental problem which disturbed the *bakufu* and its retainers at this time was economic:
a depleted *bakufu* treasury and an indebted samurai class. Yoshimune's impulse was to place restraints on spending and
regulations on commercial activity. Beginning with a vigorous call for austerity in government and frugality in private
life (he himself drastically curtailed the expenses of the Shogun's house), he issued a flood of moral injunctions which
exhorted the samurai to a revival of their martial spirit and
integrity in office and invoked detailed sumptuary regulations
for all classes. His economic policies favored hard money and
agrarianism. One of his first acts was a recoinage which returned the currency to its pre-Tsunayoshi purity. To stabilize
the price of rice he initiated the practice of controlled buying
and selling. He cut down on the alternate attendance requirements of the daimyo and then exacted a tax on their domains
which he applied to the liquidation of the debts of the Shogun's
housemen and bannermen. In an even more drastic act he
announced a moratorium on financial suits by merchants
against samurai. In the field of agriculture he encouraged land
reclamation and the planting of new crops. At the same time
he called for a more rigorous and inflexible method for collecting the agricultural tax, namely the fixed annual payment
(*jōmen*) rather than the flexible rate tied to annual yield. His
interest in the improvement of the technology of government led him to adopt a number of special administrative pro-

grams such as the five-year census begun in 1721 and the codification of *bakufu* laws begun in 1742.

Yoshimune's reforms were vigorously conceived and implemented, yet before his death he was to see that most of his efforts had proved ineffectual and several had actually served to worsen the conditions he had hoped to remedy. His hard money policy combined with the expansion of rice production drastically reduced the price of rice, and this adversely affected the finances of the Shogun's retainers, who were paid in fixed amounts of rice. His economic policies pleased neither the merchants, who were placed under arbitrary restrictions, nor the peasantry, who were squeezed under a more severe tax system.

The next two Shoguns, Ieshige (1745–1760) and Ieharu (1760–1786) again retired from active participation in *bakufu* affairs. Ieshige was a physical weakling and had to use his Grand Chamberlain, Ōoka Tadamitsu, as his mouthpiece. Ieharu quickly fell under the domination of his Grand Chamberlain, Tanuma Okitsugu (1719–1788). A clever man who rose through favoritism from minor office to become a 57,000 *koku* daimyo, Tanuma gained a reputation for unorthodox policies. For if Yoshimune had tried to meet *bakufu* financial distress by placing restraints upon the commercial sector of the economy, Tanuma did the reverse. Under him the *bakufu* openly encouraged commercial activity, which it taxed by licensing trade associations or setting up semi-official monopolies. To aid indebted daimyo it even attempted to create a pool of capital for use by daimyo which would be filled by forced loans from merchant houses. To add to the volume of currency Tanuma began the minting of silver, which had heretofore circulated as unminted lumps. Foreign trade at Nagasaki was encouraged and expanded by promoting the export of dried sea products produced in Hokkaidō. Tanuma even considered a plan to colonize the northern island and to open up trade with the Russians.

Tanuma's policies were never systematically worked out or legitimized. In the light of hindsight, it is possible to view them as potentially "progressive," since they sought to expand the base of shogunal finances by tapping the country's mercantile economy. Yet he left shogunal finances and the temper of the country in such an unsettled state that he was credited in his day as having brought on a major rout in Tokugawa fortunes. His last years in office were plagued by a series of natural calamities and famines, followed by peasant uprisings. Upon Ieharu's death he was disgraced and stripped of his lands and honors.

The eleventh Shogun, Ienari (1787–1837; d. 1841), was to have the longest life in office of any of the Tokugawa line, one which in fact embraced two completely different periods of *bakufu* policy and mood. From 1787 to 1793 shogunal policy was directed by Matsudaira Sadanobu (1758–1829), one of Yoshimune's grandsons, who served as advisor to Ienari while the Shogun was still a minor. Sadanobu had bitterly opposed Tanuma's policies, and upon assuming office, he began a second period of vigorous reform to which historians have given the name of the Kansei era. Sadanobu adopted the slogan "back to Yoshimune." His policies were largely negative, emphasizing financial retrenchment and restriction on commerce. Again some measures may have proved of temporary benefit to the shogunal treasury and to the housemen and bannermen. But the attempt to restrain the nation's expanding commercial economy proved fruitless and served in the long run to undermine the economic position of the samurai class.

Sadanobu retired in 1793 when Ienari came of age, and thereafter the Shogun took matters into his own hands. In the ensuing decades *bakufu* policy seems to have drifted into easy routine. No longer was much thought given to retrenchment or to the control of commercial activity, for the Shogun led the way in liberal spending. As a result, while the political and fiscal health of the shogunate deteriorated, the country as a whole experienced a major spurt in its economic and cultural growth. But increased signs of merchant affluence were matched by continued poverty and distress among the rural

194

and urban poor. New and dangerous tensions were beginning to pull at Tokugawa society.

The 1830's brought Tokugawa Japan to the edge of another period of crisis compounded of financial insolvency at the top and reaction to conditions of poverty at the bottom. A series of famine years in the countryside brought the popular mood in Tokugawa territories to the breaking point, and again peasant disturbances mounted. In 1837 Ōshio Heihachirō (1792–1837), a minor officer in the command of the Ōsaka City Magistrate, deeply affected by the misery of the city poor, began an armed attack on Ōsaka Castle in an effort to gain control of the city so he could release its wealth to the poor. His rebellion, while quickly put down, shocked the *bakufu* and the country into a realization that crisis conditions were at hand. Meanwhile the appearance of British and American ships in Japanese waters had aroused renewed fear of outside interference. With Ienari's death, under the twelfth Shogun Ieyoshi (1837–1853), a final desperate and unsuccessful effort at reform was undertaken by the *bakufu*. This was the work of the Tempō era led by Mizuno Tadakuni (1793–1851). The story of the Tempō reforms will be taken up in a later chapter, for they proved to be the starting point of the final epoch of Tokugawa history. Mizuno, like his two predecessors, followed a policy of retrenchment and restrictive shogunal control over the economy. He proved no more successful than the others. By the 1850's moreover, the *bakufu*'s problems were becoming more political than economic. In the face of foreign pressures, the Tokugawa power structure was coming apart. Between 1853 and 1867 three Shoguns, Iesada (1853–1858), Iemochi (1858–1866), and Yoshinobu (or Keiki) (1866–1867; d. 1913) presided over the demise of the *bakufu*.

While the vicissitudes of shogunal politics necessarily created an impression of overall dynastic decline, the *baku-han* system as a form of government flourished for over two and a half centuries. Samurai government as a political system and as a mechanism for the management of a nation must be looked at in the light of its capacity to keep the peace for so long a period. Beneath the surface of the power struggle which the *bakufu* ultimately lost, there were broader currents of institutional development involving changes in administrative technology which cannot be dismissed simply as evidence of dynastic decline. In fact, the reverse is true. Japanese political institutions underwent a process of maturation which was to have significant consequence for Japan's later rise as a modern state.

Government in Tokugawa Japan, both in the shogunate and the *han,* had acquired its basic shape by roughly the middle of the seventeenth century. But another half century or more was required before the particular style which distinguished the mature *baku-han* system was perfected. During the second half-century of Tokugawa rule, it was the political process itself which was to undergo the most marked change. The contours of the administrative structure had been sketched in by this time, but the mechanics of government, the procedures, and principles had yet to be clearly defined. The lines of development were primarily two: first the application of new Confucian principles to the conduct of officials produced a trend toward what the Japanese have called "rule by moral suasion" (*bunji-seiji*); and second, increasing administrative impersonality and functional differentiation in government produced a clear trend toward bureaucratization. These changes were to affect profoundly the way of life, the career patterns, and the values and motivations of the *bushi* class, and, of course, the overall style of Tokugawa government.

The samurai entered the seventeenth century in large part a rough unlettered class of military officers; they came out of the century a reasonably literate and culturally polished class dedicated to the problems of civil administration. This change in the nature of the samurai's style of life and function in society was accompanied by a fundamental change in the principles upon which administrative authority was exerted. So long as the threat of military action was real, the samurai as a full-time fighter and part-time administrator could govern with militant absolutism born of the necessity of wartime expediency. But in peace more than the threat of force was needed to justify the authority he exercised. It was here that, as we have already noted, Tokugawa government came to rely on the ethical principles of Confucianism and the concept of rule by moral suasion.

The effect upon the lives of the samurai was dramatic. Where once military training was their prime concern, they were now urged to cultivate a balance between learning and military training (*bun-bu*). Samurai were called upon to divide their attention between military arts and scholarship from the time of the first pronouncement of the *buke shohatto* in 1615. And a long line of Confucian scholars, beginning with Yamaga Sokō (1622–1685), expounded the principle that the samurai were the ordained leaders of society with the duty to protect, to govern, and to lead by example. *Bushidō* unquestionably attempted to reconcile two fundamentally incompatible value systems, the old tradition of the *bushi* as a militant man of action and the new concept of the ruler as a gentleman. The tension between these two persisted throughout the regime. The samurai remained the "two-sworded" class, and Tokugawa government continued to function as though its parts were interchangeable between civil and military service. Yet in practice, the military functions were played down and routinized. In the *bushi* code, *bun* (learning) came before *bu* (military arts), and while it was characteristic of the military conscience of the age that it bitterly deplored the loss of martial vigor in the *bushi* class, by their actions, the shogunate and the daimyo houses placed their prime emphasis on public law and civil order. Thus in 1663 the practice of "following one's lord to his death" (*junshi*), was declared barbarous and illegal. The precedence of civil law over the law of military vengeance was upheld in 1702 in the famous case of the 47 *rōnin*. The loyal *rōnin*, who had entered the Edo residence of a daimyo to avenge a dishonor to their lord, became the immediate sentimental favorites of the country. The question of whether they should be commended for their exemplary military behavior or punished for having broken a shogunal law divided the shogunate and even the learned Confucian scholars of the time. But the trend toward precedence of law prevailed. The 47 were obliged to perform *seppuku* and thus admit their transgression.

Increasing reliance on bureaucratic administrative techniques came as a consequence of the proliferation of administrative functions and the weakening of the feudal connective tissue within Tokugawa society. Underlying the whole process was the conversion of the samurai from the status of enfeoffed vassal to that of salaried official, particularly at the lower levels, a process that was closely related to the final withdrawal of the samurai from the land. The relationship of Shogun to daimyo, especially the *tozama* and *shimpan*, was not to change so much. They remained pretty much vassals in the feudal sense. The *fudai* and *hatamoto* fared differently, however, and were treated increasingly as officials of the Shogun. Constantly shifted from domain to domain, their importance to the shogunate was measured in terms of the specific office they filled. The oath of allegiance became increasingly perfunctory while the oaths of office were taken seriously and often sworn in person.

The conversion of the rank and file of the samurai into salaried officials could be seen most clearly in the daimyo domains. As the daimyo became increasingly institutionalized as the symbolic heads of their *han*, the bond between them and their retainers became less personal and more of an accepted matter of abstract loyalty. Concurrently the daimyo worked to limit the independence of their retainers by cutting them away from their land holdings and placing them uniformly on their stipendiary rolls. By 1800 over 90 percent of the *han* paid all retainers by stipend (*hōroku*), having abolished the fief (*chigyōchi*) system entirely. As salaried officials, the samurai became completely dependent upon the daimyo for their livelihood and upon the military and administrative service which centered in the lord's castle headquarters.

The proliferation of *bakufu* and *han* administrations led to further modifications in what had started out as a closed military system of selection for office. The Japanese style of elite society in which status was essentially hereditary and assignment to office was consequently restricted to certain status ranges proved too limiting for the needs of an evolving bureaucracy. Various practices which would permit selection on the basis of ability were invented. Within the *bakufu*, the practice of "incremental stipends" (*tashidaka*) was adopted first by Yoshimune to permit able men of low base salary (and status) to qualify for higher office. Moreover, while for the highest offices it had been expected that the appointee rely on his own household staff to carry out the duties of office, in time actual office stipends and funds for office expenses were provided.

These trends did not transform the *baku-han* system. Samurai government retained weaknesses which it had no capacity to remedy. The samurai class itself, some five to seven percent of the whole Japanese population, was a holdover from the days of civil turmoil and incessant warfare. Its numbers were far beyond the needs of government, and as a result most *han* were grossly overstaffed at almost every level. The technique of multiple holding of office and joint responsibility greatly aggravated this condition. But above all, samurai government clung to a reliance on precedent in determining policy which incapacitated it for dealing with major change. Particularly toward the end of the regime, samurai government labored under a heavy burden of formalism which inhibited its flexibility. Ultimately the problems which it faced both internally, in the fields of economic and social affairs, and externally, as a new foreign menace showed itself, proved too much.

Economic Growth and the Problems of Agriculture and Commerce

Of the domestic problems which the Tokugawa authorities confronted, none proved so frustrating as those of economic origin. It may well be that the Tokugawa political system was unusually sensitive to changes in the economic sector, for few societies were so isolated from outside contact or so rigidly structured internally. From the beginning of the period of seclusion, Japan began to experience a profound struggle between the process of economic growth and the limitations imposed upon the economy by the political system. The struggle was accentuated by the fact that the Tokugawa policy restraining foreign trade and internal diversification had been adopted at the very time when the economy had acquired new capacities for growth and overseas expansion.

In few areas of Tokugawa policy was the discrepancy between the model which guided the administrator, and the real conditions which required his attention, more pronounced than in the economic field. The ideal economic world invisaged by Tokugawa administrators derived from the experience of the sixteenth-century daimyo and the new Confucian book-learning of the seventeenth century. It postulated a fundamentally agrarian economy with minimum development of trade—a society in which the samurai governed, the peasants produced, and the merchants took care of distribution. Yet such a vision was no longer tenable even at the beginning of the Tokugawa period. It was made obsolete almost immediately by the growth of commerce and craft production under the stimulus of the inhabitants of the newly emerging cities. It had, in fact, been made fundamentally anachronistic by the fact that the samurai, having been withdrawn from the land, had become an urban consumer class congregated almost entirely in the castle towns of the daimyo. The urban style of life which, to use Ogyū Sorai's phrase, obliged the entire samurai class to subsist "as in an inn," that is to become dependent upon the services of others, was further accentuated by the development of Edo as a residential center for the daimyo and large bodies of their retainers. The *baku-han* political system which centered so much on the castle city was itself a denial of the basic conditions which formed the premises of its economic policy.

Yet the inadequacy of an economic policy which emphasized agriculture to the neglect of trade and industry was not at first apparent. During the first century or more, expansion of the land economy proved possible, and this provided certain outlets for economic growth. As the Tokugawa "Great Peace" was turned into reality, the authorities were able to devote their attention to agrarian improvements, particularly to the expansion of the land base. Under daimyo and *bakufu* stimulus reclamation projects were carried out throughout Japan, so that the national figure for total land assessment, which was 18.5 million *koku* in 1597, had jumped to 25.8 million *koku* by 1700. Thereafter the rate of expansion dropped off somewhat, but by 1832 the total had nonetheless climbed to 30.4 million *koku*.

Assessment figures were not the only measure of the growth in the agrarian base. Production itself was expanded through improvement of tools and seeds, the more common use of draft animals and the more frequent use of iron in plows and hoes. The use of fertilizers increased tremendously, as the Japanese turned to the bulk application of fish and vegetable products and of night soil collected from city privies in order to replenish the soil. Areas of double cropping expanded.

All told, it is estimated that cereal production doubled between 1600 and 1730. Nor was the improvement accomplished simply on the basis of trial and error or the haphazard spread of folk knowledge. The circulation of books on agriculture such as Miyazaki Antei's *Nōgyō zensho* (*The complete agriculturalist*, 1697) illustrates a purposeful effort toward technological improvement. Eighteenth-century Japan probably had as efficient and productive an agricultural base as any country in Asia.

Village economy was not limited to cereal production alone. Rice was already produced for commercial purposes in many parts of Japan. Cotton, tea, hemp, sugar, mulberry, indigo, and tobacco became major commercial crops, so much so that the authorities had to restrict their encroachment upon the taxpaying paddy lands. Subsidiary products such as lumber, paper, dried sea products, salt, and specialized products such as horses in the north and cattle (for draft purposes) in central Japan were to add to the diversified growth of agriculture.

By the 1720's, however, a wide variety of agrarian problems had come into being. Underlying all others was the elementary problem of livelihood in its relation to economic production. Historians have cited Japan as a classic example of the Malthusian principle of the relationship of population to the sources of food. For population changes appear to parallel rather closely the figures of land area and assessed production of rice. Yet in actual fact the discrepancy between these sets of figures was as significant as their apparent correlation. Japan's population is thought to have increased by roughly 50 percent between 1600 and 1721, when the first accurate census was taken. The figure for 1721, adjusted to include members of the samurai class, would probably run to 30 million. Thereafter, statistics show a leveling off of the population curve, though by the middle of the nineteenth century the likelihood is that there had been a rise to about 32 million, a somewhat lower percentage of increase than for the agrarian base. This leveling off of Japanese population has never been adequately explained. The common assumption has been that it reflects the evidence that many portions of the Japanese population were existing on the fringe of subsistence. Famines which followed years of drought and poor harvest often had terrible consequences. Peak periods of crop failure, which came in 1675, 1680, 1732, 1783–84, 1787, and 1833–37 gave rise to some 20 recorded great famines. The one in 1732, for example, is said to have brought 1.6 million persons to the edge of starvation in western Japan. Both the *bakufu* and the daimyo administrations did what was possible to alleviate famine conditions, usually by the distribution of relief rice. But famines persisted and undoubtedly became a factor in the falling off of the Tokugawa population growth rate. Fear of famine may also have been a factor, for voluntary reduction of population, particularly by infanticide (euphemistically known as *mabiki*, i.e. "thinning"), is known to have taken place.

Evidence of peasant unrest is found in the great number of "peasant uprisings" (*hyakushō ikki*) which occurred during the Tokugawa period, and this too is cited as testimony that the economy was in trouble. All told, some 1600 incidents have been recorded, but many of these were comparatively small-scale affairs motivated by specific grievances. After the turn into the eighteenth century, however, mass protests became more common. Often the peasants of an entire region would march upon the daimyo's castle to protest a new impost or the raising of the tax rate. In 1764, for instance, the inhabitants of two provinces, Musashi and Kōzuke, pushed towards Edo to complain about a special tax levied to pay for the shogunal progress to Nikkō. Toward the end of the century such protests took on a more destructive nature. Often the residences of wealthy peasant moneylenders or the storehouses of rice merchants were broken into. Such smashings (*uchikowashi*) also became prevalent in the cities as an increasing number of rural poor drifted into the urban centers.

But whether the evidence of population stagnation and peasant unrest is to be explained in simple Malthusian terms is open to question. During the last century of the Tokugawa period it was not population that outstripped production, but the reverse. Population control can be evidence of more than just a blind reaction to fear of starvation, and violent protest can reflect rising expectations. The "economic problem" of the late Tokugawa period was more a matter of differentials in regional development and of the unequal distribution of wealth. At the village level it was as much as anything the spread of landlordism and commercial activity which led to the breakup of the traditional village economy and to many of the social dislocations which troubled the authorities.

While the Tokugawa laws were rigorous and explicit about the non-alienation of paddy land or the fragmentation of farm holdings, land tended throughout the Tokugawa period to gravitate into the hands of a small number of wealthy members of village society. Shifts in holdings were often covered over by subterfuges such as "permanent mortgages," but also, since land was reclaimed under official encouragement, the acquisition of large holdings through reclamation became quite legal. Moreover since taxes were assessed on the *mura*, not the individual, the authorities were not motivated to interfere with readjustments of ownership within the village units.

The emergence of a wealthy farming class inevitably affected social and economic conditions within the village. Economic surplus made possible numerous secondary activities such as moneylending or the manufacture of *sake, shōyū* (soy sauce) or textiles, while economic diversity led to changes in the family structure. Wealthy villagers began to break out of the traditional structure of the village by turning to hired, or contract, labor rather than relying on the extended family system which had provided pools of labor in the past. Landless families turned to tenant farming or wage earning in the villages or cities. Thus village society began to separate out at two levels, at the top a small group of wealthy, partially commercialized, families and at the bottom the general run of tenant and part-time cultivators and laborers. The differential development of Tokugawa economy, in which the economically underprivileged may well have found conditions unbearable, may help to explain why evidence of agricultural commercialization and signs of affluence could coexist with a heavy incidence of peasant uprisings.

Signs of affluence were plentiful. Village society had never been without its own internal social and economic hierarchy. From the outset each village contained families of more than usual wealth, often descendants of samurai, or families which might have aspired to samurai status at the time of the Taikō land survey. In time these were joined by others with more recently acquired wealth. Together they formed a village upper class, often well educated and in close contact with samurai officialdom, able to partake of the cultural products of the castle town or the great cities. Rural society eventually acquired something of a higher cultural life of its own and was able to produce substantial leadership in local administration and economic development.

Yet much of what was happening in the villages was looked upon as undesirable by the samurai officials. Any sign of affluence in the lives of the wealthy villagers was taken as an indication that they had exceeded the limits set upon the peasant estate. The spread of wealth in the rural areas was thought to reflect a decline in the moral fiber of both the samurai and peasant classes. The major "reforms" attempted by the Tokugawa *bakufu* showered sumptuary laws upon the peasantry and prohibitions against neglect of land, while Confucian scholars urged the country to return to the agrarian ideal. Throughout the Tokugawa period the nostalgic vision of a society in which the samurai would join the peasantry in the simple life upon the soil was kept alive. As Kumazawa Banzan (1619–1691) put it, if only the samurai and farmer classes were again reunited, the samurai would regain their martial spirit and sense of frugality. They could live on but a fraction of the rice they had begun to consume. And the peasantry, thereby released from burdensome taxation and brought again under the direct paternalistic supervision of the samurai, would be made content as well. This "back to the soil" policy was frequently voiced and even occasionally attempted by daimyo whose housemen found themselves in extreme financial straits. But conditions in Japan worked constantly in the opposite direction, towards economic complexity and commercialization.

One of the most obvious signs of economic growth in Tokugawa Japan was to be seen in the general improvement of the standard of living of the four classes. Evidence of better housing, clothing, food, and more entertainment and leisure was everywhere apparent after the middle of the seventeenth century, and these in one form or another revealed the spread of commercial activity and the growth of a money economy. While from the traditional point of view this was looked upon as a trend toward "luxury" and was considered undesirable, the samurai class in its own pragmatic way was willing enough to rely on the merchant class if it meant an easier life and more services. From beginning to end of the Tokugawa period, official theory which denigrated commerce contrasted with actual practice which recognized the necessity of the commercial function in the economy.

The position of the merchant in the Tokugawa social and economy scheme reflected the failure of the commercial estate to achieve independence either under Confucian theory or Japanese law. Mercantile activity was first of all denied free access to foreign trade and was placed under extensive government interference in the production and distribution of key commodities. From the economic point of view, seclusion was merely the culminating step in the Tokugawa effort to deny the western daimyo access to profits from foreign trade. Monopolization was the main technique of economic control known to the *bakufu* officials, who resorted as well to strict regulation of the country's mines as a means of securing control over the nation's currency.

The theory which prompted government interference in commercial activities derived from Confucian doctrines which placed the merchant at the bottom of the four classes on the assumption that as a "mover of goods" he was by definition unproductive. Traditionally the feudal aristocracy had considered money matters unclean and beneath the samurai's dignity. As in Medieval Europe, usurious profit was held in disesteem. The *chōnin* style, which included profit taking and accumulation of capital, was consequently misunderstood and suspect. Thus the Tokugawa merchant remained far more vulnerable to the arbitrary actions of government than his European counterpart. But on the other hand his profits were never as systematically taxed.

While the samurai scorned the merchant's way of life, in actual fact he became deeply dependent upon his services. Restricted to an "inn-like existence" in the castle towns, the samurai was forced to rely upon the *chōnin* to bridge the gap between town and country. From the outset of the Tokugawa period therefore the shogunate and the daimyo took special procurement merchants (*goyō-shōnin*) into their service. Many of these were in fact ex-samurai who had specialized in the handling of certain commodities (often military supplies) during the years of civil war. In the new castle towns, merchant quarters were laid out close under the walls of the daimyo's castle. And here the class came to rest, encouraged on the one hand to serve the needs of the samurai authorities and, on the other, closely regulated by the daimyo's officials and rigidly excluded from participation in the political affairs of the domain or of the nation. This position, which at first glance seems so restrictive and precarious, had, however, its advantages, for few merchant communities in premodern East Asia managed to acquire as vital a place in its nation's economy.

Since the Tokugawa merchant was never really free, *chōnin* made their way as handlers and agents for the ruling authorities. Thus in actual practice something of an alliance grew up between the merchants and the authorities as revealed by the reappearance of guilds and licensed organizations. The *bakufu* had from the first recognized a number of monopoly guilds (*za*) such as the silk thread monopoly and the gold monopoly. Later under Tanuma monopolies were established to handle silver (*ginza*), copper, lime, and vegetable oil. Private protective organizations were at first prohibited by the *bakufu*, but the ten Edo wholesale guilds (*Tokumidonya*) and the 24 guilds of Ōsaka made their appearance before the end of the seventeenth century. In 1721 Yoshimune turned to the licensing of merchant associations (called *kabunakama*) and the practice was greatly expanded under Tanuma. Such associations, organized by commodity or trade, were looked to by the authorities to stabilize prices and to assure adequate distribution; they were also obliged to pay annual license fees (*myōga-kin*). The merchants received in return official sanction and some protection.

The interdependence of the samurai and merchant houses became particularly complex when it came to the commercial and fiscal operations of the shogunal and daimyo territories. In the country, rural wholesalers bought up commodities from the villages for sale in the castle towns or in the national entrepots of Ōsaka and Edo. In the *han* capitals some merchant houses took over the handling of goods and rice for shipment to the daimyo's Edo residences, others for shipment to Ōsaka for exchange. Such middle-level wholesalers, generally called *tonya,* were also licensed to trade with the great wholesale guilds of Ōsaka and Edo on their own. Soon the need for *han* financial agents in the exchange cities led to the establishment of domain warehouses (*kura-yashiki*) superintended by domain financial representatives (*kuramoto*). Such agents were at first appointed from among the daimyo's housemen, but increasingly they were selected from wealthy and financially influential Ōsaka business houses. Increasingly too the *han* resorted to monopoly sale of their own local products through specially licensed commercial organizations and to the control of exchange between the *han* capitals and Ōsaka or Edo. Larger *han* turned to the use of rice or silver certificates which were made legal tender within the *han* boundaries, restricting species payment to commercial operations involving Ōsaka or Edo. To carry out trade and fiscal regulation practices of this sort they set up within the domain capital special agencies or factories (*kaisho*) which served as yet another organ of "alliance" between samurai and merchant interests.

The gradual establishment of a unified national economy centering on Ōsaka and Edo and involving the exchange of commodities with the *han* and the farflung shogunal territories is visible in all these developments. Ōsaka and Edo became the locus of exchange houses (*ryōgae*) and rice and commodity markets. The Ōsaka rice exchange at Dojima dealt in futures and acquired the capacity to affect the price of rice on a national scale. Ōsaka in the mid-eighteenth century had over 130 *han* warehouses and the annual flow of rice into its docks was in the neighborhood of one million *koku*. Increasingly under these circumstances the samurai class became dependent on financial agents: the shogunate on its currency monopolists and its large financial agents, the *hatamoto* on money changers (*fudasashi*) who converted their rice stipends to cash, the daimyo on their Ōsaka or Edo warehouse agents. Conversely, as the commercial houses became involved in nearly every aspect of the fiscal transactions of the administrative class, they were bound to become a major creditor group.

The merchant community of Tokugawa times went through certain stages of development in its rise to economic prominence. In the early years, the important merchants were those specially patronized by the Shogun and daimyo, the so-called "house merchants." By the eighteenth century a number of great commercial houses had grown up in Ōsaka and Edo whose diversified activities focused upon moneylending and exchange. By the nineteenth century, houses based on manufacturing and cottage industry had begun to make their appearance. The growth of commercial capital is revealed in the estimate that by 1761 there were in Japan over two hundred commercial houses each valued at over 200,000 gold *ryō*. (The *ryō* was roughly equivalent to a *koku* of rice.) Thus in total capital worth the great merchants had become the equivalent of many daimyo.

By the middle Tokugawa period most of the outstanding *chōnin* houses which were to retain their status into modern times had been established. The founder of the Mitsui house had his start in the 1620's as a *sake* brewer in the province of Ise. He subsequently turned to local usury and rice and money exchange. His son in 1673 moved into Edo and established a drygoods store, the Echigoya. By the 1680's the house had branches in Kyōto and Ōsaka and had entered the exchange business. During the 1690's, Mitsui became financial agent for the shogunate and the imperial house, in addition to serving several daimyo. By then also it managed a large network of wholesale associations for which its stores provided outlets. It developed a runner service for rapid communication between Ōsaka and Edo, and had even gone into the acquisition of land through its financing of large-scale reclamation. The Kōnoike house also started as *sake* brewers in Settsu province near Ōsaka. In 1616 its founder moved to Ōsaka to engage in shipping and moneylending. By the 1650's it had become an important exchange house and served as *kuramoto* for several daimyo. By the 1690's the Kōnoike handled the financial affairs of nearly 40 daimyo. The fees from such services alone are said to have amounted to 10,000 *koku* of rice annually, an amount greater than the disposable income of most of the daimyo he served. From this point the Kōnoike also entered the land reclamation business. The Sumitomo house began as drug and iron-goods merchants in Kyōto. In the early years of the Tokugawa period it began to trade in copper through Ōsaka and to operate copper refineries in Kyōto and Ōsaka. When Tanuma established the *bakufu* copper monopoly in 1783, the Sumitomo served as agents in the Kansai area and later in 1791 began development of the rich Besshi mines.

By the eighteenth century it is clear that Japan had entered a new phase of urban-centered commercial economy. Urban growth had been astounding. Edo may well have acquired a population of one million, certainly more than contemporary London or Paris. Ōsaka and Kyōto had populations of around 400,000, while Kanazawa (capital of the Maeda domain) and Nagoya (capital of the Owari domain) may have attained close to 100,000 inhabitants. Nagasaki and Sakai, chiefly commercial towns, each had about 65,000 inhabitants. Probably, all told, ten percent of the Japanese of this time were living in cities of over ten thousand inhabitants and were thus acquiring an entirely urbanized way of life. The trend towards urbanization was to continue at the expense of the countryside, thus beginning the modern trend away from agriculture.

Transportation and communication facilities also increased tremendously through both the efforts of the authorities and private companies. Japan was slow to develop the wagon and relied on the packhorse for light-weight transport. Bulk commodities, rice, *sake,* vegetables and the like were transported by boat along the coast. The overland highway system flourished, however, as daimyo and their retinues travelled the roads and as hordes of common travellers passed to and fro. Post stations and inn towns prospered to the amazement of even European travellers such as Kaempfer, who passed along the Tōkaidō in 1690. And runners (*hikyaku*) kept postal services operating for daimyo and commoners alike. Shogunal and daimyo authorities along the roads saw to the maintenance of the road system, though bridges were sometimes neglected in order to discourage hostile movements of troops. Shipping lines emerged with great vitality to funnel goods into the great cities of Ōsaka, Edo, Kyōto and Nagasaki. While tonnage was limited, small vessels in large numbers were organized to perform specific functions such as navigating the short shallow rivers into the interior or running along the coast. Rice shipment from northern Japan to Ōsaka along the Japan Sea coast and then around the Straits of Shimonoseki and up the Inland Sea became a major industry as did the shipment of rice into Edo from the north along the Pacific coast. To meet the needs of foreign trade at Nagasaki, ships brought down sea products from Hokkaidō. Express lines developed between Ōsaka and Edo to serve the great wholesale guilds, and these in turn formed the competitive Higaki and Taru lines.

Commercial growth was served as well by the rapid development of a currency and exchange system. After the unification of currency by Hideyoshi, the *bakufu* managed to maintain a reasonably stable currency utilizing a parallel system of four media of exchange: rice, gold, silver, and copper. Increasingly rice became simply a unit of taxation and of accumulation, limited however by its perishability. Metallic currency thus became the real medium of exchange based on a theoretical convertibility of one *ryō* of gold $= 60$ *momme* of silver $= 4$ strings (*kan*) of cash. Silver, as we have noted, was not minted until Tanuma's day. Before that silver was calculated by weight and transferred in lumps. Scarcity of precious metals and complexity of exchange led to the development of various kinds of commercial paper and localized paper currencies. Banking and exchange houses developed in Edo and Ōsaka to handle letters of transfer or of credit between the cities. Paper currency, which was largely in the form of *han* rice or silver certificates, gradually reached major proportions. At the end of the Tokugawa regime it was discovered that 244 *han* and 21 localities within Tokugawa territory had issued some 1,600 varieties in all. When converted to the new national currency these certificates amounted to over 24 million *yen* (the *yen* being roughly equal to the Mexican dollar at the time).

By the late Tokugawa period signs of yet a new stage of economic development were visible at two levels. Urban growth and the expansion of the consumer market had injected a new spirit of enterprise into the countryside. Wholesale organizations and village entrepreneurs developed new techniques of mass production exemplified in the silk-weaving, paper-making, and lacquer-work industries. In Kiryū, for instance, by the mid-nineteenth century factory-style weaving establishments had brought some 5,000 looms under less than three hundred roofs. In mining and *sake* brewing, as well, large groups of laborers were handled on a hired labor basis. These new developments in the rural areas were to have important consequences for the city-based licensed merchants, with whom they competed, and for some of the daimyo. Toward the end of the Tokugawa period *han* authorities began to take up with vigor a new line of mercantilist economic policy. New practices which emphasized local production for export sale to Edo and Ōsaka on a monopoly basis began to lure the fiscal agents of the *han* still further into collaboration with the commercial class.

But before the major *han* could convert totally to mercantilist practices in the effort to solve their financial difficulties, samurai policy toward commerce and the merchant had to undergo a fundamental rethinking. Even in as late a work as Ogyū Sorai's *Seidan* (*Political essays,* 1727) the assumption remained that the merchant's contribution to society was insignificant. Townsmen merely absorbed the stipends of samurai and hence were useless destroyers of grain. This official attitude was constantly held over the heads of the merchants who remained vulnerable to arbitrary acts of the authorities such as cancellation of debts, forced loans (*goyōkin*), or the sudden confiscations of property. The most celebrated case of confiscation was that of Yodoya Saburōemon who was ruined in 1705 on the accusation of ostentation. The passing of Yodoya, one of the richest Ōsaka merchants and head of the Dojima rice market, is said to have permitted the cancellation of vast sums of daimyo debts and yielded a fabulous treasure reported at 121 million *ryō*. There is doubt about the authenticity of this story, but the legend of Yodoya has persisted as evidence of the precariousness of the *chōnin's* life in Tokugawa Japan.

There is some indication that economic theory in the late Tokugawa period attempted to keep up with economic realities and that from out of the body of Confucian orthodoxy there emerged a few theorists who argued for a more pragmatic approach to the economy. One of the pioneers in this respect was Ogyū Sorai's pupil Dazai Shundai (1680–1747), who argued for the acceptance of money economy as a legitimate extension of economic growth. Another, Kaiho Seiryō (1755–1818), perhaps influenced by his knowledge of royal enterprises in Europe, wrote that the samurai who converted his rice stipend into money at a profit was no different from a merchant. Nor could he see that the merchant differed from the samurai, since the profit he took was equivalent to a hereditary "stipend." The later years of the Tokugawa period found a number of writers, often of *rōnin* or merchant status, who toured the country, offering advice on economic projects, suggesting new crops or better mining techniques and in general emphasizing the possibilities of economic growth. But it was probably the dire necessity of improving *han* finances and the possibility of doing so by playing the *han* regional economies against the great city markets of Ōsaka and Edo that drove *han* authorities into the arms of merchant houses and gave rise to the numerous *han* commodity monopolies which emerged after the middle of the eighteenth century. Such monopolies tied in with debt flotation through currency issues became the main expedient of the *han* in late Tokugawa times.

In Tokugawa Japan the *chōnin* remained from first to last a "problem" for the samurai authorities, and official policy remained at odds with the commercial trend of the age. Yet along with the rural entrepreneurs, the merchant found it possible to prosper. Certainly from a purely economic point of view he occupied a deceptively favorable position. As the Mitsui house laws state so emphatically, the merchant was obliged to understand his place and acknowledge the fact that he was a servant in the samurai's world. But in his own world he was master. Relieved of the temptation to strive for noble status either by purchase or infiltration, the Japanese merchant could concentrate his energies on the struggle for business success. It was perhaps this feature of the Tokugawa system which more than any other induced the *chōnin* to press for the economic growth which so marked the latter half of the Tokugawa period.

213

Samurai Culture and Thought

The class-based legal concepts and separate living conditions of Tokugawa society affected the cultural style of the several classes profoundly. Tokugawa culture was class-based both in theory and to a large extent in practice, for samurai, *chōnin*, and peasants necessarily lived in different environments and according to different routines and values. Admittedly there were large areas of fusion, particularly in the new urban environment where samurai and commoner shared a variety of interests and pastimes. Yet in the minds of the Japanese, and particularly the authorities, the line between noble and vulgar ways of life and between rural and urban remained strongly drawn. That later generations have looked upon the achievements of the Tokugawa bourgeois society as more noteworthy than those of the samurai would have startled the people of the time, for the aristocratic ideal still lingered, and the products of the "floating world" (*ukiyo*) of the urban lower classes were considered beneath the dignity of cultivated society. Yet like samurai government, samurai culture has been harshly dealt with by modern historians and connoisseurs who have found in bourgeois activities of the age the most dynamic and creative impulses of the time.

Certainly one of the distinguishing features of Tokugawa life was the emergence of a bourgeoisie into national prominence for the first time. The creation of a distinct cultural style which was of and by the common classes illustrated as nothing else the growth in urban population, its affluence and its energy. And it was characteristic of bourgeois culture, produced as it was by a stratum within Tokugawa society which was less tied to the necessity of keeping up a noble, and at times artificial, tradition that its content dealt largely with matters of the moment and of the heart. Undoubtedly it is this more common or universal quality which has proved so attractive to later observers. Yet the achievements of the samurai class were both considerable and important. Their poor reputation or neglect by later writers is due largely to the fact that much of the samurai's efforts were directed to the more esoteric fields of philosophy and classical scholarship and that in strictly artistic fields the scale of creativity fell off considerably. Moreover the whole aristocratic class structure, the metaphysical concepts of Confucianism, and the *bushi* military values which supported the samurai mode of life were gradually to be discarded after 1868. And so the *chōnin*'s culture of entertainment, with its less particularistic concerns, was to find more ready appeal in the twentieth century.

The military houses of the Tokugawa age maintained a cultural life based upon a distinct consciousness of what was "appropriate to the *bushi* status." Its elements were not by any measure new. In architecture, painting, and drama the patronage of daimyo and Shogun did little more than perpetuate without great modification the genre and styles which had originated in the Ashikaga age. Tokugawa architectural monuments were not greatly inspired and tended toward the heavy and ornate. The great mausolea at Nikkō and Kan'eiji may be admired for their grandeur and obvious display of conspicuous wealth and power. The Yōmei gate at Nikkō, so intricately carved in flowers and figures, may elicit wonder from the untrained eye, but to a Bruno Taut it seems a "barbaric and ostentatious sepulchre." Nijō castle in Kyōto exemplifies the high residential style using lacquered pillars, richly decorated and gilded ceilings, and elaborately painted wall screens. Castle architecture in its use of massive stone walls and gateways of blackened wood studded with iron, reinforced the feeling of authority and strength. Daimyo and Shogun also built spacious gardens set with tea houses and outdoor stages for the performance of *nō* drama. In their Edo residences and their castled headquarters they patronized the visual and performing arts which had become the mark of aristocratic culture since Ashikaga days. Their level of living gave impetus, as well, to the production of fine porcelain, lacquer ware, silk brocade, and metal work in large quantities. In the minor arts where lower class craftsmanship met aristocratic patronage, in fact, some truly remarkable artistic achievements became possible.

In general, however, the noble arts of the Tokugawa age tended increasingly towards formalization. Tea ceremony and *nō* drama, perpetuated as a prerogative of the military class, became stereotyped. Special hereditary schools of actors, tea masters and flower arrangers perpetuated their styles under official patronage. In painting, the Kanō school of decorative artists monopolized the field and relied with little modification on the techniques and the themes which had been invented by their predecessors. In literature classical Chinese and Japanese texts were preferred, while in music the *koto*, the hand drum, and the singing of *nō* excerpts relied on styles and scripts which had long been considered classical. All of these accomplishments tended to become formalized as schools of instructors, each with its specific style, guided the training of the samurai class in the polite arts.

Yet samurai culture was occasionally saved from the ostentatious and the derivative by both the strong continuity of Zen taste and the waking of new intellectual currents. The detached palaces of Katsura and Shūgakuin outside Kyōto are perhaps the finest examples of a domestic style of architecture, combining the aesthetic principles of the tea house and the needs of the aristocratic way of life. Their simplicity of line, use of natural woods, integration with surrounding gardens and overall restraint are illustrative of the best in the Japanese architectural tradition.

In painting, several new styles showed more vitality than the work of the Kanō artists. A school of extreme stylization and simplification developed by Hon'ami Kōetsu (1558–1637) and Tawaraya Sōtatsu (?-1643) out of the Yamato tradition was applied to decorative screens, lacquer boxes, and pottery. Under the brush of Ogata Kōrin (1658–1716) this style became established as a major component of Japanese artistic expression. At the other extreme men like Maruyama Ōkyo (1733–1795) instilled new life into the Chinese monochrome tradition by giving attention to realistic detail. Ōkyo made careful studies from life and adopted techniques of perspective and shading introduced from Western painting. It is interesting to note that all of these developments in the field of painting were the work of commoner artists working out of existing traditions, though of course for upper-class patrons.

More properly, the property of the samurai class was the style of "literati" painting (*bunjinga* or *nanga*) which became popular along with the spread of Confucian philosophy. Indulged in by amateurs as well as professionals, it cultivated a deliberate sense of academism and sketchiness which emphasized the thought behind the painting. Yosa Buson (1716–1783) and Ike-no-Taiga (1723–1776) brought the style to a high point in their pictorial essays.

It was in the field of scholarship and philosophy, however, that the samurai showed their most creative and industrious capacities. Especially distinguished was the work in history, for Tokugawa scholars laid the basis of objective historiography and began as well the accumulation of archives and libraries upon which modern historical research first depended.

Leading the list of historical compilations of this period is the *Honchō tsugan* (*Comprehensive mirror of our country*), a chronological history of Japan completed around 1670 by members of the Hayashi family of Confucian scholars and modeled after the Chinese work by Ssu-ma Kuang, the *Tzu-chih t'ung-chien*. Other shogunal projects included the *Tokugawa jikki* (*Veritable records of the Tokugawa House*), prepared between 1809 and 1849, which covers in great and exact detail events at the Shogun's court, and the *Kansei chōshū shokafu* (*Collated genealogies of the Kansei era*) completed in 1812 and containing the house records of all daimyo and important retainers of the Shogun.

Paralleling this shogunal effort were works of daimyo sponsorship. A "national" history rivalling the product of the Hayashi house was the *Dainihon-shi* (*History of great Japan*) begun in 1657 by the daimyo of Mito, Tokugawa Mitsukuni (1628–1700). The work of the Shōkōkan, a domain-sponsored historical office, its first 250 chapters were made public in 1720, but the work was not completed until 1906. Other *han* devoted their efforts chiefly to the compilation of "house records" or local gazetteers.

217

Numerous private histories were produced by the ever increasing body of Confucian scholars and historiographers who served the *baku-han* establishment. Arai Hakuseki is noted for his *Tokushi yoron*, a rationalistic study of the passage of political power from the hands of the nobility to the military aristocracy. Iida Tadahiko (1816–1861) wrote the *Dainihon yashi* (*Private history of great Japan*), conceived as a continuation of the Mito history. Rai Sanyō (1780–1832) prepared a popularized and somewhat nationalistic version of Japanese history in his *Nihon gaishi* (*Unofficial history of Japan*). Meanwhile the *bakufu* bibliographer Hanawa Hokiichi (1746–1821) was at work on the voluminous *Gunsho ruijū* (*Classified documents*), a collection of basic historical texts completed in 1794. This work together with its successor prepared by Hanawa's son stands today a monument of archival compilation containing over three thousand items in 91 volumes.

Scholarship was not limited to the samurai class, of course, and the list of significant academic and philosophic writers of the Tokugawa age includes many a man from *chōnin* or even peasant background. What the spread of erudition indicated was that the opportunities for education had expanded greatly at all levels of Tokugawa society. Japan was, in fact, entering upon a period of widespread literacy fed by an expanding network of schools and consuming vast quantities of publications. Among educational facilities, the *bakufu's* Shōheikō continued as the prime official college, adding a medical school to its facilities in 1765. Daimyo-sponsored *han* schools grew rapidly after 1700, and by the end of the Tokugawa regime numbered over 270. In addition over 375 academies are said to have been supported by the *han,* and more than 1,400 private schools had made their appearance in the larger cities and towns. Such facilities were chiefly dedicated to the education of samurai, but commoner education was not neglected. Several *han* schools were open to the sons of merchants and peasants, especially those from headmen families, for reading and writing were essential skills for the keeping of administrative records. In addition common people were provided for

218

in the so-called "temple schools" (*terakoya*), small private elementary schools, often but not necessarily attached to local temples. Over 10,000 schools of this type are recorded as having come into existence by the middle of the nineteenth century. The result, as estimated by R. P. Dore, was that by the 1860's the Japanese had achieved a literacy rate of from 40 to 50 percent among males and about 15 percent among females. Certainly all samurai were literate, and the higher levels of the peasantry and merchant classes had been educated to some extent. In terms of literacy Japan thus compared favorably with England of the same time, a surprising fact when one considers the isolation of the Japanese from outside intellectual currents.

The nature of education was itself a prime formative element in Tokugawa culture. Confucian-based for the most part, bookish and highly moralistic, it was nonetheless taken with great seriousness, for it was a necessary element of success for members of the samurai and *chōnin* classes. The Tokugawa mind was therefore scholastic but practical. Its style of inquiry was derivative, perhaps, but within certain limits remarkably flexible and pragmatic. Tokugawa scholasticism, though based on Chinese Confucian thought, developed along its own lines and led the samurai to a diversity of intellectual inquiries within the realms of moral philosophy, political economics, and history. Above all the samurai kept alive the ideal of training in *both* the military and civil arts. He thereby remained true to his calling and his sense of cultural identity as a Japanese.

Confucian scholarship in Japan embodied from the first large areas of heterodoxy, either because the Japanese failed to comprehend the niceties of Chinese philosophy or because they could not detach themselves from Japanese realities. The early Tokugawa Confucianists, to be sure, tended to be dogmatists who looked to the Neo-Confucian texts almost as revealed scriptures. And throughout the Tokugawa period the Chu Hsi school, over which the Hayashi house presided, kept to the orthodox line. Proscription of heterodox teachings in the *bakufu*'s college was attempted in 1790 by Matsudaira

Sadanobu. But while the shogunate might seek to regiment the doctrines of its own educational institutions, it had less control over policies in the daimyo domains and in the private schools in Kyōto or Ōsaka. Despite its generally conservative social influence, Confucian doctrine had within it the seeds of intellectual inquisitiveness and even of skepticism. Japanese Confucianists, once they were familiar with basic principles, began to apply their learning to Japanese problems with the inevitable result that they were drawn to novel answers.

Ogyū Sorai (1666–1728), the advocate of "ancient learning" (*kogaku*), proposed to look at the original sources for justification of his strongly idiosyncratic advice to the shogunate on government policy. His work *Seidan* (*Political essays*) urged practical reforms upon the shogunate and called for a firmer assertion of shogunal absolutism. Arai Hakuseki's objective approach to Japanese history was matched by his detached appraisal of Christianity. His *Seiyō kibun* (*A report on the Occident*) was written in 1715 after interviews with Giovanni Sidotti (1668–1715), an Italian priest who had been taken prisoner by the *bakufu* while trying to smuggle himself into Japan in 1708. In it Arai showed a frank admiration for Western science, and proclaimed in matter-of-fact fashion that Christianity was too irrational to be of any harm to Japan. Miura Baien (1723–1789), a scholar of non-samurai origin, devoted a lifetime to the quest for explanation of such questions as, "Why do eyes not hear and ears not see?" Unable to accept the formalized explanations he found in Confucian doctrine, he developed a skeptical philosophy which looked for proof in empirical evidence. Kaiho Seiryō (1755–1817) developed economic theories which urged samurai government to tap commerce as a source of wealth. Why should the samurai disdain trade and profit, he asked, when the king of Holland actively patronizes commercial ventures? Honda Toshiaki (1744–1821) studied what he could of world geography and concluded that Japan's seclusion policy was misguided. He envisioned Japan as striking out across the seas and developing its northern frontier for self-protection. Satō Nobuhiro (1768–1850), broadly read in Dutch works, astronomy, botany, geography and history, spent a vigorous life travelling about Japan advising daimyo on agricultural improvements and gratuitously recommending to the *bakufu* that it impose more strenuous controls upon the country.

By the nineteenth century it is clear that Japanese writers in almost every field were being influenced to some extent either by knowledge of Western science and geography or by fear of Western encroachment. Late developments in Confucian thought were thus not all self-generated. The necessity of confronting new and often contradictory ideas from abroad impelled some Japanese to rejection and alarm, others to eclectic accommodations with their Confucian heritage. Yamagata Bantō (1748–1821), for example, sought to integrate Western heliocentric theory with Confucian cosmology and even equated Western science with the Confucian concept of reason or ultimate principle (*ri*). But Confucian rationalism lacked the essential drive to deny its premises in the quest for science, and the main line of orthodox thinking with its moralistic and class-based attitudes still weighed heavily upon the Tokugawa mind.

The rationalistic element in Tokugawa Confucianism not only caused modifications in the orthodox tradition itself, it induced new lines of intellectual inquiry which carried beyond the Confucian base in Japan. The Confucian emphasis on the past naturally led to interest in Japan's own historical heritage and in its literary tradition. Confucian scholars could not avoid the fact that the doctrines they admired were of Chinese origin. Yet samurai society had little respect for the rabid sinophile. Most Japanese Confucianists maintained a strong nationalistic pose while admitting their admiration for things Chinese. Hayashi Razan, having found in Shintō an ally against Buddhism, began the effort to rationalize the imperial myths by the use of Confucian theory. For him the three sacred imperial treasures became symbols of basic Confucian ideals. Yamaga Sokō's doctrine of *bushidō* continued this eclectic trend which in Yamazaki Ansai (1618–1682) found expression in a new brand of Shintō thought (*Suikashintō*) interpreting the "way of the *kami*" as the way of the sage kings. Ansai discovered Confucian virtues in the *Kojiki* and *Nihon shoki* legends and saw in the ancient *kami* a reflection of Confucian reason.

It was merely a matter of time before this philosophical interest in Shintō would combine with the vogue of historical and literary scholarship to produce a school of indigenous studies based on a supposed body of "Japanese classics." The resulting "national learning" (*kokugaku*) movement began in the eighteenth century as an effort to recover for Japan a literary and historical heritage. It became in time a full-fledged school of intellectual return to Japan's origins.

Kokugaku studies gained national recognition when in 1728 Kada Azumamaro (1668–1736) memorialized the *bakufu* for the establishment of a "school of national learning." A Shintō priest from the Kyōto area, Kada had been influenced by the recent trend in Confucian scholarship which sought to return to the original "ancient way." Kada's student Kamo Mabuchi (1697–1769) advanced the study of the *Manyōshū* and added the first anti-Confucian note in his writings. In the ancient poems of the Nara period he claimed to hear "the voice of our divine land."

The towering figure of the *kokugaku* movement was Motoori Norinaga (1730–1801), the man who spent thirty years recapturing the meaning of the *Kojiki*. Norinaga became convinced that the *Kojiki* revealed a unique Japanese "ancient way," a state of natural utopian goodness exemplified in the age of the *kami,* and that this had been contaminated by the influence of Buddhism and Confucianism, Motoori's tremendous influence stemmed from his dedication to teaching. He is said to have had nearly five hundred students in his forty years of active instruction.

After 1800, *kokugaku* spread widely as a branch of scholarly inquiry into Japanese literature. But it also encouraged a revival of interest in the theological aspects of Shintō. Hirata Atsutane (1776–1843), a violently nationalistic and antiforeign thinker, wrote of Japan's unique polity (*kokutai*: i. e.

Japan as a land of the *kami*, ruled by a unique imperial line). The logical extension of his argument was that Japan must revive Shintō as its only religion and the emperor as its only ruler. His ideas proved sufficiently subversive to the shogunate to have him placed under house arrest in 1841.

While much of what the Shintō revivalists wrote seems irrational and highly emotional, they nonetheless led the way in developing new ideas of Japan's historical identity and destiny. By enshrining a new body of Japanese classics, and by pointing to the emperor as a new focus of loyalty, they gave impetus to political action in defense of their nation. Their scorn of China began the process which cut Japan away from its undue reliance on a cultural mentor it had so long admired, just as new influences were beginning to reach Japan from the West.

Knowledge of the lurking presence of Western vessels in waters off the coast of Japan in the early nineteenth century was not the only intimation the Japanese had of the existence of an outside world vastly different from their own. Information about the West and study of Western languages and scientific subjects were kept alive, albeit by a small body of inquisitive individuals, throughout the Tokugawa period. Foreign studies (*yōgaku*) or Dutch studies (*Rangaku*) thus comprise still another unorthodox line of inquiry pursued by Japanese scholars, sometimes with great difficulty and personal sacrifice. The source of such study was of course Nagasaki where the only contact with Europe was provided through the Dutch factory on Deshima.

For about eighty years after the adoption of the seclusion policy, the *bakufu* authorities placed increasingly severe restrictions on Japanese contact with Westerners. A prohibition was issued against the importation of Western books, or Chinese translations of such books, and knowledge of the Dutch language was restricted to a few official "interpreters" attached to the Nagasaki Commissioner's office. Arai Hakuseki is credited with having made possible the relaxation of extreme

223

vigilance by the Nagasaki officials when publication of his *Seiyō kibun* in 1715 revealed that there was much in Western science from which Japan could learn. The Shogun Yoshimune in 1720 lifted the ban on the importation of foreign books and Chinese translations (except those directly concerned with Christianity) and encouraged the private study of the Dutch language and such subjects as astronomy and military tactics.

Through this narrow crack in the wall of seclusion began the school of Dutch studies which was to absorb with avid and often distorted eagerness knowledge of Western subjects. A Dutch-Japanese dictionary was produced by Aoki Konyō in 1745. Sugita Gempaku (1733–1817) and others translated the *Tavel Anatomia* in 1774 under the title *Kaitai shinsho* and thereby introduced Western medical techniques into Japan. Ōtsuki Gentaku (1757–1827) openly established a school for the study of Dutch and Western subjects. His *Explanation of Dutch Studies* (*Rangaku kaitei*), published in 1788, became the first popularly available explanation of the Dutch language for the general reader.

During the period of Tanuma's ascendancy in the *bakufu* Japan's suspicion of foreigners was relaxed considerably. Contact with members of the Dutch factory became much more free, and the importation of Western curiosa took on the proportions of a fad. Daimyo collected clocks and fieldglasses, drank out of glass goblets and even watched experiments in electricity. Between 1769 and 1786 the Swedish physician Thunberg and the Dutch trading captain Titsingh imparted a great deal of first-hand scientific information to the Japanese who flocked to their quarters. The *rōnin* Hiraga Gennai (1726–1779), briefly patronized by Tanuma, made his way to fame for his study of botany and his experimentation with asbestos and electricity. An eccentric genius, he wrote satirical novels and comical plays and dabbled in oil painting techniques learned from the West.

Much of this open enthusiasm for things Western was dampened by Matsudaira Sadanobu when he came to power in

224

1787. Hayashi Shihei's works, which had mentioned the approach of the Russians in the north, were suppressed in 1792, and new restrictions were placed on contact with Westerners in Japan and on the acquisition of Western books. Yet in 1811 the *bakufu* itself recognized the need to keep abreast of developments in the West by establishing a body of official translators of Western books (*Bansho wage goyōkata*) within the shogunal astronomical observatory. One of these was Ōtsuki Gentaku.

Dutch studies thus became a firmly established subject of study by the beginning of the nineteenth century, though it is difficult to assess the influence of the ideas and techniques it may have made available to the Japanese. Students of Dutch and of Western science never constituted a large group, nor did they become a dissident force in Tokugawa society. The political and social implications of their study were particularly weak, for few if any of these men broke out of the Confucian ethical framework or the confines of Tokugawa official policy. Yet in the long run, the spread of a heterodox discipline coming from the West was to have important consequences. Accepted first because of demonstrated technological superiority, Western techniques of medicine, astronomy, agriculture, and military science were studied under the official patronage of both *bakufu* and daimyo. Once established, the new methods undermined the supremacy of the established Chinese techniques and the Confucian theory behind them.

The late Tokugawa intellectual climate was thus far from stagnant or committed to an inflexible orthodoxy. Showing a wide diversity of opinion and of lines of inquiry, the samurai's world was open to many currents. Still strongly Confucian in its basic ethical commitment, it yet had made room for the independent study of Japanese history and of Western science and medicine. Above all, however, it was a world in which the samurai and his values remained dominant, a world in which a growing awareness of Japan's identity as a nation carried with it a renewed consciousness of the samurai's role as political and intellectual leader.

The Culture of the *Chōnin*

While by the end of the eighteenth century there were large areas of urban life in which it had become difficult to differentiate the separate contributions of the samurai and non-samurai classes, it is still valid to talk about a distinct style of *"chōnin"* culture which had its origins in the great cities of Ōsaka, Kyōto, and Edo. It was the urban populace of Tokugawa times which first gained the means and the leisure to support a mass-participant culture in contrast to the "noble" tradition in the arts and letters. In their new urban quarters the *chōnin* patronized their own arts and pastimes, adding thereby a new and vital element to the totality of the nation's cultural life. Theirs was a distinctively bourgeois creation, confined to its specific place and status within the social environment. Unconcerned with matters of state or metaphysics, *chōnin* culture was nourished mainly by the search for enjoyment. It avoided the "noble" for the human and entertaining. It dwelt on the personal, the immediate, and the erotic. Its ideal became the "floating world" (*ukiyo*), the world of fashion and popular entertainment.

But we should not suppose that the *chōnin* lived without compelling ideals or that they had no sense of moral form. The merchant and artisan lived in a world of obligations and aspirations as demanding in its way as that of the samurai. The merchant felt obligated to make his business prosper and thereby honor the name of his family. The artisan was obliged to maintain the quality of his particular craft. There existed a "Way of the Chōnin" which urged the merchant to work diligently for honest profits and to dedicate his labors to his calling and to the enrichment of his business. The merchant's way, perhaps in imitation of the samurai's, stressed no less severely the requirements of loyalty (to the business) and frugality (so as not to dissipate profits). *Chōnin* life could be demanding and confining, involving long years of apprenticeship and supervised internship.

Thus while what we call *chōnin* culture was largely a prod-

226

uct of the merchant's desire for diversion and relaxation, *chōnin* life itself was not without its serious demands and its areas of practical achievement. In the first instance the *chōnin* subscribed to values and even to religious beliefs which added dignity and meaning to their calling. Great merchant houses such as the Mitsui lived by codes of conduct as strict as any which applied to the samurai. Ishida Baigan (1685–1744), the Kyōto merchant-philosopher, blended a mixture of Shintō beliefs and Confucian and Buddhist maxims into a new religion which spoke directly to the daily needs of the common people. "Heart Learning" (*Shingaku*), as this new eclectic system was called, stressed acceptance of the natural (i.e. four-class) social order, and urged each individual to live out his assigned lot with diligence, compassion, and honesty. Merchants, it stated, were as important in the scheme of nature as the other classes, and it was important for them to live up to their "way" in order to do honor to their calling.

Merchant ingenuity also had much to do with the remarkable development of some of the practical lines of inquiry and technology. Mathematics, applied both in the counting house and to problems of astronomy and engineering, achieved a sophistication which claims for Japanese mathematicians such as Seki Takakazu (1642–1708) abilities comparable to their European contemporaries. Inō Tadataka (1745–1818) prepared a remarkably accurate map of Japan after 17 years of surveying. In the fields of astronomy, agronomy, botany, medicine and civil engineering, men of non-samurai origin frequently led the way to improved methods. What the Japanese historian Nishida Naojirō has called "the spirit of calculation and measurement," the practical pitting of the mind against real problems, owed a good deal of its early spread to the activities of *chōnin*.

But the culture of the merchants as a distinct form was by and large a product of the *ukiyo*, the world of entertainment. Its elements were the female entertainer, the music of the *shamisen*, the popular story, the new drama and the wood block print. Of these the courtesan was of predominant importance, for she was both central to the urban world of entertainment and also a very distinct product of Japanese social tradition. As a professional female entertainer, the *geisha* ("gei" refers to the performing arts) of Tokugawa times was descended from a long line of courtesans and dancing girls who had commonly formed part of the aristocratic world of entertainment. But it was during the Tokugawa period that she became established as an institution available to a new and broader urban population. In a society in which home life, for both samurai and commoner, was so institutionalized as to preclude free entertainment, in which there were no mixed social functions such as balls, dances, and dinners, in which arranged marriage eliminated courtship, the professional entertainer had an essential function. The courtesan and the environment she created provided the only opportunity for free association between men and women other than on a purely routine basis at the brothel.

The *geisha* congregated in certain special quarters of the new cities, the "nightless cities" such as Shimabara and Gion in Kyōto, Shinbashi in Ōsaka, or Yoshihara in Edo. Here she became the central element in the world of restaurants, theatres, baths and brothels. Created in the main by the wealthy merchants, the world of the *geisha* was off limits for the samurai, yet increasingly the samurai also partook of the diversions of the gay quarters, leaving their long swords behind in order to do so. Thus for both the samurai and the sober business-minded merchant the nightless city provided a place of relaxation from the rigors of office or the abacus. It also proved a major source of temptation. For the *geisha* often became the pivotal figure in the conflict between duty (*giri*) and passion (*ninjō*), as much of the popular theatre and fiction of the times was to record.

About a century after the founding of the new castle towns and the expansion of the new urban societies of Kyōto and Ōsaka, the city milieu began to produce its own literature and art. Cultural historians identify two periods of florescence, the Genroku age (1688–1705) and the Bunka-Bunsei period (1804–1829). During the first of these Kyōto and Ōsaka served as primary centers. During the second, Edo became the center of a more sophisticated though somewhat less vigorous phase of urban life. Since most of the *ukiyo* genre were brought to their first creative height during the Genroku age, it is customary to emphasize this period somewhat to the exclusion of the second. But the growth of *chōnin* culture was continuous, and the later periods of development which saw an increased fusion between *chōnin* and samurai achievements were historically of great importance.

Short stories and longer fictional writings produced for popular consumption developed with tremendous vitality during the early Tokugawa period, reflecting the new wealth and leisure of the *chōnin* and the spread of literacy among all classes. By the eighteenth century the main cities had developed lucrative publishing businesses. Publishing houses acquired stables of writers and illustrators and brought out with skillful publicity love stories or illustrated guides to the entertainment quarters, often devising the most ingenious ways to avoid the censorship efforts of the *bakufu* officials. Like the modern paperback market, this genre of literature dealt mainly with the gay quarters and the affairs of the heart. It featured stories of *chōnin* dandies who knew their way around the *geisha* quarters or of the beautiful *geisha* themselves. It was often risqué and frequently banned.

Ihara Saikaku (1641–1693), an Ōsaka merchant, was the first great figure in the field of *ukiyo-zōshi* (stories of the *ukiyo*). A genius at writing linked verse, he turned to the subject of sex toward the end of his life. His *Amorous Man* (*Kōshoku ichidai otoko*) appeared in 1682 and told the story of a precocious youth who, having exhausted the possibilities for love in Japan, sailed off for the "isle of women" at the age of sixty. His *Amorous Woman* (*Kōshoku ichidai onna*) tells of a woman who in the style of Moll Flanders goes step by step to her degradation as a prostitute kept in a Buddhist monastery. Saikaku turned to homosexual stories of samurai society in 1687, but these having been banned, he took to the writing of uplifting stories about the road to commercial success. His *The Everlasting Storehouses of Japan* (*Nihon eitaigura*) told of successful merchants and how they made their

229

money. Saikaku's contribution to Japanese literature was chiefly through his realism and the conviviality of his subject matter. His was a true literature of the merchant class, depicting the *chōnin*'s life, values, and foibles.

Another somewhat later and tremendously popular writer was Ejima Kiseki (1667–1736), who followed Saikaku's style, but with even greater realism, and added a critical, almost satirical dimension. His works on personal character described the lives of various types of *geisha*, merchants' sons and daughters, shop clerks and the like, commenting particularly on weakness of character in the second generation. Once started, the new genre of popular writing found a ready market among the new urban class. Much of the flood of comical books, popularized renditions of classical stories, love stories, guides to theatres, restaurants, or famous spots proved to be ephemeral. But from time to time works of note were produced, as for instance Jippensha Ikku's (1775–1831) comical story of travel on the Tōkaidō (*Tōkaidō chū hizakurige*). In modern English translation it has attracted attention for its picaresque qualities.

The appearance of a popular literature and of a large number of night spots in the *ukiyo* world which required advertisement, stimulated the work of popular illustrators. Since the Japanese still found the carved wood block most efficient for the printing of books, it was natural that the wood block should form the basis of this popular pictorial genre. The wood block print (*ukiyo-e*) became in time a major art form, appearing first as simple line cuts, with color added by use of new techniques learned from China through Nagasaki. By the end of the seventeenth century a multi-block technique had been perfected by which pictures of great sophistication in line and color could be produced. Wood block prints were produced for utilitarian and mass consumption purposes, as illustrations for books, as handbills for theatres or *geisha* houses, or as mementoes of famous spots. They were thus considered ephemeral and vulgar, and their recognition as art worthy of appreciation did not come until the close of the Tokugawa period. Ironically it was in Europe that the *ukiyo-e* first attracted serious attention. Among wood-block artists Hishikawa Moronobu (1618–1694) was the first of note. Suzuki Harunobu (1725–1770) developed the subtle rendition of color to a high point. Kitagawa Utamaro (1753–1806) specialized in idealized female types. Katsushika Hokusai (1760–1849) and Andō Hiroshige (1797–1858) portrayed with great vigor and visual effect landscapes and famous spots.

The drama of the common people began with wandering ballad singers and dancers but evolved during the Tokugawa period into a serious puppet drama (ningyō jōruri) and an elaborate stage theatre (kabuki). As in Elizabethan England, the theatre suffered at the hands of the official censor. The low morality of early female actors was such that the stage acting was placed under several bans. Thus theatrical performance was first brought to its peak in the puppet theatre where large, two-thirds life size puppets were manipulated by several highly trained puppeteers. By the time stage theatre came into its own as kabuki, it had been limited to performance by male actors alone. This fact, plus the strong influence of nō drama and the puppet and ballad-dance media, led to a unique theatrical tradition of great diversity ranging from highly stylized dance dramas to realistic domestic tragedies. The greatest of the writers for both the jōruri and kabuki theatres was Chikamatsu Monzaemon (1653–1724) whose interest ranged from historical samurai plays to works about chōnin life. Many of the latter were drawn from current happenings, such as actual double suicides among chōnin and geisha lovers. Nowhere is the emotional life of the chōnin and samurai more powerfully depicted than in Chikamatsu's plays, which hinge on the tragic tensions between loyalty and human sentiment or family duty and emotional attachment (the giri-ninjō conflict). Chikamatsu was followed by other playwrights; among them Kawatake Mokuami (1816–1893) was able to bridge the gap between the Tokugawa and Meiji dramatic worlds.

While the samurai was generally only a surreptitious participant in the ukiyo world, the field of poetry bridged all levels of Tokugawa society. The major poetic form of the period was the short haiku which employed three lines of 5-7-5 syllables.

The *haiku* became the poetic vehicle of ultimate popularity in Japan, for it could be cultivated by high and low for serious or comical purposes. In fact, during the Tokugawa period several styles of *haiku* writing developed, such as a comical genre known as *kyōka* (crazy verse), satirical poems, and even poems of social protest. But it is the serious form of *haiku* (or *haikai*) writing which has attracted the most attention as having produced a form of poetic expression both simple yet deeply expressive. During the Tokugawa period serious *haiku* poets came from numerous walks of life, both samurai and *chōnin*, but the best known were on the fringes of the priestly life or the world of samurai scholarship. Matsuo Bashō (1644–1694), the first and greatest of the serious *haiku* writers, was born a samurai and received a good education before he took up the life of a wandering recluse. Making a living by instructing disciples, he frequently travelled the country, and wrote of his love of nature and of his search for the meaning of life. His poems are tinged with the typical Buddhist melancholy over evanescence and change in nature and man. His *The Narrow Road of Oku* (*Oku no hosomichi*), a deeply poetic account of his travel in northern Japan, contains some of his finest writing. Bashō's followers perpetuated his style and developed it into a more systematic form. Among them Yosa Buson (1716–1783) and Kobayashi Issa (1763–1827) have written some of the most perfect *haiku*.

No better example is to be found of the manner in which life had begun to change for the vast majority of urban dwellers in Japan than in the "*haiku* communities" of the great cities. Here in the urban environment which ranged on the one side from the life of official service for the daimyo to the merchant gay quarters on the other there was coming into being a new fusion of values and interests which lay between the two. The new secular, rationalistic approach to life which characterized the outlooks of both samurai and *chōnin* was beginning to form into something quite new, and one is tempted to say modern. Tokugawa urban culture had become far less religious and far less socially stratified than anything which had preceded it in Japan.

The Tempō Era (1830–1844) and the Mounting Domestic Crisis

The preceding chapters have revealed the range of economic and cultural change which affected Tokugawa Japan despite the lack of outside contact. By 1830 Japan had obviously become a far different country from what it was in 1600. During the years of the Tokugawa "great peace," the country had grown significantly in population and wealth; the values by which its leading classes lived had been remade by Confucian teachers and in the teeming urban environments of Edo and Ōsaka. Both inside and outside the confines of the daimyo's castles, the Japanese now found the leisure for education and the pursuit of scholarship and entertainment on a mass scale. But peace had brought its problems as well, in terms of over-staffed and overrigid administrations and of economic dislocations which brought suffering to some and affluence to others. How, therefore, is one to assess the overall condition of the country? Was Japan sick, as some historians would have it, from being too long withdrawn from outside contact, a country technologically retarded, economically depressed, and inflexibly committed to an outmoded political system? What would have happened had not the Perry expedition pushed open Japan's doors in 1854, thereby forcing upon the country an unwanted challenge from the West? Could Japan have continued on its own or perhaps even revitalized its political institutions? Or was it doomed to a slow decline into stagnation or civil war?

Questions of this sort, of course, can have no final answer, and in any event it is impossible to imagine Japan after 1800 as moving solely under its own momentum, completely without awareness of the outside world. By the turn of the century, and certainly by 1830, the country was acutely conscious of the presence of a new foreign menace from out of the West. Yet it is also true that Japan in 1830 was not complacent or asleep, and it was not the foreign issue which alone gave the Japanese cause for alarm. The Tempō era (1830–1844) has

233

given its name to a pivotal period in the late years of the
Tokugawa regime when a general sense of crisis gripped the
nation and urged upon its leaders the necessity of reform. The
causes of alarm were at first more internal than external.

By 1830, few Japanese could escape a distressing sense of
"malaise" which had set in upon the shogunate and the daimyo
establishments. Perhaps it was the samurai who had the most
cause to feel restive about the future, for as a class they were
faced with the most disheartening economic conditions. *Bakufu* financial policies, particularly currency debasement, had
continued to undermine the economic position of those on
fixed rice stipends. Between 1819 and 1837 there had been
nineteen debasements. The amounts were great, yielding
enough profit to account for from one-third to one-half of the
bakufu's annual expenditures, and the inflationary pressures
were severe. Rising prices added to the already severe problems of livelihood for the samurai, for most of them by this
time were on short salaries, having been obliged to take "voluntary" cuts in their stipends to aid the domain finances. That
many samurai were in dire economic straits is indicated by the
number of incidents in which shogunal retainers took high-
dowried wives from among merchant families or even sold
their birthrights. In many *han* the lower levels of samurai went
into handicraft production, working for merchants on a putting
out arrangement to manufacture small items such as lanterns,
umbrellas, fans, brushes and the like. By the 1830's, in most
of the castle towns the samurai suffered from too little income
and too little work. They were simply too numerous for what
they were expected to do. Yet they were obliged to live under a
stern discipline, mindful of their status, which prevented them
from changing occupations.

Yet the samurai were no worse off individually than were
the public instruments of finance under which they lived.
Daimyo domains had begun to run into debt by the turn of
the eighteenth century. Required to keep up an official level
of outlay which included the constant drain of *sankin-kōtai*
travel, saddled with overstaffed bureaucracies and unnecessary
armies, periodically called upon to rebuild their castles or

234

their Edo residences after fire or flood, and beset by the constantly expanding routine expenditures, most daimyo domains slipped into a pattern of indebtedness to merchant financial houses with no prospect of reversing the financial trend. To take but two examples, the domain of Owari with an annual rice income of about 250,000 *koku* was obliged in 1801 to borrow 127,000 *ryō*. (If we assume a rough equivalence between the *koku* of rice and *ryō* of gold, we can see that the debt was more than one half of the domain's annual income.) Between 1849–1853, Owari borrowed 1.8 million *koku* secured by mortgages on the domain's annual rice taxes. The Satsuma domain was in even more serious condition. A domain assessed at 770,000 *koku*, it had a debt of 1.3 million *ryō* in 1807 and by 1830 this had increased to nearly 5 million *ryō*. The amount was equivalent to twenty years of domain taxes. Such conditions were endemic, and by 1840 it is estimated that Ōsaka merchants held daimyo debts totalling 60 million gold *ryō*; annual interest alone, if paid off in regular installments, would theoretically absorb a quarter of the normal tax income of the country.

Most *han* had somehow learned to muddle through with debt-ridden finances, making do with a number of expedients such as floating paper certificates or engaging in various monopoly projects in cooperation with merchants. In fact it may well be that the debtor-creditor dichotomy was not so extreme or dangerous as was then believed, for *han* finances and tax operations had become so dependent upon financial agents that many of the domain expedients would appear to modern eyes as attempts at deficit financing. But this was not by any means understood at the time. By the 1830's, therefore, most *han* were, like the *bakufu*, in a state of bewilderment, trying various policies but having little confidence of extricating themselves from debt. No clear-cut alternatives to the traditional policies of retrenchment and frugality had presented themselves other than to plunge further along the path of involvement with the merchants.

In the tense years of the 1830's those who were doing best economically were, of course, the successful merchants and

235

village entrepreneurs. But balancing the wealthy few in the upper levels of the urban and village communities, were the great masses of peasant and urban poor who lived on the edge of starvation. Caught in a highly regimented economic order between the pressures of inflation and the spread of money economy, they found that more and more of their necessities of life had to be purchased from their insufficient earnings. In an overwhelmingly agrarian economy, natural conditions of disease or crop failure had immediate influence. Crop failures, as we have noted, were widespread from 1824 to 1832. A severe famine struck northern Japan in 1833, and in 1836 there was a nation-wide famine. By the mid-1830's, the country was seething with displaced peasants and the cities choked with peasants seeking menial employment. The *bakufu* and *han* governments opened relief stations. But the poor were in a desperate mood. Outbreaks of violence and rice warehouse smashings became frequent. Highlighting the seriousness of the plight of the masses was Ōshio Heihachirō's attempted uprising in Ōsaka in 1837. Ōshio had called upon the peasants of the four provinces around Ōsaka to rise up and kill "the heartless officials and luxury-living merchants who profited while the poor starved." His naive plan to capture Ōsaka castle and thereby to take over the commercial metropolis of Japan was put down in a day. But his revolt made a deep impression upon the country—both upon the *bakufu* whose authority had been challenged and on the peasantry.

The general state of rural unrest is associated with yet another mass phenomenon of the countryside which had end-of-the-regime overtones. Beginning in 1814 there came into being in the course of several decades a number of popular messianic religious movements all of peasant origin. Lumped together today under the category of "sectarian Shintō" most of these movements stressed faith-healing and material happiness. Kurozumi Munetada (1780–1850), a Shintō priest of the Bizen domain, claimed mystical vision as the result of severe illness. His Kurozumi sect founded in 1814 stressed faith in the power of Amaterasu. The Tenri movement was founded in 1838 by Nakayama Miki (1798–1887), the wife of a farmer of Yamato province, who also claimed faith-healing powers. The Konko sect was founded in 1859 by Kawade Bunjirō (1814–1883), a farmer in central Japan. All three movements gained extensive followings among the peasant masses and appealed to them by promising a utopian life and protection from illness.

Yet for all the evidence of economic distress and dissatisfaction, one is struck by the lack of more overt or effective protest. To be sure, the age gave rise to considerable evidence of what might be called a "desertion of the intellectuals." In almost every field one could find examples of critics and those who looked with alarm, "Forerunners of the Restoration Movement" as Sir George Sansom has called them. Andō Shōeki called for the abolition of the samurai class and a complete return to agrarianism. Honda Toshiaki urged Japan to strike out on the course of empire, establishing its new world capital in Kamchatka. Takashima Shūhan (1798–1866) devoted a lifetime to convincing the *bakufu* of the need to modernize its military defenses. Sakuma Shōzan (1811–1864) and Takano Chōei (1804–1850) urged Western style armaments upon the *bakufu*. The philosophers of the Mito domain demanded greater concern for the needs of the country in the name of the emperor. But it is significant that these voices of alarm were raised in the main by isolated individuals. None developed a following dedicated to revolutionary action or created a lasting political organization. The same is true also of the outbreaks of mob violence in the cities and villages. Discontent was strong, but it did not feed political or social theories calling for action against the regime. Revolution was not in the air, nor can one find more than the vaguest expression of subversion toward the existing order. Rather, the Tempō era witnessed yet another diligent round of reforms by the *bakufu* and many of the *han*, within the confines of the existing political system.

The reforms of the Tempō era tried again to use traditional weapons against well-known problems which had so far escaped remedy. If there was anything new in the reform attempts it was the quality of desperation and the increasing resolve on the part of the samurai officials to intensify their authority in order to cut through the difficulties which confronted them. Some historians have seen this period as marking the beginning of a trend toward political absolutism which was to carry through into the early years of the modern period. They claim to detect, for instance, a new fusion of interest between lower class samurai and local producers which led to a compromise stage between feudalism and industrial capitalism. But analogies with European history are particularly dangerous at this point.

Mizuno Tadakuni (1793–1851), the leader of the *bakufu* Tempō reform, was certainly more extreme in his policies than the two reformers who had preceded him; his failure was even more dramatic. Behind his reform attempt the sense of crisis was also quite apparent. Mizuno, who had become *rōjū* (Senior Councilor) in 1834, was a man of considerable administrative experience, having served as both Keeper of Ōsaka castle and Governor General of Kyōto. He was also in touch with Tokugawa Nariaki (1800–1860), head of the Mito domain, who had increasingly taken alarm at the aimless policies of the *bakufu*. Nariaki had memorialized the Shogun on the need for reform in 1838, following the Ōshio rebellion. His words hit hard on traditionalist themes: return to the martial spirit of the past, restriction of foreign trade and contact with foreigners, suppression of Dutch studies, and elimination of "luxury" from government and the personal lives of the samurai. There were many who sympathized with Nariaki, but so long as the old Shogun Ienari lived no change of policy could be contemplated. In 1840, Nariaki, upon hearing about the Opium War in China, was roused to action in his own domain. He began a vigorous program of "spiritual strengthening" among his retainers, coupled with a domain-wide cadastral survey in order to tighten up on the collection of agricultural taxes. His efforts had little long-range economic effect, but the domain was stirred up to a high emotional pitch.

When in 1841 Ienari died, Mizuno was made chairman of the *rōjū* and encouraged to take firm action. He began by a drastic house cleaning in which some 1,000 hired officials and service personnel were dismissed from *bakufu* employment. He issued the usual round of sumptuary laws and efforts to "rectify the classes." His censorship of lewd literature caught up Tamenaga Shunsui (1790–1843), a popular writer of comical stories, who died in prison following the cutting off of his hands. Mizuno's agricultural policy called for the usual efforts at reclamation and return of the peasants to their farms. This time the *bakufu* attempted forcible return of peasants found in the cities without the necessary transfer of residence papers. Mizuno's approach to *bakufu* finances was no different from his predecessors'. Recoinage of 1.7 million *ryō* in 1841–1842 was followed in 1843 by a demand of nearly 2 million *ryō* in forced loans from a list of 700 merchants in Edo, Ōsaka, Kyōto, and other cities.

It is clear that Mizuno recognized the failing capacity of the shogunate to maintain its authority over the country at large, and several of his measures were conceived as means of strengthening the *bakufu* at the expense of the daimyo. Strangely anachronistic was the costly progress to Nikkō staged in 1843, presumably as a means of boosting Tokugawa morale and *bakufu* prestige. More practical, but unhappily ill-conceived, was the plan to create a solid geographical base for *bakufu* rule by physically moving certain bannermen and daimyo out of the immediate environs of Edo and Ōsaka. The plan, which was never executed, was to clear an area twenty-five miles square around Edo and twelve miles square around Ōsaka, thereby giving the *bakufu* unimpaired control over the two centers most crucial to the shogunate's economic and political power.

Most controversial of Mizuno's reform policies was his abolition in 1841 of all *bakufu*-licensed monopolies (*kabunakama*) and wholesale organizations (*tonya*). His motives appear to have been sincere enough, for he hoped thereby to pull down what he thought was the artificially high price level, and his abolition decree was followed by others which called for a 20 percent cut in prices, wages, and rents. But chaos followed this act. Circulation of commodities was thrown into confusion, and as a result prices soared even higher. The

239

bakufu simply did not have the means of regulating the economy.

Mizuno's Tempō reforms not only failed but stirred up widespread resentment. Tokugawa Nariaki bitterly opposed the Nikkō progress. The Lord of Kii opposed the plan to transfer territory, since it would have affected him. The abolition of commercial associations brought such confusion into the commercial world that they were reinstated in 1851. Thus all in all the reforms demonstrated the ineptitude of the *bakufu* and opened up dangerous fissures of conflict within the Tokugawa camp. The main collateral houses were now becoming concerned over the way the *rōjū* were running the *bakufu*. And between the *bakufu* and the country at large ill will was also gathering.

The *bakufu* was not alone in attempting to meet the crisis of the Tempō era. Most of the large *han* were also caught up in the reform spirit. Some had begun their efforts earlier. The Yonezawa domain, for instance, had recovered from a bankrupt state by the most drastic practice of reduction in expenses and aid to the agricultural sector. The Mito reform, also based on retrenchment, had proved less successful, however. The two best-known, and ultimately the most significant, reforms were those of Chōshū and Satsuma. Chōshū, saddled with a debt of some 1.6 million *ryō*, had been shaken by a violent peasant uprising involving some 2,000 persons (some estimates go as high as 60,000) in 1831 over various grievances including high taxes, produce monopolies, and maladministration. In 1837, under the leadership of Murata Seifū (1783–1855), the *han* was placed under a strenuous retrenchment program. One of Murata's first moves was to call for a full-scale resurvey of the land, after which the *han* adopted a more equitable tax procedure which quieted peasant unrest. Unprofitable *han* monopolies were converted to protect merchant enterprises. Reorganization of *han* finances provided for the establishment of a revolving fund for the repayment of private (largely samurai) debts. The *han*'s main debt was readjusted so as to permit long-term repayment. Meanwhile services rendered ships and goods in transit through the Straits of Shimonoseki brought in important profits which could be turned to the improvement of Chōshū's military organization and the purchase of Western equipment.

Satsuma began its reform in 1840 under the direction of Zusho Hirosato (1776–1848), a samurai of administrative ability who rose to become *karō* in the Shimazu service. Zusho started by converting the *han*'s staggering debt into a 250 year non-interest-bearing loan and then proceeded to build up the *han*'s commercial advantages, using the Ryūkyū trade and the area's sugar production. A sugar monopoly was established which obliged farmers to plant assigned quotas of sugarcane and sell their crops to the *han* authorities at fixed low prices. The cane was then processed and sold in Ōsaka through a monopoly organization at enormous profit.

Satsuma and Chōshū were relatively successful in their reforms, which represented different but basically similar approaches to the Tempō crisis. Chōshū tended to work on the agrarian base, tightening it and improving the overall management of *han* finances. Satsuma used the *han* monopoly system. Both techniques required a strong hand at the helm. Both required the vigorous assertion of political authority over the commercial sources of capital, and both emphasized the mercantilist slogan "enrich the territory and strengthen its military capacity" (*fukoku-kyōhei*).

By the mid-1840's domestic problems had clearly created something of a crisis mood in the country. Failure of the *bakufu* reform caused resentment and frustration. With the shadow of the Western powers now falling upon Japan, the urge to take strong authoritarian action was in the air. And in the process new administrative and economic policies were being attempted. Yet a final assessment of Japan's condition in 1844, the last year of Tempō, cannot dwell completely on the sense of malaise—of frustration and failure. The essential residue of any assessment must be that Japan was a country in motion. Internal problems were recognized for what they were, and the threat of the West was not minimized. That a will to reform had been aroused is significant. And while the efforts were often misguided, the variety of responses which the *baku-han*

241

system elicited was bound to produce successes if only by chance. As of 1844, decentralization was one of Japan's major national assets, for in every part of the country the daimyo and their samurai administrators were aroused to their political and economic needs, not simply as local elements of a centralized bureaucracy, but in terms of their own territorial well-being and security. When the crisis worsened after 1853, vast numbers of the samurai class entered the political arena filled with the zeal to defend their country and to reform its political structure.

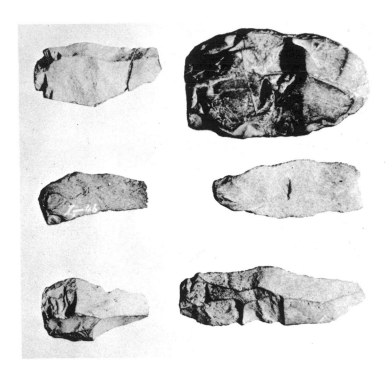

1. Stone implements found at Iwajuku: evidence of a pre-ceramic culture in Japan

2. Middle period Jōmon vessel with incised decoration and on its base the typical "rope pattern"

3. Wheel-turned Yayoi pottery

4. *Haniwa* figurine in the form
of an armor-clad warrior

5. Shrine at Ise dedicated to
Amaterasu Ōmikami

6. Tomb of Nintoku Tennō showing the typical
"keyhole" style construction

7. A remarkably preserved example of seventh-century Buddhist
architecture: Hōryūji, founded by Shōtoku Taishi

8. Ganjin, the Chinese priest, founder of Tōshōdaiji

9. The Shaka Trinity, dated 623, the central figure at Hōyūji

10. Aerial view of
the Okayama Plain
showing remains of
the *jōri* field system

11. Audience hall: The Imperial Palace, Kyōto.
The building is an eighteenth-century reconstruction

12. Courtiers mourn the death of an emperor

13. A petty samurai with his peasant attendants

14. Minamoto-no-Yoritomo, founder of the Kamakura shogunate

15. The Kamakura Daibutsu, erected in 1242

16. Ashikaga Takauji, founder of the Ashikaga shogunate

17. Daitokuji: a major Zen center in Kyōto

18. Ginkakuji (the Silver Pavilion), part of Yoshimasa's Higashiyama villa, completed in 1493 after his death

19. The garden at Daisen'in, one of the sub-temples of Daitokuji

20. A modern performance of *nō* drama

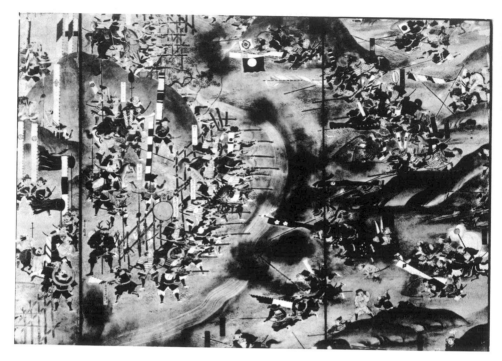

21. Battle of Nagashino, 1575.
Here firearms, first used on a large scale,
won the day for Nobunaga

22. Toyotomi Hideyoshi in court robes

23. The martyrdom of 1596
(an illustration published in Manila by the Franciscan press, 1744)

24. The Dutch at Deshima

25. Himeji castle,
typical of the
daimyo headquarters of
the Tokugawa period

東海道
五拾三次
之内

日本橋

26. Nihombashi, the center of Edo's commercial quarters,
from a print by Hiroshige

27. Scene from a *kabuki* play

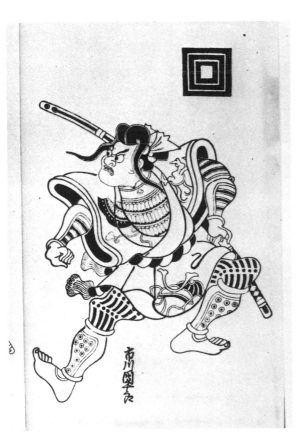

28. Ichikawa Danjūrō I,
the actor, in a
characteristic pose
(about 1697)

29. Geisha and attendant as depicted by Kiyonaga

30. Commodore Perry confronts the Japanese in 1853

31. The foreign concession at Yokohama

32. Members of the Iwakura Mission, 1871
From left to right: Kido, Ōkubo, Iwakura, Itō, and Yamaguchi

33. Prince Itō

34. Traffic in downtown Ōsaka, 1929

35. The London Naval Conference, 1930

36. The first Konoe cabinet, 1937

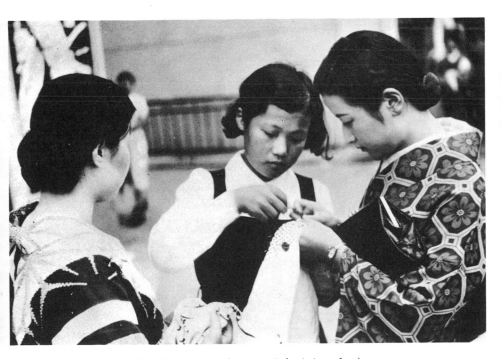

37. Women sewing *senninbari* (amulets)
for soldiers fighting on the continent

38. The destruction of Pearl Harbor, December 7, 1941

39. General Tōjō as Premier, 1941

40. The Diet Building

41. Downtown Tokyo, 1966

42. The superspeed train, the Hikari (speed: 155 m.p.h.)

43. Mechanics building the Japan Material Testing Reactor

44. A 276,000-ton tanker under construction
at the Second Yokohama Shipyard of the Ishikawajima-Harima
Heavy Industries

45. Tōkai power plant of the Japan Atomic Power Generation Co.
—Japan's first nuclear power plant

11

The Gathering Foreign Crisis

From the domestic frustrations of the Tempō period, Japan was plunged into the uncertainties of foreign crisis. One decade after Mizuno's failure at shogunal reform, Japan found itself on the threshold of what was to prove the most traumatic chapter in its entire history, when within a brief century nearly every aspect of its life—its government, economy, social structure, and style of living—were all to be radically altered under Western influence. Japan's confrontation with the West, like the earlier encounter with Chinese civilization, was to force a major turning point in its history. But the common assumption that Japan was simply overwhelmed by foreign influence holds no more for the nineteenth century than it did for the seventh. Japan was not simply the passive object of "Westernization" after 1853, but was to become an active participant in its own development as a modern society.

Our thinking about Japan's transformation after 1853 is helped, therefore, if we differentiate between two processes: Westernization and modernization. To say that Japan was Westernized after 1853 implies too great a cultural passivity on the part of the Japanese, a willingness literally to abandon their traditional culture for something new from out of the West. To say that Japan "became modern" after 1853 puts the emphasis on a more universal process, one in which the Japanese themselves served as active and creative participants. For surely the last hundred years of Japanese history showed more than a blind effort on the part of the Japanese to imitate the ways of Western Europe and North America. In twentieth-century Japan a long established cultural tradition and deep-running internal currents of change commingled with influences from the West to produce a modern society which nonetheless has retained an identity of its own.

Historically, of course, it was in the West that societies first underwent the many interrelated changes which produced the modern condition, and it is certainly hard to imagine that Japan would have initiated the revolutionary reforms of the 1860's and 1870's had there not been a "Western impact." Japan in the years of the Tempō crisis may have been groping toward some form of "new society," yet the necessary drive to break the restrictions of the Tokugawa system was missing. This impetus first came from the West.

The modern condition, being historically the result of the evolution of Western society, originated with changes which became evident in Europe during the eighteenth century. The new European societies were, first of all, the product of the eighteenth century wars of consolidation which forged a new style of nation state; they were the product of social revolutions which brought the individual into closer participation with national life, supported by ideas of political representation, universal education, and universal military service; they were the products of spiritual revolutions which came in the wake of the Protestant Reformation and the growth of rationalistic, scientific thought; and finally they were the products of an economic revolution marked by the growth of science and industry. By the outbreak of the French Revolution in 1789 the people of Europe were on the verge of an explosion which was to carry them across the globe in a new wave of expansion and colonization. After 1800, at first traders, then diplomats and soldiers, then missionaries, educators, and scholars spread out through the world in such numbers and with such persistence and superior force that they placed their imprint on the entire world. This was the modern "Western impact" which was to strike Japan so dramatically in 1853.

We can assume that no people, even the pioneers among the modernizers, were able to undergo the profound changes

244

involved in modernization without the most disturbing internal consequences. For non-European people such as the Japanese and Chinese, the experience was made all the more traumatic because it was to greater or lesser degree forced upon them by the influence of a radically different and alien culture. Since for them modernization literally began with Westernization, an element of cultural shock was added which made the process of institutional and intellectual revolution doubly difficult and complex. The late-modernizing societies of Asia were each faced with a remarkably similar series of challenges as they met the Western impact. The "opening" of China and Japan involved the forceful intrusion of the Western presence in these countries as each was obliged to open trading ports to Western commercial activity, to open their interiors to Western travellers and missionaries, and eventually to rewrite their laws and constitutions to emulate Western practices. The contrasting responses of Japan and China to these challenges are particularly interesting, since Japan had so long subscribed to many of the fundamental premises of the Chinese way of life.

In the nineteenth century both China and Japan faced first what might be called their crises of identity. In other words, both countries were required somehow to acquire a will to survive in the face of Western pressure and to remake themselves into definable national entities. Each nation moreover was obliged to defend its identity if it was to maintain its security in a hostile environment. These initial crises of identity and security were not easily met, and it was only after vigorous new leaders had come to the fore to take command of new governments capable of uniting the previously fragmented human and material resources of their countries, that new nations were brought into existence which could compete in the modern world. But new leadership appeared only after the old political structure had been broken and long-entrenched vested interests had been weakened. In both China and Japan, then, modernization was closely associated with political revolution against the old regime.

Having been brought into existence, however, the new nations faced further problems of development. Technological

245

change and industrial growth were essential if they were to survive economically. A continuous evolution of the political system was needed if their citizenry was to be rallied behind the state and its policies. Changes at first rapid and chiefly inspired from the West, then long range and increasingly the outcome of indigenous conditions, were necessary to bring these people into the modern world. Westernization, in other words, phased into modernization.

The speed with which Japan met these challenges startled the world. There were, to be sure, many special factors such as Japan's location and size, the particular timing of Perry's arrival, and above all the particular condition upon which the Western challenge fell. For whatever reason or combination of reasons, Japan's reaction to the impact of the West was rapid and purposeful from the start. Thus the initial crises of modernization were solved with minimum hesitation or failure of will. Between 1853 and 1877 Japan overcame its double crises of identity and internal security. Between 1868 and 1890 the adoption of far-reaching social, economic, and educational reforms permitted Japan to meet the crises of economic development and popular participation. By 1890 Japan was able to launch upon a program of heavy industrialization and at the same time begin to assert its independence in international affairs. Between 1894 and 1905, having defeated China and Russia in war and having concluded a treaty of alliance with Britain, Japan could sense that it had joined the Western powers on their own terms.

Yet the story of Japan's modernization was not ended at this point. And it is just at this point that historians have asked whether the business-like manner in which the Japanese established themselves as a world power did not mask a number of unresolved problems which were to inhibit the later development of the Japanese people. Had Japan's success of "nation building" suppressed a social revolution, the need for which would inevitably make itself felt at a later date? In retrospect one can say that the outstanding characteristic of Japan's reaction to the Western impact had been its success in maintaining national cohesion at the critical point of transition from a traditional to a new political order—at the point at which so many other countries have dissolved into civil war. The Japanese political "revolution" had been hardly a revolution at all, for it had been contained within the old power holding group, the samurai class, and it relied upon strong continuities in loyalty symbols and political values. Japan had carried out what was essentially a controlled political reaction, and as some have put it, experienced its modernization "from the top." Did the essentially conservative and statist reaction of the 1850's to the 1890's lead, then, to the social tensions of the 1930's and 1940's? Was the drive towards militarism and totalitarianism during the twentieth century made unavoidable by the policies of the 1870's and 1880's? We cannot attempt an answer at this point. Yet one thing is certain; Japan's second confrontation with the West in the years following its defeat in 1945 became the prelude to a second era of fundamental reform which greatly accelerated the later phases of modernization in Japan.

To return to the Japan of the 1840's, the same decades which had roused the country to a sense of domestic crisis had also revealed the existence of a new foreign menace—new in that an entirely new group of foreign powers had begun to press Japan. The initial Tokugawa seclusion policy had been enacted against the old colonial powers and had been maintained with little difficulty for well over a century. But by the end of the eighteenth century, the Japanese were forced to realize that the world about them had changed; a new group of European powers had begun to enter Japanese waters intent on breaking down Japan's wall of isolation. Although not obliged until 1853 to confront the new foreign crisis head on, there was a growing uneasiness in the country for over half a century before Perry's arrival, as the tempo of foreign encroachment into Japanese waters increased and the frequency of incidents involving foreign nationals began to cause alarm.

The first of the new Western powers to arouse the fears of the Japanese was the Russians. Having pushed across Siberia and to the Pacific by 1638, Russians had colonized the Amur

247

valley and had begun a profitable fur trade with China. The lure of furs urged their explorers along the north Pacific coast and down the island chain of the Kuriles. Desire for trade with Japan became compelling by the eighteenth century, particularly as the Russians looked for new sources of foodstuffs. Eventually Japanese and Russians came face to face in the northern island of Ezo (Hokkaidō). Ezo was to the Japanese of the Tokugawa period still a little-explored frontier. It was permanently inhabited by the Japanese only in the southern portion where the daimyo of Matsumae retained a special frontier status, being exempted from the necessity of appearing at Edo for *sankin-kotai* service. But in the eighteenth century Ezo had become important to the shogunate as a source of marine products which served as one of the main items of trade with the Chinese at Nagasaki. Thus a contract trade in dried seaweed and sea ears was maintained by Ōsaka merchants who were licensed to ship to Nagasaki for export.

News of Russian penetration into the Kuriles filtered through several channels into the ears of the shogunate and a few scholars alert to the outside world. The early reaction, when not apathetic, was alarmist, resulting in fantastic reports and recommendations. Kudō Heisuke (1734–1800) of the Sendai *han* memorialized the *bakufu* to colonize Ezo and to develop its "fabulous mineral wealth." Hayashi Shihei (1738–1793) wrote in alarm that Japan must be prepared for a Russian attack from the north. Honda Toshiaki (1744–1821) suggested that Japan move its capital to Kamchatka as a base for world domination.

The event which forced the Russian problem into the open occurred in 1792. A Lieutenant Laxman, serving as envoy of Catherine II, sailed into Nemuro harbor in an effort to open trade relations with Japan. He was met by the local authorities of the Matsumae *han*. The daimyo of Matsumae communicated with Edo, and in due time a reply was received denying Laxman's request on the grounds that foreign relations were conducted only at Nagasaki. He was, however, given a permit for a Russian vessel to enter Nagasaki. In this incident we have the first illustration of the sensitivity with which the

Japanese authorities viewed their foreign relations. For following the Laxman visit the shogunate moved quickly to rectify its neglect of the northern frontier. In 1798 the shogunate began an official mapping of Ezo and started an effort to colonize the northern island. By 1802 the Matsumae *han* had been taken over by the *bakufu* and a Commissioner for Ezo (*Ezo bugyō*) was established at Hakodate with responsibility for colonization and defense.

Russian interest in Japan continued to mount, particularly after 1799 when the Russo-American Company received its charter. In 1804 the director of the new company, N. P. Rezanov (1776–1807), entered Nagasaki harbor with Laxman's permit. But the Japanese steadfastly refused to make trade concessions, and after a wait of six months, Rezanov left in disgust. His officers in the course of the next few years perpetrated a number of retaliatory raids on Japanese outposts in Ezo and Sakhalin, the result of which was to further alarm the Japanese. In 1811 a Japanese defense post captured the Russian naval officer V. M. Golovnin in the southern Kuriles and held him prisoner at Hakodate. Here he and his companions were well treated but hounded for information on all imaginable subjects. The Russians meanwhile having captured the *bakufu* monopoly merchant Takadaya Kahei (1769–1827) were able to negotiate Golovnin's return in 1813. This was the last incident of note between the Japanese and Russians for several decades, however. Russia had been invaded by Napoleon, and the Russian presence in the Far East was to be almost negligible until after the Crimean War.

Meanwhile the British had begun to probe Japanese coastal waters. During the eighteenth century, having turned their interest to East Asia, the British rapidly pushed the French and Dutch out of the Canton trade. During the Napoleonic Wars, Britain briefly held Java and prevented the Dutch from sending their trading vessels to Nagasaki. In 1808 the English frigate *Phaeton* entered Nagasaki under a Dutch flag in search of Dutch ships. Although it left without carrying out a threatened bombardment of the harbor, the Nagasaki Magistrate, Matsudaira Yasufusa, committed suicide to absorb the responsibility for permitting a violation of Japan's seclusion policy. By the 1820's British whalers had entered the north Pacific in large numbers, and their efforts to secure supplies from the Japanese created a series of incidents. A British ship entered Uraga Bay in 1819, and another landed on an island near the coast of Satsuma in 1824, provoking an armed clash with its inhabitants. As a consequence the shogunate issued in 1825 its order that all Japanese authorities should "drive away foreign vessels without second thought."

British concentration on China during the 1830's and 1840's, and particularly after the outbreak of the Opium War (1839–1842), momentarily relieved direct British pressure on Japan. Thus it happened that it was the United States which became the Western nation most directly responsible for the "opening of Japan." American interest in Japan had been growing for some time. Its ships had been engaged in the Canton trade since the last decades of the eighteenth century, and its whalers entered the north Pacific shortly thereafter. With the opening of the Chinese treaty ports, a new era was opened up in the Far East not only for the British but for the Americans and Russians as well. With the American acquisition of California in 1848 and the development of San Francisco as a port of direct trade with Canton and Shanghai, American interests turned increasingly toward the West Pacific. As they did so, Japan loomed larger and larger on the American horizon.

United States interest in Japan sprang from a number of considerations. There were the practical problems incidental to the China trade and the whaling industry: protection of shipwrecked sailors, the need for provisions, and later on, the desire for coaling stations. There was the hope of trade as well. But two less tangible factors provided the primary motive force behind the effort to open Japan. One was what might be called the sense of cultural destiny, the belief that what had happened to China was inevitable, that the light of Western civilization and progress must eventually be made to shine on all people. By extension, Japan's stubborn refusal to deal with the civilized world and to share its ports with others seemed morally wrong. Secondly there were the pressures of national rivalry between the Western powers which urged the United States to press into the Pacific along the lines of its "manifest destiny."

Americans had made several futile attempts at opening up relations with the Japanese. In 1837, the merchant ship *Morrison* carrying Japanese castaways entered Edo Bay, but was driven off by the batteries at Uraga. In 1846 Commodore Biddle with two American naval vessels approached Uraga, but not wishing to use force, left without securing concessions. It was in this context that President Fillmore commissioned Commodore Matthew C. Perry in 1852 to lead an expedition in a major effort to break Japan's isolation. Commodore Perry, with his squadron of four ships, of which two were steam frigates, anchored off Uraga on July 8, 1853 and demanded the right to present a letter from President Fillmore to the Japanese "emperor" (i.e. the Shogun). The "black ships" with their mysterious dignity and their obvious power symbolized the new capacity of the Western powers to violate at will the land of the *kami*.

News of the American arrival, when it reached Edo, threw the city into turmoil. And in the samurai residences and fencing schools there was many a proud boast that the enemy would be driven from Edo's doors by force. But the *bakufu* officials who were obliged to negotiate with Perry were well aware that Japan had reached a moment of truth. The *bakufu* had not been ignorant of Perry's threatened arrival or of the changing complexion of world conditions. In 1842 Mizuno Tadakuni had relaxed the order to drive off all foreign ships, admitting Japan's apprehension over Western power. In 1844 the Dutch government had sent a naval vessel to Nagasaki bearing a letter from the Dutch King telling of the Opium War and urging the Japanese to open their ports before being forced to do so as China had been. In 1852 the Dutch warned the shogunate of Perry's mission and revealed the contents of the demands he would make. Yet the Tokugawa government was not ready either psychologically or militarily to meet Perry. The presence of the American ships at Uraga revealed the futility of the hastily prepared coastal defenses and proved the utter vulnerability of the city of Edo to foreign attack or starvation through blockade. Abe Masahiro (1819–1857), who as head of the Senior Councillors had the responsibility of dealing with Perry, realized that he lacked the means to retain inviolate the seclusion policy. When Perry left Uraga after delivering the President's letter with the promise to return for an answer, he set in motion a chain of events which would shortly open Japan to the world and bring the Tokugawa shogunate down in ruins.

12

The Opening of Japan and the
End of the Tokugawa System

The nineteenth century "Western impact" on Japan led first
to the opening of the country to foreign commerce and then in
1868 to the end of the Tokugawa hegemony. By 1871 the last
remnants of the Tokugawa system went out with the abolition
of the daimyo domains. The new leadership which seized
power in 1868 proceeded to create a unified nation state and
to enact fundamental reforms calculated to put Japan on the
road to rapid modernization. These events are known as the
Meiji Restoration.

Perhaps the distinguishing feature of the period from 1853
to 1871 is the powerful influence external pressures exerted
on the entire cycle of Japanese behavior. The Western presence was acutely felt first as a threat to national security and
secondly as a stimulus to reform. Fear and chagrin, the desire
to protect the country from possible foreign conquest, incited
the Japanese to alarm and restrained them from the kind of
irresponsible political rivalry which might have led to internal
chaos and even civil war. One senses throughout the period a
remarkable element of control as the contenders for leadership
kept constantly in mind the need to preserve Japan's identity
in the face of an external threat. Hence from the outset, the
internal political struggle in Japan demonstrated a strong
counterplay among the leaders between the desire to defend

the country and the ambition to gain control of it—to serve as protector of the state and to serve private interests.

Yet a definite struggle for power took place. Among the participants in the Meiji Restoration struggle, once the fear of the West was upon them, there was a precipitous rush to tighten the country's defenses against the foreign menace. But the efforts to meet the crisis through the existing political structure failed. The shogunate proved inadequate to the task, and this failure created a power vacuum which brought on a bitter contention for control of the nation. The result was to redirect attention upon the emperor as the historic transcendent authority. Under the imperial symbol, first a desperate attempt was made to patch up new combinations of power between the Shogun and daimyo. The failure of compromise led eventually to the movement to abolish the shogunate and create a new unified state in the name of the emperor. The movement succeeded in 1868, and the effort of the new government to maintain itself in power and to raise Japan into the ranks of the Western powers brought on the radical reforms which completed Japan's modern revolution.

It is only by hindsight that we can look upon the shogunate as a doomed institution in 1853. Certainly, it was inconceivable to contemporary Japanese that within fifteen years the mighty Tokugawa edifice would be torn down. Yet the once proud and all-powerful shogunate had by 1853 become a cumbersome and routine-ridden bureaucracy. And the efforts at coastal defense and military preparation which it was obliged to undertake after 1853 were not only belated and inadequate but a drain on an already embarrassed treasury. Thus the *bakufu* found itself unable either to meet the foreign crisis with firmness or to assert its accustomed authority over national affairs. In 1853, moreover, the Tokugawa leaders were thoroughly divided among themselves over what to do. The *rōjū*, who bore the routine responsibility for policy, were inclined to be pragmatic and accept the need for compromise with the foreign powers. But there were strong interests which called for maintenance of seclusion at any cost. The Tempō crisis had already brought daimyo such as Tokugawa Nariaki of Mito to the fore in the role of critic of the *bakufu*. Over the foreign issue Nariaki was even more intransigent. Claiming that Japan's only hope for the future was to prepare immediately for war and to direct all the nation's energies to driving the foreigners from Japan's shores, he called for the *bakufu* to lead a spiritual awakening in the country to meet the foreign challenge.

The man who bore the brunt of the crisis of 1853 was Abe Masahiro, chief member of the Senior Council. A fairly enlightened and vigorous administrator, he realized that although as "barbarian subduing generalissimo" the Shogun was expected to maintain the seclusion policy and protect Japan from violation by foreigners, it would be futile for the *bakufu* to attempt at the moment to drive the Americans off. Yet the shogunate no longer possessed a mechanism for the assertion of arbitrary policy in dictatorial fashion. The Shogun had become a figurehead, and the Senior Councillors timidly attempted to ride the sense of consensus among the Tokugawa house daimyo. Thus it was that Abe, confronted with an unprecedented problem and lacking the real power to deal with it arbitrarily, "consulted" widely throughout the *bakufu* and the nation. Letters requesting opinions were sent to all daimyo, including the *tozama*, and a report was made to the imperial court. This act, while reasonable under the circumstances, had unfortunate consequences, for it made *bakufu* policy for the first time a matter of public discussion. Of the fifty or so replies of which we have evidence, thirty-four called for rejection of Perry's request; fourteen were equivocal but advised conciliation. Only two openly advocated opening up the country to foreign trade. Abe had not received a mandate to negotiate with the Americans, yet only eight of the daimyo, among them Mito Nariaki, had advocated resort to military action. And on the basis of this, Abe proposed to justify a compromise course. Toward Perry he made every effort to minimize concessions, while at home he put into effect a vigorous policy of military preparation.

Almost every move Abe made led to new difficulties. The 1854 Treaty of Kanagawa—the provisions of which opened up Shimoda and Hakodate to American ships for provisioning (water, food, coal), guaranteed good treatment for American sailors, and anticipated the appointment of an American consul to reside at Shimoda—was itself not a major concession. But an opening wedge in Japan's seclusion policy had been inserted. Meanwhile the act of requesting opinions from the daimyo had placed the foreign issue into the public domain, and the *bakufu* was being criticized or advised from all directions. Abe continued his effort to draw powerful daimyo to his support, appointing Nariaki as commissioner in charge of national defense, and entering into consultation with other collateral and *tozama* daimyo. It was clear that the *baku-han* system simply was not designed to facilitate a united national effort except under the coercive leadership of the Shogun. Abe's effort to bring the daimyo into voluntary support of the *bakufu* only weakened the Shogun's position. His lifting of the traditional limitations on *han* military establishments and on the tonnage of ships that might be built, while calculated to improve the nation's defenses, proved detrimental to the *bakufu*'s absolute position. Abe was well aware that the *bakufu* must exert itself to retain its military leadership. In 1854, warships and armaments had been ordered from the Dutch and new forts were set up to guard the major ports. The next year a naval training school with Dutch instructors was founded at Nagasaki and a Western style military training center in Edo. In 1856 a new translation bureau for Western books was created. But most of these efforts were too modest and too late, and they put a heavy burden on the already shaky *bakufu* finances. In 1855 an earthquake destroyed parts of Edo, killing key personnel in the *bakufu* and putting a further strain on the *bakufu* treasury. Nariaki made himself thoroughly unpopular with the *rōjū*, and the general run of *fudai* formed a sullen faction opposed to opening *bakufu* councils to outside opinion. In the fall of 1855 Abe turned over chairmanship of the *rōjū* to Hotta Masayoshi (1810–1864) in hopes of easing the rift in the Tokugawa ranks.

Meanwhile the problem of dealing with the foreign powers continued to be troublesome. Townsend Harris (1804–1878), the American consul-general at Shimoda, persistently pressed the *bakufu* officials to accept a treaty of commerce. Meeting with Hotta, Harris argued the positive benefits of trade, backing his arguments with the evidence of history. China, he explained, had been opened at the point of the gun, and Britain was engaged in a second war with China (the Arrow War of 1857–1858) which would wring further concessions from it. Convinced of the inevitable necessity of opening Japan to trade, Hotta determined to sign the treaty which Harris proposed. Moreover by diligent work on his part, he managed to convince most of the *bakufu* higher officials and *fudai* daimyo of the wisdom of his decision. A second round of letters sent to the major daimyo revealed that the mood of the country was decidedly more favorable. And so in early 1858 Hotta proceeded with the drafting of an acceptable treaty. The final terms upon which agreement was reached included fourteen provisions. These called for exchange of diplomatic officials, unsupervised trade at Kanagawa (Yokohama), Nagasaki, Niigata, and Hyōgo in addition to Shimoda and Hakodate, residence of foreigners at Ōsaka and Edo, a conventional tariff, and extraterritoriality.

Once the provisions of the proposed treaty were announced, however, opposition rose from all quarters. Mito Nariaki again led the attack. In desperation, Hotta went in person to Kyōto to obtain imperial sanction for the treaties. But here he met unexpected obstacles. The once docile court officials, suddenly finding themselves in a position where their actions had political importance, and still profoundly out of touch with the world situation, refused his request.

By 1858 Kyōto suddenly had become the prime focus of internal politics. Not only had the *bakufu* brought the emperor publicly into the policy-making process, but factional splits within the *bakufu* and among the daimyo had reached Kyōto and had begun to compete for possession of the imperial sanction. Moreover, at this very time, Tokugawa factionalism had been suddenly and seriously deepened by an internal controversy. In 1858 the Shogun Iesada had died without heir. As

257

successor, the *rōjū* and other *fudai* daimyo, led by the greatest
of the *fudai*, Ii Naosuke, favored Tokugawa Yoshitomi, lord
of Kii. The Tokugawa collaterals and other outside daimyo
favored Hitotsubashi Yoshinobu (also referred to as Keiki),
son of Tokugawa Nariaki. Thus the succession issue further
polarized the controversy over foreign policy. Hoping to frus-
trate the work of Hotta and to secure the succession for his
son, Nariaki had actually appealed to the court for support,
thus permitting it to enter into what was essentially an internal
bakufu problem. Nariaki had begun, in other words, an attack
upon the *bakufu* in the name of the emperor.

The unexpected turn of events in 1858 pushed the *rōjū* to
action. Ii Naosuke (1815–1860) was precipitously put in
command of *bakufu* policy as Great Councillor (*Tairō*) with
a mandate to bring order out of the factionalism. Ii had been
one of the two daimyo advocating abandonment of seclusion
in 1853. He now proceeded to sign the American treaty of
commerce without reference to imperial sanction and to settle
the succession dispute arbitrarily in favor of Yoshitomi. Within
a few months commercial treaties were signed with five
nations, thus bringing to an end Japan's two-hundred-year-old
seclusion policy. Simultaneously, to quiet factionalism in Edo
and intrigue in Kyōto, Ii dismissed numerous *bakufu* officials
who had sympathized with the opposition, ordered into house
arrest Mito Nariaki, Hitotsubashi Keiki, and several daimyo
including those of Owari, Tosa and Satsuma, and executed
agitators or outspoken critics of the *bakufu* such as Yoshida
Shōin and Hashimoto Sanai. With this so-called Ansei Purge,
Ii reasserted the traditional dominance of shogunal authority,
and both internal and external problems seemed to have been
settled for the moment.

Yet the quiet was only on the surface. Ii's actions served
merely to drive factional opposition underground, and his
arbitrary assertion of *bakufu* authority left a smoldering resentment. When in the succeeding year foreigners began to
take up residence in Yokohama and foreign diplomats entered
Edo, strong anti-*bakufu* sentiments combined with anti-foreign
feelings throughout the country. In March of 1860 a group

of Mito samurai, resentful of Ii's treatment of their lord and bitter over his foreign policies, assassinated him at one of the entrances to Edo castle. Ii's death struck a fatal blow to *bakufu* morale and the attempt to assert firm authority. For the *bakufu* it was the beginning of the end, for hereafter all efforts turned towards conciliation and compromise. Throughout Japan, moreover, the assassination gave a signal for further direct action. The calm produced by the Ansei Purge suddenly burst into violence.

The years 1860–1863 were marred by terrorist activity directed toward the new foreign residents of Japan and men in authority in the *bakufu* and the *han*. A new element was now abroad in Japan in the form of extremist agitators ready to use the sword for a cause. Japanese have called them *shishi* ("men of determination"). While coming from all parts of the country, these men nonetheless had remarkably similar backgrounds. As young men, they had been excited by the domestic crises of the 1840's and by the growing menace from abroad and had begun to take up military training or national studies in their *han* with a new sense of dedication and mission. The more able of these were sent, or went on their own, for advanced training to Edo, where they tended to congregate in certain well-known fencing schools. There many of them came in contact with the teachings of such Mito thinkers as Fujita Tōkō (1806–1855), whose lord, Nariaki, had so steadfastly clung to a policy of national honor and military preparedness and whose emphasis upon the emperor as a symbol of Japan's identity had become increasingly vigorous. Thus in the course of their training, they had acquired a strong element of political consciousness. Perry's haughty violation of Japanese soil fell particularly severely on such men, who were uniformly anti-foreign at the time and increasingly pro-emperor. Thus in the years after 1853 these men returned to their *han* carrying with them the slogans of *joi* ("expel the barbarian") and *sonnō* ("revere the emperor"). Many of them became organizers of new *han* defense forces, others became advisors to their daimyo or were used as liaison officers to run messages

259

between *han*. These were new positions created by the changing political and military requirements of the day, positions which required youth and vigor. Others became disgruntled and turned to direct agitation, often requesting permission to leave their lord's service and become *rōnin* so as to be free to use their swords without embarrassment to their superiors. *Shishi*, then, it was who cut down Ii Naosuke; who left Ando Nobumasa, chief of the *rōjū*, near death in 1862; who in 1861 cut down Townsend Harris' Dutch interpreter, Heusken, and attacked the British legation in Edo. In 1862 an Englishman named Richardson was cut down by the body guard of the Satsuma daimyo, and Chōshū men turned their swords on foreigners in Yokohama. Early in 1863 men of Chōshū burned the British legation, and later in the same year Chōshū shore batteries fired on American, French and Dutch ships in Shimonoseki Straits.

These acts of terrorism had immediate repercussions both among the Western representatives and upon domestic politics. The powers, determined to secure compliance to the letter of the treaties and to retaliate for the acts of violence against their nationals, resorted to strong-arm tactics. Furthermore, since it had become evident that the shogunate did not have the power to enforce the treaties (in fact the *bakufu* had begun to talk of the necessity of closing Yokohama), the Western representatives determined to take their message to the several *han* and the imperial court directly. In 1863, in retaliation for the Richardson killing, a British fleet bombarded Kagoshima and burned the city. A year later an allied fleet, predominantly British, knocked out Chōshū's coastal batteries and reopened the Shimonoseki Straits. In 1865, determined to obtain imperial ratification of the commercial treaties and to hasten the opening of Hyōgo, an allied fleet pushed into Hyōgo Bay, in a further show of naval power. Meeting *bakufu* officials in Ōsaka, the allied representatives were able to force the emperor to sign the treaties.

During these same years the internal political situation in Japan was undergoing profound change. In the atmosphere of terrorist activity and Western pressure, those in authority, including *bakufu* officials and daimyo, were shocked into taking common cause to preserve the status quo. After 1860, *bakufu* leaders, admitting their loss of national support, sought to make public use of the backing of the emperor and to work toward a coalition of interest with the daimyo. Increasingly the Shogun was obliged to work through the emperor. In 1862, as a concession to the daimyo, Hitotsubashi Yoshinobu was made regent to the Shogun who had once been his rival, and the *sankin kōtai* system was greatly modified. Almost overnight the entire center of political activity moved to Kyōto. In 1863 the Shogun travelled to Kyōto in response to an imperial request, again admitting the revived prestige of the court. The Shogun was now forced to seek political compromise by calling for a coalition of daimyo which would unite with the Shogun under imperial auspices to set national policy. This so-called *kōbu-gattai* ("court-daimyo coalition") arrangement was given its most hopeful form in an agreement reached in early 1864 whereby the Shogun was to conduct the affairs of state in the name of the emperor. An advisory group of daimyo was to participate in policy decisions; but it lacked sufficient unity to function as a group, and it broke up before the year was out.

By 1864 the coalition efforts had proved unsuccessful, and the crisis of internal leadership entered a new and critical phase. It was by now evident that real changes in the power balance were inevitable and that the Tokugawa shogunate was running into increasing opposition throughout the country. Among the *han* a certain few, by virtue of recent financial reforms, or because of the forceful leadership of their daimyo, had been able to undertake basic military reforms, thereby increasing their real power in the *baku-han* balance. Satsuma and Chōshū, in particular, through their contact with the Western powers, had begun to overtake the shogunate in modernizing their armed forces. In these and other *han* a vigorous new leadership emerged to command the new forces or to serve as *han* agents in the increasingly complex and intense rivalry which had begun to develop between the *han*.

Many of the new *han* agents were men of *shishi* temperament whose inclinations were to drag their *han* into the anti-*bakufu*, pro-emperor movement which was swirling around the court. In the years after 1860 some, in fact, had led pro-emperor movements within their *han*. Thus by 1864, with the frustration of the conservative attempt at coalition, the country was literally thrown into a free political competition. And while the daimyo were to remain fairly conservative in their thinking about the future, their activist agents and officers were moving toward the abolition of the shogunate and the creation of a new government under the emperor.

From 1864 through 1866 various groups in Japan were obviously probing for weakness in the *baku-han* system. Kyōto became a hotbed of loyalist agitation, as young members of the court nobility such as Iwakura and Sanjō secretly plotted against the *bakufu*. The shogunate, its initiative lost to the major collateral houses, tried its best to keep order, a task which called into being two military expeditions against Chōshū for having attempted a military putsch on the capital. The first of these was a qualified success but resulted only in the establishment of revolutionary leadership in Chōshū. Another "chastisement" proved necessary. But before a second expedition could be launched, in March of 1866, the daimyo agents of Satsuma and Chōshū (Saigō and Ōkubo for Satsuma, Kido and Takasugi for Chōshū), who heretofore had been at odds, entered a secret compact of mutual support. The second Chōshū expedition proved disastrous to the *bakufu*, whose reluctant units were routed by the newly trained Chōshū troops equipped with arms imported from the British. The once mighty military superiority of the shogunate had been undone by a single *han*. It was obvious that the *bakufu* would have to make a supreme effort to recapture its hegemony or face dissolution.

In early 1867, two nearly simultaneous events brought the political situation to its climax. The conservative emperor Kōmei died, to be succeeded in February by his 14-year-old son Mutsuhito. In January, Hitotsubashi Yoshinobu at length succeeded to the office of Shogun, henceforth to be known as

Tokugawa Yoshinobu (or Keiki). These critical changes in leadership helped bring the political agitation to its conclusion. For the remainder of 1867 three lines of frantic activity are visible through the clouds of political struggle: a last-ditch effort of the *bakufu* to stay in command through internal reform, a continuing effort to work out a conservative coalition by some of the daimyo, and the increasingly vigorous anti-Tokugawa agitation aimed at a restoration of imperial government.

Yoshinobu had accepted the post of Shogun reluctantly. But once in command he gave his support to a vigorous reform program aimed at strengthening the *bakufu* under French guidance. The French, who appeared as the chief rivals of the British at this time, had been backing the *bakufu* in opposition to the British who supported Satsuma and Chōshū. Léon Roches, the French minister, had since 1864 been vigorously at work in Edo, hoping to shore up *bakufu* power. The new *bakufu* plan called for both the expansion of the Shogun's military base and a complete administrative reorganization using the French system of cabinet, ministries and prefectures. But again the reforms came too late.

Meanwhile Yoshinobu worked in Kyōto for a restructuring of the power balance under the emperor, hoping to salvage a position of leadership for the Shogun. He therefore continued to push for the idea of a daimyo coalition, but without success. At this point, the daimyo of Tosa, fearing the growing power of Satsuma and Chōshū, proposed a compromise solution to the problem of political organization. The so-called Tosa Memorial called for the Shogun to resign in favor of a council of daimyo working under the emperor. The Shogun's political authority would be returned to the emperor, but the head of the Tokugawa house would retain his lands, and, as the greatest power in the land, would continue to serve as prime minister. Yoshinobu accepted this proposal in November of 1867. His resignation brought into being an "imperial restoration" in the name of the shogunate.

This solution was not acceptable to either the more radical members of the court nobility or the activist leaders of Satsuma,

Chōshū and a number of other *han*. On January 3, 1868 (according to the Japanese calendar, the 9th day of the 12th month of 1867) armed contingents from Satsuma *han*, along with those of Echizen, Owari, Tosa and Aki, seized the palace against the Tokugawa and announced a new restoration. A council was called, from which Tokugawa partisans were excluded, and a formal return of administration to the emperor was announced. A government structure which purportedly went back to the "time of Emperor Jimmu" was drawn up, the shogunate was declared abolished and its lands confiscated, and Yoshinobu was reduced to the level of a common daimyo. This was the Meiji Restoration of 1868.

A civil war followed the Meiji *coup d'état* but was short-lived and essentially half-hearted. Yoshinobu, who had accepted the January 3rd announcement and had withdrawn his troops to Ōsaka, was unable to restrain some of his commanders. On January 27 an attempt by Tokugawa forces to recapture Kyōto was beaten off by the superior arms of the Satsuma, Chōshū and Tosa contingents. This battle fought at Toba-Fushimi ended the Tokugawa hegemony just as surely as the great engagement of Sekigahara had created it two hundred and sixty eight years before. The revolutionary government now branded the Tokugawa "enemies of the throne." An imperial prince, Arisugawa, was put in command of an "imperial army" (mostly Satsuma and Chōshū troops) which marched upon Edo. There Yoshinobu surrendered peacefully. North of Edo, the Aizu *han*, one of the Tokugawa collaterals, held out for several months of bloody fighting but capitulated in November. The shogunal navy, retreating to Hokkaidō, held out until May of 1869. With its surrender, Tokugawa resistance ended, and the new government acquired control of the entire country. Already the new leadership had begun to move in the direction of far-reaching political and institutional change.

13

The Meiji Restoration and Its Meaning

The events of January 1868 brought to sudden demise the Tokugawa shogunate and created in its stead a new center of authority under the symbol of the emperor. Japan had achieved a new national unity by destroying the dual system of government which had existed since the time of the Kamakura shogunate. At a crucial moment the emperor had been returned to the center of government. The long historic separation between a reigning sovereign and a ruling authority had in fact proved a blessing. For in the moment of crisis, when Japan faced the Western menace, the emperor provided a new rallying point for the nation. The old order was attacked in the name of a transcendent and still more ancient sanction which was moreover supremely "Japanese." Japan's initial reaction to the Western impact was taken in the name of a "return to the past" (*fukko*). To this extent a "restoration" had taken place. The new government returned to a direct public reliance on the supreme authority of the emperor (*ōsei*), though in characteristic fashion the emperor continued to stand above the machinery of government and the struggle for power.

The Restoration proved to be more than just a reshuffling of political influence. While the initial political settlement of January 1868 had resulted in a distinctly conservative coalition composed of imperial princes, court nobles, daimyo and their agents, the momentum of political change, and further of social and economic reform, eventually carried far beyond the simple act of destroying the shogunate. Of transcendent importance to the men who engineered the Restoration was the objective of strengthening the country to meet the threat from abroad, and to this purpose they adopted the slogan *fukoku-kyōhei* ("to prosper the state and strengthen its armed forces"). By 1871 in the name of this slogan, the daimyo had been dispossessed, the samurai class had been abolished, social equality and freedom of individual movement had been promulgated, and an all-out effort to recreate Japan along Western lines had been begun. The Restoration thus marked Japan's transition to modernity, and as such it proved to be one of the pivotal events in Japanese history.

Historians have debated long and heatedly over the meaning of the Restoration in this larger sense. The question of whether the Restoration should be considered a "revolution" is generally asked in the context of comparison with European history. But while Japan underwent the most dramatic political and cultural changes during the 1860's and 1870's, the framework of action and motivation differed in many fundamental ways from those of the modern revolutions of Europe. Japan saw little of the social antagonisms or political ideologies which fired the French or Russian revolutions. There were no mobs in the streets nor rolling of heads. That economic and social factors had much to do with the events of the Restoration period is undeniable. There were peasant uprisings. But though they had increased in numbers and violence, they remained local and non-political to the end. They gave rise to no universal slogans of social or political protest. The merchants, too, though perhaps dissatisfied with the restrictions they were forced to endure, had, in the main, found ample scope for their economic ambitions. The Meiji Restoration was neither a bourgeois nor a peasant revolution, although both peasants and merchants were found among the individuals who led the attack on the shogunate. The leadership for a change came mainly from another source, from within the samurai class itself. Thus while it is possible to make limited comparisons between the anti-Tokugawa movement and the early phases of the revolutionary movement in Russia, it would be difficult to find valid comparisons between the Restoration and the later course of the Russian Revolution or of the French Revolution. The two outstanding features of the entire Restoration period were the overwhelming sense of foreign crisis which gripped the country and the manner in which a new leadership drove to the fore from out of the samurai class.

Moments of crisis have a way of throwing great men upon the stage of history. Japan has rarely if ever produced a larger number of able leaders than during the period from the 1850's through the 1880's. It was these men who gave the main thrust to the Restoration movement and to the reforms which followed. What motivated them, and why they appeared when they did, is probably the most fundamental question which can be asked about the Restoration era. The explanations that these men were simply seized with an overwhelming sense of loyalty toward the emperor or that they were inspired mainly by the desire to emulate the West are clearly too simplistic. A theory made popular by E. H. Norman—that they were an extrusion from out of the ranks of disaffected lower class samurai and that they represented indirectly the momentum of a bourgeois revolution—has been undercut by recent scholarship. The Restoration leaders came from many levels of the samurai class, and their actions carried little sense of class or group motivation; nor did they conceive of themselves as using the resources of their class for revolutionary purposes. The theory most prevalent among postwar Japanese scholars—that the Restoration represented a reconsolidation of the samurai class in an effort to retain control of the country in the face of the revolutionary forces of peasant unrest and expanding mercantile capital, that it was in other words a counter-revolutionary drive toward political absolutism—is also too clearly an effort to put Japanese history into an illustrated European mold.

It is in terms of a group of individuals of heterogeneous background and varying private ambitions that we must see the motivations behind the Restoration. While all told there are well over a hundred individuals who have been identified

267

as leaders of the Restoration movement, we need in fact consider only a much smaller group of primary leaders:

FROM THE COURT:

Sanjō Sanetomi (1837–1891)
Iwakura Tomomi (1825–1883)

FROM SATSUMA:

Okubo Toshimichi (1830–1878)
Terashima Munenori (1833–1893)
Godai Tomoatsu (1835–1885)
Saigō Takamori (1828–1877)
Kuroda Kiyotaka (1840–1900)
Matsukata Masayoshi (1837–1924)

FROM CHOSHU:

Takasugi Shinsaku (1839–1867)
Kido Kōin (1833–1877)
Ōmura Masujirō (1824–1869)
Itō Hirobumi (1841–1909)
Inoue Kaoru (1835–1915)
Yamagata Aritomo (1838–1922)
Hirosawa Saneomi (1833–1871)

FROM TOSA:

Itagaki Taisuke (1837–1919)
Gotō Shōjirō (1837–1897)
Fukuoka Kōtei (1835–1919)
Sakamoto Ryōma (1835–1867)

FROM HIZEN:

Etō Shimpei (1834–1874)
Ōkuma Shigenobu (1838–1922)
Soejima Taneomi (1828–1905)
Ōki Takatō (1832–1899)

OTHERS:

Yokoi Shōnan (1809–1869, Kumamoto)
Katsu Kaishū (1823–1899, *bakufu*)
Yuri Kimimasa (1829–1909, Fukui)
Inoue Kowashi (1844–1895, Kumamoto)

About this group there are a number of elementary generalizations which come first to mind. Most of them came from four large *tozama han* of western Japan, which shared a traditional antagonism to the Tokugawa house. They were as a group remarkably young, the average age being slightly over thirty in 1868. They were for the most part brought up in families of lower-class samurai, though some, such as Kido, were of high status. As youths they were vigorous and ambitious, and most began their careers in the traditional manner, pressing up the ladder of preferment in their *han,* notably in military service. Not being of a landed aristocracy, their ambitions could be met by success only in government service. And because of the decentralization of the *baku-han* system they found a large number of political arenas in which to prove themselves. As in prerevolutionary America, the Japanese "founding fathers" learned to become leaders of men in their home territories before they became leaders of the nation.

Characteristic of the Restoration leaders was their uniformly high level of education and specialized training. Most had gained recognition in their *han* for military skills or scholarship. As a consequence they all had active early careers, serving as advisors to their daimyo, as diplomatic agents or as organizers of new military units. The military career was perhaps the most common. Saigō, Ōmura, Etō, Hirosawa, Itagaki and many others were foremost military commanders of *han* units. Itō was used as an interpreter, Kido was a chief daimyo advisor. The kind of education these men received was also significant. Brought up as samurai to endure rigorous military discipline (many of the group became excellent swordsmen), they were trained to be men of action and to cultivate a martial disposition. The intellectual content of their schooling was predominantly Confucian, stressing loyalty and dedication to society. Thus, though their personal ambitions were strong, they also were highly sensitized to national problems and inculcated with the idea of service to higher authority. *Shishi* that they were, most had been fired by the desire to save their country or serve their daimyo. Yet few could be considered bigoted or blind in their political views. Several had been abroad by

269

1868 (Godai, Itō and Inoue had been to England; Katsu had taken a Japanese ship across the Pacific), others had had associations with Westerners in Japan (Ōkubo, Saigō and Ōkuma had had long talks with Satow, the English interpreter). Though most *shishi* started out in 1853 violently anti-foreign (Itō had taken part in the attack on the British legation in 1863), the most fanatical had been killed off early, and those who remained were, by 1868, convinced of the superiority of Western civilization. This change of heart which came to nearly all of the Meiji leaders was in most instances the incident which converted them from being strictly restorers to becoming reformers.

As of 1867 it is hard to generalize on the overall aims of the Restoration leaders. They were, in fact, still a diverse group of individuals working within their *han* or as independent agitators. Many were known to each other from fencing school days or because they had negotiated with each other on behalf of their domains, but they were not joined in a concerted plan of action. They were still not individually powerful, and they were able to influence events only by maneuvering the resources of their *han* and using the prestige of their superiors. Most were in fact still serving as the appointed commanders of *han* military units or as political agents for their daimyo. Thus the first move was to eliminate the *bakufu* and gain control of the emperor on behalf of their daimyo. Having done this their next two objectives were, as we have noted, to secure the state and to strengthen it against the West. In the process of achieving these objectives, personal ambition combined with statesmanship to draw the active agents into positions of leadership from which they could direct their nation toward fundamental reform.

In the early months of 1868 the new government was little more than a new coalition of *han* held together chiefly by the superior strength of Satsuma and Chōshū and the prestige of the court. Tosa and Hizen were brought in to give stability. (Hence the phrase Satchō-dohi, referring to the four primary *han*.) But the balance of power was still precarious. Gradually, behind the facade of daimyo and high courtiers who provided the public face of the new power coalition, the samurai activists to whom most of the practical affairs of government were delegated drew together as a conscious oligarchy and began to conceive of a transcendental form of government, over and above the *han*. But they proceeded cautiously.

In 1868 the territory confiscated from the Tokugawa House was organized into prefectures (*ken*) and municipalities (*fu*), and young leaders from the western *han* were appointed governors. At the same time agents of the central government were sent into the 273 *han* to work toward administrative uniformity and conformity to central directions. During 1868, through a series of reorganizations of the central government, the figurehead courtiers and daimyo were dropped from positions of prestige, and the active leaders moved up to take their positions. Among them Ōkubo of Satsuma began to emerge as the leading force. In March of 1869 Ōkubo became convinced of the need for further centralization. After seeing to it that the regiments drawn from Satsuma and Chōshū to form an imperial army were strong enough, he and Kido convinced the daimyo of the four principal coalition *han,* Satsuma, Chōshū, Tosa and Hizen, to return the titles to their domains to the emperor. Other daimyo followed suit, and the first step in the abolition of the *han* was complete. While the *han* remained in name, they were now treated as subdivisions of a unified state; and while the daimyo remained on as "governors," they too were theoretically appointed by the central government.

But further centralization proved necessary, and the spring of 1871 found Ōkubo and Kido working toward this end. At a secret meeting which included Kido, Inoue, Yamagata, Ōkubo, Saigō, Ōyama, Sanjō and Iwakura, the decision to abolish the *han* was finally taken. The move was prepared for again by securing a compact of acquiescence from among the leading ex-daimyo, and by reinforcing the central military forces with units from the major coalition *han*. In August of 1871 the ex-daimyo were called into the presence of the emperor and he issued the decree abolishing the *han*. The old domains were converted into prefectures headed by newly appointed governors. The former daimyo were to be pensioned into retirement. The existing *han* armies and guards were abolished, the former castle headquarters of the daimyo were confiscated by the central government. All told, 305 new units of local administration were created. But by the end of the year these had been reduced by merger to 75, all under governors appointed by the central government. If there were those opposed to this move, they had no chance to express themselves; the daimyo meekly accepted retirement to titled and pensioned lives in the new capital. And so Japan was converted into a fully centralized state. From here on the new leadership appeared in full command—an oligarchy able to undertake further reforms with little opposition.

As in the aftermath of the Taika Reform, the Japanese had again executed a revolutionary change in political structure and the distribution of power without carrying out a revolution. Why did the daimyo, especially the four most powerful, collaborate so readily in the abolition of their positions? They were not powerless to resist, nor were they too stupid to know what was happening. The common Japanese explanation, and the one they themselves held to, was that they were motivated by loyalty to the emperor. But we would be naïve to accept this as a sufficient answer. More likely, as in the seventh century, a combination of pressure and inducement was involved. First of all, the steps toward abolition of the *han* were taken slowly and were not made explicit at the start. Each step was prepared for by the acquisition of military power at the center. And hence each step became harder to resist. But also the alternatives offered the daimyo were not so hard to take. There were no guillotines awaiting the dispossessed daimyo, rather they received generous financial settlements at the same time they were freed from the burdens of office. Even the old *han* debts and paper currencies were absorbed by the new government. The fact that the political change was not so drastic (even Tokugawa Keiki was given a comfortable settlement, becoming a Prince in 1903) together with the sense of national crisis created by the presence of the Western powers, gave rise to an environment in which the activities of a handful of purposeful men were able to remake the Japanese state.

14

Creation of a Modern State

The relative moderateness of the political change which accompanied the Restoration meant that the task of creating new institutions of government did not require a complete remaking of the political apparatus. While the shogunate and the *han* were abolished, it nevertheless proved possible to utilize many of the old channels of authority and much of the existing machinery of administration, and thus to satisfy modern needs with small incremental changes. The Restoration leaders in 1868, as they faced the necessity of erecting a modern state structure, were conscious of two prime requirements: first the practical one of maintaining power and gaining a national following, and second the long-range one of giving durable and effective form to the government.

Again the pressures placed upon the government, and the opinions held among its leaders, were divisive and to some extent contradictory. New models of government based on representative principles were advocated by those who had been abroad, while the desire to retain a tight grip on internal affairs reinforced the traditional inclination toward authoritarianism. The new leaders dealt with these problems pragmatically, steering a remarkably astute course between tradition and innovation, between centralized authority and representation of diverse interests.

Faced with a still precarious hold upon the country and still uncertain of the outcome of military operations against the Tokugawa, the new government in early 1868 took two revealing moves to gain a wider following within the nation. In March it summoned delegates from all the *han* to form a consultative assembly, and in April it issued the so-called Charter Oath, a pronouncement of five articles in the emperor's name which set forth the new philosophy of government the Restoration government proposed to adopt. While extremely general and at some points ambiguous in its wording, this document, which was drafted by Yuri and Fukuoka (both men who had been influenced by Western political thought) and later modified by Kido, emphasized four main points: that government policy would be based upon wide consultation (presumably among *han* interests), that individuals would be free to pursue their private aspirations, that national interests would transcend all others, and that "base customs of the past" would be abolished in favor of modern practices derived from the West.

Two months later the first experimental effort was made to draft a national constitution and administrative code. The *Seitaisho*, prepared by Fukuoka and Soejima, proved to be a strange mixture of traditional bureaucratic forms and new Western ideas of representation and division of powers. Under it a new central organ of government, the Dajōkan (thus reviving the name of the Nara Grand Council of State) was established and vested with full powers of administration. The activities of government were divided among seven departments. Of these, the Legislative Department was itself composed of two houses, the upper a Council of government officials and the lower an Assembly (*Kōgosho*) of *han* representatives. The other departments were Executive, Shintō, Finance, War, Foreign Affairs, and Civil Affairs. A separate Department of Justice was established in an effort to effect a threefold separation of powers.

With the capture of Edo, the new government acquired as its main base of direct administration the old Tokugawa *tenryō*. Because of this, and because Edo was the real political capital of the country, the new government in late 1868 transferred its operations to Edo, renamed Tōkyō ("eastern capital"). In early 1869 the emperor was ensconced in the old

274

shogunal castle enclosure with great pomp. A revision of the governmental structure made in August of 1869 further tightened the organs of central administration along more traditional lines. Abandoning the idea of division of powers, the leaders adopted a structure even more closely modeled after the old Nara system. A Department of Shintō Affairs was placed alongside the Council of State. The Assembly was retained, though it met only once before dissolution. And the main operations of government were centered in a Council of Advisors (*Sangi*) and six (later eight) Ministries (Civil Affairs, Finance, War, Foreign Affairs, Imperial Household, Justice, Public Works, and Education). By now most of the figurehead members of the government had been eliminated and the real leaders behind the Restoration were in public view as members of the Council or as chiefs and vice-chiefs of the Ministries. An oligarchy was beginning to take shape, composed at this time of somewhat less than twenty men drawn almost evenly from the court and the four main *han*, though behind them in the lower ranks of the central government there was a great preponderance of men from Satsuma and Chōshū. Hence Japanese have referred to this as the "*han* clique" (*hambatsu*) government. The *Dajōkan* system remained in effect until the adoption of the cabinet system in 1885. Minor changes were made, for instance in 1871 after the abolition of the *han*, and in 1873 with the conversion of the Ministry of Civil Affairs into the Home Ministry (*Naimushō*). The importance of the Home Ministry is shown by the fact that Ōkubo, by then the strongest member of the government, left the Ministry of Finance to become its head. Given authority over the prefectural governors and the national police, it became the prime office through which internal security was achieved and some of the most controversial reforms were carried to completion.

These changes within the central organs of government would have been of little consequence had not the Meiji leaders been able to extend their system of control to the local level. While the new imperial government in 1868 appeared to face an almost superhuman task of bringing unity out of scattered daimyo domains, the Tokugawa territories and the many special holdings of the court and monasteries, in actuality a sufficient uniformity of administrative practice had already developed so that assimilation into a national prefectural system proved relatively easy. We have already followed the procedure by which the *han* were converted into prefectures in easy stages. First in 1868 the central government infiltrated the *han* and prepared them to accept central authority. In 1869 the daimyo turned back their domains to the throne, but stayed on as "governors" of the *han*, then in 1871 the *han* were converted into prefectures, and within a few months were amalgamated into 72 prefectures and 3 municipalities. (In 1888 the prefectures were still further reduced, to 43.) By 1873, with the creation of the Home Ministry, most of the new governors were hand picked from Tōkyō (a large number were Satsuma or Chōshū men), and local administration was fully under central control.

Within the prefectures, at the lesser level of town and village administration, something of the same sort of cautious amalgamation took place. Throughout the period of political adjustment which accompanied the abolition of the *han*, higher authority managed to remain in force so that even the collection of taxes went on uninterrupted. In 1871 an effort was made to rationalize local administration by dividing the entire country into large squares of uniform size called *ku*. These served primarily as units of new and accurate census and cadastral information. For a while, the central government attempted to create a system of local administration based on those arbitrary units. The idea proved a failure, however, and the government went back to a more familiar and congenial arrangement after 1877. The prefectures were now divided into medium-size units by reviving the old Nara period *gun* (districts) and these in turn were divided into the familiar units of town (*machi*) and village (*mura*). But the new villages were larger than the Tokugawa communities, and were created by amalgamation of several older units. The Tokugawa villages generally retained their identity as sub-villages (*aza*) in the new system.

One may well wonder why the gradual tightening up of prefectural and local administration did not meet more resistance from the former *han* administrators and village headmen. Perhaps one reason is that the rapidly changing political situation after 1868, while disrupting the old *han* and village systems, created at the same time a variety of new opportunities for the more ambitious among the former samurai and village officials. Tōkyō became a major attraction for the more capable of the *han* administrators and the prefectural governments provided employment for former *han* samurai and the more able of the village headmen. But aside from this, the new leaders skillfully provided a series of safety valves in the form of new, and for the most part powerless, local assemblies, which made it possible to absorb the energies of a large number of politically ambitious individuals without endangering the force of central authority. The *han* Assembly created under the *Seitaisho* gave even the minor *han* a sense of participation in the new government. In 1871 the government encouraged the establishment of Consultative Assemblies (*Kaigi*) at the lower levels of government within the new prefectures. In most parts of the country these came into being quickly at the village, district, and prefectural levels. Village assemblies thus became a repository for men of local influence (generally former village heads) who might otherwise be deprived of any status. District assemblies were drawn from the membership of village assemblies, and prefectural assemblies were formed by representation from the districts. These groups served both as bodies for the voicing of political ideas and also as agencies through which the government was able to secure backing for some of its more controversial reforms in land ownership and taxation. Since the assemblies were given powers of debate only, they did little to impede the course of policy determined from Tōkyō.

One of the most important consequences of the ability of the new government to maintain its strong and continuous hold on the countryside is that it was able to solve its most critical fiscal problems in a relatively short time. In fact the financial measures of the Meiji government, though less visible than those in the political sphere, contributed equally to the ultimate stability of the new regime. In early 1868, it should be remembered, the central government had no independent source of income. In its early months it was obliged to rely on the backing of certain *han* and on forced loans from domestic fiscal agents. By 1869 the new government had obtained the income from the former Tokugawa lands, but this met barely half of its overall expenditures. New issues of paper currency filled the immediate gap. With the abolition of the *han* the situation was somewhat improved, but the government had also absorbed the old *han* debts (about 78,130,000 yen) and had saddled itself to a staggering expenditure in pensioning off the daimyo and samurai (190 million yen in bonds, 200 million in cash). Financial reforms carried out by Itō and Ōkuma in 1871 and 1872 reorganized the national currency on a standard decimal system using the *yen* as the standard coin. A banking system modeled after the American Federal Reserve plan was adopted at this time and provided the machinery for absorbing government bonds as the basis for new note issues. One of Japan's few foreign loans, 2.4 million pounds from England, also provided a critical element of stability. In 1873 reform of the land tax placed the government on the road to long-range financial stability.

The 1873 land settlement is generally treated as a measure similar to the freeing of the serfs in Russia. No event better reveals the difference between conditions of land ownership in mid-nineteenth century Japan and feudal Europe than the history of Japan's first modern "land reform." In Japan the motivation for reform was largely economic, not social. Centralization and rationalization of the "agricultural tax system" was the major incentive. For this purpose three new procedures were adopted which thoroughly revised Tokugawa practices. Taxes were to be paid by the individual, not the *mura*, on the basis of the assessed value of the land, not the crop. They were to be paid to the central government, not the daimyo. To carry out this revision, "ownership" of the land had to be clarified and new certificates were issued to the individuals who had been held responsible for tax payments under the Tokugawa system. Since the rights of the samurai class had long since been withdrawn from the cultivated land, this meant that the new settlement left no feudal estates to be dealt with, and only portions of forest and mountain land remained in possession of daimyo families, Buddhist institutions, and a few high-ranking samurai. Former "common lands" were taken over by the government.

Japan thus entered upon its new national development with a particularly modern land base in which economic factors were the prime determinants. But the new system carried into the Meiji period certain conditions of tenancy which had come into being in the late Tokugawa period. Thus, rather than give rise to an enclosure movement or to the spread of large farms operated under high-capital entrepreneurial management, the system of intensive farming with its high level of tenancy continued into modern times. With the elimination of the restrictions on alienation of land and the newly systematized tax system the flow of rice land into the hands of wealthy landlords in fact increased. It is estimated that as of 1873 over a quarter of the land was already tenant farmed; by the 1890's this figure had increased to 40 percent. Under these circumstances a large portion of the Japanese farmers continued to pay rents in kind without formal tenancy agreements.

In the final analysis, of course, it was the ability of the new Meiji government to muster military power that gave force to its reform measures and its claim to speak for the nation and its security. Since the samurai leaders of the Restoration were either military officers or men with considerable military training, their skill in maneuvering military force and their sensitivity to national military needs were highly developed. To a large extent the fall of the shogunate had come about as a result of military defeat inflicted by groups in the country which had mastered the latest Western techniques of warfare. The defeat inflicted by Chōshū on the *bakufu* forces in 1866, partially through the vigor of volunteer army units (Kiheitai) which included commoners as well as samurai, and the defeat of the Tokugawa forces at Toba-Fushimi in 1868 were both assured by the superior equipment and modern training of the anti-Tokugawa forces. Having forced the Restoration, the new Meiji leaders were obliged to look to their military power from the outset, first to complete the conquest of the Tokugawa and beyond that to maintain a sufficient force to be able to exert dominant authority over a country in which independent *han* armies continued in existence.

From 1868 through 1869, most of the fighting on behalf of the Meiji imperial government was done by *han* forces under central command. In 1869 a Department of War was created and placed under the direction of Ōmura Masujirō, the Chōshū military genius. Ōmura created the base for a modern national army by founding military schools and establishing arsenals, but he was unable to gain acceptance for a national conscript army. By early 1871, however, an Imperial Guard (*Goshimpei*) of roughly 10,000 men contributed from the *han* armies of Satsuma, Chōshū, and Tosa had been put under the single command of Saigō Takamori. Meanwhile Ōmura had been assassinated in 1869 and was succeeded by Yamagata Aritomo, also from Chōshū. Following an inspection tour of Europe, Yamagata pushed for a military system modeled after that of France. With the abolition of the *han* in the summer of 1871, the old *han* guards were brought under central control, all weapons and military establishments were nationalized, and a national military force without local ties was created. By the end of 1872 plans were complete for the enforcement of a conscription system, and in January 1873 a conscription law was promulgated. The law was epoch-making, since it coincidentally abolished the difference between samurai and commoner. According to the conscription law, all males at age 21 were placed on the conscript registers and made liable for three years of active service and an additional six years in the reserves. Exceptions were made for family heads, heirs, officials and certain professions, and service could be commuted by payment of 270 yen. The country was divided into six military districts, and a peacetime army of 46,000 men was immediately planned. Within a few years Japan was on the way toward the creation of a conscript army fully based on the European system of recruitment and organization.

The social repercussions of the conscription law were as far-reaching as any of the early Meiji reforms, for its effect was to eliminate the last of the privileges of the samurai class. Since the Restoration the effect of several separate actions of the Meiji Government had been to force a social revolution, though one would suspect an unplanned one. Whether the Restoration leaders were impelled by any clear-cut social policies is difficult to determine. Certainly at the time of the Restoration there was no strong expression of egalitarian principles. The young samurai were certainly frustrated by the social restrictions which had hampered their own free mobility, and they did write into the Charter Oath an expression of freedom of occupation. But obviously more important to them than abstract principles of equality was the concept of service to the state. The dominant idea of strengthening the state (*fukoku-kyōhei*) was thus only incidentally concerned with social policy. Moves toward social equality were therefore most often the result of measures taken for other more practical reasons. Class barriers were abolished as a result of the desire to secure freedom of employment, the lifting of the Tokugawa restrictions upon the peasant class came in the wake of a new tax law, abolition of the samurai class came as the side effect of the building of a conscript army. On the other hand special treatment of ex-samurai and ex-daimyo continued for some time, and a new aristocracy was even created. Modern Japan continued to accept a hierarchal conception of society when it seemed appropriate.

Yet revolutionary social changes were consciously adopted by the modern Japanese state. The four-class system was abolished. A free economic society made wealth, education or political influence the new measure of prestige. And in the wake of these changes, Japan was to experience a tremendous release of human energy. The measures which accounted for the abolition of class restrictions were first, in 1869, a simplification of class status. Courtiers and daimyo were designated

281

nobles (*kazoku*), samurai were classed as gentry (*shizoku*) or soldiers (*sotsuzoku*), and all remaining classes, including *eta* and *hinin*, were lumped together as commoners (*heimin*). Before long most of the soldiers were dropped into the commoner status as well. In 1870 commoners were permitted to take surnames and given freedom of occupation and residence. Ex-samurai were permitted to marry nobles. By 1871 the wearing of swords had been made optional. With the abolition of the *han*, ex-samurai ostensibly lost their employment, but as a class they retained their hereditary income in the form of government pensions calculated at new rates which were from one-half to one-tenth of their earlier stipends.

As can be imagined, the financial burden on the government created by the samurai settlement was tremendous. Gentry and nobility accounted for some 2 million individuals (458,000 households), and their pensions alone accounted for about a third of the government's annual outlay. Thus the government step by step reduced these pensions to lump-sum payments, completing the task in 1876 with a compulsory conversion to government interest-paying bonds on a sliding scale of from four to fourteen years in one lump sum. A total of 170 million *yen* was issued in bonds in average amount to each household of about 550 *yen*, not enough at all to support most families on interest alone. The vast majority of ex-samurai were thereby cut adrift from their former positions and thrust upon a new world to fend for themselves. The conscription law of 1873 had in effect undercut their hereditary status as an officer class, and in 1876 they were prevented from wearing their swords. Already their special dress and hair style had gone out of fashion. In the interval since the Restoration, some of course had made their way into the new central and local administration. Others had become officers in the new army or the police. Some entered professions or business and industry, but the majority went downward in the economic (and social) scale, ending up as common workers or even paupers. The ex-samurai who relentlessly pushed forward the policies which dispossessed their colleagues were not unmindful of the suffering of the class. Both through the central government and the various prefectural offices efforts were made to help the ex-samurai by liberal provisions for entering business, by land reclamation, and by government sponsorship of new industries. The opening up of Hokkaidō was in part conceived of as a means of aiding the samurai.

The policies which abolished the samurai class and carried so many other basic changes before it could not have had the uniform support of all government leaders. While the government was united in the objective of building a strong state there were differing opinions on how to proceed. Moreover in the country at large, groups of disgruntled individuals banded together to express their dissatisfaction through the only means they knew, assassination or armed uprising. The conscription law and the tax revisions had stirred up among many farmers a blind opposition to the government. A statement that conscription was a "blood tax" was particularly frightening to the class which had so far been exempted from military service. Rural uprisings averaged nearly thirty incidents a year from 1869–1874.

But it was the opposition of the ex-samurai class which was particularly disturbing to the government. Resentment had been brewing particularly after 1871 when, with the abolition of the *han*, the extent of the Satsuma-Chōshū monopoly of the central government and its ministries became increasingly pronounced. Demands for greater representativeness in government, more public debate of policy, and retention of the *han* system and samurai status mounted. These issues came to a head within the government over the question of policy toward Korea. The possibility of a Korean war had become attractive to several government leaders, particularly Saigō and Itagaki. In 1873, while Iwakura, Ōkubo and other important officials were on a tour of the West, the remaining leaders reached a decision to provoke war with Korea. Upon his return from abroad, Ōkubo, more than ever convinced of Japan's need for internal reform and economic growth, managed to overturn the Korean decision. As a result, Saigō, Itagaki, Etō, Gotō and Soejima left the government in disgust. Shortly thereafter Etō led some 2,500 former Hizen samurai in

283

an attack on the government. His group was easily suppressed, but other uprisings sprang up in Kumamoto, Hagi and elsewhere. Saigō, who had returned to Satsuma and had begun a series of private military schools, soon found himself at the center of a group of some 30,000 ex-samurai set on opposing the government. In 1877 Saigō was at the head of a major rebellion. It took the Tōkyō government some six months of bitter fighting by 40,000 troops to put down the Satsuma rebellion (called by the Japanese the Seinan engagement). Saigō took his own life in defeat, and most of his following was killed. The new conscript army, despite its obvious newness, had proved its effectiveness against the last stand of the samurai.

15

Modern Reforms and
Western Influence

By 1877 the new Meiji state had weathered its crisis of domestic order. Already it had sanctioned momentous changes in social and economic institutions and had adopted a vigorous policy of modernization under Western influence. The process of Westernization was soon to hit full stride. Yet the interaction between Japanese tradition and Western influence was never to be completely one-sided. From the beginning there had been a dialectic process at work in the relationship between Western impact and Japanese response, and this was to continue in the years that lay ahead.

Simply in terms of policy we have noted the extreme ambivalence of attitude with which most groups in the country viewed the foreign problem after 1853. Some favored ending seclusion temporarily to give Japan time to acquire the foundations of modern national power. Others publicly called for expulsion of the foreigner, knowing full well that to do so would be impossible. By 1868, of course, the men of Satsuma and Chōshū were fully convinced of the necessity to learn from the West (at least in military matters) and believed that if Japan was to avoid the fate of China voluntary intercourse on peaceful terms was preferable to involuntary submission to terms dictated by the West. In the years that followed, Japan's leaders were constantly obliged to accept concessions on the basis of expediency or because resistance would be hopeless.

Thus permission for the revival of Christian missionary activity was granted to avoid foreign intervention. Western legal and court systems were adopted in large part in order to induce the Western powers to relinquish their extraterritorial privileges.

But fear or sense of weakness was not the only reason for Japan's quick acceptance of Western practices. Of all the people of Asia the Japanese showed the most frank and unrestrained fascination for Western civilization and its products, and the greatest inclination to dedicate themselves to acquiring knowledge from the West. The Charter Oath had publicly placed Westernization alongside the creation of a powerful state as the two foremost objectives of the new regime. The two were in fact necessarily related in the minds of the drafters of the oath.

The process of Westernization began early. Once Japan's doors had been opened there was little hesitancy about going abroad. The *bakufu* in 1860 had sent a mission of 80 samurai officials to the United States to ratify the commercial treaty. The group was accompanied by the ship *Kan'in Maru,* a Dutch-built warship which made the trip to San Francisco and back with a Japanese captain and crew. One of its passengers was Fukuzawa Yukichi, later to distinguish himself as one of Japan's prime advocates of modernization. A second *bakufu* embassy travelled to England, Holland, and France in 1862 and 1863. In 1863 Chōshū had secretly sent five of its young samurai to England. The group included Itō Hirobumi and Inoue Kaoru. In 1865 Satsuma sent 19 men abroad including Terashima Munenori and Godai Tomoatsu. In the wake of these early *bakufu* and *han* ventures came an immediate stimulus to the creation of Western-style armament and ship-building works and military and language schools. After the Restoration the tempo of exchange picked up. The most conspicuous of the official trips abroad undertaken by the Meiji government was the Iwakura Mission of 1872–1873 when Iwakura, Ōkubo, Kido, Itō, and more than forty other government leaders travelled to the United States and Europe ostensibly to seek revision of the 1858 "unequal treaties."

The lengthy report prepared by the mission emphasized Japan's backwardness and the need to learn from the West, but it also pointed out Japan's strong points (such as freedom from religious bigotry) and the fact that the nations of the West had acquired their power only in the last fifty or one hundred years. Japanese went at the task of modernization with confidence and a sense of purpose.

After the Iwakura Mission the government systematically began to hire foreign advisors in anticipation of needed reforms. The practice had already been started by the *bakufu* and some *han* before the Restoration and ultimately by 1875 there were to be some five or six hundred foreign experts hired by the Japanese government. All told, perhaps 3,000 foreign government advisors were brought to Japan between the signing of the commercial treaties and 1890. German experts were used to organize new universities and medical schools, and somewhat later men like Hermann Roesler and Albert Mosse (1846–1925) were to help in the drafting of a constitution. A German scholar, Ludwig Reiss (1861–1928), was to establish a school of historical studies at Tokyo University. American advisors helped to set up agricultural stations and a national postal service. Horace Capron became a senior advisor in the development of Hokkaidō. David Murray of Rutgers, invited to Japan in 1873, helped establish the new elementary school system. Erasmus P. Smith, as an advisor to the Foreign Ministry, taught the Japanese a new diplomatic technology. British advisors were active in railway development, telegraph and public works. The navy was almost entirely based on the English system. The army, meanwhile, depended on French military instructors. The French jurist Gustave Boissonade served as advisor in adapting the French legal codes to Japanese use. Even Italian painters and sculptors were employed to reveal the secrets of Western art. It was characteristic of Japan's jealous concern over its own identity that all such advisors were placed in Japanese administrative organs under Japanese supervisors. Their services were also terminated as quickly as the Japanese felt they could manage by themselves.

The West, of course, became known to the Japanese in ways other than through official advisors. The treaty ports, particularly Yokohama and Kōbe, became beachheads of Western influence where foreign communities grew up and gave rise to their own cultural manifestations. Besides the rows of business firms and warehouses, the Western communities built residences, churches, schools, and hospitals. The new port communities became the centers from which educators and missionaries pushed into the interior towns and cities of Japan. The inroads of Western civilization into Japan were quickly made and widely spread. And meanwhile private Japanese by the hundreds travelled overseas for observation and education.

It is well to reflect a moment on the nature of the Western world which so fascinated the Japanese. To some extent it must have presented a more hostile front to Japan than does the West of the twentieth century. It came with no offers of foreign aid, for this was the age of competitive imperialist expansion. Yet once the Japanese had managed to hold their own against the Western powers, another element was introduced. The West, proud of its religion and its progress, mindful of its cultural burden and mission, offered advice and aid with solicitous care. In an age of laissez-faire permissiveness in international affairs, the world was open to the inquiring Japanese. The West was proud to share its secrets. In this respect the West presented a more unified facade to Japan than it does today when a major cleavage divides it into two opposed camps. The West in 1870 stood for "progress, Christianity and science."

Yet the West also presented Japan with numerous conflicting words of advice, which posed alternative models for national development. In political organization there were the separate examples of British or French liberalism and Prussian monarchal authoritarianism. In essential values the spiritual demands of the missionaries contrasted with the secular views of scientists and social Darwinians. And so the Japanese of the 1870's and 1880's faced not only the trauma of modernization through imitation of a foreign culture but also the necessity of deciding what features of Western life most deserved their emulation.

As in any case of cultural borrowing, what has been called the "Japanese reaction" was a composite of numerous separate and even contradictory patterns of individual and group behavior. On the one hand there were those who advocated all-out acceptance of everything foreign, those who literally came to detest their own past and its values. "Japan must be reborn," they said, with "America its new mother and France its father." Suggestions, born of the prevalent theories of social Darwinism, that the Japanese would do well to draw superior Western blood into their veins through intermarriage, even had the momentary support of high-ranking political figures like Inoue and Itō. Modification, even abandonment, of the Japanese language was considered essential for Japan's "progress." Rabid converts to Western ways turned their iconoclastic attacks on all of Japan's past, its government, art, literature, philosophies, as products of a benighted, barbarous culture. Western ways for many became a compulsive fad, as Japanese avidly put on Western-style suits and hats, grew out their hair, sported watches and umbrellas, and learned to eat meat. The country as a whole rapidly adopted Western material culture, sometimes with thoughtless avidity. Railroad and telegraph lines were pushed through the countryside, new styles of architecture were adopted for government buildings and factories. German, French and Anglo-American political and social ideas were injected into education and were debated by a score of discussion groups.

From the early 1870's a heated controversy over fundamental issues of Westernization had been in process. Numerous discussion clubs formed in Tōkyō debated the latest ideas from abroad and their application in Japan. Of these groups the Meirokusha, founded in 1873 by Mori Arinori, was the most significant, since many of its members were to become influential in the world of thought and education. Included in its membership were Fukuzawa Yukichi, founder of Keiō Uni-

289

versity, Katō Hiroyuki, later president of Tōkyō University, Nishimura Shigeki, tutor to the emperor, Nishi Amane, later principal of Tōkyō Normal College, and Nakamura Masanao, founder of Tōkyō Women's Normal School. Though the organization had a short life, it published a journal which popularized Western ideas and also discussed the essential differences in values between Japanese and Western culture.

The spirit of early Meiji modernization is best revealed in the slogan which inspired so many of the intellectuals of the Meirokusha variety. "Civilization and enlightenment" (*bummei-kaika*) became the theme of those who saw Japan as emerging from barbarism. For such persons the West offered the hope of progress by its example of enlightened civilization, its science and its social values of equality and individualism. Outstanding among the advocates of "civilization and enlightenment" was Fukuzawa Yukichi, whose *Conditions in the Western World* (*Seiyō-jijō*), published in 1866, became immensely popular as a description of the marvelous new world of parliaments, railways, steamships, banks, museums, and universities which he had discovered on his Western travels. During the 1870's Fukuzawa emerged as a real intellectual leader, interpreting Western ideas for Japanese use and lecturing the country on the need for reform. His chief antipathy was to "feudal" social values and the Confucian dogmas which supported them. His *Encouragement of Learning* (*Gakumon no susume*), published in 1872, contained the famous opening lines "Heaven did not create one man above another nor one below another." His *Outline of Civilization* (*Bunmeiron no gairyaku*), which appeared in 1875, attempted to interpret the meaning of modern civilization for the Japanese. His call was for the Japanese to emancipate themselves from the past, for once freedom is acquired "there is nothing in the world which can withstand man's courage and intellect."

To Fukuzawa, the enlightened qualities of progress and individualism were exemplified in the worlds of politics and education. But the enquiring Japanese mind probed deeper in search of the secret of Western success. To become fully civilized, did not the Japanese have to live like Europeans and even believe like them? For many the real issue became that of Christianity. Nakamura Masanao, one of the Meirokusha, had claimed in 1872 that Western art and technology without Christianity was a hollow shell without a soul. Niishima Jo (1843–1890), returning from years of Christian education in the United States, founded The Dōshisha in 1875 as a college for the inculcation of Christian principles into Japan. With the lifting of the ban on Christian missionary activity in 1873, missionaries began to catch the imagination of the Japanese. For a while they were immensely successful among the ex-samurai, many of whom transferred their deep personal loyalties from their daimyo to the new God of the enlightened West. By 1880 perhaps some 30,000 Japanese had been converted, and the number had tripled by 1890.

Christianity raised the ultimate question of identity and nationality for the Japanese. Was it necessary to become Christian to be modern and progressive? And to be Christian, did the Japanese have to give up their *kami* and their emperor? Below the surface of initial exuberance the struggle for basic values continued. Nor were the Western residents in Japan united in their views. Business men and science teachers were quick to draw the line between science and religion. The ideas of Herbert Spencer undercut the message of the missionaries. The tide against Christianity had more than turned in 1890 when Uchimura Kanzō, instructor at the First Higher School of Tōkyō, refused to worship the imperial portrait because of his Christian beliefs. The storm of protest, which resulted in his dismissal, merely brought to the surface the general hostility to Japan's acceptance of a "foreign religion."

Not only did the pendulum swing away from Christianity, it pulled back from the liberal ideal and from overly enthusiastic Westernization as well. For inevitably the early enthusiasm for Western life set up countercurrents of ethnocentric reaction. Traditionalist reaction, always close to the surface, emerged during the 1880's to urge Japanese to retain their sense of cultural identity in the face of foreign influence. Again one heard the argument that Western civilization was useful for its technology but that Japanese spiritual and ethical values were

291

superior to those of the West and must be preserved; Japan's essence, its "national polity" (*kokutai*) must never be lost. Reaction followed two lines, one which found justification in Western thought itself and another which called for a return to the spiritual traditions of Shintō and Confucianism.

Not all intellectuals, even the most convinced of the Meirokusha group, had been comfortable with the liberal gospel, and many a second thought had been raised over whether liberty would invite license or individualism lead to anarchy. For such persons ideas of social Darwinism and German statism proved particularly congenial. German political theory became the prime rationale for the new constitution of 1889.

The most influential advocates of the revival of Japanese values were located within the government, particularly in the Imperial Household Ministry. Traditionalists concentrated their attention on the field of education and the effort to influence the ultimate principles upon which education should be based. In no area of reform had the Japanese moved more quickly and purposefully than in the development of a new educational system, for the Meiji leaders realized the importance of education as a prime agent of modernization. Yet from the first the question of ultimate values became an issue. Should education be based on the search for knowledge "throughout the world" or should it strive to inculcate the spirit of loyalty and dedication to the state? The Restoration of 1868 had brought to the fore a group of Shintō scholars who demanded the elimination of Confucian-based education in the name of Japanese imperial values. Their influence was successfully countered by advocates of Western scientific training. The 1872 Education Ordinance called for a fully Westernized system of elementary education. But the possibilities of a coalition of interests which would bring a strong Shintō-based support for the emperor together with Confucian principles of personal and public morals remained latent in Japan's drive for national strengthening. The final resolution of these competing ideas came with the promulgation of the Imperial Rescript on Education in 1890, a document which fused elements of Shintō statism, Confucial ethics, and modern attitudes towards the education of the subject for service to the state.

The Japanese search for national identity in the face of Western influence had thus gone through three distinct phases—from eager all-out advocacy of Westernization, to assimilation and modification, to a return to certain aspects of Japanese tradition. The resultant amalgam of thought typified the "enlightened conservatism" of the late Meiji intellectual. Still desirous of the elements of Western progress, he had begun to turn some of his sense of shame in his country's backwardness into a new nationalistic pride which fed both on the evidence of Japan's success in modernization and on the deeply felt sense of attachment to traditional values. Confucian social attitudes and Shintō political ideas were thus drawn to the support of a new sense of national prestige.

16

The Meiji Constitution and the Emergence of Imperial Japan

Despite the many institutional innovations adopted by the Meiji government, the task of creating a new political system remained unresolved for some years. The Dajōkan system had brought into effect by 1873 a highly centralized government in a style particularly congenial to the Japanese political leaders. This essentially authoritarian structure had proved effective in the early years of rapid social and economic reform, and by 1877 it had even defended itself against armed rebellion. Yet it still faced opposition from a variety of quarters, and it still had not solved two fundamental problems: that of meeting the expectations of the Western powers through the adoption of some form of constitutional structure, and that of winning the popular endorsement of the nation as a whole. In 1878 Ōkubo, the Home Minister, had been assassinated for having, as his assailant put it, "obstructed public discussion, suppressed popular rights . . . erred in the conduct of foreign affairs and caused decline in national power and prestige." These words echoed the anti-government grievances of the so-called popular rights (*minken*) movement, which had been gaining momentum since 1873.

Opposition to the central government in the late 70's came first of all from those Restoration leaders who for one reason or another found themselves on the outside of the controlling leadership and from various bodies of ex-samurai who desired more voice in the affairs of government. The claim that the Meiji government had become an oligarchy dominated increasingly by men from Satsuma and Chōshū had already led some to rebel and others to demand more accessibility to the avenues of political participation. Pressure for the creation of an elected assembly started with the early efforts of certain samurai for *han* representation but soon grew into a more vigorous and widespread political movement. Private or regional political interests were fed by ideas of liberty, popular sovereignty, and popular representation which circulated in Japan through the translated works of Mills and Rousseau.

In 1874 a group of political leaders who had left the government over the issue of war with Korea, among them Itagaki, Fukushima, Etō and Gotō, issued a memorial in favor of an elective assembly. Itagaki thereupon took up the cause of popular political action, urging the formation of political interest groups throughout the country. In 1875 at a meeting in Ōsaka he headed an amalgamation of a number of local groups into a national organization called the Aikoku-sha (Patriotic Society). Though hardly extensive enough to be called a political party, this society used a variety of means, such as public discussion and journalism, to bring pressure on the government for the establishment of a national assembly, for the lessening of land taxes, and for the revision of the unequal treaties.

By 1875 the Meiji government leaders were forced to take cognizance of this pressure. Not that they were fundamentally opposed to the eventual adoption of some form of representation in Japanese government. Kido had long advocated the preparation of a constitution which would provide for a parliament and limited ministerial responsibility. But others, notably Ōkubo, had refused to go along. In 1875, however, Ōkubo changed his views and, compromising with Kido and Itagaki, permitted the issuance of an imperial rescript which promised the establishment of constitutional government by gradual stages. A new body of imperially appointed officials called the Senate (*Genrōin*) was brought into existence for the purpose of drafting a constitution.

Between 1876 and 1878 the Senate prepared four draft constitutions, all of them highly liberal in their conception, and therefore unacceptable to Iwakura and Ōkubo. To clear the air, in 1879 Iwakura requested the chief members of the oligarchy to submit their views on constitutional government. All complied with cautious statements except Ōkuma, who held out for political reasons. When finally Ōkuma submitted his reply, he advocated a system of cabinet responsibility similar to the British. Ōkuma had thus broken with the main body of government leadership, who accused him of seeking to use the *minken* movement to enhance his political interests. In 1881 he was expelled from the government, and the occasion was taken by the remaining leaders to issue an imperial statement promising a constitution by 1890. Iwakura had already put a set of fundamental principles into writing for the guidance of Itō, to whom the task of drafting the constitution was given. The constitution should emanate from the emperor, the ministers should be responsible to the emperor, and legislation should be initiated by the government. Japan was obviously already looking to Prussia as the most suitable model for emulation.

Between 1881 and 1889 both the government leadership and the leaders of the *minken* movement worked toward the day when constitutional government would become a reality. Itō made his tour of Europe and returned with a group of German political theorists to serve as his advisors. As the shape of the constitution began to clarify, the government put into operation ahead of time the major non-representative organs of government which would serve as the pillars of the new establishment. In 1884 a new nobility of five classes was established, thus creating the basis for a House of Peers. Five hundred patents were issued to former courtiers, ex-daimyo, and to a select number of ex-samurai leaders of the Restoration who by that time had become recognized members of the oligarchy. In 1885 the Dajōkan was supplanted by a Cabinet in which ministers remained responsible to the emperor. In 1888 a Privy Council of life-time imperial appointees was created for the immediate purpose of approving the constitution. This group was to continue in existence after 1890, as a high advisory board to assist the emperor. Thus by 1888 most of the apparatus of government which would appear under the constitution was in working order. The only missing element was the Diet, which was to become the oligarchy's major concession to the concept of representation.

Meanwhile those out of the government, in anticipation of the new political roles which they would acquire through the elective process, began to organize their followings. Itagaki and Gotō organized the Jiyūtō (Liberal Party), while Ōkuma formed the Rikken Kaishintō (Constitutional Reform Party). These groups, with the support of other intellectuals, newspaper editors, various new financial interests and rural landlords in some parts of the country, were able to mount considerable political agitation in anticipation of the establishment of the Diet. Their activity was sufficiently disturbing to the government that an attempt was made to quiet it. In 1882 the government organized a captive political party, the Teiseitō (Imperial Rule Party), and a year later gave new powers to the police to disband political rallies and to censor newspapers. Itagaki and Ōkuma found it impossible to maintain harmony within their organizations, and by 1884 the Jiyūtō had disbanded and Ōkuma had left the Kaishintō.

The Meiji Constitution, promulgated in 1889, proved to be a remarkable combination of Western political technology and traditional Japanese political ideas. Its philosophy of government, particularly in its handling of the question of sovereignty and the relationship of the emperor to government and to the people, was based on principles which Japanese for centuries had looked upon as their inherited polity (kokutai). The emperor was legalized as an absolute, sacred monarch, above the government and yet the very embodiment of the state. The people of Japan were his subjects, admonished to serve him loyally.

The machinery of government provided for by the constitution remained highly bureaucratic and centralized. The emperor was served by a Ministry of the Imperial Household and an Imperial Household Law which existed outside the constitution and normal government channels. The emperor was advised by a Privy Council and was placed over the Prime Minister and Cabinet, both of which remained responsible to the emperor alone. The Army and Navy Ministers were also placed under the emperor, who served as Commander in Chief, independent of civilian control. Local administration was directly controlled through the Home Ministry, and governors were appointed by the central government.

The small avenue of popular participation provided for in the constitution was found in the Diet and the largely powerless local assemblies. The Diet was composed of a House of Peers and a Lower House filled by a carefully limited elective process. About 450,000 persons, slightly over one percent of the population, were eligible to vote in the first election. Conceived primarily as a body for the debate of government measures, the Lower House had no real powers of initiative. It did, however, exploit its capacity for obstruction and criticism rather quickly. As it turned out, the sole effective power given to the Lower House was that of withholding its vote on the national budget, and even this was weakened by the provision that if the budget for one year was rejected, that of the previous year would automatically go into effect.

Yet to characterize the Meiji Constitution as a blindly reactionary document, as some have done, is not altogether just. While it safeguarded the powers of the establishment, and while it reinforced conservative political and social values, it was nonetheless a modern document, particularly when one considers the age in which it was drafted. Certainly in terms of Japan's own political history the document was a major innovation. For it formed the basis of modern rule by law, and it established institutions through which the further political growth of the Japanese people could be achieved. The establishment of the Diet had been no mere concession tossed to a noisy opposition. Itō had worked hard against heavy resistance in the government to gain its acceptance, and he himself believed that he had provided the apparatus for a true sounding of public opinion and the eventual expansion of popular participation in the decisions of government. The constitution was carefully devised to maintain the political *status quo*, to be sure, but it proved far less authoritarian than some members of the high bureaucracy would have wanted. And once it was promulgated it had the approval of the Japanese press and of constitutional scholars and lawyers the world over, including such men as Herbert Spencer and Oliver Wendell Holmes.

Two constitutional provisions in particular helped to broaden the political process in Japan. Article IV, which provided that government should be conducted "according to the constitution," opened the way for theorists to claim that there could be a law above the emperor and hence that government should be responsive to popular will. Secondly, the Diet and the electoral process provided an arena for party political activity that eventually obliged the government to respond to party pressures and to relax the rule by oligarchy which predominated during the late Meiji period. The constitution therefore provided the vehicle for a highly controlled process of political modernization.

But the Meiji Constitution also had severe defects. Not only did it institutionalize sovereignty in the person of a "divine emperor," it gave a cloak of credibility to the myths and dogmas of sanctification which had historically supported the Japanese monarch. Figuratively and emotionally the emperor remained the most cherished symbol of national identity. The constitution also perpetuated that particular form of Japanese political decision-making which obscured the locus of responsibility behind a "sovereign without accountability" who spoke for the consensus of his political advisors. It was this combination of imperial absolutism and undefined responsibility vested in a centralized bureaucracy which proved so impervious to the representative process in the years which followed.

Whatever its defects, however, the constitution of 1889 placed Japan among the "civilized nations" in the eyes of Western political writers, and this was shortly to be reflected in Japan's relations with the Western powers themselves. One of the major objectives of the Meiji leaders had been to have their country take a place among the advanced nations and thus overcome the shame of the unequal treaties. That by the turn into the twentieth century Japan had largely achieved this objective is generally accepted as one of the great success stories of modern history. For in a brief fifty years Japan was to transform itself from a defenseless collection of little-known islands into a modern empire, victorious in war against China and Russia.

If there had been no subsequent Japanese invasion of the Chinese mainland, no Pearl Harbor, and no atomic bombing of Hiroshima in 1945, the success-story view of Japan's post-Restoration history would no doubt stand unchallenged. But subsequent events were to lead many historians to a more cynical view of Japan's rise as an imperialistic power. Was it to the advantage of the Japanese people as a whole, they ask, that their country attempted to compete so vigorously in the "age of imperialism"? Did the authoritarian nature of the Meiji Constitution and the international policies of the Meiji oligarchy wilfully place Japan upon a path linking national policy to war and expansion to the detriment of the general welfare? Did Japan wilfully choose imperialism as its national style and hence bring disaster upon its people in 1945?

In reply one can only ask what alternatives were open to Japan of the 1890's. Certainly we cannot subscribe to the thought that a plot concocted in the 1880's placed the country on an inevitable path to ruin in 1945. Japan's international behavior was a resultant of many pressures and interests. And if there is any thread of consistency which runs through the years between 1853 and 1945 it would be less an appetite for territory than a desire for recognition and security. From the beginning of the modern phase of contact with the West, Japan showed a determination "not to be second" among the world's nations, and this necessarily placed certain requirements upon its leaders.

As of 1853, if Japan was to do no more than stand still as an independent nation, it was required to build up an apparatus of diplomacy backed by a national capacity to protect its own international interests. Beyond this, to gain some freedom of

300

action required that Japan meet the institutional forms by which the West considered itself "civilized," to establish acceptable laws at home, and to play the game of treaties and agreements abroad. And beyond this, to seek not to be second, that is to enter the field of international affairs competitively, required still more assertiveness. It required a willingness and an ability to harness the cutting edge of national power to diplomacy—ultimately the willingness to take the risk of war. Japan entered the field of imperialist competition with certain advantages. Its leaders took foreign relations seriously. They were willing to put the best national talent into the field of international diplomacy and to put behind that talent the necessary national resources: a modern army and navy, and a vigorous voice of public opinion.

The diplomatic story of Japan's rise as a modern world power proceeded in several phases up to the dramatic moment when Japan emerged victorious over Russia in 1905. From 1853 to 1871 Japan's leaders were necessarily engaged in trading away time and concessions while they learned to master the new diplomacy and the new requirements of international negotiation and national defense. It is sometimes forgotten how much the Japanese were able to learn even before 1868. For on both sides of the domestic struggle Japanese officials, whether in the shogunate or the *han*, had begun to deal directly and often quite effectively with foreign diplomats. Already they had learned from Sir Harry Parkes of Britain or Léon Roches of France some of the fine points of Western international politics. Thus after 1868 the government moved quickly to meet the demands of the Western powers for the protection of foreign nationals in Japan, and in a variety of ways attempted to reduce the pressures the West was placing upon it. It was not until 1871, however, with the appointment of Soejima as Foreign Minister and shortly thereafter, the hiring of Erasmus P. Smith of the United States as his advisor, that the Japanese were able to begin a phase of positive diplomacy.

Between 1871 and 1894 Japanese leaders concentrated on two main objectives: first to define and secure Japan's international status in terms of modern diplomatic language, and second to secure revision of the unequal treaties. The first objective was achieved purposefully and with surprising ease by the new leadership in the Ministry of Foreign Affairs. In 1871 Japan concluded a commercial treaty with China which also recognized the equality of the two nations in terms of the new language of international diplomacy. In 1872 the Japanese asserted administrative control of the Ryūkyū Islands, and in the next year placed the Bonin Islands under control of the Japanese navy. In 1875 the Kuriles were acquired from Russia by treaty and the boundary beween Japan and Russia in Sakhalin was clarified.

The first real crisis in foreign relations came over Korea. It was Korea's refusal to offer immediate recognition to the Meiji Government that aroused members of the government to suggest that Japan force Korea into war. The suppression of this policy by Iwakura and Ōkubo caused, as we have noted, a major split within the government leadership. In 1874, partially in order to mollify the losing faction in the Korean controversy, the government dispatched a naval expedition to Taiwan, in direct retaliation over an incident in which Formosan aborigines had killed some Ryūkyūan sailors. The expedition was costly and not too successfully handled, but it provided another diplomatic victory for Japan. By skillful diplomacy the Japanese managed to outmanoeuver China by casting legal doubt on China's claim to Formosa, and securing recognition of Japanese sovereignty over the Ryūkyū Islands.

In 1876 the Japanese opened Korea, using the same gunboat technique that the West had used against Japan in 1853. The resulting treaty of Kanghwa not only opened Korea to Japanese trade but also included a clause on Korean independence that became the opening wedge for the eventual detachment of Korea from Chinese control. Having established a powerful legation guard in Seoul, the Japanese now began to engage directly in the game of imperialism, competing against Russia and China for influence on the continent.

The same 1870's and 80's that saw these diplomatic advances proved extremely frustrating to Japan's desire to secure treaty revision. Throughout these years the treaties remained a dominant political issue, and prominent figures such as Terashima and Inoue were nationally humiliated because of their inability to negotiate revision with the foreign powers. In 1889 Ōkuma, who was serving as Minister of Foreign Affairs, lost a leg to an assailant who attacked him for his failure to eliminate the mixed court provision in the treaties. But already the tide had begun to turn in Japan's favor. As the Western powers realized that Japan had adopted a new constitution and had put into effect commercial and judicial codes based on Western models, resistance to Japan's demands for abolition of extraterritoriality began to weaken. The break finally came in 1894 when Foreign Minister Aoki negotiated with British Foreign Secretary Kimberley an agreement that was to eradicate extraterritoriality by 1899. The other powers soon followed suit. Tariff autonomy was not to be recovered until 1911, but the most annoying feature of the unequal treaties had been eliminated.

From 1894 Japan entered a new phase in its international relations, a phase which began with its war with China and ended eleven years later with a military victory over Russia. It is an unavoidable fact that the 1894–95 war with China marked Japan's coming of age in the eyes of the world. The relatively easy victory which the Japanese won caught the world by surprise and demonstrated to the Western powers Japan's quick mastery of the modern weapons of warfare. The war also proved that Japan was a power to contend with in the Far Eastern arena. For, despite its still relatively modest forces, its geographical location gave it the capacity to place troops on the continent with great speed. The possible threat which Japan posed to the Western powers gained quick recognition in the Triple Intervention of 1895. Alarmed by the prospect of Japan's further expansion into mainland Russia, Germany and France moved to block Japan's acquisition of the Liaotung Peninsula as part of the spoils from war with China.

In 1900 the Japanese joined the Allied relief expedition to Peking at the time of the Boxer Uprising. Again the Japanese impressed Western observers, especially the British, by the excellent discipline and training of their troops and by their qualities of "pluck, heroism and reserve." Two years later Japan made world history by signing a treaty of alliance with Britain. By this, the first such treaty between a Western power and an Asian nation, Japan secured its most tangible recognition of diplomatic equality. Fear of Russian expansion into Manchuria and Korea still haunted Japan's leaders, however. In 1904 Japan attacked the Russians at Port Arthur and, after two years of savage warfare, inflicted the first major Asian defeat of a European power.

Japan's ability to win its international security and to compete successfully among the imperialist powers was not simply the result of its dramatic political reorganization after 1868 and its skill in the diplomatic game. Underlying these achievements were far-reaching institutional and technological reforms which started Japan on a remarkable course of economic growth and provided the means of competition in the spheres of international trade and industrial development as well. Japan's success in becoming a modern economic complex was less dramatically apparent in these early years but nonetheless remarkable.

The early phases of Japan's social and economic reform have already been described. The 1860's and 70's saw most of the old restrictions on social mobility and economic innovation removed, while structural and institutional changes helped create an environment favorable to economic development. Much of what took place was done without long-range systematic planning, but it was by and large premised on the slogan of *fukoku-kyōhei*. The lifting of class and occupational restrictions, while placing a burden on the samurai class, nonetheless served to release tremendous sources of human energy, driving talent into a variety of new occupations and professions. Meanwhile the government through its revision of the land tax and its establishment of a unified currency and banking system provided the environment within which the new energy could operate.

In the early years after the Restoration, the surpluses that supported the government and built up the financial reserves upon which new industries got their start came chiefly from the agrarian sector of the Japanese economy. Historians such as E. H. Norman have been critical of the Meiji government for a policy which squeezed the farmer in the interest of an imperialistically motivated state. More recent studies by Lockwood and Rosovsky have shown that the government did not play so dominant a role in the national economy and that Japan followed much the same pattern as most European countries in depending upon agriculture as the main support for the first stage of economic growth. What is most remarkable about the early years in Japan was the great energy shown by the small businessman, the steady improvements in agricultural production, and the remarkable willingness of the Japanese to put money into savings even at a low standard of living. In some areas of course the government necessarily exercised its leadership, particularly in the development of arsenals and certain heavy industries. Government patronage was also turned towards the encouragement of steamship lines and railroads. Postal and telegraph service developed rapidly under government management. But the real secret of Japan's economic modernization lay elsewhere.

The real start of Japan's modern economic growth can be placed in the twenty-year period between 1886 and 1905. The former date marks the end of the so-called Matsukata deflation, by which time Japan came into possession of a sound monetary system capable of sustaining large-scale industrial growth. Between 1876 and 1881 the government had been obliged to expand its note issue dangerously to cover expenses of the war in Satsuma and the program of commutation of samurai stipends. A sharp inflation created a serious budgetary crisis and caused a severe shift in the balance of payments. Matsukata, on becoming Finance Minister in 1881, instituted a strenuous deflationary policy, reorganized the banking system by creating the Bank of Japan, and put the government on a sound budgetary system. Under his direction the government became financially solvent and the country at last was given a modern currency system. At the same time an adventurous group of entrepreneurs who had weathered the shock of deflation stood ready to engage in a variety of new enterprises.

Yet it was not the conspicuous heavy industries which accounted for the first statistics of economic growth or gave Japan the base from which to gain its economic security in the world at large. One of the most significant developments at this time was the expansion of silk production for foreign export. Here was an industry which had its roots in the traditional village economy, yet served a growing international need. Once the Japanese were able to modernize the industry and work out the requirements of quality control sufficient to meet the European market, Japanese silks came into great demand. Between 1899 and 1903 Japan produced more than 15 million pounds of raw silk annually, to become the world's largest source.

Next to silk it was cotton spinning that became Japan's great moneymaking industry. With the introduction of mechanized cotton-spinning techniques the Japanese quickly adapted their domestic labor structure to the requirements of the new industry. By moving large segments of surplus farm labor (largely female) into new factories on a short-term basis, industrialization could proceed without undue disruption of the traditional economic base in the rural areas. By 1907 Japan had 1.5 million spindles and was producing nearly 400 million pounds of cotton yarn annually.

With these two industries carrying the main burden in the balance of trade, Japan gradually moved into more diversified production of industrial goods, but it was not until after 1905 that this had much effect upon domestic or world markets. Yet by 1905 there was evidence that Japan had begun to move into a new phase of economic development. In the early 1880's raw silk, tea, and rice had accounted for two-thirds of Japan's exports, and during the next fifteen years only copper and coal had been added as major items in the export trade. By 1905, however, more than half of Japan's exports were machine-made, consisting of cotton yarn and cotton and silk piece goods. Tōkyō, Ōsaka, Yokohama and Kōbe had become the centers of new heavy industries and growing commercial and financial combines. A period of raw industrialization was in the making.

By the end of the Russo-Japanese war Japan had become a regional power in the true sense of the term. Japan was now with justice called "Imperial Japan" (Dai Nippon Teikoku). Possessing an empire consisting of Formosa, acquired in 1895, and the Liaotung Peninsula, acquired in 1905, and shortly to acquire Korea, Japan was a full partner in the imperialist rivalries on the continent. At the head of state was the imposing figure of Emperor Meiji, now grown in stature to fill out the symbol of national dignity. A mature man, heavyset with a strong profile, and generally seen on horseback in his Field Marshal's uniform, he symbolized to the world Japan's newfound national strength, while to his people he became a benevolent father-figure.

Toward this emperor the Japanese people directed their sense of nationalism, which now for the first time welded them into a national community. By 1905 Japan had fought and won two wars against foreign enemies. The wars against China and Russia had been total wars, requiring total national effort. Conscription had cut through all classes; the newspapers and government propaganda had dramatized the national effort and the national aims for which Japanese youth were dying. A new shrine to the war dead, Yasukuni Jinja, became the focus of a new feeling of patriotic sacrifice. Not only had Japan developed a formidable military machine, it had also created a nation unified behind that machine and behind its government as symbolized in the emperor.

17

The Decade of the 20's—Political Parties and Mass Movements

Emperor Meiji's death in 1912 symbolically brought to a close the first era of Japan's struggle to become a modern nation. The new emperor, Taishō, ascended the throne under circumstances which contrasted dramatically with those which had confronted his father. The basic foundations of the imperial state had been laid; the initial tasks of nation-building had been achieved. Japan in the Taishō era (1912–26), faced a new order of challenges arising from the pressures of growth and differentiation within the structure given form by the Meiji Constitution. By 1920 the problems Japan faced were those of bigness, of spreading industrialization, mass political participation, and of increased world involvement. In the words of the political scientist, Japan confronted the challenge of integration within a rapidly modernizing society.

The new demands placed upon Japan in the Taishō era, whether at home or abroad, were in some respects more difficult to cope with than those of the previous period. Increasingly after 1920 Japan looked out upon a hostile world. By 1918 the international scene had changed greatly from what it had been in the early 1900's. The tragedy of the Great War, and the shock of the revolution in Russia, had sobered the Western powers. Ideas of international democracy, fed by thoughts of national self-determination or hopes that a "war had been fought to end all war," and the expectations which surrounded the League of Nations, brought an end to the age of uninhibited imperialism. Japan, however, entered the postwar era in quite a different mood. The country had not suffered from military action, nor had it been drawn into the grip of national hatreds which had so affected the countries of Europe. Japan had done well at the expense of Germany and other Western powers, improving its world trade position and acquiring new strategic territories in China and the Pacific. There was, as a consequence, little incentive for a disavowal of imperialistic policies. Moreover, Japan still felt insecure in its relationship to the great powers and resented the special interests and privileges which Western nations retained on the continent. If the ill-conceived twenty-one demands expressed a hidden desire to settle Japan's difficulties with China, the military thrust into Siberia seemed, from Japan's point of view, a logical aftermath to the East Asian phase of the First World War.

Thus, just as the Western powers had begun to settle down to what they hoped would be a stable world order, Japan, a latecomer in the era of imperialistic rivalry, was still in a state of disquiet. Newly admitted to the high international councils with Britain, the United States and France, Japan found itself committed to a context of international agreements determined by the great Western powers. The prestige of the democracies was high, and so was their vision of a peacefully coexisting world of democratic states. Yet for Japan this Western vision became an increasingly restrictive and even hostile reality. While at first Japan made the effort to accommodate to the postwar order and to play the international game according to the diplomatic settlements of Versailles, Washington, and London, her defensive needs and national aspirations increasingly came into conflict with the interests of the Western powers.

Meanwhile Japan faced domestic problems of new magnitude and complexity. By 1918 the context of political action at home—the nature of politics and the voices raised in leadership or protest—had undergone drastic change, as had the social and economic circumstances of the majority of the

309

people. Japan was now a heavily urbanized, industrial society; by 1920 its population had reached more than 55 million. Tōkyō had grown to over 2 million inhabitants, and Ōsaka to well over 1 million. The industrial labor force had reached over 1.6 million. Japan was no longer a country which could be dominated by a small handful of politically influential individuals placed in high office. With the appearance of new professions and occupations, the spread of literacy through the national education system and of nationalist sentiment as a result of military conscription, Japan was becoming a "mass society" in which large new class and group interests had begun to separate out. These in turn found new ways of self-expression: through mass media and large membership organizations, or through new types of leaders who could exploit mass media or could master the techniques of political organization and direct political action. The new context of political action now involved, in addition to certain clearly defined elite factions, large interest groups, party organizations, mass associations, and unions. The main domestic political problem had become one of maintaining a balance among these groups and of adequately meeting their needs and expectations without undue conflict or tension with the interests of a state which sought to achieve domestic stability and international security.

In conceiving of the politics of the 1920's historians have resorted to something of a shorthand of terms in their effort to identify the several interest groups which competed for control of government policy. In a dominant position in Japanese politics of the 1920's was an entrenched coalition of elite interests constituting a definite establishment. Its most prominent elements were, according to this shorthand, the aristocracy, the upper bureaucracy (called *mombatsu* by the Japanese), conservative political party leaders, big business interests (the *zaibatsu*), rural landlord interests, and the military bureaucracy (*gumbatsu*).

Opposed to the dominant power coalition, there came to the fore during the 1920's certain newly vocal mass interests. The common concerns of the industrial workers and tenant farmers were largely those of their own economic security and social welfare. City white-collar workers, journalists, educators, and other types of intellectuals, tended to represent neglected "consumer interests" and to voice an intellectual opposition to the establishment. Thus the politics of the twenties was played out on two levels as a struggle for balance of power *within* the plural elites which made up the establishment and as a struggle *between* the establishment and the forces representing the interests of various mass groups.

There were real issues at stake. By the 1920's a major complaint was that the country was suffering from over-population. Since World War II, we have been able to look back upon these claims of over-population and see that the real problem was not so much population size—Japan now has a population nearly double what it was in 1920—but rather that there were gross inequities in the distribution of economic opportunity. Nonetheless the existence of large groups of unemployed or underemployed persons was real enough for the Japanese at the time. The narrowness of the Japanese islands, the miserliness of natural resources, and the relatively low standard of living from which Japan started its economic development, meant that there had been from the beginning of the Meiji period an intense competition for livelihood. Rapid change in the structure of Japan's economy after the 1880's and in the technological foundations of the economy, created acute imbalances in rates of development. Modern industrial growth had been achieved in only a small portion of the total economy, so that in the 1920's this sector was in the hands of a small group of industrial combines which both exploited and depressed the traditional sector of the economy. In 1913 for instance there were only 52 companies with over 5 million *yen* capitalization. Yet these companies, holding 38 percent of the total national capital, represented hardly a third of one percent of all of the business enterprises in Japan. The result was what economists have called a "dual economy" in which modern industry existed side by side with traditional enterprises in such a way that the latter, serving a depressed domestic standard of living, set the standard for wage and labor practices and took on the main burden of absorbing the surpluses of labor.

Japan faced two primary problems of domestic adjustment after 1920. First the needs of the growing body of workers employed by the large industrial enterprises required attention. Labor legislation and unionization had not kept pace with the expansion of industry, nor had wages reflected the scale of profits which "big business" was realizing. The result was increased pressure upon management and government for improved labor conditions and higher wages. Second, there was the agrarian problem. Industrial development and urbanization had not changed the pattern of Japanese agriculture. Rents remained extremely high. The technology remained at the level of small-scale labor-intensive production. Increasingly Japanese farmers were reduced to the status of tenants on the farms of large landholders where they continued to pay rents in kind and remained unprotected by legally backed tenant contracts. Meanwhile the modern requirements of trade and food supply had begun to remake the agricultural market. The beginning of large-scale imports of grains from Korea, of specialized foodstuffs (fruits and sugar) from Taiwan, and of wheat and other agricultural products from the United States, began to destroy the favored position and self-sufficiency of the Japanese farmer. Added to this was the fact that the Japanese farmer continued to rely heavily upon the production of raw silk as a secondary source of income. Thus the well-being of the farmer varied with fluctuations in the silk market, and a depression of the price of raw silk, as happened in 1920, from roughly 4,000 to 1,000 *yen* per hundred pounds, could bring disastrous results to rural Japan. Land under tenancy was close to 50 percent by 1920.

Agitation for the improvement of laboring conditions and better treatment of tenants gave rise to political movements which sought to represent the interests of the depressed sectors of the population. During the 20's labor unions and tenant-farmer associations increased enormously in numbers and aggressiveness. Demands for an expansion of the suffrage and effective welfare legislation on behalf of both farmers and laborers became a major element in socialist thought and in left-wing political platforms. The demands of the dissidents were not readily heard by those in political power, however, and political tempers mounted. Ultimately, as the entire nation became embroiled in issues such as the suffrage, taxes, and labor legislation, the specter of social upheaval was raised by the appearance of an active communist party.

All of these domestic issues were exacerbated by the problem of Japan's external relations. Japan's foreign and domestic sectors continued to be linked in an extremely sensitive fashion. The relationship of the Japanese domestic economy to the outside world had always been precarious, due first to the lack of accessible raw materials and second to the extremely competitive market into which the Japanese as latecomers had to move. This forced the Japanese economy into an unusual degree of dependence upon external sources of materials, especially China, which by 1920 had become a dominant source of coal, iron and cotton fibers as well as the market for over 50 percent of Japan's textiles production. It also continued Japan's heavy reliance on raw silk as a major domestic source of exportable goods. Protection of these foundations of economic stability consequently became matters of great concern and constantly placed before Japan the question of whether to rely on world cooperation or to resort to direct action in creating close at hand a defensible economic bloc of its own.

Before the end of World War I, political issues, both domestic and foreign, had been decided outside of public view by the great figures who then dominated the government. Remnants of the Meiji oligarchy, now referred to as *genrō*, were still the unchallenged leaders of the nation. By the 1920's, however, of the old leadership only Yamagata remained, and he was to die in 1922. Saionji, a late addition to the ranks of the *genrō*, lived on until 1940, but his influence was muted. The political scene of the 1920's was consequently more open and less controlled. The factional disputes which divided the elite interests, or the efforts of mass interests to secure recognition became matters of public knowledge and debate. The country was forced to devise new mechanisms for political

313

participation if the conflicting interests which divided it were to be satisfied and resolved.

In the Western democracies, the political party linked to a parliamentary process had become the accepted means of broadening the base of political participation and the scope of interest conciliation. The party was less congenial to the Japanese political process. Yet with the breakdown of "oligarchy politics" and the increased participation of parties in the political process after 1920, there was some expectation that they might become the central instrument of the political process in Japan as well. Western observers consequently looked upon the 20's in Japan as an era of incipient democracy and party government. Japanese historians, while acknowledging the important role played by parties in the political process, have more often described the decade as one of political confusion and international weakness. The truth undoubtedly lies somewhere between. A study of the nature of Japanese political parties of the 20's and their role in the governmental process shows that they were hardly representative of liberal or democratic forces, nor did they adequately establish themselves as brokers of interest groups in the political marketplace. The political party in Japanese politics functioned in a quite different manner than those of England or America. Yet they did serve an important role in opening up the highly elitist structure of Meiji politics and in pointing up the necessity of creating a parliamentary mechanism capable of resolving the kind of broadly based conflicts of interest which characterized the 20's.

With the adoption of the Meiji Constitution and the creation of the Diet, Japanese politics had provided an arena for party activity, although on a limited basis. The early parties served largely as organs of factional competition within a government still largely dominated by independently powerful political figures and members of the professional bureaucracy. Increasingly, however, the parties came to represent interests lying outside the official bureaucracy, such as those of the *zaibatsu* or of rural landowners. By the end of the Meiji era they were regularly looked to as means of mediating the struggle between the plural elites which comprised the establishment: between the several remaining oligarchs (the *genrō*) or between the civil bureaucrats and the military. Thus, as the Meiji leaders began to fade from the Japanese political stage, the parties became increasingly significant as nodes of political influence or as channels through which political backing could be secured by those less influential leaders who succeeded the *genrō*.

The first indication that the parties had real power to influence political decisions came in 1912 when a united front of political parties backed certain elements in the bureaucracy to oppose the attempt of the armed forces to force through the Diet an enlarged military appropriations bill. But more significant, the formation of the Dōshikai Party in 1913 as a rival of the dominant Seiyūkai had laid the base for two-party politics. Five years later the first truly party government, one in which the head of the majority party in the Diet became Premier, ushered in a new era in Japanese politics. The circumstances which brought this about were both foreign and domestic. The world sentiment in favor of democracy and the success of the Russian Revolution, combined to create a mood of resistance to establishment politics even in Japan. Then in August of 1918 Japan was shaken by a series of "rice riots." The government was clearly culpable. Bad economic planning in the previous years had led to critical consumer goods shortages and a precipitous rise in the rice price in the summer of 1918. Discontent in the cities exploded into destructive riots, mostly against rice stores and warehouses, lasting for over three weeks. The government proclaimed martial law, and troops were sent into every major city. There were clashes between mobs in the streets and government troops, and this left a residue of bitterness across the country. The government of General Terauchi was forced to resign, and the *genrō*, in an effort to placate the aroused populace, turned toward the political parties. Hara Kei, a commoner and head of the Seiyūkai, was named Premier.

The appointment of Hara marked the appearance of a new type of political leader as well as a new style of government.

315

Heretofore premiers had been selected from out of the "inner oligarchy." Hara, though a highly placed bureaucrat, was primarily a party man. His strength came mainly from his party and from his connections in the worlds of journalism and big business. Spoken of as the "Great Commoner," he was well suited to capture the confidence of the newly awakened public, yet his fundamental conservatism made him acceptable to the establishment as well.

The so-called party governments which continued with some gaps from 1918 to 1932, represented a coalition of political interests differing appreciably in mix and in policy from those that had existed up to 1918. The leading parties were now two: the Seiyūkai, essentially the successor to the Jiyūtō, and the Kenseikai (renamed Minseitō after 1927) which followed the course of the old Kaishintō, and more recently the Dōshi-kai. Both were conservative in that they represented elite interests. They inclined, however, toward civil interests as against military, and they cooperated with business much more than did the bureaucracy itself. It was common knowledge that the Seiyūkai supported the *zaibatsu* interests of Mitsui while the Minseitō supported those of Mitsubishi. Both parties represented a commitment to parliamentary government and as such served as a means of bringing politics into the public arena of the Diet.

Party leaders in government tended to steer a moderate course both in international and domestic affairs. Thus during the 1920's there was a steady though cautious accommodation to the demands of the anti-establishment groups and an expansion of popular participation in government through an enlarged electorate. There was also a general readiness to follow a policy of world cooperation and reduction in armaments. The trend toward internationalism began in 1921 when Japan attended the Washington Conference where she agreed to abide by a *status quo* of defenses in the Pacific and re-affirmed the "Open Door" policy in China. In 1920 Japan had joined the League of Nations; in 1928 she was among the signers of the Kellog-Briand Pact renouncing war. In 1930, after bitter debate, Japan ratified the London Naval (limitation) Treaty. The agreement, which restricted Japan's defensive edge in the Pacific, marked the farthest extent of Japan's co-operation with the Western powers. Already tensions were building up with Britain and the United States. The armed forces in Japan were convinced that the London Treaty had gone too far in compromising essential defensive requirements, while Japan's growing effort to dominate China was destined to come in conflict with the long established interests of the other "Open Door" powers.

In domestic politics the major public issues during the decade of the 20's were those of achieving universal suffrage and extending the scope of parliamentary government. The newly emerging anti-establishment forces realized that if they were to obtain a voice in government they must secure an expansion of the electorate. Yet the existing parties were by no means the most reliable supporters of universal suffrage. Operating still as extensions of elite factionalism, they did not look with favor on the enlargement of an electorate over which they might have little control. Thus when student demonstrations and mass agitation in 1919 forced the issue of universal manhood suffrage to the fore, Premier Hara refused to permit the matter to come to debate in the Diet. The Seiyūkai, at least, was not committed to a larger suffrage, and Hara proved unwilling to disrupt the balance of political support which had brought this party to power in exchange for the uncertain advantage of wider popular participation. When Hara was assassinated in 1921, he had done little to advance the cause of manhood suffrage.

But agitation for extension of the suffrage continued with growing violence in the streets and in the Diet. Parties in opposition to the dominant Seiyūkai ultimately saw an advantage in espousing the suffrage cause. When in 1925 a Kenseikai-led coalition gained a majority position in the Diet, the post of Premier went to Katō Takaaki. Katō proved amenable to the passage of a new suffrage bill. In May, 1925, a bill granting suffrage to all males over the age of 25 was made into law, and at one stroke the electorate was increased from three to 14 million. A few days prior to this, government action had

317

reduced the size of the Japanese army from 21 to 17 divisions. Both acts were hailed as major victories for the "people" against the "government." Yet they could hardly be taken as signs of a general liberalization of Japanese politics, as the events of the next few years were to prove. Reaction against the granting of popular concessions and the adoption of a "soft" international policy was close to the surface. Despite expansion of the electorate, "party government" as a means of securing political integration was eventually repudiated.

The weakness of the conservative parties after 1925 lay in the fact that they were unable either to legitimize themselves as spokesmen of the new electorate or to defend themselves against a growing opposition from the bureaucracy and the armed forces. Thus violence was a constant accompaniment to the Japanese politics of the late 20's, as extremists of both the right and left resorted to direct action. The roots of representative government were still very shallow. Although the period from 1918 to 1932 is called the era of party governments, in actual fact only 6 out of 11 premiers were party men; the other five were career bureaucrats or military officers. And of the six party premiers, three were assassinated in office. The 1925 legislation was also less a victory for participatory government than appeared on the surface, for the suffrage bill was linked to a new "Peace Preservation" bill which enlarged police control over freedom of speech and assemblage and marked a new stage in the control of "dangerous thoughts." Even the effect of the reduction in the size of the army was nullified by the fact that many army officers displaced by the cut were moved into the schools to begin a new program of expanded military training. On top of this the late years of the decade were complicated by the effects of world depression which reduced large segments of the labor and farm population to poverty. In the dark years from 1929 to 31, as labor agitation mounted and the activities of new mass parties inflamed the electoral scene, the efficacy of the parliamentary process was seriously brought into question. When in 1930 Premier Hamaguchi pushed through ratification of the London Naval Treaty over the vigorous protests of the Navy, violent popular opposition erupted in Tōkyō, and the whole nature of Japan's international posture came under attack. Hamaguchi's assassination followed shortly thereafter. The last party premier, Inukai Tsuyoshi, already faced with the independent action of Japanese military forces in Manchuria, sought to forestall the inevitable decline of civil parliamentary government by coming out against military expansion and calling for an enforcement of discipline in the army. He was killed by junior military officers, members of a "patriotic society," in May 1932. With his passing Japan's first era of party government was brought to an end.

For many writers the decade of the 1920's proved only the inadequacy and ultimate failure of the party system in Japan. For others it demonstrated the inevitability of a militarist and "fascist" takeover in a Japan burdened by an antiquated constitution and an anti-democratic "emperor system." Still others see the key to the decade in the weakness of "liberal" forces in Japan in contrast to the particular potency of the military and bureaucratic elites. Certainly an essential element in the understanding of this period is to be found in a study of the left-wing movements and their potentiality in the decade of the 20's.

The voices which were raised in favor of civil rights and social welfare, in favor of universal suffrage, and against the powerful influences of the aristocracy and big business, found expression through a number of separate "social movements." During the early 1920's, the so-called "democratic" movement caught the imagination of the country. Its demise led anti-government leadership increasingly towards socialism and communism. While the first of these movements was chiefly the property of the newly articulate urban intelligentsia, the latter two were heavily dependent on the support of organized labor.

There is no question but that mass political movements had to work against strong odds in Japan. The achievement of popular representation, which was the prime objective of the anti-establishment interests of the 20's, faced two overpowering obstacles. First was the coalition of elite interests itself and its reluctance to share political power with a mass electorate.

319

Second was the manner in which the Meiji Constitution placed the locus of sovereignty above the political arena and protected the organs of government decision from popular control. If the new mass interests were to secure a voice in government, some shift toward popular sovereignty and some relaxation of elite control over the power of initiative in government was essential.

It was the characteristic of the "democratic" movement of the early 20's that it took an essentially parliamentary and legalistic approach to the problem of achieving the popular will in government. This rather moderate break with the strongly statist theories which had grown up around the emperor since 1889 was first popularized by Professor Minobe Tatsukichi (1873–1948) of Tōkyō University who began in 1911 to expound the theory that the emperor was an "organ of the state" rather than being the state itself. The point was a technical one in the realm of constitutional theory, but it did permit a reinterpretation of the status of the emperor and his government, leading to the view that the emperor was accountable for the welfare of his people.

Following World War I another Tōkyō University professor, Yoshino Sakuzō (1878–1933), a Christian who had gone abroad to study the roots of democracy in Europe, carried Minobe's theories still farther in an effort to justify representative government within the existing "emperor system." Stopping short of the demand for popular sovereignty, he called for "government *for* the people" (*mimponshugi*) as against "government *by* the people" (*minshushugi* or democracy). Thus while avoiding an attack upon the status of the emperor as defined in the constitution, he acquired the benefits of democracy by placing upon the emperor the injunction that "in politics the fundamental end of the exercise of the nation's sovereignty should be the people."

Yoshino for a brief moment in his life entered politics. Organizing a party known as the Reimeikai in 1918, he conducted public rallies and made speeches attacking vested interests such as the Privy Council and the House of Peers and calling for universal suffrage so that the popular will could be expressed. Yoshino's movement, resting on a strange blend of Christian socialism, Confucian political morality and labor unionism, found for a moment a fervent following among students and labor leaders. But the public displays of vocal anti-government feeling, the rallies and parades which he sponsored, frightened rather than convinced the establishment. With the failure to adopt the suffrage bill in 1920 the movement died, and Yoshino went back to his books.

The cause of moderate political change was rather timorously carried into the existing party platforms by a few political leaders such as Inukai and Hamaguchi, both of whom were assassinated. The experience of Yoshino merely convinced most of the dissident elements in Japan that it would take men of more dogmatic temper and more forceful involvement in politics to influence the establishment. And so the intellectual leadership moved increasingly toward Marxist political philosophy and away from any effort to work within the party system. The new spearheads of popular participation in politics became the socialist-labor movement and, for a brief period, the Communist Party.

Socialism as a political movement had a spotty history in pre-World War II Japan. First introduced into Japan by missionary Christian socialists, it had an immediate appeal to young Japanese idealists with a strong social conscience. In 1901 an effort was made to form a socialist party based on principles of universal brotherhood, abolition of classes, redistribution of wealth, and public ownership of utilities. The organization was quickly crushed by the Home Ministry. The execution in 1911 of twelve purported anarchists, including Kōtoku Shūsui, proved a severe psychological blow to the movement, and for nearly a decade it was hardly heard from. One of the most prominent socialists of the period, Katayama Sen (1859–1933) left Japan for Europe at this time. Eventually he turned communist and lived out his life in the U.S.S.R.

A second phase of socialist activity began after World War I. The country's intellectuals had been stimulated by news of the Russian Revolution, and the 1918 rice riots became a further spur to their revolutionary aspirations. Socialist intellectuals and labor union leaders now found themselves working together to create a base for mass political action. In 1921 an effort was made to revive the socialist party. Remnants of the prewar leadership, together with representatives of various student groups and labor unions, founded what they called the Socialist Alliance, but this was quickly disbanded by the government. Organized labor, however, continued to carry socialist principles into the political arena. The Japan Federation of Labor (Nippon Rōdō Sōdōmei) founded in 1919 by Suzuki Bunji (1885–1946) became a fighting organization dedicated to political as well as economic aims. Its influence was felt by big business interests which created a counter organization known as the Harmonization Society (Kyōchōkai). Labor's first major success came in the great dockyard strike at Kōbe in 1921, during which some 30,000 workers left their jobs and for several months staged mass rallies and demonstrations in defiance of the police. Management eventually compromised with the union leaders and thereby put the first stamp of legitimacy on the new tactics employed by labor. The labor movement expanded tremendously as a result, and by 1929 union membership in industry had reached 300,000 workers.

Passage of the manhood suffrage act opened up new possibilities for any group which could mobilize the new industrial and farm labor vote. Organized labor made the effort, but it is clear that the Seiyūkai and Minseitō absorbed the bulk of the new votes created by the electoral changes. So-called "mass parties" proliferated after 1925, but they were dominated by labor and tended to espouse causes that restricted their appeal. The Marxist-oriented Rōdō Nōmintō (Labor-Farm Party), formed in 1926, was the first of the new parties. After passing through several transformations and factional splits which included at various times the Shakai Minshūtō (Social Democratic Party) and the Musan Taishūtō (Proletarian Mass Party), the labor parties managed to combine in 1932 into the relatively middle-of-the-road homogenous Shakai Taishūtō (Social Mass Party). The party received over 600,000 votes in 1935 and seated 18 members out of 466 in the lower house of the Diet. The following year it acquired 37 seats to reach the height of its influence.

The difficulty with the labor-farm parties was that they lacked a stable leadership and depended too directly on labor unions for support. Their leftist inclinations made them the constant object of government harassment. For all their claim to speak for the masses, the new parties did not solicit broad mass involvement and remained elitist in their party organization and hence prone to factionalism. One of the reasons for this was that already by the mid-1920's the political movement of the left was being affected by communist infiltration. The result was to drive political action increasingly toward radicalism and emotionalism.

Despite its early connection with Comintern activities in Shanghai, the Japanese Communist Party developed very differently from the party which eventually came to power in China. Its history followed a pattern much more like that exemplified in the countries of Western Europe. Organized and led by a few active leaders, often working underground, supported by a strong elitist intellectual element, never achieving a mass base, it was obliged to meet police suppression from the very outset. The fact that communism called for an elimination of the emperor system and a complete break with the traditional polity (*kokutai*) in Japan made the doctrine anathema to the Japanese establishment and even to most of the people. The party, of course, was able to exploit the sentiments of real grievance held by the laboring classes and could champion the attack against the aristocracy, capitalism, the corruption of the parties and the lack of political freedom in Japan. But the extremity of its break with traditional values kept it in a bitterly subversive minority role.

The first Communist Party founded in 1922 by such leaders as Tokuda Kyūichi, Ōsugi Sakae and Arahata Kanson was poorly organized. It was destroyed by police purges in 1923 following the discovery of party documents in the possession of Sano Manabu, a Waseda University professor. The great Tōkyō earthquake of the same year gave the police an opportunity to round up leftist suspects of all coloration. Ōsugi was

323

killed while under detention. A "second party" organized in 1926 adopted the first official platform, calling for abolition of the emperor system and the Diet, redistribution of wealth, and a foreign policy favorable to the U.S.S.R. During 1926–28 Communist Party members infiltrated the labor unions and became active on university campuses. But counter action by the police through the newly created Peace Preservation (antisubversive) Bureau was rapid. Massive arrests in 1928 and in 1929 literally obliterated the party. During 1931–1932 the public trials of nearly 400 jailed communists led to renunciation of communism by all but a handful of hard-core leaders. Already the country was being aroused by the successes of Japanese troops in Manchuria. And while intellectuals continued to read Marxist literature in private, the drift toward "dangerous thoughts" was not to go much further. Japan's first flirtation with communism was over.

In retrospect the decade of the 20's was a time of intense political awareness for the Japanese people. The nation was beset by deep-seated social and economic problems, and its people were played upon by conflicting ideologies which reflected the powerful tensions separating the establishment from proletariat, farmer, and intellectual. And while the widening of the electorate marked a significant advance toward greater representation, the fundamental problems of mass participation in the political process remained unsolved. The centrist political parties in particular proved inadequate to the task of providing a mechanism which could both maintain a balance of interest within the establishment and at the same time provide the avenues through which popular desires could be served. By the end of the decade, changes in Japan's international environment and the disastrous effects of world depression had given rise to new crisis conditions. Placed under unusual pressure, the tendency of Japanese politics was to move to the extremes of right and left. Under the circumstances socialist policies had no possible chance of success. The swing toward an enforced national unity under rightist leadership became the alternative which Japan followed.

18

From Manchuria to War
in the Pacific

The year 1931 stands as a major turning point in Japan's modern history, for in September of that year Japanese armed forces overran southern Manchuria, committing their government to a course of direct action on the continent and, ultimately, to the rejection of the entire structure of international relations which had come into being during the 1920's. The Manchurian Incident, of course, was less the cause of Japan's turn toward military expansion than a symptom of deep-set domestic problems and of mounting world tensions. Nor was Japan alone among the world's nations in taking the course it did. Superficially at least, the similarities with Germany and Italy, with which Japan entered a military alliance in 1940, were strong. Like the Axis powers of Europe, Japan in the 1930's underwent a drastic political transformation which stirred its people to a frenzy of ultra-national spirit while offering them expectations of prosperity through foreign expansion and of solace through the achievement of an integrated welfare state.

Japan's alienation from the community of democratic powers with their "Open Door" protestations toward China had been growing since the end of World War I. Disillusionment with the United States grew rapidly after the Washington Conference, which the Japanese interpreted as an effort at containment by the Western powers. The 1924 Exclusion Act and the high tariff policy adopted by the United States in the wake of the Great Depression further strained Japan's relations with America. Simultaneously Japan's "special interests" in China were being thwarted by a stubborn Britain and a resurgent Nationalist government in China. Meanwhile in Europe, with the rise of Fascist Italy and Nazi Germany, concepts of state socialism and of bloc economic organization had gained acceptance. Depression had tarnished the prestige of the democracies and their economic and political systems. It was easy to argue that the world was being controlled by the "have" nations while the "have-nots" were excluded from their rightful opportunities to achieve security and self-fulfillment. Japan's destiny, it seemed to many, lay on the continent, not in cooperation with the Western powers.

The demand for "positive policies" abroad and at home came from many quarters. For Japan, depression had been a bitter experience. The failure of many small businesses and the impoverishment of the lower levels of the farming populace created social welfare problems of vast proportions. Party leadership, its image damaged by its reputation for corruption and opportunism, had failed to secure the confidence of the people. Yet fear of communism inhibited most Japanese from following left-wing leaders. For many segments of the country, the crying need seemed to be strong authoritarian government, aggressive military preparedness, and humane concern for the underprivileged masses. For while socialism and communism would have destroyed the emperor and the Japanese polity in the name of the masses, state socialism and militarism would deify the state in the name of its concerned subjects. Japan's drift towards extreme military mobilization came both as a result of an aggressive determination to go it alone in East Asia and a mounting sense of national insecurity, as Japan felt itself placed on the defensive by what it judged to be the growing hostility of the Western powers.

To describe Japan as having gone fascist or totalitarian in 1941, as some writers have done, is actually beside the point. The final stage of Japan's reorganization under military mobilization and ultra-nationalist ideology resulted in social and

326

political conditions quite different from those which characterized Nazi Germany or Fascist Italy. The so-called "New
Structure" in Japan did not depend on a Hitler or Mussolini.
Nor was it the strong-arm creation of an aggressive political
party. Japan in 1941 was more nearly what the Japanese themselves called it, a "defense state" in which the nation was
drawn together around collectivist goals for defensive purposes, turning ideologically inward toward its traditional
sources of psychological security and crushing out all political
dissidence in the interests of national unity. In the Japanese
defense state the emperor-centered political structure of the
Meiji Constitution remained intact to protect the vested interests of the establishment elites. The new elements which entered
the political scene were militarism and the concepts of state
socialism.

In Japan of the late 20's the ingredients of rightist upsurge
were already close at hand. An apparatus of state-supported
Shintō shrines provided a ritual base for a return to semi-
religious belief in Japan's historical uniqueness. A number of
secret and patriotic societies provided avenues for the spread
of ultra-national and Japanist ideas as well as the new concepts of state socialism. And the armed forces, independent of
civilian control, existed as a powerful vehicle for the eventual
application of such concepts in domestic and foreign affairs.
Not one of these elements need have proved critical in pushing
Japan toward the course it took, but taken together, and in
combination with the failure of party government at home and
of world cooperation abroad, they created the necessary
environment.

The Meiji government had consciously used the network of
Shintō shrines in existence at the time of the Restoration for
national purposes. In 1871 the shrines were given state support
and graded into twelve classes from the Ise Shrine at the top
to small village shrines at the bottom. Priests received official
appointments, and a Bureau of Shrines developed a new style
of state ritualism. Shintō theology and the myths of national
origin and imperial sanctity were also taught in elementary
school in the so-called "morals" (shūshin) courses. Thus while

327

the new Shintō was not immediately linked to the spread of popular nationalistic sentiment, it kept alive the ingredients of "emperor worship"—i.e. the veneration of the imperial portrait and the ritual reading of the Imperial Rescript on Education—and provided the means of reinforcing communal or national solidarity through shrine-centered patriotic observances. Shintō gave to Japanese patriotism a special quality of mysticism and cultural introversion.

Rightist societies also had their origins in post-Restoration Japan. Early secret societies such as the *Genyōsha* (Black Ocean Society, 1881) or the *Kokuryūkai* (Amur Society, 1901, and more often called the Black Dragon Society) were not by origin rightist in their objectives. Both were elite movements designed to press for overseas expansion of Japanese interests, particularly in Korea and Manchuria. After World War I, and with the mounting social tensions of the 20's, such societies shifted their emphasis to domestic problems, raising the alarm against "dangerous thoughts" and political radicalism. At the same time a number of new mass patriotic societies dedicated to domestic harmony and patriotic nationalism were also formed. The Japan Patriotic Society (Nihon Kokusuikai) founded in 1919 by Tokonami Takejirō, Premier Hara's Home Minister, and other members of the Seiyūkai leadership, brought bureaucrats and businessmen together around a platform that called for harmony between labor and industrial management, a patriotic unity of the nation around the emperor, and a disavowal of radical politics. It is said to have quickly acquired over 100,000 members. The Anti-Red League (Sekka Bōshidan) was founded in the same year as was the Japan Communist Party. The Society for the Foundation of the State (Kokuhonsha) founded in 1924 by Baron Hiranuma, then Minister of Justice and later Premier, found its membership chiefly within the civil and military bureaucracy. Its objectives emphasized preservation of Japan's "unique national character" and pursuit of Japan's "special mission in Asia."

During the 1920's such societies with their followings drawn from government and business circles were concerned chiefly with the protection of Japanese society from radicalism and the dilution of patriotic fervor. By the 1930's, however, a new element had been injected into the thinking of the rightist groups. As domestic problems increased in magnitude and as Japan's international position weakened, at least in Japanese eyes, the conviction that a "national reorganization" along state socialist lines was called for caught the imagination of a number of individuals, particularly those on the fringes of the military establishment. The belief began to be heard that Japan was fundamentally in danger of subversion and that the work of the Meiji Restoration still remained to be achieved—i.e. that a "Shōwa Restoration" was called for.

The man who is credited with injecting the ideas of state socialism into the thought stream of the rightist movement of the mid-1930's was Kita Ikki (1885–1937). A member of the Amur Society and a worker for Japanese interests on the continent, he wrote in 1919 a work entitled *An Outline Plan for the National Re-Organization of Japan* (*Nihon kaizō hōan taikō*) in which he advocated a military coup d'état to achieve the true objectives of the Meiji Restoration which, he claimed, were being betrayed by incompetent men around the emperor. The book was quickly banned, but it circulated secretly within military circles during the early 30's. Kita's plan called for a takeover of the government by military leaders so as to free the emperor from his weak advisors and permit him to assume his rightful authority. After suspending the constitution and dissolving the Diet, the emperor and his military supporters would work toward the establishment of a "direct collectivist will" uniting leaders and people. Eventually a new government would be created, served by an assembly freed of factionalism and corruption. Meanwhile the peerage would be abolished, the emperor would renounce his wealth, big businesses would be reduced in size, the working classes would be supported, and a new harmony would be achieved in Japanese society. Abroad Japan should provide the leadership to free Asia of Western influence. By the late 1920's the intellectual basis for a Shōwa Restoration movement had been laid. Advocating revolution *within* the framework of the imperial system, it proposed ideas

329

which were basically anti-parliamentary, hyper-national and anti-capital.

The group that eventually became the most powerful vehicle for the spread of nationalist-militarist thinking in Japan was the military establishment. Always a powerful political interest group, the armed forces had become increasingly critical of and even alienated from the policies of party government during the 20's. At the top of the military hierarchy, high officers of the Army and Navy became disillusioned by the willingness of the civilian-led government to cut military appropriations or to compromise Japan's security interests. Among the middle- and lower-grade officers, many came from families which had suffered during the depression, and as a consequence they remained acutely conscious of the economic problems of the country's farmers and factory workers and of the danger of communist thinking. The armed forces were in a particularly sensitive position to influence the nation's politics. At the top, the Army and Navy commands could touch government policy directly without being subjected to civilian control. They could exploit large areas of independent influence, for instance in the field of military training and in the colonial areas. Moreover, through its conscript system and an extensive reservist organization, the armed forces affected a growing segment of the population. The military man exploited as well a sentiment in his favor which persisted from the mystique which had once surrounded the samurai class. Officers, by contrast with the "corrupt politicians," were considered by definition pure of private motivation, "above politics" and filled with a sense of responsibility for the welfare and security of the country.

During the 1920's, the armed forces had reluctantly accepted party leadership in government and had played along with the system which required them to compete for a voice in national affairs along with other elite interests. But increasingly the army became disillusioned with party politics. Criticism of civilian leadership was particularly vehement among the new groups of younger officers who, as narrowly trained products of the War College with little political experience and almost no opportunity for travel abroad, combined a strong sense of social responsibility with a narrow view of world affairs. Impatient with both the technique of international negotiation and representative government, these young officers were attracted to the concept of a Shōwa Restoration which would put the country in the hands of leaders who would move resolutely to take care of its problems. Impatient even with their more cautious superior officers, they ultimately resorted to political activism and military insubordination as a means of forcing their superiors to take action. By the late 20's, the army in particular had a distinct "young officer problem." Radical elements in the army found two main arenas of activity: the relatively autonomous Kwantung command in Manchuria and the newly-formed secret societies.

The late 1920's witnessed an ominous spread of small conspiratorial societies dedicated to direct action. Their names indicate the nationalist nature of their objectives: Jimmu Society (Jimmu-kai), Heavenly Sword Party (Tenkentō), Blood Brotherhood (Ketsumeidan), the Cherry Society (Sakura-kai). The last of these was particularly noteworthy, since it was one of the first to resort to violence. Its membership included a number of young military officers, like Hashimoto Kingorō, who later became involved in the Manchurian Incident. A key bridge between its military membership and the ideas of Kita Ikki proved to be a civilian by the name of Ōkawa Shūmei, a lecturer at the Colonization Academy and a radical advocate of military expansion abroad and military takeover at home.

What triggered the thrust into Manchuria, thus opening the way for the ascendancy of the military approach to Japan's national predicament, must be understood in the context of the "continental problem" which faced Japan, for it was not simply the work of a handful of fanatics. By the 1930's, a large percentage of the Japanese had become convinced of the need to protect their "special interests" in China and above all, both for strategic and economic reasons, to secure control over Manchuria. Yet with each passing month Chiang Kai-shek's

331

government in Nanking appeared to be growing in strength and Soviet troops along the Amur became increasingly menacing. To the military mind particularly, it seemed like insanity that Japan should at this critical time weaken its security in the Pacific by agreeing to the London Naval Treaty. By 1930, a growing sense that "something had to be done" was in the air. At the Dairen headquarters of the Kwantung Army the seriousness of Japan's national situation was gravely discussed and preparations were made for possible military action.

On September 18, 1931, the field command of the Kwantung Army commenced hostilities near Mukden and proceeded to take over Manchuria according to a preconceived plan. The responsibility for the Manchurian Incident, as it was to be called, is no longer in doubt. While certain lower echelon officers set the spark (among them Colonel Hashimoto, of the Cherry Society), it is now clear that the senior officers in the Kwantung Army as well as the War Ministry and General Staff in Tōkyō were party to the action or were sufficiently predisposed so as not to interfere with it once it had started. The civilian leaders of the government, faced with a *fait accompli*, were not able to control the military action.

The crisis created by full-scale military operations in Manchuria had a profound impact on Japan's domestic politics, upon its economy, and upon Japan's international position. At home a mood of exhilaration temporarily swept the country following reports of Japan's easy military successes. The feeling of nationalism ran high, and a climate of chauvinism encouraged further direct action. In late 1931 two terroristic plots by secret-society members were uncovered before they were set off. In February 1932 the campaign manager of the Minseitō Party and the chairman of the board of directors of the Mitsui Company were assassinated in symbolic attacks upon the parties and the *zaibatsu*. Then, on May 15, 1932, a group of young army and navy officers made the first extensive attempt to achieve the Shōwa Restoration by terror. Although they succeeded in killing Premier Inukai and made attacks upon the Tōkyō police headquarters, the National Bank of Japan, and the house of the Privy Seal Makino, they failed to create the national crisis which they hoped would lead to martial law and a military take-over.

Yet though the May 15 incident was unsuccessful, its effect upon Japanese politics was lasting. When the smoke cleared after the shooting, the senior statesmen, who traditionally selected the new premier, were faced with the fact that the parties had lost their ability to maintain the confidence of the country. They turned, therefore, to the formation of a non-party "national unity cabinet" under Admiral Saitō. With this move, the era of party government was essentially brought to an end. Thereafter the Army and Navy, through their exploitation of the posts of War and Navy Ministers, increasingly managed to influence the choice of premiers and the makeup of cabinets. Furthermore, the appointment at this time of General Araki as Minister of War and General Mazaki as Inspector General of Military Education brought into positions of high sensitivity men who were favorably inclined to the "restorationists."

The impact of the May 15 rebellion upon army morale and popular opinion was also enormous. While the Army high command technically disavowed the rebel hotheads, they nevertheless revealed considerable ambivalence of attitude in the court martial trial which followed. The rebels were treated as misguided patriots. At the trial itself they were permitted to speak vigorously in their own behalf, expounding the objectives of the Shōwa Restoration and freely attacking the existing society and the members of the government.

If the Manchurian Incident created a new political mood in Japan, the acquisition of Manchuria had a profound effect upon Japan's strategic position in East Asia and upon Japan's world economic role. Organized in February 1932 into the puppet state of Manchukuo, the entire area was controlled by the commander-in-chief of the Kwantung army, who also served as Japan's ambassador to Manchukuo. Being ostensibly an independent state, separated from Japanese civilian government control, Manchukuo became a testing ground where the Japanese Army could try out its concepts for a planned economy. In the years after 1931, every effort was made to develop

Manchuria into a self-sufficient economic region with an industrial base to support the army's presence on the continent. Manchuria was never profitable to the home islands, and in fact the army squeezed billions of *yen* from the homeland *zaibatsu* for its development. But Manchukuo proved the capacity of the Japanese for large-scale overseas economic development. Almost overnight, the small town of Hsingking was created into a new capital city of over 300,000 inhabitants, with large public buildings, parks, and asphalt roads. In less than ten years, the Japanese had built some 2000 miles of railroad, several strategic airports, dams and power plants on the Yalu, and even a new port, Rashin, on the Japan Sea coast of Korea, in order to facilitate direct ship communications with Japan's industrial heartland. By the time of the war in the Pacific, Manchuria had become the most highly industrialized and militarized area on the continent, next only to Japan in its industrial potential, and Japan had joined it, at considerable sacrifice to its domestic economy, into a vast strategic complex stretching back to the homeland through Korea.

More significant in the long run for the total Japanese economy than the development of Manchuria was the effect of the 1931 military action in creating a new relationship between government and business and in hastening Japan's recovery from world depression. The crisis mood which prevailed after 1931 permitted the government to adopt emergency measures leading the way to a spectacular surge of economic growth. Military action in Manchuria was matched by a new "trade offensive" which literally doubled Japan's exports between 1931 and 1936. Though under strong competition from Britain, the United States, and Germany, Japan became the first major power to recover from depression. The techniques used in this offensive created resentment among Japan's competitors, who claimed that Japan's unnaturally low standard of wages, combined with questionable business practices and the sale of shoddy goods, gave Japan an unfair edge. But the real reasons for Japan's success were more orthodox and depended upon sound use of economic theory and the strenuous channelling of the entire national effort. By abandoning the gold

THE RISE AND FALL OF THE MODERN JAPANESE STATE

standard in 1932, Japan depreciated the *yen* to a point that its goods could sell competitively in the world market. The Major Industries Control Law of 1931 permitted the government to "rationalize" industry, sponsoring mergers, eliminating "wasteful" competition, and streamlining industry for foreign competition. In the process, many small-scale industries and businesses were sacrificed, it is true, and the standard of living for the nation as a whole was kept low. The Japanese consumer therefore gained little from the statistically remarkable economic recovery. Toward the consumer and worker, the crisis in Manchuria provided the government with the excuse to conduct a propaganda campaign which built up a sense of crisis and called for the creation of a "domestic front" or a "workers army" to parallel the activities of the men in the field. Hard

335

work, austerity, patriotism, were successfully urged upon the worker in hopes of a prosperity which lay ever in the future.

Perhaps the most critical effect of the Manchurian Incident was its effect on Japan's international position and its foreign policy. The thrust into Manchuria had obviously been in defiance of Japan's international agreements with the Western powers. Britain and the United States in particular were disturbed by Japan's action, though they took no retaliatory measures other than to point the finger of "moral" censure through the League of Nations. The Lytton Commission investigation was equivocal when it came to naming Japan the aggressor in Manchuria, but the report adopted in the League recommended against the recognition of Manchukuo as an independent state. The action of the League, therefore, merely aroused ill will while demonstrating to the Japanese that it was possible to flaunt the "fence of treaties" which hemmed them in. In 1933, Japan withdrew from the League, and the following year the Tōkyō Foreign Office issued the so-called Amau statement (sometimes referred to as the "Asiatic Monroe Doctrine"), which substituted for the Open Door a claim that Japan would take full responsibility for peace in East Asia and would exert what amounted to a protectorate over China's relations with the Western powers. Japan had begun the process of diplomatic extrication from the company of the Open Door powers which was to lead eventually to the 1940 alliance with the Axis.

All told, then, the Manchurian Incident and its aftermath brought dramatic changes to Japan, both at home and abroad. At home, there was an immediate shift in the national mood. The success in Manchuria encouraged the spread of extremist thinking, while a feeling of resentment set in against the rest of the world, which had criticized Japan's actions. The popular trend moved quickly away from the advocacy of "internationalism" which had characterized the 1920's. Bitter attacks were now launched upon all thought and action considered unpatriotic or detrimental to the national interests. In 1935, for instance, Professor Minobe was denounced and forced to resign from the House of Peers for his earlier writings setting forth the "organ theory" with regard to the emperor. Mass media carried diatribes against liberal thinkers and exalted military virtues and nationalist sentiment.

It was in this climate of opinion that army extremists made several further attempts to achieve the Shōwa Restoration. In November 1934 a plot of serious proportions was discovered within the army involving officers up and down the line of command. Among those implicated was General Mazaki, the Inspector General of Military Education. Conservative leadership in the army, alerted to the seriousness of the breakdown of discipline within the services, attempted a thorough housecleaning, and quickly ordered over 3000 changes of command, beginning with General Mazaki. In August of 1935 Lieutenant-Colonel Aizawa of the extremist group killed General Nagata, whom he blamed for Mazaki's transfer. The trial of Aizawa that ensued was again permitted to become a public display of ultranationalist sentiment. Aizawa claimed purity of intent and brought to his defense letters from school girls signed in blood. At the climax of the trial, as a means of reducing tension in the capital area, the army First Division, which had by tradition been placed on duty near Tōkyō since 1905, was suddenly ordered to prepare for transfer to Manchuria. On the night of February 26, 1936 the First Division mutinied. Nearly 1400 men with their newly issued arms followed a group of extremist officers in a bloody attempt to capture the government and to "safeguard the Fatherland by killing all those responsible for impeding the Shōwa Restoration and slurring the Imperial prestige." The troops succeeded in occupying the Police Headquarters, the War Ministry and General Staff Headquarters, and the new Diet Building for three days, killing several cabinet members and terrorizing the center of Tōkyō. Eventually saner heads in the Army, obtaining the support of the imperial voice, managed to secure the surrender of the rebellious troops. This time punishment was swift and quiet; 103 men were sentenced, 17 of them to death. The rebellion was followed by another round of purges

337

and a conscientious attempt to re-establish discipline within the army. The February 1936 incident proved to be the last open effort at achieving the Shōwa Restoration by assassination.

The common assumption that the revolt by the First Division was part of a direct chain of events which pushed Japan into calculated war with China has been brought into question by later research. The outbreak of hostilities with China in July 1937 was predictable, perhaps, but it did not result, as did the Manchurian Incident, from any preconceived plot on the part of the army's field officers. Japan blundered into the war with China. Yet once fighting started, the expansion of hostilities on a wide scale was made inevitable by predisposition on both sides. Both civilian and military leaders in Japan, appeared ready to press for what they felt to be Japan's national interest in China, while Chinese leaders showed a new willingness to stand up against Japanese penetration of China below the Great Wall.

Ironically, in the interval between February 1936 and July 1937 there occurred in Japan a brief revival of party activity and party-based criticism of army interference in government. Economic recovery from the depression had now brought full employment. The election of 1937 brought to a high point the popularity of the Social Mass Party, giving it 37 seats in the Diet. Party leaders struggled to reassert an anti-army voice within the government coalition. But by and large the trend in government was in the direction of further civilian compromise with the military and a build-up in nationalist spirit. The Hirota cabinet which came to power in the spring of 1936 publicly adopted a more aggressive foreign policy calling for the establishment of a "special anti-communist, pro-Japanese, pro-Manchukuo area" in North China as part of the "fundamental principle" of Japanese national existence. Increasingly Japan's leaders had begun to confuse the nation's military-strategic goals with its economic and moral expectations. When in June of 1937, in order to resolve the now aggravated tension between the parties and the army, Prince Konoe Fumimaro was named premier, Japan received a leader even more calculated to place the aura of mission and destiny on aggressive action on the continent. As a man of aristocratic lineage, close to the sources of imperial charisma, his appointment heightened the feeling that Japan was returning to its "fundamental values."

As of 1937 Japanese army planning looked upon Soviet Russia as the major threat in East Asia. Yet the problem of North China had become increasingly perplexing. Since the takeover of Manchuria, the army had moved steadily into the borderlands toward Peking, using the subterfuge of "autonomous" regimes or independent buffer zones to gain indirect control. Yet increasingly it became evident that a firm hold over North China with its sources of cotton and coal and its tremendous market for Japanese goods was essential to a viable national defense bloc. What was needed, it was claimed, was an "independent" North China friendly to Japan. The reluctance of the Chinese to "cooperate" built up in Japan a powerful urge to settle the China problem by some sort of direct action.

Meanwhile Chiang Kai-shek had consolidated the Nanking regime and had begun to stiffen his resistance to Japanese demands. In the spring of 1937, Chiang had agreed to a united front with his communist antagonists in order to combat the Japanese penetration of North China. When unplanned fighting broke out between Chinese and Japanese troops near Peking on July 7, 1937, a border incident quickly flared into a general war. The areas of flexibility between Japan and China had become too narrow to permit a negotiated settlement.

The outbreak of fighting at Marco Polo Bridge thus marked the beginning of the long-drawn-out China Incident which in essence lasted until Japan's total defeat in 1945. No Japanese leader expected such a lengthy war, and civilian leaders in particular hoped for a quick Manchuria-like victory. Yet in the end the war proved unwinnable, and the Japanese were drawn further and further into an all but fruitless effort which hastened the conditions of militarism and regimentation at home

339

and led ultimately to Japan's attack upon the United States in 1941. Caught in a situation in which only victory would satisfy the national honor, the Japanese bled themselves in a cause in which simple military victory was essentially impossible.

The course of war in China proceeded in three distinct stages. Between July and December, 1937, the Japanese army moved rapidly to occupy major portions of North China, capturing Chiang Kai-shek's capital of Nanking. The fall of Nanking was expected to end China's will to resist, and the Japanese army, perhaps as punishment for the "anti-Japanese" activities of the Nanking regime, engaged in an orgy of rape and murder. In two days 12,000 non-combatant Chinese were killed in what has gone down in history as "the rape of Nanking."

Yet Chiang Kai-shek moved his capital inland to Hankow from which he directed further resistance. The second stage of Japanese operations was consequently concerned with the capture of Hankow and Canton. The latter city fell in October 1938. But Chiang again moved his capital inland above the Yangtze Gorges to Chungking. In the third phase of fighting which ensued, the Japanese bogged down into an amorphous stalemate in which the Chinese, resorting to guerrilla fighting, exchanged geography for time. After 1938 Japan controlled China's major cities and railroad lines but was constantly harassed by Chinese guerrillas who occupied the countryside.

By 1940 the China Incident was costing the equivalent of $4 million daily, and over 1.5 million Japanese had been sent overseas. Casualties among troops were high, and the rationing of essential commodities had begun at home. The "incident" had become a serious affair. And increasingly a note of desperation crept into the political and propaganda efforts to terminate it. Toward China the Japanese waged a vigorous propaganda campaign claiming that Japanese troops were engaged in a selfless "holy war" to free China from communism and the influence of the West. The effort to create a regime in North China friendly to Japan culminated in the establishment in Nanking of a puppet government under Wang

Ching-wei. Yet the Japanese attempts at political control and economic exploitation proved clumsy and ill-coordinated.

The domestic repercussions of war in China were profound. Japan now moved toward full-scale military mobilization and centralized economic planning. The government passed increasingly under military domination, while nationalist and patriotic slogans were used to exhort the people to dedicate themselves to the national effort. Thus while the extremist goals of creating a military based state-socialist structure in the name of the emperor had been crushed in 1936, by 1940 the country had been pushed so far into wartime mobilization and inculcated with statist ideology that it came to resemble very much what the military extremists had envisioned. As some observers have claimed, Japan in fact achieved the Shōwa Restoration, but *from the top.* The Japanese went to war with the United States in a state of near hysterical commitment to their "national mission," their emperor, and their "holy war" in China.

Late in 1937 Japan undertook the first major steps toward increased centralization of government control over the private sectors of the country—chiefly the political parties and the private business interests. A Cabinet Advisory Council, consisting of 4 representatives of the armed forces, 3 party men, 2 from finance and business, and 1 from the field of foreign affairs, was established to provide a balance of interests. A Cabinet Planning Board of 20 men, drawn from the now proliferating government bureaus, was looked upon to coordinate national policy. In November 1937 the Imperial Headquarters (Dai Hon Ei) was created to coordinate planning and operations within the two services. In March 1938 Premier Konoe aided the army in pushing through the Diet a National General Mobilization Law (Kokka Sōdōin Hō) which gave the Premier broad discretionary powers over the conduct of domestic affairs. The government, now able to by-pass the Diet, began to enact extraordinary measures for the control of the national economy, enforcing price controls and rationing, and allocating materials and labor.

341

From this point it was but a short step to the adoption of a coordinated plan for the mobilization of all aspects of national life. In 1940, after Prince Konoe had acquired the premiership for the second time, he announced the formation of a New National Structure (Shintaisei) for the purpose of turning Japan into an "advanced national defense state." Early in 1940 the political parties were coerced into dissolution, and their place was taken by the Imperial Rule Assistance Association (Taisei Yokusankai). Based on the single-party concept, the Association was to bring about the unification of all Japan's bureaucratic and political effort in support of "imperial objectives." All differences of opinion were to be submerged in a single collective cause. At the same time the few remaining labor unions were amalgamated into a single patriotic association of workers dedicated to the war effort.

The IRAA, though modeled in part on the Nazi Party, was typically Japanese in its composition and style of activity and differed fundamentally from its European counterpart. Not a party used to gain support in taking over the government, it was essentially the reverse, a mechanism by which Japan's leaders sought to create a facade of national consensus. Thus the Association had no active agents and relied very little on rallies and speech making. Rather more like the Communist one-party system, it worked through social pressures to grind down disaffection and to produce a single-minded unity behind the government. In all its ramifications it served more as a means of quieting opposition or heresy toward wartime goals and nationalist dogmas than as an active agent of political control. Thus while in Germany the Nazi party first seized control of government, then created a totalitarian state, and then went to war, Japan's "defense state" resulted from a reaction to an existing war and a growing sense of national insecurity. In the course of Japan's commitment to what eventually became total warfare, the nation was pushed towards a greater and greater mobilization of its resources, both material and human. But the resulting pattern of national regimentation differed greatly from the German or Italian models.

The mobilization efforts conducted under the IRAA fell into

three classifications. First was what was called popular mobilization, i.e., the effort to completely unify the home front. By mid-1941, the entire country was systematically organized into small neighborhood associations (called *tonarigumi*). These were linked into a nation-wide organization through town, city, prefectural, and national committees, to comprise a pyramidal structure of interrelated cells. The neighborhood units, organized by residence, absorbed every Japanese household into a system of compulsory councils. Patterned on the neighborhood groups of the Tokugawa period, they became a tremendous force in bringing about conformity, for the dissident or laggard literally had no place to hide in such a system. The neighborhood associations became means of boosting home front morale and spreading government propaganda. They served as units for rationing, civil defense, and for the collection of home front offerings to the war effort, such as cash for airplanes or gold for the government.

The second feature of the IRAA program was called "national purpose mobilization" and consisted of the effort to achieve an amalgamation of all political, social, and cultural agencies in the country. The parties and unions had already been united to an extent. Pressure was placed upon the newspapers, various professional organizations, and on the universities to merge facilities and to speak with a single voice.

That voice was the concern of the third area of IRAA effort, namely "spiritual mobilization." Increasingly as the Japanese people found themselves on the defensive and faced with external and internal problems of frustrating magnitude, the struggle to assert national identity and self-assurance created pressures towards conformity in thought and unity behind Japanist and nationalist slogans. Negatively, every effort was made to stamp out all dissident thinking. Positively, the Japanese hoisted such slogans as "the Imperial way" (*kōdō*), Yamato spirit (*Yamato damashii*), Imperial mission as exemplified in the phrase "all the world under one roof" (*hakkō-ichiu*), and "unity of government and religion" (*saisei-itchi*). Spiritual mobilization also called for overt anti-Westernism and the purging of Western influence from Japanese life. Foreign movies were increasingly dropped from the movie house bills, English was removed from train station signs, golf was given up in preference to Japanese archery. In school a new text, *Kokutai no hongi* (*The Essentials of Japan's National Polity*), inculcated acceptance of Japan's historical myths and the Shintō dogmas of the divinity of the emperor, the uniqueness of the Japanese people, and the mission Japan possessed to unify the world by bridging East and West. Irrational as much of the Shintō mythology was, the Japanese were able to convince themselves of the necessity of believing in their own national righteousness and in the essentially creative mission they held in the modern world.

By 1940 Japan was caught up in a cycle of events which forced it farther and farther along the course of ultranationalism, world isolation, and ultimately war with the United States. In Europe war had broken out in 1939, and the initial German successes had contrasted markedly with the frustrating circumstances which confronted Japan. With the fall of the Netherlands and France in June of 1940, many Japanese were convinced that the Axis powers were sure to win Europe. The time seemed ripe for Japan to create her own self-sufficient bloc in Asia. Thus in late 1940 Japan completed its diplomatic revolution against the Open Door powers under the leadership of Foreign Minister Matsuoka. In September he put the Japanese signature to the Tripartite Pact which forged a military alliance between Germany, Italy and Japan, and gave Japan recognition of her primacy in East Asia. When in April 1941 Matsuoka completed a non-aggression pact with Soviet Russia, Japan had acquired a free hand to move southward toward the French, Dutch and English colonies. While in 1938 Premier Konoe had issued a statement expounding Japan's "New Order in East Asia," by 1940, in restating his New Order policy, Konoe developed the idea of a *Greater* East Asia Co-prosperity Sphere, one which placed Japan at the hub of a defense bloc whose perimeter swung through the colonial areas to the south. But already Japan's expansive designs had begun to agitate the United States.

That an ultimate confrontation between Japan and the United States was possible had worried observers from the time of the Washington Conference, for Japanese interests were obviously at odds with the *status quo* efforts of the Open Door powers. Until the outbreak of World War II, however, it was Britain which stood most to lose by Japan's continental expansion and hence which offered the most tangible resistance. After 1939, however, the American reaction to Japan's continued fighting in China and to the spectre of a Japanese push to the south built up an image of Japan as a major menace to American security in the Pacific. Yet the stiffening of a positive American policy toward Japan was slow to come. President Roosevelt found his advisors divided between men like Ambassador Grew, who believed that patience would permit the "moderates" in the Japanese government to gain control of policy and so contain the military leadership, and former "old China hands" in the State Department who advised that a show of firmness was the only policy which the Japanese militarists could understand. The United States in fact had a considerable weapon to use against Japan, for the Japanese war industries depended heavily on U.S. iron and oil shipments. In 1939, when President Roosevelt delivered his rather mild "moral embargo" speech, he refrained from placing an embargo on these commodities but nonetheless put Japan in the camp of the totalitarian powers. In the summer of 1940, however, as a result of Japanese moves into French Indochina, the president permitted the existing U.S.-Japan trade treaty to expire and placed limited restrictions on the sale of strategic goods to Japan. The situation was worsened for the United States by the signing of the Tripartite Pact which merged the European and Pacific problems. When Japanese troops moved into south Indochina in the summer of 1941, America, Britain and Holland placed a total embargo on all exports to Japan, thus cutting off Japan's essential oil and rubber supplies. Japanese military officers calculated that reserves of these supplies in Japan would last for only two years. For them the situation was intolerable. Japan was already being "squeezed to death" by what they called the ABCD (American, British, Chinese and Dutch) encirclement. To the military in particular, the encirclement had to be broken.

By the time of the Nomura-Hull talks in the summer of 1941 the two countries had come to an impasse. The United States was determined that Japan should not only withdraw from Indochina but also from China. Japan was determined that the United States must abandon its support to Chiang Kai-shek, recognize Japanese hegemony in the Far East, and let up the oil embargo particularly on shipments from Indonesia. On both sides the escalation of objectives and commitments made retreat impossible. The Japanese had come to believe that one-time aspirations were now matters of absolute necessity and that their attainment was made legitimate in terms of national defense needs. The United States had come to believe that further Japanese expansion was unthinkable in view of the dangers posed by the totalitarian threat in the world. On both sides were grave miscalculations. Japan had joined the Axis powers in expectation that the United States would be intimidated; the United States, in adopting its "get tough" policy, expected the Japanese to back down.

In September 1941 at a meeting of the Liaison Council of high military and civil officials, Japan's leaders decided to go to war with the United States if agreement on oil shipments had not been reached by October. In October, General Tōjō became premier in anticipation of the possibility of war. At a November Imperial Conference, December 1 was set for mobilization, if final diplomatic negotiations failed. The decision was desperate, yet the prospect of war with America seemed more acceptable than retreat from China and possible civil rebellion at home. The Japanese military plan was well calculated. By knocking out the U.S. Pacific fleet at Pearl Harbor and destroying American forces in the Philippines, Japan could wait out the German victory in Europe in hopes that the U.S. would not move wholeheartedly against Japan. The plan contained a fatal miscalculation. The attack without warning on Pearl Harbor united the United States behind an all-out determination to crush Japan.

The war in the Pacific lasted for four years, bringing untold misery to the Japanese people and leading to the complete destruction of the Japanese empire and its military institutions. Yet for a year the Japanese *blitzkrieg* carried everything before it. At Pearl Harbor on December 7, the United States lost 7 battleships, 120 aircraft, and 2400 dead. In short order the Japanese overran the Philippines, captured Hong Kong, Singapore and Indonesia. By March 1942 Japanese troops were on New Guinea and were poised for the attack of Australia. By May they had occupied Burma and were considering the conquest of India. Yet Pearl Harbor had unified America in a fierce determination, and ultimately the massive military and industrial capacities of the United States and its allies began to turn against Japan. At Midway in June of 1942 the Japanese Navy lost four of its best carriers, and in August Allied forces on Guadalcanal made the first amphibious landing against Japanese troops. Japan's overextended empire was placed on the defensive.

Between the summer of 1942 and 1944 the Allies were primarily engaged in Europe, yet Japan suffered tremendous losses in shipping to Allied submarines, and several strategic islands in the Gilbert and Marshall Islands were reconquered. In the summer of 1944 the Allies directed two massive island-hopping amphibious thrusts toward the Japanese home islands. One pushed into the Marianas, capturing Saipan in June and Iwo Jima in March of 1945. The other recaptured the Philippines in October 1944. The two movements converged on Okinawa in May of 1945 and succeeded in taking it from the Japanese in June. Allied forces were now on Japan's doorstep and within bombing range of the home islands. Beginning in late 1944 Allied planes began the systematic bombing of Japanese cities. The single incendiary attack on Tōkyō on March 10, 1945 is estimated to have killed 100,000 persons. In all, 668,000 civilians died in Japan during these raids. By the summer of 1945 Japan was militarily beaten but still unwilling to accept the unconditional surrender demanded by the Potsdam Declaration. Then in August Japan received two blows that made surrender inevitable. On August 6 the U.S. dropped its first atomic bomb on Hiroshima. On August 8 the Russians

347

declared war and began to overrun Manchuria. On the 9th a second atom bomb was dropped on Nagasaki. Against the continued protests of the military, the emperor on August 14 took upon himself to "endure the unendurable." The next day Japan officially accepted the Potsdam Declaration.

19

Occupation and Recovery

The Allied Occupation of Japan is one of the most remarkable
chapters in world history. Certainly no occupation, other than
one of outright conquest, has been so dedicated to political and
social reform. And certainly few other societies have been as
thoroughly "made over" in so short a time as was Japan between 1945 and 1952. Japan's response to the Allied Occupation was the more remarkable since the country had never
before experienced a defeat in war which brought a foreign
occupation to its soil.

Japan in the summer of 1945 was a nation totally exhausted
both physically and morally. Since the outbreak of the China
War 3.1 million Japanese—of whom 800,000 were civilians—
had lost their lives. The country had experienced the most
frightful of shocks: the great incendiary raids on its cities and
the explosion of two atomic bombs. Over 30 percent of the
Japanese had lost their homes. For nearly a year Japan had
been virtually without sea communication, and inland transportation had all but collapsed. Acute food shortages brought
much of the country to near starvation; civilian morality broke
down as farmers reaped tremendous profits by selling food on
the black market and as wealthy families bartered heirlooms
for the necessities of life. Industry had been smashed to one
quarter of its previous potential, the country was on the verge
of an inflation that reduced the *yen* to barely a hundredth of
its prewar value. The people also were emotionally and intellectually bewildered, having been brought up on exaggerated

wartime propaganda and hyper-nationalist values, all of which collapsed with Japan's unconditional surrender.

Yet out of the debris of war and the collapse of Japan's wartime value system, Japan made a remarkably speedy and complete recovery. Three factors in particular helped to account for this achievement. First the breakdown of the Japanese state and the existing social system was checked by the final decision by the occupying forces to retain the essential structure of the Japanese polity and to modify but not abolish the position of the emperor. Second, and perhaps as a corollary to the first, the Japanese as a people retained their sense of social and political discipline. Third, the Japanese managed to avoid the worst psychological aftermath of defeat by passing the guilt of war on to the military sector of the society. Having faced defeat in expectation of the worst consequences, the Japanese reacted to the benevolent nature of the occupation with relief and then enthusiasm. A pragmatically inclined people, the fact that they had been defeated by "democratic powers" made them overnight converts to the efficacy of the democratic system.

In the long run, of course, Japan's postwar transformation could not have taken place had it not been for the long era of modernization which had preceded World War II. To this extent the postwar era was a direct legacy from the era of party government of the 1920's. Yet Japan could probably have made its recovery to become a model socialist state as well, if the circumstances had demanded it. It is significant therefore that the policy which was applied to Japan in 1945 was largely made in the United States and that its two main agents of application were General MacArthur on the American side and Premier Yoshida on the Japanese. For MacArthur, while essentially a deep conservative, had come to view himself briefly as a messenger of democracy in the most idealized terms. And Yoshida, as a convert to representative government, was able to stand up for the dignity of the Japanese people and their cultural independence.

The Allied Occupation was distinguished, then, by the fact that SCAP (the Supreme Commander for the Allied Powers) was personified in General MacArthur and was almost exclusively an American show. Japan was not partitioned as was Germany or Korea, as a result of the primary American effort in the Pacific War and because of the prestige which accrued from the Atom Bomb. SCAP policy, while set in terms of fundamentals in Washington, was rather freely interpreted in Tōkyō. It is fortunate that a remarkable degree of rapport was worked out between the American military advisors sent to Japan and the Japanese government officials who remained in office to carry out SCAP directives.

Occupation policy fell under three major headings: demilitarization, democratization, and rehabilitation. To begin with, the first two categories were emphasized, for resentment over Japanese militarism ran high at the outset. Under the heading of demilitarization, Japan was stripped of all its wartime gains and obliged to abolish the institutional supports upon which the military establishment rested. First the Japanese empire was literally cut back to the four main islands with which Japan had started in 1868. Thus Japan lost outright Manchuria, Korea, Taiwan, Sakhalin and the Kuriles; Okinawa and the Bonin Islands were placed under U.S. trusteeship. The contraction of the Japanese empire necessitated the repatriation of 6.5 million Japanese, many of whom had been firmly settled in colonial areas. Demilitarization called for the destruction of Japan's armed forces, abolition of the ministries of Army and Navy, of all war industries, air transportation and even for a time Japan's merchant marine. To eliminate persons who had "participated in Japanese expansion," SCAP ordered a purge of some 180,000 individuals from positions of leadership in government, the services and education. A war crimes trial brought to public prosecution 25 leaders who were presumed to have been most involved in wartime atrocities and the responsibility for the outbreak of war. Leading the list of 7 who were hanged in 1948 was ex-Premier Tōjō.

Other measures less strictly concerned with the reduction of Japan's military potential were calculated to lay the roots of democratic behavior in Japanese soil. The abolition of state Shintō, the cutting off of state support from all Shintō shrines, and the cessation of the Shintō-based "morals" courses in Japanese schools was pressed in order to purge from Japanese thought the traditional dogmas upon which ultra-nationalism had flourished. The emperor, also, was obliged to take to the radio to "deny his divinity."

The single most important political change adopted by SCAP was the establishment of a new constitution. Put through as an amendment of the Meiji Constitution in 1947, the new document altered fundamentally the political structure of the Japanese state, creating a truly representative form of government in which the locus of sovereignty was firmly placed in the hands of the people. The new constitution began with the phrase "We, the Japanese people." It wrote into its clauses a new definition of the emperor as "symbol of the state and of the unity of the people, deriving his position from the will of the people with whom resides sovereign power." It established a cabinet responsible to the electorate on the British model, it provided for an extension of the franchise to all men and women aged 20 or over, and made both houses of the Diet elective. (The Upper house was to be called the House of Councillors.) It created an independent judiciary and made high office in local government elective, including the office of prefectural governor. It decentralized the police system. Human rights were guaranteed by the new constitution through a Bill of Rights. And Article 9 contained the now famous provision for the disavowal of warfare except for self-defense. All told the constitution was probably more "liberal" than could have been adopted in the United States at the time.

The new constitution, though purportedly the work of Japanese framers, was largely identical with the working draft provided by the Government Section of SCAP. Yet its acceptance by the Japanese leadership shows that the Japanese people were in large measure prepared for the changes set down in it. In the years since 1947 it has withstood efforts at revision, and its system of government has proved congenial to the Japanese, providing for a fuller development of representative government.

Occupation reforms were directed toward the economy as

well. A major effort was made to break up the great *zaibatsu* combines so as to decentralize the economy. Anti-monopoly legislation was passed to preclude re-combination. Labor unions were given support and encouraged to counterbalance the power of management. And within a year union membership rose to 4.5 million. One of the most influential achievements of the Occupation was land reform. Attacking the problems of tenant farming and absentee landlordism at their roots, the reform obliged all absentee owners to sell their paddy land holdings beyond 2½ acres. Cultivator owners were permitted to retain up to 7½ acres. In a short while over 5 million acres changed hands, and owner-cultivated land rose from 53 to 87 per cent of the total. The collection of rents in kind was virtually eliminated. These reforms, combined with postwar agricultural prosperity, accounted for a remarkable period of both economic and political stability in the village communities of postwar Japan.

Finally there was education reform. The Occupation sought to decentralize the state educational system, though it did not abolish the Ministry of Education. The 6–3–3–4 system culminating in a college curriculum of general education was introduced. Local school boards were given power over portions of the curriculum, P.T.A. associations were created, and efforts made to diminish the authoritarian atmosphere of the classrooms. To spread the base of higher education new prefectural universities were created. Perhaps the most significant of all was the thoroughgoing curriculum and textbook revisions sponsored by the Occupation. These eliminated the "morals" courses, for which were substituted "social studies"; modified history textbooks to set forth a new pluralistic viewpoint; and introduced such new social science subjects as political science. A further step was also taken toward simplification of the written language.

The Occupation lasted until 1951 but its basic policies had been carried out by the end of 1947. The early years were filled with remarkable idealism both on the part of the Occupation authorities, many of whom were ex-Fair Deal bureaucrats, and for the Japanese, who found the reforms congenial. By

1948 the nature of the Occupation changed. Increasingly SCAP turned decision-making over to the Japanese. American basic policy also changed, as opposition to Fair Deal policies increased at home and as difficulties with Russia and the Chinese Communists brought cold war tensions into East Asia. Japan, the former enemy, gradually emerged as a major ally of the United States in Asia. After 1948, therefore, American strategic interests in Japan began to outweigh those of de-militarization and reform, and basic policy turned toward rehabilitation and reconstruction. With the outbreak of the Korean war Japan suddenly became an invaluable asset to the American forces. With economic recovery a major objective, earlier economic and fiscal restrictions were relaxed. A "National Police Reserve" was permitted Japan in 1950, and by 1960 this was to become a 200,000 man "National Defense Force" fully provided with tanks, airplanes, and naval units. While the letter of Article 9 was retained, Japan was encouraged to participate in its own self-defense.

In 1951 the United States and 47 other nations signed a peace treaty with Japan. Soviet Russia and Communist China still refrained from acknowledging diplomatic relations with Japan. The Occupation formally came to an end in 1952. However, a security treaty and an administrative agreement signed between Japan and the United States provided for the continuation of American military bases in Japan and committed the United States to protect Japan in case of war. Thus Japan remained under the American protective umbrella and continued to provide important military facilities upon which American power in East Asia could be based. Increasingly, however, Japan regained its freedom of action and its status in the world. In 1956 diplomatic relations were restored with Soviet Russia, and Japan was admitted to the United Nations.

The Occupation years—"Japan's American Interlude"— and the years of adjustment immediately following clearly constitute a major watershed in Japan's history. Ranking next to the Meiji Restoration as a time of drastic change toward modernization, it has been looked upon by some as marking

Japan's final break with tradition and acceptance of institutions and values uncolored by feudal or Confucian ideas. Yet it is difficult to separate out the factors of history, tradition, and enforced change which culminated in the Occupation era. Certainly without the changes of the 1870's and 80's, and without the experience of the 1920's, the institutional reforms of 1945–1947 would hardly have taken root. It is hard to know, of course, how much wartime privation and the shock of defeat had to do with the depth to which social and economic reforms penetrated. The Occupation was more than catalyst, but it was not the sole moving force in postwar Japan. Let us say then that it was the combined force of wartime suffering, defeat, disillusion, and occupation which pushed Japan over its second major watershed in the course of modernization, creating a mass participation society with sovereignty invested in the people, a mass consumption society with one of the most remarkable economic growth rates of any society in modern times.

As of the mid-1960's, Japan, though lacking its own military power and still exercising restraint in voicing its opinion in world affairs, had produced a remarkable set of statistics to document its rise into what by 1968 had become third place among the world's industrial powers. With a population already over 100 million, a life expectancy of 65 for men and 70 for women, a per capita income of over $600 by 1965, and only 25 percent of its labor force engaged in agriculture, Japan had taken on the demographic features of an advanced modern society. In 1950 Japan passed the United Kingdom in shipbuilding and in 1961 in steel production. In the 1960's Japan became second only to the U.S. in the manufacture of radios and television sets. In the same period it passed West Germany to become third in the manufacture of autos. Japan ranked fifth in giving foreign aid to underdeveloped countries, having contributed to economic projects in India and Pakistan and to the launching of the Asian Development Bank. Japan's "new capitalism," as W. W. Lockwood has called it, had seemingly overcome most of the problems which kept Japan's prewar economy so unbalanced in its structure.

Yet the Japanese themselves, living in a land of new television sets and high-speed trains, found it difficult to believe that their country was still not in a precarious economic position. One of the reasons may be that there remained considerable uncertainty about the country's political leadership. Japan came through the Occupation years with a political organization which probably came the closest of any Asian nation to being a practical working democracy. Politics in postwar Japan looked increasingly like that in Western societies, with a stable balance between two parties and with some 75 percent of the electorate voting for candidates on a multiple-choice basis. Japan, in other words, was far advanced in its solution of the problem of the popular relationship to the political process. Yet a certain uneasiness could be seen to pervade the balance of interests and ideologies upon which Japanese politics rested. Deep-seated cleavages were still in evidence. Behind the strong Liberal-Democratic Party coalition the government still operated under the shadow of establishment interests. Between 1950 and 1951 over 80,000 men had been depurged, thus helping to bring back into political leadership men who had grown up in the prewar atmosphere of elite politics. Meanwhile the Socialist Party had its difficulties as a "permanent minority party." Part of this was due to the manner of its emergence as a major party and the difficulties it had in bringing unity out of the factionalism which had always plagued the Left. Early Occupation policies had been extremely liberal in political matters. Wartime political prisoners, among them communists, were released from jail, and freedom of political assembly was encouraged. For a brief period from June 1947 to March 1948 Katayama Tetsu of the Socialist Party became premier. But a legacy of the prewar factionalism and involvement with both communism and labor unionism continued to divide socialist leadership over policy, both national and foreign. The conservative party soon returned to power under Premier Yoshida and was to stay in power ever since. The socialists, while growing in importance, still constituted a minority, relatively untested by the responsibilities of being in power. Because of their heavy reliance on labor support they precluded the kind of political consensus between major parties as in the United States or Britain. The claim that Japan's has been a "one and a half party" system has some validity. Thus when in 1960 the Socialists attempted to block acceptance of the U.S.-Japan Mutual Defense Treaty, they were reduced to obstructionist tactics in the face of what they called the "tyranny of the majority." Adding to the sense of ideological tension between the conservative and leftist parties in Japan was the continual anti-establishment role of the academic and intellectual elite and of the great newspapers. Fear of radicalism, through violent moves either to the right or the left, remained to haunt the Japanese people.

Domestic uncertainties were closely interrelated to the problem of Japan's recovery of a sense of world security. Japan's road back to international respectability has been slow going, and the Japanese, remembering the suffering of war, have been reluctant to assert themselves. Also in the postwar world in which Japan has been so dependent upon the United States, a move toward greater freedom of action has immediately placed before Japan the problems of cold war tension and of dealing with Communist China. By the end of the 1960's Japan was still cautious in its response to the world. Its future depended very much on an open world economy and a free balance of power; and the openness of its own political system depended greatly on its ability to maintain a profitable relationship with the world at large.

Chronology of Japanese History

ca. 150,000 B.C.–Evidence of preceramic culture

ca. 7000–250 B.C.–Jōmon pottery culture

    ca. 250 B.C.–Introduction of Yayoi culture

      660 B.C.–Mythical date of the accession of Jimmu, first Emperor

ca. A.D. 300–645–Yamato Period

  552 or 538–Introduction of Buddhism from Korea

    593–622–Regency of Prince Shōtoku (Shōtoku Taishi)

       607–First embassy to China

       645–Taika coup d'état, followed by Reform

       702–Taihō Law Codes promulgated

710–784–Nara Period

       752–Dedication of the Great Buddha (Daibutsu) of Tōdaiji in Nara

    781–806–Reign of Kammu; revival of Taihō institutions

794–1185–Heian Period

       805–Introduction of Tendai sect

       806–Introduction of Shingon sect

       838–Twelfth and last embassy to China

858–1160–Fujiwara Period

   995–1027–Supremacy of Fujiwara-no-Michinaga

ca. 1002–1019–Writing of *Genji monogatari* (*The Tale of Genji*) by Murasaki Shikibu

 1086–1129–Establishment by Shirakawa of *Insei* (rule by the retired Emperor)

 1159–1160–Heiji conflict; military supremacy gained by Taira-no-Kiyomori (d. 1181)

1175–Founding of the Jōdo (Pure Land) sect by Hōnen Shōnin (1133–1212)
1180–1185–War between the Minamoto and the Taira (Gempei War)
1185–1333–Kamakura Period
1192–Title of Shogun granted to Yoritomo
1203–Hōjō-no-Tokimasa appointed *Shikken* (Shogunal
Regent)
1232–*Jōei shikimoku* (Kamakura Law Code) issued
by Hōjō
1274, 1281–Mongol invasions
1334–Kemmu Restoration under Go-Daigo
1338–1573–Ashikaga (or Muromachi) Period
1368–1394–Yoshimitsu (1358–1408), third Shogun
1449–1473–Yoshimasa (d. 1490), eighth Shogun
1467–1477–Ōnin War
1542 or 1543–Portuguese at Tanegashima; introduction of
Western firearms
1549–St. Francis Xavier (1506–1552) arrives in Japan
1568–1600–Azuchi-Momoyama (or Shokuhō) Period
1568–Occupation of Kyōto by Oda Nobunaga
1582–Nobunaga assassinated by Akechi Mitsuhide
1586–Ōsaka Castle built by Toyotomi Hideyoshi
1590–Hideyoshi supreme in Japan
1592–Hideyoshi's first invasion of Korea
1595–Nationwide cadastral survey (*kenchi*) ordered
1598–Death of Hideyoshi and withdrawal of troops
from Korea
1600–Victory of Tokugawa Ieyasu at the Battle of
Sekigahara
1600–1868–Tokugawa (or Edo) Period
1603–Title of Shogun acquired by Ieyasu
1614–1615–Capture of Ōsaka Castle
1622–1623–Period of the greatest Christian persecutions
1623–1651–Institutional foundations of the Tokugawa shogunate completed by Iemitsu, third Shogun
1637–1638–Shimabara uprising
1639–Sakoku-rei (seclusion order) promulgated
1641–Dutch factory moved to Deshima at Nagasaki
1688–1704–Genroku Era

1716–1745–Kyōhō Reforms initiated by Yoshimune (1648–1751), eighth Shogun
1769–1786–Supremacy of Tanuma Okitsugu (1719–1788)
1787–1793–Supremacy of Matsudaira Sadanobu (1759–1829), author of the Kansei Reforms
1804–1829–Bunka-Bunsei Era
    1804–Arrival of Nikolai Rezanov at Nagasaki
    1837–Rice riot in Ōsaka led by the Confucian scholar Ōshio Heihachirō
1841–1843–Tempō Reforms undertaken by Mizuno Tadakuni; *kabunakama* (merchant guilds) abolished
    1853–Arrival of Commodore Perry at Uraga
    1854–Treaty of Kanagawa with the United States
1858–1860–Ii Naosuke as *Tairō* (Great Councillor)
    1858–Commercial treaty with the United States
    1862–*Sankin kōtai* (alternate attendance) relaxed
    1865–Imperial ratification of treaties with foreign powers
1866–1867–Yoshinobu (Keiki, d. 1913), fifteenth and last Shogun
    1867–Enthronement of Mutsuhito (Meiji)
1868–1912–Meiji Period
    1868–January 3, resumption of rule by the Emperor; Emperor's Charter Oath
    1869–Return of daimyo domains to the Emperor
    1873–New national military conscription law; new land tax system; establishment of the Home Ministry (*Naimushō*)
    1877–February-September, Satsuma rebellion
    1881–Decree promising constitution
    1885–Beginning of the Cabinet (*Naikaku*) system; Itō, first Premier
    1889–Promulgation of the Constitution; Gen. Yamagata Aritomo (1838–1922), Premier
    1890–Imperial Rescript on Education
1894–1895–Sino-Japanese War
    1899–Revision of treaties; extraterritoriality ended
    1902–Signing of the Anglo-Japanese alliance
1904–1905–Russo-Japanese War
    1910–Annexation of Korea

1912–1926–Taishō Period

1914–Ōkuma as Premier; Japanese declaration of war on Germany

1915–Twenty-one Demands pressed on China

1918–Beginning of "party government"; Hara Kei (Takashi) of the Seiyukai as Premier

1921–1922–Washington Conference

1925–Passage of the Universal Manhood Suffrage Bill and the Peace Preservation Law by the Diet

1926– –Shōwa Period

1930–Signing of the London Naval Treaty

1931–Outbreak of the "Manchurian Incident"

1933–Japan quits League of Nations

1937–Prince Konoe Fumimaro (1891–1945) as Premier; July, outbreak of war with China

1940–Announcement by Premier Konoe of *Shintaisei* (New National Order); Tripartite Alliance with Germany and Italy; inauguration of the Imperial Rule Assistance Association

1941–Gen. Tōjō Hideki as Premier; December 7, attack on Pearl Harbor

1945–Surrender of Japan

1946–Gen. Douglas MacArthur appointed SCAP; disavowal of "divinity" by the Emperor; new constitution promulgated; Yoshida Shigeru as Premier; Occupation reforms

1950–Creation of the National Police Reserve by the Japanese

1951–Peace Conference in San Francisco

1952–Occupation of Japan terminated

1953–United States-Japan Mutual Security Agreement

1956–Japan admitted to the United Nations

1960–Demonstrations against the continuation of United States-Japan Mutual Security Treaty

1964–Satō Eisaku as Premier; Tōkyō Olympiad

Glossary

bakufu: headquarters of the shogun; the shogunate.

baku-han: a modern term referring to the Tokugawa system of government in which the shogunate (*bakufu*) exercised authority over the several daimyo (*han*).

be: "service community" in early Japan, attached to an *uji;* abolished after 645.

bugyō: commissioner; an official charged with a specific administrative function.

buke shohatto: "code of the military houses," the basic set of regulations applied by the Tokugawa shogunate to the daimyo. First issued in 1615.

bushi: the military aristocracy; the samurai.

chigyō-chi: land held in fief.

chō: a land area: about 3 acres in the eighth century, 2.5 acres after the sixteenth century.

chōnin: non-samurai urban dwellers; merchants and artisans.

daimyo: after the fifteenth century, a local magnate with territory producing 10,000 *koku* or more of rice.

fudai: "house daimyo" of the Tokugawa shogun; i.e., those created by the shogun.

fukoku kyōhei: "to prosper the nation and strengthen its defenses," a primary slogan of the early Meiji state leaders.

genrō: elder statesmen, men who because of their role in the Meiji Restoration served as imperial advisers from the 1890's to the 1930's.

gokenin: "housemen"; commonly used to refer to the close vassals of the shogun.

gun: district; a subdivision of a province.

han: a daimyo domain.

hatamoto: "bannermen"; enfeoffed vassals of the Tokugawa shogun of less than daimyo rank.

hyakushō: farmer

in: cloister; retired emperor. In 1086 the retired emperor Shirakawa began the practice of exercising political influence through the "office of the cloister."

jitō: "military land stewards" appointed to facilitate *shōen* administration by the Kamakura shogunate.

kami: central concept of Shinto referring to spirit or deity.

kampaku: imperial regent; title acquired by the Fujiwara family in the ninth century.

kan: "string"; unit of measure for copper cash; 1,000 cash.

karō: elder; chief vassal of daimyo.

kanrei: chief official of the Ashikaga shogunate.

kenchi: land survey, particularly of agricultural land for tax purposes.

kofun: prehistoric burial mound or tumulus.

Kojiki: history of Japan written according to native tradition, in contrast with the *Nihon shoki*. Presumably completed in 712.

koku: a measure of grain, roughly 5.2 bushels.

kokugaku: "national learning," the school of national (Shintō) studies which flourished during the late Tokugawa period.

kuge: the civil court aristocracy.

kuni: term for the area under the control of a territorial chieftain in ancient Japan. After 645, groups of several such units were combined into new and larger *kuni,* or provinces, of which eventually there were 66.

kuni-no-miyatsuko: title of territorial aristocracy prior to the Taika Reform (645).

minken: popular rights.

momme: unit of weight used to measure silver in financial transactions.

mura: village.

muraji: aristocratic title of high rank prior to 685.

Nihon shoki: officially commissioned history of Japan, completed in 720 under Chinese influence.

omi: early aristocratic title indicating kinship to the imperial line; it lost its significance after 685.

rōjū: "elders," senior councillors in the Tokugawa shogunal administration.

ryō: unit of gold currency.

sankin-kōtai: "alternate attendance." The system whereby daimyo under the Tokugawa were obliged to spend half their time "in attendance" on the shogun at Edo.

sengoku daimyo: daimyo of the Sengoku period; the first true daimyo.

shiki: rights and obligations pertaining to land tenures under the *shōen* system.

shikken: shogunal regent during the Kamakura period.

shimpan: daimyo houses collaterally related to the main Tokugawa shogunal line.

shōen: landed proprietorship exempted from central government control. Private estate.

shogun: from the twelfth through the nineteenth century, the chief military figure of Japan.

shōyū: soy sauce.

shugo: "military governor" appointed by province under the Kamakura and Ashikaga shogunates.

Taihō: era name for the years 701–703. It has given its name to the administrative and judicial codes issued in 702.

tennō: the emperor.

tenryō: the territory held directly by the Tokugawa shogun.

tozama: "allied daimyo" of the Tokugawa shogun; i.e., those who pledged allegiance as peers of the Tokugawa shogun.

uji: aristocratic lineage consisting of a main family and an extended group of branches.

uji-gami: deity worshipped as the guardian or founding spirit by the members of an aristocratic lineage.

ukiyo: "fleeting world," the stylish world of the urban entertainment quarters.

za: trade or commercial guild in medieval Japan.

zaibatsu: the "business clique," the great commercial-industrial cartels which emerged during the 1920's.

Bibliography

Much of the content of this volume is dependent upon the work of Japanese historians writing in their own language. I have not listed these works, but those who have an interest in the nature and extent of the field of history in Japan may consult my *Japanese History: A Guide to Japanese Reference and Research Materials*, the Kokusai Bunka Shinkōkai bibliographic series, and the reports prepared by the Rekishigaku Nihon Kokunai Iinkai cited below.

The list which follows is weighted toward political and social history and thus neglects the very large body of literature in translation which is so useful in filling in the cultural environments of the several periods of Japanese history. Any of the standard bibliographies which appear below, beginning with that by B. S. Silberman, should serve to open up this field. Recommended for its completeness is the bibliography published by the P. E. N. Club.

Akita, G., *Foundations of Constitutional Government in Modern Japan 1868–1900*. Cambridge, Mass., 1967.

Allen, G. C., *Japan's Economic Expansion*. London, 1965.

———, *Japan's Economic Recovery*, New York, 1958.

———, *A Short Economic History of Modern Japan,* rev. ed. London, 1962.

American Embassy, Tōkyō, Daily Summary of the Japanese Press; Trends of Japanese Magazines; Summaries of Selected Japanese Magazines. Mimeo.

American Historical Association, The American Historical Association's *Guide to Historical Literature*. New York, 1963.

Anesaki, M., *History of Japanese Religion*. London, 1930. Reprint, Tōkyō, 1963.

Asakawa, K., *The Documents of Iriki*. New Haven, 1929. Tōkyō, 1955.

———, *The Early Institutional Life of Japan*. Reprint, New York, 1963.

———, *Land and Society in Medieval Japan*. Tōkyō, 1965.

Asia Major. Leipzig, 1924–35, 1944. London, 1949.

Association for Asian Studies, *Bibliography* (annual September issue), 1955.

———, *The Journal of Asian Studies*. Ann Arbor, 1956– (Formerly the *Far Eastern Quarterly*, 1941–1956.)

Aston, W. G., *Nihongi; Chronicles of Japan from the Earliest Times to AD 697*. London, 1896. Reprint, 1956.

Beardsley, R., Hall, J. W., and Ward, R., *Village Japan*. Chicago, 1959.

Beasley, W. G., *Great Britain and the Opening of Japan, 1834–1858*. London, 1951.

———, *Japan. Geschichte der letzten 150 Jahre*. Spich, 1964.

———, *The Modern History of Japan*. London, 1963.

———, (ed. and trans.), *Select Documents on Japanese Foreign Policy, 1853–1868*. London, 1955.

———, and Pulleyblank, E. G., (eds.), *Historians of China and Japan*. London, 1961.

Beaujard, A., *Sei Shōnagon, Son Temps et Son Oeuvre (Une Femme de Lettres de l'Ancien Japon)*. Paris, 1934.

Beckmann, G. M., *The Making of the Meiji Constitution: The Oligarchs and the Constitutional Development of Japan, 1868–1891*. Lawrence, Kansas, 1957.

Bellah, R. N., *Tokugawa Religion: The Values of Pre-Industrial Japan*. Glencoe, Ill., 1957.

Benedict, R., *The Chrysanthemum and the Sword*. Boston, 1946.

Benl, O., and Hammitzsch, H., *Japanische Geisteswelt: Vom Mythus zur Gegenwart*. Baden-Baden, 1956.

Bennett, J. W., and Ishino, I., *Paternalism in the Japanese Economy*. Minneapolis, 1963.

Bernard, Henri, S. J., "Les Débuts des Relations Diplomatiques entre le Japon et les Espagnols des Iles Philippines 1571–1594)." *Monumenta Nipponica*, 1.1 (1938), pp. 99–137.

———, "Les premiers rapports de la culture européenne avec la civilization Japonaise." *Bulletin de La Maison Franco-Japonaise,* 10.1 (1938), pp. 1–74.

Bersihand, Roger, *Geschichte Japans von den Anfangen bis zur Gegenwart,* übers. V. S. Scharschmidt. Stuttgart, 1963.

Blacker, C., *The Japanese Enlightenment: A Study of the Writings of Fukuzawa Yukichi.* New York, 1964.

Bohner, H., "Shōtoku Taishi." Deutsche Gesellschaft für Natur- und Völkerkunde Ostasiens, *Mitteilungen.* Supplementband XV., Tōkyō, 1940.

Borton, H., (ed.), *Japan Between East and West.* New York, 1957.

——, *Japan's Modern Century.* New York, 1955.

——, *Peasant Uprisings in Japan of the Tokugawa Period.* New York, 1968.

——, et al., *A Selected List of Books and Articles on Japan in English, French and German.* Cambridge, Mass., 1954.

Boxer, C. R., *The Christian Century in Japan, 1549–1650.* Berkeley, 1951. Second edition, 1967.

——, *Jan Compagnie in Japan 1600–1850.* The Hague, 1950.

Brower, R. H. and Miner, E., *Japanese Court Poetry.* Stanford, 1961.

Brown, D. M., *Money Economy in Medieval Japan: A Study in the Use of Coins.* New Haven, 1951.

——, *Nationalism in Japan: An Introductory Historical Analysis.* Berkeley, 1955.

Bulletin of the School of Oriental and African Studies. London, 1920– .

Bunce, W. K. (ed.), *Religions in Japan.* Rutland, Vt., 1955.

Butow, R., *Japan's Decision to Surrender.* Stanford, 1954.

——, *Tōjō and the Coming of the War.* Princeton, 1961.

Chamberlain, B. H. (trans.), *Kojiki, or Records of Ancient Matters,* 2nd ed. Kōbe, 1932.

Chambliss, W., *Chiaraijima Village: Land Tenure, Taxation, and Local Trade, 1818–1884.* Tucson, 1965.

Chikamatsu, M., *The Major Plays of Chikamatsu,* trans. by D. Keene. New York, 1961.

Cohen, J. B., *The Japanese Economy in War and Reconstruction.* Minneapolis, 1949.

Conroy, H., *The Japanese Seizure of Korea, 1868–1910.* Philadelphia, 1960.

Craig, A. M., *Chōshū in the Meiji Restoration.* Cambridge, Mass., 1961.

Crawcour, E. S., "Changes in Japanese Commerce in the Tokugawa Period." *Journal of Asian Studies,* 22.4 (1963), pp. 387–400.

Crowley, J. B., *Japan's Quest for Autonomy.* Princeton, 1966.

Dettmer, H. A., *Die Steuergesetzgebung der Nara-Zeit.* Wiesbaden, 1959.

―――, *Grundzüge der Geschichte Japans.* Darmstadt, 1965.

Dore, R. P., *City Life in Japan.* London, 1958.

―――, *Education in Tokugawa Japan.* Berkeley, 1965.

―――, *Land Reform in Japan.* London, 1959.

―――(ed.), *Aspects of Social Change in Modern Japan.* Princeton, 1967.

Dumoulin, H., Kamo Mabuchi, "Ein Beitrag zur japanischen Religions- und Geistesgeschichte." *Monumenta Nipponica* Monograph No. 8., Tōkyō, 1943.

―――, *Zen: Geschichte und Gestalt.* Berne, 1959.

Duus, P., *Party Rivalry and Political Change in Taishō Japan.* Cambridge, 1968.

Earl, D., *Emperor and Nation in Japan, Political Thinkers of the Tokugawa Period.* Seattle, 1964.

Embree, J. F., *Suye Mura: A Japanese Village.* Chicago, 1939.

―――, *The Japanese Nation, 1945.* The Smithsonian Institution, October, 1950.

Eliot, C., *Japanese Buddhism.* New York, 1959.

Esthus, R., *Theodore Roosevelt and Japan.* Seattle, 1966.

Fairbank, J., Reischauer, E. O., and Craig, A., *A History of East Asian Civilization,* Vol. II., *The Modern Transformation.* Boston, 1965.

Feary, R. A., *The Occupation of Japan, Second Phase, 1948–1950.* New York, 1950.

Feis, H., *Japan Subdued.* Princeton, 1961.

―――, *The Road to Pearl Harbor.* Princeton, 1950.

Fukutake, T., *Man and Society in Japan.* Tōkyō, 1962.

Fukuzawa, Y., *Autobiography.* Tōkyō, 1940. New translation, Tōkyō, 1960.

Gaspardone, E., "La Chronologie Ancienne du Japon." *Journal Asiatique,* 230 (1938), pp. 235–77.

Ginsburg, N. S., *The Pattern of Asia.* Englewood Cliffs, New Jersey, 1958.

Gonthier, A., *Histoire des Institutions Japonaises.* Brussels, 1956.

Groot, G. J., *The Prehistory of Japan.* New York, 1951.

Grousset, R., *Les Civilisations de l'Orient*. Tome IV; *Le Japon*. Paris, 1930.

Gundert, W., *Japanische Religionsgeschichte*. Tōkyō, 1943.

Haguenauer, C., *Origines de la Civilisation Japonaise*. Paris, 1956.

Hall, J. W., "The Castle Town and Japan's Modern Urbanization." *Far Eastern Quarterly*, Vol. 15, No. 1 (1955), pp. 37–56.

——, "The Confucian Teacher in Tokugawa Japan." Nivison, D. S., and Wright, A. F. (eds.), *Confucianism in Action*. Stanford, 1959.

——, "Feudalism in Japan—A Reassessment." *Comparative Studies in Society and History*, Vol. 5 (1962), pp. 15–51.

——, "Foundations of the Modern Japanese Daimyo." *Journal of Asian Studies*, Vol. 20, No. 3 (1961), pp. 317–29.

——, *Government and Local Power in Japan, 500–1700: A Study Based on Bizen Province*. Princeton, 1966.

——, "Historiography in Japan." *Teachers of History*, Hughes, H. S., (ed.). Ithaca, 1954.

——, *Japanese History: A Guide to Japanese Reference and Research Materials*. Ann Arbor, 1954.

——, *Japanese History: New Dimensions of Approach and Understanding*. Service Center for Teachers of History, Publication 34. Washington, 1961.

——, *Tanuma Okitsugu, 1719–1788: Forerunner of Modern Japan*. Cambridge, 1955.

——, and Beardsley, R. K., *Twelve Doors to Japan*. New York, 1965.

——, and Jansen, M., *Studies in the Institutional History of Early Modern Japan*. Princeton, 1968.

Hall, R. K. (ed.), *Kokutai no Hongi: Cardinal Principles of the National Entity of Japan*, trans. by J. O. Gauntlett. Cambridge, 1949.

Hammitzsch, H., "Die Mito-Schule and ihre programmatischen Schriften: Bairi Sensei Hiin, Kōkōkanki, Kōdōkangakusoku, Seiki no Uta." *Mitteilungen* der Deutschen Gesellschaft für Natur- und Völkerkunde Ostasiens, 31 B (1939).

——, "Literaturbericht über japanische Geschichte." *Historische Zeitschrift* Sonderheft 1 (1962), pp. 443–66.

Hara, Katsurō, *Histoire du Japon des origines à nos jours*. Paris, 1926.

371

Harrison, J. A., *Japan's Northern Frontier*. Gainesville, Fla., 1953.
————, *New Light on Early and Medieval Japanese Historiography*. Gainesville, Fla., 1959.
Harvard Journal of Asiatic Studies. Cambridge, 1936–
Hearn, L., *Japan, An Attempt at Interpretation*. New York, 1904.
Henderson, D. F., *Conciliation and Japanese Law*. Seattle, 1965.
Herbert, J., *Aux sources du Japon: Le Shintō*. Paris, 1964.
————, *Les Dieux nationaux du Japon*. Paris, 1965.
Hirschmeier, J., *The Origins of Entrepreneurship in Meiji Japan*. Cambridge, 1964.
Holtom, D. C., *Modern Japan and Shinto Nationalism*, rev. ed. Chicago, 1947.
————, *National Faith of Japan*. London, 1938.
Honjo, E., *Economic Theory and History of Japan in the Tokugawa Period*. New York, 1965.
————, *The Social and Economic History of Japan*. New York, 1965.
Ienaga, S., *History of Japan*. Tourist Library, Vol. 15., Tōkyō, 1959.
Ike, N., *The Beginnings of Political Democracy in Japan*. Baltimore, 1950.
————, *Japan's Decision for War*. Stanford, 1967.
Ikle, F. W., *German-Japanese Relations 1936–1940*. New York, 1956.
Inoue, Mitsusada, *Introduction to Japanese History before the Meiji Restoration*. Tōkyō, 1962.
International Military Tribunal for the Far East, Judgment. Documents. Evidence. Mimeo, Tōkyō, undated.
Iriye, A., *After Imperialism: The Search for a New Order in the Far East, 1921–1931*. Cambridge, 1965.
Ito, H., *Commentaries on the Constitution of the Empire of Japan*. Tōkyō, 1906.
Iwao, S., and Bonmarchand, G., (comp.), *Dictionnaire Historique du Japon*. Tōkyō, 1963–
Iwata, M., *Ōkubo Toshimichi, The Bismarck of Japan*. Berkeley, 1964.
Jansen, M. B. (ed.), *Changing Japanese Attitudes toward Modernization*. Princeton, 1965.
————, *The Japanese and Sun Yat-sen*. Cambridge, 1954.
————, *Sakamoto Ryōma and the Meiji Restoration*. Princeton, 1961.

Japan Quarterly. Tōkyō, 1954– .

Jones, F. C., *Japan's New Order in East Asia.* London, 1954.

Joüon des Longrais, F., *Age de Kamakura: Sources (1150–1333) —Archives.* Tōkyō, 1950.

————, *L'Est et L'Ouest: Institutions du Japon et de l'Occident comparées.* Tōkyō and Paris, 1958.

————, *Tashi: Le Roman de Celle qui épousa deux Empereurs (Nidai no Kisaki) (1140–1202).* Paris, Vol. 1., 1965.

Kaempfer, E., *The History of Japan, Together with a Description of the Kingdom of Siam, 1609–1692.* 3 vols. London, 1727–1728; Glasgow, 1906.

Kawai, K., *Japan's American Interlude.* Chicago, 1960.

Kawano, K., "Révolution française et révolution de Meiji: Aspects économiques et sociaux." *Annales historiques de la Révolution Française* 35 (1963), pp. 1–14.

Keene, D. (ed.), *Anthology of Japanese Literature from the Earliest Era to the Mid-19th Century.* New York, 1955.

————, *The Japanese Discovery of Europe.* London, 1952.

————, *Japanese Literature.* London, 1953.

————, *Living Japan.* New York, 1959.

————, *Modern Japanese Literature, an Anthology.* New York, 1956.

Kidder, J. E., *Japan Before Buddhism,* 2nd ed. New York, 1959.

Kitabatake, C., *Jinnō Shōtōki, Buch von der Wahren Gott-Kaiser-Herrschaftslinie,* trans. and ann. by H. Bohner. Tōkyō, 1935.

Kitagawa, J., *Religion in Japanese History.* New York, 1966.

Kluge, I. L., *Miyoshi Kiyoyuki, Sein Leben und Seine Zeit.* Berlin, 1958.

Kokusai Bunka Shinkōkai, K. B. S., *Bibliography of Standard Reference Books for Japanese Studies with Descriptive Notes.* Vol. III, *History and Biography.* 3 Parts. Tōkyō, 1963–1965.

Kōsaka, M., *Japanese Thought in the Meiji Era,* trans. by D. Abosch. Tōkyō, 1958.

Kublin, H., *Asian Revolutionary: The Life of Sen Katayama.* Princeton, 1964.

de la Mazelière, A. R., *Le Japon. Histoire et Civilisation.* 8 vols. Paris, 1907.

Langer, W. L., *The Diplomacy of Imperialism,* 2nd ed. New York, 1951.

Laures, J., "Nobunaga und das Christentum." *Monumenta Nipponica* Monograph No. 10. Tōkyō, 1950.

————, *Takayama Ukon und die Anfänge der Kirche in Japan*. Münster Westfalen, 1954.

Lockwood, W. W., *The Economic Development of Japan, Growth and Structural Change, 1868–1938*. Princeton, 1954.

————, (ed.), *The State and Economic Enterprise in Japan*. Princeton, 1965.

Lu, D., *From the Marco Polo Bridge to Pearl Harbor*. Washington, 1961.

Malm, W. P., *Japanese Music and Musical Instruments*. Tōkyō, 1959.

Martin, J. M., *Le Shintoisme, religion nationale du Japon*. 2 vols. Hong Kong, 1924–1927.

Maruyama, M., *Thought and Behavior in Modern Japanese Politics*. London, 1963.

Maxon, Y. C., *Control of Japanese Foreign Policy: A Study of Civil-Military Rivalry, 1930–1945*. Berkeley, 1957.

McCullough, H. C. (trans.), *The Taiheiki: A Chronicle of Medieval Japan*. New York, 1959.

————, *Yoshitsune*. Stanford, 1965.

McEwan, J. R., *The Political Writings of Ogyū Sorai*, Cambridge, 1962.

McLaren, W. W., "Japanese Government Documents." *Transactions of the Asiatic Society of Japan*. XLII, Part 1, 1914.

————, *A Political History of Japan during the Meiji Era, 1867–1912*. New York, 1916. Reprint, 1965.

Miller, F. O., *Minobe Tatsukichi: Interpreter of Constitutionalism in Japan*. Berkeley a.u Los Angeles, 1965.

Monumenta Nipponica. Tōkyō, 1938–43; 1951–

Moréchand, Guy, " 'Taiko Kenchi' Le Cadastre de Hideyoshi Toyotomi." *Bulletin De L'École Française D'Extrême—Orient*, 53.1 (1966).

Morley, J. W., *The Japanese Thrust into Siberia, 1918*. New York, 1957.

Morris, I. I., *Nationalism and the Right Wing in Japan: A Study of Postwar Trends*. London, 1960.

————, *The World of the Shining Prince: Court Life in Ancient Japan*. New York, 1964.

Murasaki, S., *The Tale of Genji*, trans. by A. Waley. 2 vols., Boston, 1935. 1 vol., New York, 1960.

————, *Die Geschichte vom Prinzen Genji*. 2 vols. Zürich, 1966.

Nachod, O., *Geschichte von Japan*. 3 vols. Gotha, 1906; Leipzig, 1929.

Najita, T., *Hara Kei in the Politics of Compromise*. Cambridge, 1967.

Nakamura, J., *Agricultural Production and the Economic Development of Japan, 1873–1922*. Princeton, 1966.

Nish, I., *The Anglo-Japanese Alliance*. London, 1966.

Noda, Y., "La réception du droit français au Japon." *Revue internationale de droit comparé* 15 (1963), pp. 543–56.

Norman, E. H., *Andō Shōeki and the Anatomy of Japanese Feudalism*. Tōkyō, 1949.

———, *Japan's Emergence as a Modern State: Political and Economic Problems of the Meiji Period*. New York, 1940.

———, *Soldier and Peasant in Japan. The Origins of Conscription*. New York, 1943.

Ogata, S., *Defiance in Manchuria*. Berkeley and Los Angeles, 1964.

Okakura, K., *The Book of Tea*. New York, 1906. Reprint, Rutland, Vt., 1957.

Ōkuma, Count S. (comp.), *Fifty Years of New Japan*. 2 vols. London, 1909–1910.

Oriental Economist. Tōkyō, Monthly, 1934– .

Pacific Affairs. Vancouver, B.C., 1928– .

Packard, G., *Protest in Tokyo, The Security Treaty Crisis of 1960*. Princeton, 1966.

Papinot, E., *Dictionnaire japonais-français des noms principaux de l'histoire et de la géographie du Japon*. Hong Kong, 1899. Reprint, Ann Arbor, 1948, in English.

Passin, H., *Society and Education in Japan*. New York, 1965.

———, (ed.), *The United States and Japan*. Englewood Cliffs, N.J., 1966.

P. E. N. Club, Japan, *Japanese Literature in European Languages: A Bibliography*, 2nd ed. Tōkyō, 1961.

Piovesana, G., *Recent Japanese Philosophical Thought, 1862–1962*. Tokyo, 1963.

Pittau, J., *Political Thought in Early Meiji Japan*. Cambridge, 1967.

Plath, D. W., *The After Hours: Modern Japan and the Search for Enjoyment*. Berkeley, 1964.

Quigley, H., *Japanese Government and Politics*. New York, 1932.

Ramming, M., *Japan-Handbuch*. Berlin, 1941.

Rein, J. J., *Japan nach Reisen und Studien im Auftrage der Königlich Preussischen Regierung.* 2 vols. Leipzig, 1881–1886.

Reischauer, E. O., *Japan, Past and Present,* 3rd ed. New York, 1964.

————, *The United States and Japan,* rev. ed. Cambridge, 1957; 3rd ed., 1965.

————, and Fairbank, J., *A History of East Asian Civilization,* Vol. I., *East Asia: The Great Tradition.* Boston, 1960.

————, and Yamagiwa, J., *Translations from Early Japanese Literature.* Cambridge, 1964.

Reischauer, R. K., *Early Japanese History.* 2 vols. Princeton, 1937.

Rekishigaku Nihon Kokunai Iinkai, *Le Japon au XIe Congrès International des Sciences Historiques à Stockholm.* Tōkyō, 1963.

————, *Japan at the XIIth International Congress of Historical Sciences in Vienna.* Tōkyō, 1965.

Renondeau, G., "Histoire des moines guerriers du Japon." *Bibliothèque de l'Institut des Hautes Études Chinoises.* XI Paris, 1957, pp. 159–344.

Robinson, G. W., and Beasley, W. G., "Japanische Geschichtsschreibung. Entstehung und Entwicklung einer Eigenen Form vom 11. bis 14. Jahrhundert" *Saeculum,* 8 (1957), pp. 236–48.

Roggendorf, J. (ed.), *Das moderne Japan: einführende Aufsätze.* Tōkyō, 1963.

————, *Studies in Japanese Culture.* Tōkyō, 1964.

Rosovsky, H., *Capital Formation in Japan, 1868–1940.* Glencoe, Ill., 1961.

Sansom, Sir G. B., *Japan, A Short Cultural History,* rev. ed. New York, 1943.

————, *A History of Japan.* 3 vols. Stanford 1958–1963.
Vol. I., *A History of Japan to 1334.*
Vol. II., *A History of Japan, 1334–1615.*
Vol. III, *A History of Japan, 1615–1867.*

————, "Early Japanese Law and Administration." *Transactions of the Asiatic Society of Japan* (2): Vol. 9, pp. 67–109 (1932); Vol. 11, pp. 117–149 (1934).

————, *The Western World and Japan.* New York, 1958.

Scalapino, R., *Democracy and the Party Movement in Prewar Japan.* Berkeley, 1953.

————, *The Japanese Communist Movement, 1920–1966.* Berkeley, 1967.

————, and Masumi, J., *Parties and Politics in Contemporary Japan*. Berkeley, 1962.

Schwind, M., *Das japanische Inselreich. Eine Landeskunde nach Studien und Reisen*. 3 vols. (in press) 1967–

Sheldon, C. D., *The Rise of the Merchant Class in Tokugawa Japan, 1600–1868*. Locust Valley, N.Y., 1958.

Shibusawa, K. (comp. and ed.), *Japanese Life and Culture in the Meiji Era*, trans. by C. S. Terry. Centenary Cultural Council Series. Tōkyō, 1958.

Shigemitsu, M., *Japan and Her Destiny*. New York, 1958.

Shimmi, K., *Die Geschichte der Bukeherrschaft in Japan: Beiträge zum Verständnis des Japanischen Lehnswesens*. Basel, 1939.

Shinoda, M., *The Founding of the Kamakura Shogunate, 1180–1185*. New York, 1960.

Siebold, P. F. von, *Nippon, Archiv zur Beschreibung von Japan und dessen Neben- und Schutzländern*. 2 vols. 1852.

Siemes, J., "Hermann Roesler und die Einführung des deutschen Staatsrechts in Japan," *Der Staat* 2 (1962), pp. 181–196.

————, *Hermann Roesler and the Making of the Meiji State*. Tōkyō, 1966.

Silberman, B. S., *Japan and Korea: A Critical Bibliography*. Tucson, 1962.

————, (ed.), *Japanese Character and Culture: A Book of Selected Readings*. Tucson, 1962.

————, *Ministers of Modernization*. Tucson, 1964.

————, and Harootunian, H. (eds.), *Modern Japanese Leadership*. Tucson, 1966.

Smith, B., *Japan: A History in Art*. New York, 1964.

————, *Japan–Geschichte und Kunst*. Zürich, 1965.

Smith, T. C., *The Agrarian Origins of Modern Japan*. Stanford, 1959.

————, "The Japanese Village in the Seventeenth Century." *Journal of Economic History*, vol. 12, pp. 1–20 (1952).

————, "Japan's Aristocratic Revolution," *Yale Review*, vol. 50, pp. 370–383 (1961).

————, " 'Merit' as Ideology in the Tokugawa Period," in R. P. Dore, *Aspects of Social Change in Modern Japan*. Princeton, 1967.

————, "Old Values and New Techniques in the Modernization of Japan," *Far Eastern Quarterly*, vol. 14, pp. 355–363 (1955).

————, *Political Change and Industrial Development in Japan: Government Enterprise, 1868–1880.* Stanford, 1955.

Smith, W., *Confucianism in Modern Japan.* Tōkyō, 1962.

Spae, J., *Itō Jinsai, A Philosopher, Educator and Sinologist of the Tokugawa Period.* New York, 1967.

Spaulding, R. M., *Imperial Japan's Higher Civil Service Examinations.* Princeton, 1967.

Storry, R., *The Double Patriots.* Boston, 1957.

————, *Histoire du Japon moderne.* Paris, 1963.

————, *A History of Modern Japan.* London, 1962.

Swearingen, R., and Langer, P., *Red Flag in Japan.* Cambridge, 1952.

Taeuber, I. B., *The Population of Japan.* Princeton, 1958.

Takahashi, K., "État Actuel et Tendances générales des Etudes Historiques au Japon depuis la Guerre." *Revue Historique* 216 (1956), pp. 59–66.

————, "La Place de la Révolution de Meiji dans l'histoire agraire du Japon." *Revue Historique* 210 (1953), pp. 229–270.

Teng, S. Y., *Japanese Studies on Japan and the Far East.* Hong Kong, 1961.

Thunberg, Ch.-P., *Le Japon du XVIIIe Siècle.* Reprint, Paris, 1966.

Titsingh, I., *Nipon O Daï Itsi Ran, ou Annales des Empereurs du Japon,* J. Klaproth, ed. London, 1834. Reprint, 1965.

Totman, Conrad, *Politics in the Tokugawa Bakufu, 1600–1843.* Cambridge, 1967.

Totten, G. O., *The Social Democratic Movement in Prewar Japan.* New Haven, 1966.

Toyoda, T., "Révolution française et révolution de Meiji: Étude critique des interprétations de Kōsa et Rōnō." *Annales Historiques de la Révolution Française* 35 (1963), 16–24.

Transactions of the Asiatic Society of Japan. Tōkyō, 1872–1922, 1924–1940, 1948 ff. Comprehensive index to all series is found in issue of December, 1958 (series 3, vol. VI).

Tsuchiya, T., "An Economic History of Japan." *Transactions of the Asiatic Society of Japan* (2), vol. 15 (1937).

Tsukahira, T. G., *Feudal Control in Tokugawa Japan.* Cambridge, 1966.

Tsunoda, R., et al. (comps.), *Sources of Japanese Tradition.* New York, 1958.

Varley, H. Paul, *The Ōnin War.* New York, 1967.

Vogel, E., *Japan's New Middle Class: The Salary Man and his Family in a Tōkyō Suburb*. Berkeley, 1965.

Waley, A. (trans.), *The Nō Plays of Japan*. London, 1921.

Wang, Y.–T., *Official Relations between China and Japan, 1368–1549*. Cambridge, 1953.

Ward, R. B. (ed.), *Political Development in Modern Japan*. Princeton, 1968.

——, and Rustow, D. (eds.), *Political Modernization in Japan and Turkey*. Princeton, 1964.

Warner, L., *The Enduring Art of Japan*. Cambridge, 1952.

Webb, H., *An Introduction to Japan*. New York, 1957.

——, *The Japanese Imperial Institution in the Tokugawa Period*. New York, 1968.

——, *Research in Japanese Sources: A Guide*. New York, 1965.

White, J. A., *The Diplomacy of the Russo-Japanese War*. Princeton, 1964.

Wilson, R., *Genesis of the Meiji Government in Japan, 1868–1871*. Berkeley, 1957.

Yamagiwa, J., *The Ōkagami*. London, 1967.

Yanaga, C., *Japan Since Perry*. New York, 1949.

Young, J. *The Location of Yamatai: A Case Study of Japanese Historiography*. Baltimore, 1958.

Yoshida, S., *The Yoshida Memoirs*. Boston, 1962.

Yoshihashi, T., *Conspiracy at Mukden. The Rise of the Japanese Military*. New Haven, 1963.

Zachert, H., "Die Tokugawa-Zeit und ihr Einfluss auf Wesen and Nationalgeist der Japaner." *Mitteilungen* der Deutschen Gesellschaft für Natur– and Völkerkunde Ostasiens 28 G, 1938.

Acknowledgments

The publishers wish to thank the following for providing illustrations for this volume: Shogakukan, Tokyo, for plates 1, 2, 3, 4, 5, 6, 7, 8, 9, 10, 11, 12, 13, 14, 15, 16, 19, 20, 21, 22, 23, 24, 26, 27, 28, 29, 30, 31, 32, 33, 34, 36, 37, and 39, from *Zusetsu Nihon Bunkashi Taikei,* edited by Professor Kota Kodama, 1956; K. B. S., Tokyo, Japan, for plates 17 and 18; John Whitney Hall, for plate 25; United Press International Photos, for plates 35 and 38; Jetro (Japan External Trade Organization), for plates 40, 41, 43, 44, 45; and Japan National Tourist Organization, for plate 42.

Index

INDEX

Hamaguchi Yuko, 318, 321
Han dynasty, 19, 20, 39
Hanawa Hokiichi, 218
Hankow, 340
Han shu, 25
Hanzei rights, 109
Hara Kei, 315–17
Hara Martino, 140
Harima, 145, 150
Harmonization Society, 322
Harris, Townsend, 256–57, 260
Hashimoto Kingorō, 331–32
Hashimoto Sanai, 258
Hatakeyama, 107–108, 133
Hayashi family, 182, 217, 219
Hayashi Razan, 182, 221
Hayashi Shihei, 225
Heavenly Sword Party, 331
Heian Period, 114
  chronology of, 358
  Court life in, 72–74
  Fujiwara ascendancy and, 61–74
Heijō (imperial city), *see* Nara
Heike Monogatari, 85, 101–102
Heusken (Dutch interpreter), 260
Hidetata, *see* Tokugawa Hidetata
Hidetsugu, 150–51
Hideyoshi, *see* Toyotomi Hideyoshi
Hieizan, 144
Higaki shipping line, 211
Higashiyama, 116, 159
Hikaru Genji, 72
Hikone, 157, 167, 176
Himeji, 157
Himiko, Queen, 25–26
Hirado, 137, 139, 187
Hiraga Gennai, 224
Hiranuma Kiichiro, Baron, 328
Hirata Atsutane, 222
Hirohito, Emperor, 348, 352
Hirosawa Saneomi, 269
Hiroshima, 149, 157, 300
  atomic bombing of, 347
Hirota Koki, 338
Hishikawa Moronobu, 231
History of great Japan, 217
Hitler, Adolf, 327
Hitotsubashi Yoshinobu, *see* Tokugawa Yoshinobu
Hizen, 268, 270–71
Hōgen conflict, 83
Hōjō family, 115, 116, 121, 132, 143–44, 147–48, 162
  fall of, 104–105, 155

Kamakura under, 88–102
Hōjō Tokimune, 101
Hōjōki (Record of a Ten-Foot-Square Hut), 101
Hōjō Masako, 91
Hōki, 111
Hokkaidō, 193, 211, 264, 283, 287
  See also Ezo
Hokke, *see* Fujiwara family
Holland, 286, 345
Holmes, Oliver Wendell, 299
Hon' ami Kōetsu, 216
Honchō tsugan, 217
Honda, 163
Honda Toshiaki, 220, 237, 248
Hōnen Shōnin, 97, 99
Honganji monastery, 133–34
Hong Kong, 347
Honshū, 11, 145
Hōō, *see* Dōkyō
Hosokawa family, 107–108, 126–28, 133
Hosokawa Yoriyuki, 111
Hotta Masatoshi, 191
Hotta Masayoshi, 256–58
Hsingking, 334
Hua-yen, 59
Hull, Cordell, 346
Hung-wu, Emperor, 114, 125
Hyōgo, 257, 260

Ieharu, *see* Tokugawa Ieharu
Ihara Saikaku, 229–30
Ii, 163, 167, 176
Ii Naosuke, 258–60
Iida Tadahiko, 218
Ike-no-Taiga, 217
Ikkōshū (Single Minded Sect), *see* Shinshū
Ikoma family, 163
Imagawa family, 108, 131, 133, 143, 162
Imagawa Yoshimoto, 143, 162
Imperial Household Law, 297
Imperial Household Ministry, 292, 297
Imperial Rescript on Education (1890), 292, 328
In (cloister), 89
Inaba, 145
Inari, 33
India, 136, 156, 347, 355
Indochina, 345–46
Indonesia, 347
Inō Tadataka, 227

386

NOTE ON THE AUTHOR

JOHN WHITNEY HALL is A. Whitney Griswold Professor of History at Yale University and former Master of its Morse College. Born in Tōkyō, Japan, he received his Bachelor of Arts degree from Amherst College in 1939 and his Ph.D. from Harvard University in 1950.

After his graduation from Amherst, Dr. Hall taught at Doshisha University, Kyōto, until shortly before the outbreak of war in the Pacific, in 1941. During the war he served with the United States Naval Intelligence, leaving the service with the rank of Lieutenant Commander.

Dr. Hall taught until 1961 at the University of Michigan, where he also served as Director of the Center for Japanese Studies. He has been a member of the editorial board of the *American Historical Review*, and was for several years Chairman of the Association for Asian Studies' Conference on Modern Japan. He is presently Chairman of the SSRC-ACLS Joint Committee on Japanese Studies. Among his books are: *Japanese History: A Guide to Japanese Research and Reference Materials; Twelve Doors To Japan* (with R. K. Beardsley); *Government and Local Power in Japan: 500 to 1700;* and *Studies in the Institutional History of Early Modern Japan* (with M. B. Jansen).